THE CHURCH'S BIBLE

General Editor

Robert Louis Wilken

•   •

The Song of Songs

Richard A. Norris Jr.

THE SONG OF SONGS

*Interpreted by Early Christian
and Medieval Commentators*

Translated and Edited by

Richard A. Norris Jr.

WILLIAM B. EERDMANS PUBLISHING COMPANY
GRAND RAPIDS, MICHIGAN / CAMBRIDGE, U.K.

© 2003 Wm. B. Eerdmans Publishing Co.

Wm. B. Eerdmans Publishing Co.
255 Jefferson Ave. S.E., Grand Rapids, Michigan 49503 /
P.O. Box 163, Cambridge CB3 9PU U.K.
www.eerdmans.com

Printed in the United States of America

08 07 06 05 04 03   7 6 5 4 3 2 1

Library of Congress Cataloging-in-Publication Data

The Song of Songs: interpreted by early Christian and Medieval commentators /
translated and edited by Richard A. Norris, Jr.
p.   cm. — (The church's Bible; 1)
Includes bibliographical references and index.
ISBN 0-8028-2579-6 (hardcover: alk. paper)
1. Bible. O.T. Song of Solomon — Commentaries.
I. Norris, Richard A. (Richard Alfred), 1930-   II. Series.
BS1485.53.S66   2003

223'.907'09 — dc21

2003049519

Selected excerpts from Gregory of Nyssa's *Homilies on the Song of Songs,*
©2003 by Richard A. Norris, are courtesy of Mr. Norris. This text will be published
in full in the Writings from the Greco-Roman Series of the Society of Biblical Literature.

Contents

CONTENTS

Series Preface

The volumes in The Church's Bible are designed to present the Holy Scriptures as understood and interpreted during the first millennium of Christian history. The Christian Church has a long tradition of commentary on the Bible. In the early church all discussion of theological topics, of moral issues, and of Christian practice took the biblical text as the starting point. The recitation of the psalms and meditation on books of the Bible, particularly in the context of the liturgy or of private prayer, nurtured the spiritual life. For most of the Church's history theology and scriptural interpretation were one. Theology was called *sacra pagina* (the sacred page), and the task of interpreting the Bible was a spiritual enterprise.

During the first two centuries interpretation of the Bible took the form of exposition of select passages on particular issues. For example, Irenaeus, bishop of Lyons, discussed many passages from the Old and New Testaments in his defense of the apostolic faith against the Gnostics. By the beginning of the third century Christian bishops and scholars had begun to preach regular series of sermons that followed the biblical books verse by verse. Some wrote more scholarly commentaries that examined in greater detail grammatical, literary, and historical questions as well as theological ideas and spiritual teachings found in the texts. From Origen of Alexandria, the first great biblical commentator in the Church's history, we have, among others, a large verse-by-verse commentary on the Gospel of John, a series of homilies on Genesis and Exodus, and a large part of his *Commentary on the Epistle to the Romans.* In the course of the first eight hundred years of Christian history Christian teachers produced a library of biblical commentaries and homilies on the Bible.

Today this ancient tradition of biblical interpretation is known only in bits and pieces, and even where it still shapes our understanding of the Bible, for example, in the selection of readings for Christian worship (e.g., Isaiah 7 and Isaiah 9 read at Christmas), or the interpretation of the Psalms in daily prayer, the spiritual world that gave it birth remains shadowy and indistinct. It is the purpose of this series to make available the richness of the Church's classical tradition of interpretation for clergy, Sunday school and Bible class teachers, men and women living in religious communities, and serious readers of the Bible.

Anyone who reads the ancient commentaries realizes at once that they are deeply spiritual, insightful, edifying, and, shall we say, "biblical." Early Christian thinkers moved in the world of the Bible, understood its idiom, loved its teaching, and were filled with awe before its mysteries. They believed in the maxim, "Scripture interprets Scripture." They knew something that has largely been forgotten by biblical scholars, and their commentaries are an untapped resource for understanding the Bible as a book about Christ.

The distinctive mark of The Church's Bible is that it draws extensively on the ancient commentaries, not only on random comments drawn from theological treatises, sermons, or devotional works. Its volumes will, in the main, offer fairly lengthy excerpts from the ancient commentaries and from series of sermons on specific books. For example, in the first volume on the Song of Songs, there are long passages from Origen of Alexandria's *Commentary on the Song of Songs,* from Gregory of Nyssa's *Homilies on the Song,* and from Bernard of Clairvaux's sermons on the Song. Some passages will be as brief as a paragraph, but many will be several pages in length, and some longer. We believe that it is only through a deeper immersion in the ancient sources that contemporary readers can enter into the inexhaustible spiritual and theological world of the early Church and hence of the Bible

It is also hoped that longer passages will be suitable for private devotional reading and for spiritual reading in religious communities, in Bible study groups, and in prayer circles.

ROBERT LOUIS WILKEN
General Editor

Acknowledgments

From the time this series was proposed to Bill Eerdmans he has been an enthusiastic and unfailing supporter, and we thank him for his interest, encouragement, and backing. We also wish to thank the Homeland Foundation and the Community of Christ in the City for their help in making this project possible.

ROBERT LOUIS WILKEN

Interpreting the Old Testament

For most of the Church's history (the early Church, the Church during medieval times, and the Reformation era) the Old Testament was a book about Christ and the Church. As the historical study of the Bible gained ascendency in the twentieth century, however, the Old Testament came to be understood chiefly within the framework of ancient Near Eastern history, culture, and literature. The books of the Old Testament were of course written before the coming of Christ; one task of interpretation, therefore, will always be to set them within the context in which they were first composed. The first Christians, however, recognized that these books were not simply documents from the past but living testimonies to the marvelous things that happened in their own time and continue to happen. St. Jerome said, "Isaiah is an evangelist and apostle, not only a prophet. . . . This book of the Bible contains all the mysteries of the Lord and proclaims him as Emmanuel born of a virgin, as a worker of glorious deeds and signs, as having died and been buried and rising from hell, and, indeed, as the Savior of all the nations."[1]

In calling Isaiah an evangelist and apostle Jerome reflects the practice of the New Testament. After Christ's ascension Philip met an Ethiopian who was returning home from Jerusalem. The Ethiopian was reading the Bible and came to the passage in Isaiah that read: "As a sheep led to the slaughter or a lamb before its shearer is dumb, so he opens not his mouth. In his humiliation justice was denied him. Who can describe his generation? For his life is taken up from the earth" (Isa. 53:7-8 as quoted in Acts 8:32-33). When the Ethiopian read this passage, he asked Philip, "To whom do these words refer, to the prophet himself or to someone else?" Philip said they referred to Christ, and beginning with this scripture "he told him the good news of Jesus" (Acts 8:26-40). The book of Isaiah spoke with uncommon clarity about Christ.

It was not only Isaiah, however, that spoke of Christ; the books of Moses, Ezekiel and Jeremiah, the Minor Prophets, the Psalms, and the Wisdom Books also spoke clearly of Christ. According to Luke, when Jesus met two of his disciples on the road to Emmaus he instructed them in the Scriptures "beginning with Moses and all the prophets" and "interpreted to them in all the scriptures the things concerning himself" (Luke 24:27). The Epistle to the Hebrews begins with seven quotations from the Psalms and other

---

1. Prologue to the *Commentary on Isaiah* (CCSL 73:1).

books of the Old Testament and applies them directly to Christ. "To what angel," he writes, "did God say, 'Thou art my Son, today I have begotten thee'? [Ps. 2:7]. To whom did he say, 'I will be to him a father, and he shall be to me a son'? [2 Sam. 7:14]. Of the angels he said, 'Who makes his angels winds, and his servants flames of fire' [Ps. 104:4], but of his Son he says, 'Thy throne, O God, is forever and ever' [Ps. 45:6]. . . ." (Heb. 1:5-14). Both the Gospel of Matthew and the Gospel of John interpret the words of Zechariah, "Lo, your king comes to you, humble and mounted on an ass, and on a colt, the foal of an ass" (Zech. 9:9), as a depiction of Christ's entry into Jerusalem (Matt. 21:5; John 12:15).

But the Old Testament is a very large book, and it is not obvious how everything that is found in it (e.g., the ritual of the Day of Atonement in Leviticus 16 or the love poetry of the Song of Songs) derives its meaning from Christ. It may be useful, in introducing these commentaries, to say a few things about how the church fathers went about the business of interpreting the Old Testament. The simple answer is that they followed the example of the writers of the New Testament. Origen of Alexandria, the first major interpreter of the Bible in the Church's history, said that "the apostle Paul, 'teacher of the Gentiles in faith and truth,' taught the Church . . . how it ought to interpret the books of the Law."[2] In 1 Corinthians Paul had written that the Israelites in the desert "drank from the supernatural Rock which followed them, and the Rock was Christ" (1 Cor. 10:4), to which he added that these things were "written down for us as types" (1 Cor. 10:11). Paul knew of course that the events recorded in the book of Exodus had taken place centuries earlier. God had delivered the Israelites from the oppression of the Egyptians and led them safely through the Red Sea into the Sinai desert. While they made their way back to the land of Israel, God sustained them with manna from heaven and water drawn from rocks. Nevertheless, St. Paul says that what happened in the desert centuries ago is not simply past history. These ancient events are dramatic rehearsals of the deeds of Christ, the Son of God.

Accordingly, Origen believed that Paul, by his example, had provided a "rule of interpretation" for understanding the Old Testament. "Take note," he writes, "how much Paul's teaching differs from the plain meaning. . . . What the Jews thought was a crossing of the sea, Paul calls baptism; what they supposed was a cloud, Paul says is the Holy Spirit." And what Exodus calls a "rock," Paul says was "Christ." Christian interpreters, says Origen, "should apply this rule in a similar way to other passages." In other words, Paul has given the Church a model of how the Old Testament is to be interpreted, and it is the task of later expositors to discern how other passages are to be understood in light of Christ's coming. Augustine made precisely the same point on the basis of the passage from 1 Corinthians. How Paul understands things in this passage, says Augustine, "is a key as to how the rest [of the Old Testament] is to be interpreted."[3]

Following St. Paul, the church fathers argued that a surface reading of the Old Testament, what Origen calls the "plain" meaning, missed what was most important in the Bible, Jesus Christ. The subject of the Scriptures, writes Cyril of Alexandria, is "the mystery of Christ signified to us through a myriad of different kinds of things. Someone

2. *Homily on Exodus* 5.1.
3. *Against Faustus* 12.29.

might liken it to a glittering and magnificent city, having not one image of the king but many, and publicly displayed in every corner of the city. . . . Its purpose is not to provide us an account of the lives of the saints of old. Far from that. Its purpose is to give us knowledge of the mystery [of Christ] through things that make the word about him clear and true."[4]

To drive home the point the church fathers also cited the passage in Ephesians where St. Paul interprets the famous words about the institution of marriage in Genesis as referring to Christ and the Church. The text in Genesis reads: "For this reason a man shall leave his father and mother and be joined to his wife, and the two shall become one flesh" (Gen. 2:24). Paul comments, "This mystery is a profound one, and I am saying that it refers to Christ and the church" (Eph. 5:31-32). In Paul's interpretation the words from Genesis do not simply signify Christ but are speaking *about* Christ; that is to say, marriage takes its meaning from the mystery of Christ. At the beginning of his *Literal Commentary on Genesis* Augustine cites this passage from Ephesians and the text from 1 Corinthians 10 to show that the Old Testament cannot be understood in a strictly literal or historical way. "No Christian will dare say that the narrative must not be taken in a figurative sense. For St. Paul says, 'Now all these things that happened to them were symbolic' (1 Cor. 10:11). And he explains the statement in Genesis, 'And they shall be two in one flesh' (Eph. 5:31), as a great mystery in reference to Christ and to the Church."[5]

The customary term for this kind of exegesis is "allegory," a word first introduced into Christian speech by St. Paul in the Epistle to the Galatians: "It is written that Abraham had two sons, one by a slave and one by a free woman. But the son of the slave was born according to the flesh, the son of the free woman through promise. Now this is an allegory; these women are two covenants" (Gal. 4:21-24). The root meaning of allegory is that there is "another" sense, another meaning, besides the plain sense. Sarah and Hagar are not simply names of the wives of Abraham; they also signify two covenants, one associated with Sinai and the other with the Jerusalem above. The rock in the desert that Moses struck and from which water flowed is not simply a rock; it is also Christ.

Allegory is not distinctive to Christian exegesis of the Old Testament. It was used by Greek literary scholars in the ancient world to interpret the *Iliad* and *Odyssey* of Homer, and it was employed by Jewish thinkers — for example, Philo of Alexandria — to interpret the Pentateuch. Christian allegory has similarities to this kind of allegory, but what sets it apart is that it is centered on Christ. Allegory in Christian usage means interpreting the Old Testament as a book about Christ. St. Ambrose wrote: "The Lord Jesus came and what was old was made new."[6] Everything in the Scripture is to be related to him. As a medieval commentator put it, "All of Divine Scripture is one book, and that one book is Christ, because all of Divine Scripture speaks of Christ, and all of Divine Scripture is fulfilled in Christ."[7] Allegory, or, if one prefers, "spiritual exegesis," is interpretation of the

4. *PG* 69:308c.

5. Augustine, *Literal Commentary on Genesis* 1.1.1.

6. *Interpretation of Job and David* 1.4.12 (*PL* 14:802a).

7. Hugh of St. Victor, *De arca Noe morali* 2.7 (*PL* 176:642c-d).

Old Testament in light of the new reality of Christ. In the words of Henri de Lubac, the distinguished theologian and historian of early Christian exegesis: "The conversion of the Old Testament to the New or of the letter of Scripture to its spirit can only be explained and justified, in its radicality, by the all-powerful and unprecedented intervention of Him who is himself at once the Alpha and the Omega, the First and the Last. . . . Therefore Jesus Christ brings about the unity of Scripture, because he is the endpoint and fulness of Scripture. Everything in it is related to him. In the end he is its sole object. Consequently, he is, so to speak, its whole exegesis."[8]

With these considerations in mind consider a few examples. Isaiah 63:1-3: "Who is this that comes from Edom, in crimsoned garments from Bozrah, he that is glorious in his apparel, marching in the greatness of his strength? 'It is I, announcing vindication, mighty to save.' Why is thy apparel red, and thy garments like his that treads in the wine press? 'I have trodden the wine press alone, and from the peoples no one was with me.'" In the early Church this passage was understood to refer to Christ's ascension. The words "who is this that comes from Edom" were spoken by the angels who received Christ in heaven after his ascension, and "crimsoned garments" was thought to refer to his garments stained by the blood of his passion. In answer to the questions of the heavenly host Christ says, "I have trodden the wine press alone. . . ." In his commentary on Isaiah 63 Cyril of Alexandria writes: "His appearance was altogether strange and foreign to the powers above. They were astonished at seeing him come up, and said: Who is this that comes from Edom? (63:1). Edom can be translated either 'of wheat' or 'of earth.' Bozrah as either 'of flesh' or 'fleshly.' And so they are asking, 'Who is this one from the earth, this earthling?' And the crimsoned garments from Bozrah means that his clothes were reddened from flesh, or, rather, from blood. He is glorious in his apparel. The heavenly powers, strong and wise and filled with heavenly glory, were looking upon Christ, even in the flesh, as a mighty one, thoroughly invincible, who manifests his divinity as well as his humanity to them."[9] Although this interpretation of Isaiah 63 may be foreign to current readers, it was almost universal in the early Church. Just as the "suffering servant" in Isaiah 53 was interpreted in reference to Christ's passion, so Isaiah 63 was an oracle about Christ's ascension.

A different kind of example can be found in an ancient paschal homily preached in the second century by Melito, bishop of Sardis in Asia Minor. Melito was a gifted orator who used his rhetorical skills to open the Scriptures to his congregation: "If you wish to see the mystery of the Lord, look

> at Abel who is similarily murdered (Gen. 4:1-8),
> at Isaac who is similarly bound (Gen. 22:1-9),
> at Joseph who is similarly sold (Gen. 37:28),
> at Moses who is similarly exposed (Exod. 2:3),
> at David who is similarly persecuted (1 Samuel 23–26),
> at the prophets who similarly suffer for the sake of Christ (Matt. 5:12).

---

8. *Medieval Exegesis* (Grand Rapids: Eerdmans, 1998), 1:235-37.
9. *PG* 70:1381b-d.

Look also at the sheep which is slain in the land of Egypt, which struck Egypt and saved Israel by its blood."[10] Here specific moments in Christ's suffering and death are seen foreshadowed in the lives of great figures in the Old Testament.

Some books, for example, Proverbs, do not yield readily to allegory. The passage, "If one gives answer before he hears, it is his folly and shame" (Prov. 18:13), stands quite comfortably on its own. Likewise there is much in the historical books of the Bible that is spiritually and morally applicable in its own right, such as the story of Joseph in Genesis or of David in 2 Samuel. On the other hand, the book of Leviticus and the Song of Songs cry out for a spiritual interpretation if they are to be read profitably by Christians. Taken only in its literal sense Leviticus, as Origen once observed, is more of an obstacle to faith than a means of exhortation or edification.[11] It is surely significant that books such as Leviticus and the Song of Songs are seldom read in Christian worship today. Without allegory, that is, a spiritual interpretation related to Christ, they languish.

The early Church read the Old Testament as the Word of God, a book about the triune God, God, Father, Son, and Holy Spirit, the God who "was and is and is to come." What the text of the Bible meant when it was written, as far as that can be determined, is part of interpretation, but it can never be the last word, nor even the most important word. A historical interpretation can only be preparatory. A Christian understanding of the Scriptures is oriented toward the living Christ revealed through the words of the Bible, toward what the text means today in the lives of the faithful and what it promises for the future. God spoke once, said St. Bernard, but he speaks to us continually and without interruption.[12]

In reading the commentaries on the Old Testament in The Church's Bible, the reader might note the ways in which interpretation turns on specific words or images. For example, the Song of Songs uses the phrase "well of living water" (4:15), an image that also occurs in Jer. 2:13, "they have forsaken me, the fount of living water," in Zech. 14:8, and in Jesus' discourse with the Samaritan woman (John 4:10-15). In its original literary setting it is crowded in with a number of other images and seems rather innocuous. In his homilies on the Song of Songs, however, Gregory of Nyssa takes "living water" to be an image of the divine life which is "life-giving." He writes: "We are familiar with these descriptions of the divine essence as a source of life from the Holy Scriptures. Thus the prophet, speaking in the person of God, says: 'They have forsaken me, the fountain of living water' (Jer. 2:13). And again the Lord says to the Samaritan woman, 'If you knew the gift of God, and who it is that is saying to you, "Give me a drink," you would have asked him, and he would have given you living water' (John 4:10). And again the Lord says, 'If anyone thirst, let him come to me and drink. He who believes in me, as the Scripture has said, "Out of his heart shall flow rivers of living water"' (John 7:38-39)." By relating what is written in the Song of Songs to other passages from the Old Testament and especially to the words of Jesus in the Gospel of John, Gregory is able to interpret the phrase "living water" in the Song of Songs as "life" flowing from the divine Word of God like water to refresh the soul.

Once a deeper significance of a word or phrase or image is discerned, texts from the

10. Melito of Sardis, *Paschal Homily* 59-60.
11. Homily 5.1 on Leviticus.
12. *Sermones de diversis* 5.1 (*PL* 183:554).

Old Testament resonate with the fullness of the revelation in Christ. The Bible becomes a vast field of interrelated words, all speaking about the same reality, the one God revealed in Christ whose work was confirmed by the Holy Spirit in the life of the Church. The task of the interpreter (and of this series) is to help the faithful look beyond the surface, to highlight a word here, an image there, to find Christ in surprising and unexpected places, to drink at the bountiful spring whose water is ever fresh. Though early Christian exegesis may on first reading appear idiosyncratic and arbitrary, it must be remembered that it arose within the life of the Church and was practiced within a tradition of shared beliefs and practices, guided by the Church's faith as expressed in the creed. Exegesis was not about novelty but about finding the triune God in new and unexpected places within the Scriptures.

The Text of the Old Testament

Most modern English versions of the Old Testament are based on the original Hebrew (and Aramaic) version as it has come down to us in the text established by Jewish scholars (the "Masoretes") in Palestine from the 6th to the 9th centuries. The Masoretic Text is the only complete version of the Hebrew Old Testament, and for centuries it has been used by Christians as well as by Jews. In recent years this text has been amended as new evidence, for example, from the Dead Sea Scrolls, has become available. But modern editions still depend chiefly on the Masoretic Text.

The early Christians, however, did not use the Hebrew version of the Bible. Few spoke or read Hebrew, and the version of the Old Testament read in the churches and used as the basis for biblical commentaries and preaching was a Greek translation of the Hebrew made by Jews before the time of Christ. This translation is usually called the Septuagint (because there were said to be seventy translators). The term may originally have referred only to the books of the Torah, the Pentateuch, that is, the first five books of the Bible. Today, however, the Septuagint (LXX) designates the Greek translation of all the books of the Hebrew Bible, including the Prophets, the Historical Books, and the Wisdom Books, as well as a significant body of other books that go by the name Old Testament Apocrypha, for example, the Wisdom of Solomon, Sirach, the books of the Maccabees, Judith, and Tobit. These latter books are available in English translation in the Revised Standard Version and in the New Revised Standard Version. This Greek Jewish Bible (or translations based on it) was the Bible of the early Church. In the early 5th century, however, St. Jerome translated the Old Testament from Hebrew into Latin, and this version, known as the Vulgate, eventually came to be used by medieval Christian commentators writing in Latin.

Besides the Septuagint, early Christian commentators had access to several other translations made in the first and second centuries A.D. These are identified by the name of the translator: Aquila, Symmachus, and Theodotion. All three were proselytes to Judaism, and Aquila's translation, which was particularly literal, came to be preferred to the Septuagint by Greek-speaking Jews.

Because the ancient commentators were basing their interpretations on the Greek version of the Old Testament (or translations based on it), the actual wording of the text sometimes differs from that of the Hebrew, and hence of modern English versions. Sometimes the differences are minor, but they can also diverge significantly. For example, at Isa. 2:2 the Hebrew reads: "It shall come to pass in the latter days that the mountain of the house of the LORD shall be *established* as the highest of the mountains. . . ." In the Septuagint the verse reads: "For in the last days the mountain of the Lord shall be *manifest*. . . ." This is of course a minor variation, yet the term "manifest" lent itself to an interpretation that highlighted that the Church that began in Jerusalem came to be known throughout the world.

A more significant variant occurs in Ps. 22:1 (LXX 21:1). In the Hebrew the verse reads: "My God, my God, why hast thou forsaken me? Why art thou so far from helping me, from the words of my groaning?" In the Septuagint the second part of the verse reads: "The words of my transgressions are far from your salvation." This reading posed a serious challenge for the interpreter because the psalm was understood to be spoken by Christ. The first words, "My God, my God, why hast thou forsaken me?" are of course the words of Christ on the cross, and other phrases in the psalm were understood to refer to Christ. Yet, if Christ is speaking, how can he say that God's salvation is far from his "transgressions," that is, from his "sins."

The Greek and Latin versions of the Song of Songs diverge significantly from the Hebrew, and the variants often suggest interpretations that would not be supported by the Masoretic Text. At the very beginning, for example, at 1:2, the Hebrew reads "For your love is better than wine," but the Greek (and the Latin following the Greek) read "For your breasts are better than wine," offering a more erotic version of the text that commentators exploited.

Because the church fathers were commenting on the Septuagint (or a version based on the Septuagint, e.g., the Latin), the commentaries in this series provide translations of the text on which their expositions are based.

In general we have tried to provide fairly lengthy selections from the commentaries so that the reader can see how the interpretation derives from the text and how the text under discussion is related to other passages in the Bible. In addition to passages from commentaries and homilies on the book under consideration, we have made a selection of occasional comments on particular verses drawn from theological writings, spiritual treatises, sermons, and other works from the early Church.

We had hoped to be able to provide material on every verse or pericope in each chapter, but that proved unrealistic for the longer books, for example, Genesis, Isaiah, and the Psalms. The ancient commentaries are lengthy and repetitive. We have tried to choose selections that are spiritually, exegetically, or theologically interesting and significant. Readers who wish to check particular passages for which we have not provided excerpts can consult the many translations of ancient commentaries that are now becoming available.

In the excerpts the specific text under discussion is printed in bold. When a passage is cited from elsewhere in the Scriptures it is placed within quotation marks.

The authors and works from which the selections are taken are given in the appendixes.

ROBERT LOUIS WILKEN

An Introduction to the Song of Songs

This volume is intended to illustrate Christian exegesis of the Song of Songs in the Church of the first six centuries and of the Latin Middle Ages. Of the sources used, the majority are either commentaries or sets of sermons dedicated to exposition of the Song. More than half of these are, at least as we now have them, incomplete; that is, they treat only a portion of the text of the Song. The remaining sources are writings in which a passage in the Song is discussed incidentally. The selections have been made to acquaint contemporary readers with the Church's traditional way of discerning in this text a guide to the character of Christian belief and vocation.

In recent times, the Song of Songs has been more a focus of literary than of religious or theological interest: for one reason or another, *erōs*, it seems, has not been thought to enter into people's relation to God. Yet in the early and medieval periods alike, the Song was counted, with the Psalms and the Gospels, among those scriptural writings that touched most deeply upon the mystery of the Church's, and the believer's, relation to God in Christ. It may be helpful, in approaching these materials, to say something about the way in which the Song was classically interpreted.

The Song of Songs and Its Classical Interpretation

The "Song of Songs, which is Solomon's" was one of the last books to be included in the canon of the Hebrew Scriptures. It is a set of poems concerned with love between a woman and a man. The immediate and most obvious problem it presents to readers is that of identifying the lovers (and their attendants). Origen of Alexandria, one of the first Christian commentators on the Song of Songs, took the Song to be a unified piece in the form of a stage play in which different characters alternate as speakers — and principally, of course, the Bride and the Bridegroom. This dramatic hypothesis, as we may call it, was accepted not only by many of those who followed Origen in the early Church but also by John Milton, who described the work as "a Divine pastoral Drama . . . consisting of two persons, and a double chorus." It has been argued in criticism of this general line that where the Song is concerned there is no real clarity about any plot or characters, and indeed no agreed assignment of speeches to characters.

It is tempting, therefore, to say that the Song is an anthology, an assemblage of love poems of one sort or another, whose collector was the first to try to set them in some reasonable order and introduced a distinctive feature of the text, its dialogue form. The late-medieval Christian interpreter Nicholas of Lyra, while not ignoring the dialogical character of the Song, insisted that the Bridegroom and Bride represent — at the "literal" level — God and God's people, and therefore that one must divide the text into two parts, assigning the first part, chaps. 1–6, to the mutual love of God and his people during "the time of the Old Covenant," and the second, to that same love as reflected in the people's life under the New Covenant.

One must, then, admit that there is significant uncertainty about the literary type or form of the Song of Songs. It is certainly poetry, and for that matter love poetry of some sort, and it does seem to have recurring figures or characters, individual or collective: bride, bridegroom, maidens, daughters of Jerusalem, and the bridegroom's companions. More than this, however, is difficult to say. Origen's introduction to the book makes it clear that he thinks the work must be read as a book about love, though he insists that the reader must "know how to listen to the language of erotic desire with chaste ears and a pure mind," and not as a "fleshling." In this way Origen agrees with Jewish interpreters. The rabbis said that "no one who has not attained full maturity [may] be allowed so much as to hold this book in his hands." Along with Genesis 1, the account of creation, and Ezekiel 1, the vision of the divine chariot-throne, the Song of Songs was reckoned among the deepest and most difficult texts in the Bible.

Accordingly, the ancient interpreters of the Song of Songs, Jews and Christians, treat the love lyrics *allegorically;* that is, they treat a human love-affair — vividly described, with scarcely veiled scenes of seduction and happy allusions to certain of the arts of love — as signifying the love between God and the people of God, or between the Word and Wisdom of God and the human soul. Rupert of Deutz, in the 12th century, develops and expands this tradition when he argues that the three works of Solomon treat of the three "theological virtues," namely, faith (Proverbs), hope (Ecclesiastes), and "the greatest of these," love (the Song). The ancient writers find no difficulty in transferring the language of erotic love to spiritual matters. Indeed, the primary reason for resorting to allegory is that they assumed that any writing included in the Scriptures treated, in one manner or another, the relation between God and human beings. They believed that human *erōs,* even when it is focused by desire for union with another human person, displays a receptivity to and a reaching out for a more ultimate love.

There is little evidence how interpreters understood the Song prior to A.D. 70. There is, however, a precedent in the Scriptures for interpreting human love allegorically. The marriage of the prophet Hosea to an adulteress is presented as an allegory of God's relation to Israel (Hos. 3:1). But in Rabbi Akiba, who lived in the second century, one can first discern an early and systematic use of allegory in interpreting the Song. He described the Song as "the Holy of Holies," a characterization that was quickly taken up by Christian exegetes. In his interpretation the Song of Songs was an allegory of God's love for Israel, manifested in the liberation of the people from Egypt, the giving of the law, and later interventions in Jewish history. In Jewish circles his approach was taken up by other interpreters, though the earliest full-blown exposition of the Song in this manner appeared only in the 7th-century Targum, an Aramaic rendering of the Hebrew in the form of a paraphrase.

This kind of exegesis was also practiced by Christians, beginning with Hippolytus of Rome and Origen, both of whom saw in the Bridegroom a representation of Christ (i.e., the eternal Word and Wisdom of God), and in the Bride a representation of the Church, that is, the people of God. The ecclesiological interpretation of the Song became a dominant, and in some cases the exclusive, theme of later Christian exegesis (and, not least, that of Nicholas of Lyra, the late-medieval commentator). Origen, however, taught that the Song could also be taken to speak of the relation between the Word of God and the individual soul — by which he means any believing member of the people of God. No doubt he thought that what is true of the Church collectively is also true, *mutatis mutandis*, of each member of the Church; and this idea was not without some precedent — or, at any rate, illustration — in Jewish treatments of the Song. Even later readings like that of Rupert of Deutz, which see in the figure of the Bride a representation of the Virgin Mary, are merely following out this tradition; for them, the Virgin Mother of God becomes the normative exemplar of the faithful souls that, taken collectively, constitute the Church.

There is, however, more to this twofold type of exegesis, with its differentiation between the Church and the individual soul, than at first meets the eye. The monk who called himself "Honorius of Autun," in the introduction to his commentary, explains that

> Sacred Scripture is interpreted and understood in four ways: historically, allegorically, tropologically, [and] anagogically. This is expressed by the table for the presentation of bread in the ark (Exod. 25:29ff.), which is supported by four feet. The ark represents the Church, in which service is rendered to Christ. The table is sacred Scripture, upon which bread is presented, that is, the food of souls. The four feet are the four kinds of meaning, that is to say: history, when the thing referred to is narrated as it happened; allegory, when the thing referred to is expounded with reference to Christ and the Church; tropology, when it is applied to soul and spirit; anagogy, when it is understood of the celestial life.

Here Honorius is explaining what by his time was, in the West, a traditional and established doctrine of the four "senses" of Scripture. This doctrine in its turn looked back to Origen's practice of interpreting the Scriptures of the Old Testament. Since they were "outward forms of certain mysteries and the images of divine things," as Origen taught, these writings were to be understood not only at the level of their "bodily," literal, or "historical" meaning but also "spiritually" or "anagogically"; and at that level they spoke of the same divine Wisdom — Christ — as did the New Testament. This second level of meaning, however, could in principle include more than one interpretation of a given passage, though Origen felt no obligation to supply more than one in all, or even most, cases. The spiritual meaning might, for example, treat of Christ's public and objective work of salvation and thus of his relation to the Church. It might also treat of that same work of salvation as it was effected in the interior life of the individual. Further still, it might treat of the full and final realization of that salvation in the age to come, that is, of eschatology.

Origen's approach lies at the root of all later Christian interpretation of the Song.

Honorius himself enjoys the distinction of having tried to go Origen one better: he attempted to supply, wherever possible, an "anagogical" — eschatological — interpretation of the verses of the Song, even though Origen had neglected that project. Most of the interpreters excerpted in this volume, however, followed Origen's policy wholly or in part. In general the medieval commentators focused on the meaning of the Song for the interior life of the faithful soul. Earlier writers, on the other hand, regularly followed Origen in providing both the "moral" and the christological or ecclesiastical application, though not in his systematic manner. Gregory of Nyssa, for example, tends, as it were, to assign these two spiritual senses to different lines or passages of the Song.

In reading the excerpts provided here, a contemporary reader needs to understand not only something about the kind of exegesis that is being practiced but also something about the scriptural texts with which these writers worked. In this connection, the first thing to note is that the Christian commentators represented in this book were with one exception, that of Nicholas of Lyra, ignorant of Hebrew. Origen, it is true, had some (secondhand) acquaintance with Hebrew, derived from a personal "consultant" who must have been either a Jew or a Jewish Christian. When later Christian commentators occasionally remark on the sense of Hebrew words, therefore, they are often drawing on Origen's work. Nevertheless, like all Christians and many Jews, Origen regarded the standard Greek translation of the Jewish Scriptures — called the "Septuagint," and, for purposes of abbreviation, the "LXX" — as inspired; and his lifelong effort to establish a reliable text of the Old Testament was focused on this Greek version, which had long been employed in Hellenistic, that is, Greek-speaking, synagogues. Even Latin-speaking Christians — for example, St. Augustine — read and interpreted the Greek Septuagint, though in Latin translation. This is not to suggest that other Greek translations were unknown. Origen, in his famous Hexapla, copied out five alternative Greek versions. Later Greek-speaking commentators like Gregory of Nyssa and Theodoret of Cyrus can be found, therefore, referring to one or more of these other versions to clarify obscurities in the (rough and uncertain) Septuagint text of the Song. Most often they refer to the translation made by Symmachus, a 2nd-century Jewish Christian.

It was only with the dissemination, starting in the 5th century, of a new Latin version composed by St. Jerome, who had learned Hebrew, that western churches came to possess an alternative to the Septuagint; and it is Jerome's translation, commonly called "the Vulgate," that was employed by the medieval scholars excerpted in this book. Needless to say, Jerome's Latin version differs in many respects from the Greek of the Septuagint. As result, *the writers excerpted in this volume are not always commenting on the same text.* Furthermore, the text they are commenting on will differ significantly at certain points from modern English translations of the Hebrew text — which themselves are uncertain and speculative at some points.

Conventions and Policies Followed in This Collection of Texts

These circumstances explain why I have supplied, at the head of each section, an English translation of the Septuagint text of the Song passage to be treated, and, parallel with it, an

English translation of the Vulgate text of the same passage. Readers should, however, understand that these English versions of mine do not profess to convey the exact sense of the original (as do the various English versions of the Song now in use). They are rather intended to render the texts in a way that will enable a reader to see how their ancient and medieval interpreters might naturally have taken them and why they explained them as they did.

For the same reason, the reader does well to understand two other policies followed here. In the first place, *all scriptural quotations in the excerpts from our commentators must be read as drawn from the text of either the Septuagint or the Vulgate.* Where the English of such quotations reproduces that of the Revised Standard Version (as is often the case), that is because the latter happens to agree with the ancient version. Furthermore, *any references given in the body of an excerpt are references to the translation the ancient or medieval writer was employing,* whether that happened to be the Septuagint or the Vulgate. If, then, readers look up a biblical reference noted in the text of one of the excerpts in a modern English translation, they will sometimes encounter what looks like a different text altogether.

Furthermore, the authors represented here were prodigal in their quotations of, and allusions to, the book of Psalms; and this presents a special problem. *The numbering of the Psalms in the Septuagint and the Vulgate differs from that of the Hebrew, and hence from that of modern English translations.* This difference in numeration is owed to the Septuagint's (correct) treatment of Psalms 9 and 10 as a single poem, with the result that the Psalm numbered "10" in the Greek and the Vulgate is called Psalm 11 in all English translations — and so it goes throughout almost the whole of the Psalter (thus Psalm 74 in the English is numbered 73 in the Septuagint and the Vulgate). The two systems of numeration revert to agreement only at the very end of the Psalter, where the Septuagint made two psalms of what in the Hebrew and English is the single Psalm 147. It is further worth noting that the numbering of the verses of individual psalms will often differ in the Septuagint and modern English versions, most often because the Septuagint likes to count a psalm's "title" as its first verse. In the light of these circumstances, I have adopted the policy, where citations of the Psalms are concerned, of supplying the Septuagint (LXX) or Vulgate (Vg) reference and after that the reference to the equivalent English psalm and verse; for example, "Ps. 44:2 LXX = 43:2."

Finally, readers should note the method followed below in arranging the excerpts from ancient and medieval authors. For each section of the Song, the passages cited are arranged in the order of the line or lines of the text each of them "explains." Only within a set of passages that treat the same line or lines are the excerpts arranged in rough chronological order. For this reason, the line or lines that it treats are printed at the beginning of each excerpt.

Sources for the Interpretation of the Song of Songs

Biographical information on the authors whose writings are excerpted in this volume is provided in an appendix. In another appendix the sources from which the individual excerpts are taken are listed in the order in which they appear.

RICHARD A. NORRIS JR.

Prefaces and Title

1:1 The Song of Songs, which is Solomon's.

[The Latin Vulgate does not contain
this title verse.]

Every ancient or medieval writer who set out to interpret the Song of Songs in a systematic way produced some sort of introduction or preface to his work. In such introductions, it was customary to say something about the title and the author (given in the first verse of the Septuagint translation), as well as about the place of the Song in the traditional list of Solomon's writings. Even more important, however, was the issue of the subject matter of the Song, and the closely connected question of the use of allegory in its interpretation. The surface or "literal" subject matter of the Song was the love that joins a bride and her betrothed, a sexual longing that the Song celebrates cheerfully. Understood in that way, however, the Song had little to say directly about the relation between God and "us"; and that relation of course defines the basic interest — the agenda — that Jews and Christians alike brought, and bring, to their reading of the Scriptures. Hence the traditional resort to allegory in interpretation of the Song: the love that it celebrates is treated as a figure or analogy for the love between God and the people of God, the Church. Thus in Christian allegory (or anagogy, "leading upward toward a higher meaning") the Bridegroom becomes Christ, the Word or Son of God, and the Bride becomes either the Church or, as Origen was the first to suggest, the individual believer. This suggestion of Origen — that the "spiritual" subject matter of the Song was not only the relation between Christ and the Church but also that between Christ and the individual soul — pretty well shaped the course of Christian interpretation of this book, and the relation between Christ and the soul dominated medieval — which is almost synonymous with "monastic" — interpretation, as the long excerpt below from William of St. Thierry (who was by no means ignorant of Origen's views) demonstrates.

(1) Origen

This little book I take to be an epithalamium, that is, a marriage song, written by Solomon and done in the manner of a drama. He sings it as if he were a bride at her wedding, burning with heavenly desire for her bridegroom, who is the Word of God. For the bride desired him very deeply — whether she be identified as the soul that is made after his image or as the Church. This very same Scripture also teaches us what words this glorious and perfect Bridegroom used when he addressed the soul or Church that has been joined to him. We also discover, from the same little book, which is called **Song of Songs**, what the young companions of the Bride, who are set in her company, had to say, and also the friends and companions of the Bridegroom. . . . And this is the point of what we said above in calling this a marriage song done in the manner of a drama; for something is called a drama — as, for example, a story acted out on a stage — when different characters are introduced, and the plot is carried through as some enter and others depart to various purposes. This writing contains such goings-on, one after another, in its own distinctive order; and at the same time the drama as a whole is put together out of mystical utterances.

But before anything else, we must be aware that, just as children are not moved by the passion of desire, so too people whose inner self is still small and infantile are not admitted to the study of these words — those, I mean, who are being fed with milk in Christ and not with strong meat, and who have only just now started to long for the "pure spiritual milk" (1 Pet. 2:2). For in the words of the Song of Songs there is found that food of which the apostle says, "Solid food is for the mature" (Heb. 5:14); and the audience it wants is composed of "those who have their faculties trained by practice to distinguish good from evil" (Heb. 5:14) in proportion to their abilities.

As to those little ones of whom we spoke, it may very well be the case that, should they approach these texts, they would neither derive profit from them nor, on the other hand, suffer much harm, whether from a reading of the words or from a review of the things that have to be said for the purpose of expounding them. On the other hand, if a man who is a mere fleshling should approach them, for such a one there would arise no little risk and danger. For anyone who does not know how to listen to the language of erotic desire with chaste ears and a pure mind will pervert what he hears and be turned from the inner self to the outward, from the spirit to the flesh; and he will foster carnal desires within himself, and it will appear to be the case that he is roused and encouraged to carnal lust by the Scriptures.

For this reason, then, I admonish and advise everyone who is not yet rid of the vexations of flesh and blood and has not withdrawn from the solicitations of our material nature to renounce entirely the reading of this book and the things said in it. For they say that among the Jews care is taken that no one who has not attained full maturity be allowed so much as to hold this book in his hands. But there is also the following observance that we have taken over from them: the custom, namely, that all the Scriptures are delivered to children by wise teachers, and at the same time that those four writings that they call *deuteroseis* — that is to say, Genesis 1, in which the world's creation is described; the opening chapters of the prophet Ezekiel, which tell about the cherubim; the last chapter of Ezekiel, which contains the building of the temple; and this book, the Song of Songs — should be held back till last of all.

To me, then, it seems first of all necessary, before we undertake to investigate what is written in this little book, to say something about desire [*erōs*], which is the principal theme of this writing. . . .

Among the Greeks, many of the learned men, wishing to undertake inquiry into the truth about the nature of erotic desire, have produced a variety of writings in the form of dialogues. They attempt to show that it is nothing other than the power of this desire that conducts the soul from earth to the exalted heights of heaven, and that there is no way to attain the highest form of happiness save at the urging of the longing that consists in desire. Furthermore, the discussions of this subject are represented as taking place at meals — between people, I suspect, among whom what went on was a banquet that consisted more in words than in meats. There are others, though, who have left us "how to" writings, with whose help this sort of desire can apparently be elicited or augmented in the soul. But carnal individuals have dragged these skills down to serve vicious desires and the mysteries of illicit desire.

It is no matter for wonder, then, if we say that in our circles too — where there are as many ignorant persons as there are folk of the simpler sort — discussions of the nature of desire are difficult and come close to being dangerous. Among the Greeks, after all, who seem to qualify as wise and learned, there were nevertheless some who did not take what was written in the sense it was intended, but seized the occasion provided by this talk to rush into fleshly lapses and fall down the precipices of immodesty — whether because, as we said above, they gathered guidance and encouragement from what had been written, or because they used the writings of the ancients as a veil for their own intemperate ways.

Lest, then, we too follow the same course, and take words that have been well and spiritually written in a base and fleshly sense, let us lift up our hands, both of body and of soul, to God, so that the Lord . . . may powerfully endow us with his Word, and we may be able, starting from these writings, to make manifest a wholesome understanding of both the name and the nature of desire. . . .

At the beginning of the writings of Moses, where he takes up the creation of the world, we find mention of the creation of two humans, the first of them made "after the image and likeness of God" (Gen. 1:26-27), and the second "fashioned out of the dust of the earth" (Gen. 2:7). Knowing this well, and having a clear grasp of these matters, the apostle Paul in his letters wrote — more straightforwardly and more plainly than Moses — that in each individual person there are two human selves. For see what he says: "If our outer self is wasting away, our inner self is being renewed every day" (2 Cor. 4:16); and again, "For I delight in the law of God in my interior self" (Rom. 7:22); and he uses similar language in some other places. For this reason it is my firm opinion that no one nowadays has any business doubting that in the opening section of Genesis Moses wrote of the creation or fashioning of two human beings; for we see Paul, who understood the writings of Moses better than we do, saying that in each individual person there are two human beings. He says that one of these — that is, the interior one — is "being renewed every day," while he asserts that the other, the "outer," is, in the saints and in people like Paul himself, "wasting away" and being enfeebled. If anything relating to this matter seems to anyone to be questionable, it will be more fully explained in the proper places.

At this point, however, let us pursue the matter on account of which we have made mention of the outer and the interior self. For we want, once this distinction is established, to show that the divine Scriptures name the members both of the outer and of the interior self by using homonyms — that is, by using similar names, to the point of employing the very same words both for the members of the outer self and for the parts and motions of that interior self; and that these are likened to each other, not only as regards the names they are called by, but as regards what they actually are. Take an example: a person is a mere child as concerns the interior self if it is possible for that person to grow and to be brought to the age of a youth, and thence attain by successive steps to the "mature man" (Eph. 4:13) and become a father.

Now our intent in using these last designations is that the expressions we employ may concur with the usage of Holy Scripture — with that passage of Scripture, in fact, which was written by John: "I am writing to you, little children, because you have known the Father. I am writing to you, fathers, because you know him who is from the beginning. I write to you, young men, because you are strong, and the word of God abides in you, and you have overcome the evil one" (1 John 2:13-14). It is perfectly apparent, and I am sure no one can doubt, that in this passage John uses the terms "little children," or "youths," or "young men," or even "fathers," not in reference to the age of the body, but to that of the soul. Yes, and Paul too says in one place, "I . . . could not address you as spiritual, but as fleshly, as babes in Christ. I fed you with milk, not solid food" (1 Cor. 3:1-2). It is beyond any doubt that the babe "in Christ" is so named in accordance with the age of its soul, not of its flesh. And finally, this same Paul also says, in another place: "When I was a child, I spoke like a child, I thought like a child, I reasoned like a child; when I became a man, I gave up childish ways" (1 Cor. 13:11). Again he says on another occasion, "Until we all come up to . . . the mature man, up to the measure of the age of the fullness of Christ" (Eph. 4:13). For he knows that all believers will come up "to the mature man" and "to the measure of the age of the fullness of Christ."

Therefore just as, in the case of the expressions we have mentioned, the names of ages are applied, in the very same terms, both to the outer self and to the interior self, so too you will find that the names of members of the body are transferred to those of the soul — or, better, these names are applied to the soul's powers and motions. That is why it is said in Ecclesiastes: "The eyes of the wise man are in his head" (Eccl. 2:14). Likewise in the Gospel: "Let anyone who has ears to hear, hear" (Matt. 13:43). Also in the prophets: "The word of the Lord that came by the hand of the prophet Jeremiah" (Jer. 50:1) — or of whomever you please. Similar is the command, "Let not your foot offend" (cf. Prov. 3:23 with Matt. 18:8), and again, "My feet were moved a little less" (Ps. 72:2 LXX = 73:2). Obviously too the womb of the soul is denoted where it says, "We have conceived in our womb, O Lord, out of thy fear" (Isa. 26:17-18 LXX). . . .

On the basis of this evidence it is apparent that these words for members of the body cannot be made to fit any visible body. They must, on the contrary, be referred to the parts and powers of the invisible soul, for although the terms do indeed refer to parts that are analogous, they openly and unambiguously bear references proper to the inte-

4

rior, and not to the outer, self. Therefore, there is a food and drink for this material human being — the one that is called "outer self" — that is akin to it: a corporeal and earthly food and drink. By the same token, however, there is also a food proper to that very self that is also called interior — that "living bread," namely, "that came down from heaven" (John 6:33, 41). It drinks, moreover, of that water which Jesus promised when he said, "Whoever drinks of this water that I give him will never thirst" (John 4:14). So it is, then, that like terms are everywhere predicated of both selves; but in each case the special quality of the entity is preserved in its distinctive character, and corruptible things are provided for the corruptible, but for the incorruptible, incorruptible things are set out.

Hence it happens that some people of the simpler sort cannot distinguish or discriminate between things that the divine Scriptures assign to the interior human being and those that they assign to the outer human being. They are deceived by the similarities of the terms, and they devote themselves to silly myths and empty fictions. Thus, for example, they believe that even after the resurrection corporeal foods will be necessary, and that drink will have to be derived not merely from that "true vine" (John 15:1) which lives forever, but also from vines and from fruit that grows on trees. But we shall see about these matters in another place.

Well then, as we have made clear in the preceding remarks, one individual is without offspring and barren as far as the interior self is concerned, and another is rich in offspring; and we note the following saying that accords with this: "The barren has borne seven, and she who has many children is weakened" (1 Sam. 2:5). One might further add what is said in the blessings: "There will be none among you that is childless and barren" (see Exod. 23:26).

Well, but if this is how things stand, then just as one kind of desire is called fleshly — the desire that the poets call *Cupid,* in accordance with which the person who desires sows "to the flesh"; so too there is a certain spiritual desire, in accordance with which that interior self, the one that desires, sows "to the Spirit" (Gal. 6:8). And to speak more plainly, any who still bear "the image of the earthly humanity" in their outer self are driven by an earthly lust and earthly love; but any who "bear the image of the heavenly humanity" (1 Cor. 15:49) in their interior self are driven by a heavenly lust and love. But the soul is driven by a heavenly desire and lust when it has detected the beauty and comeliness of the Word of God, and has been captivated by him, and at his hand has received a certain dart and wound of desire. For this Word is "the image and shining brightness of the invisible God, the Firstborn of all creation, in whom all things are created, both things in heaven and things on earth, whether visible or invisible" (Col. 1:15ff.). If, then, one has the mental capacity to hold together in one's mind and to contemplate the loveliness and grace of all these things that have been created in him, then — struck by the elegant beauty and the magnificent splendor of the things themselves and, as the prophet says, pierced through by "a chosen arrow" (Isa. 49:2) — one will receive from him the wound that is saving and will burn with the blessed fire of the desire of him.

There is another point that we must be aware of. Just as an illicit and unlawful desire may come to the outer self — as when, for example, he desires not his betrothed bride or wife but a harlot or an adulteress; so too it can come about for the interior self — which is to say, the soul — that she desires not her legitimate Betrothed, which we have identified as the Word of God, but some adulterer or debauchee. So much does the prophet Ezekiel, using this very same figure, declare when he introduces Oholah and Oholibah to stand for Samaria and Jerusalem as corrupted by an adulterous desire (Ezek. 23:4-5); and indeed this very passage of the prophetic writing demonstrates his point for those who want a fuller understanding of the matter. What is more, even the spiritual desire proper to the soul, as we have taught, flames out at some times toward certain spirits of evil, and at others, toward the Holy Spirit and the Word of God. The Word is the faithful Bridegroom and is called the husband of the enlightened soul, and it is on his account that the Bride herself, especially in the scriptural book now before us, is so named.

It seems to me, however, that the divine Scripture, wanting to take care that no moral lapse should come about in its readers because of the word "desire," and having in mind the welfare of weaker readers, assigned the name "delight" or the name "love" [*agapē*] to what, among the wise of this present age, had been called "lust" or "desire" — for example, as when it says of Isaac: "and he took Rebekah, and she became his wife, and he loved her" (Gen. 24:67). . . .

Here, therefore, and in many other passages, you will find that the divine Scripture shunned the term "desire" and instead set down "delight" and "love." Nevertheless, now and then, though rarely, it calls desire by its proper name. It summons souls and spurs them on to desire, as when, in Proverbs, it says concerning Wisdom: "Desire her intensely, and she will preserve you; embrace her, and she will exalt you; respect her, that she may enfold you" (Prov. 4:6, 8). And in the book called The Wisdom of Solomon, it is written concerning Wisdom herself: "I have become a desirer of her beauty" (Wisdom 8:2). I think, though, that the word "desire" is inserted only where there seems to be no occasion of moral lapse. For what that is shameful or liable to passion can anyone discern in the desire for Wisdom, or in someone who professes to be a desirer of Wisdom? On the other hand, if it had said that Isaac desired Rebecca passionately, or that Jacob desired Rachel, some shameful passion could indeed be understood to have affected the holy men of God, and especially by those who have no idea of how to ascend from the letter to the spirit. Obviously, though, in the little book now before us, the word "desire" has been changed to the term "love" in the passage where it says, "I have adjured you, O daughters of Jerusalem, if you find my kinsman, to tell him that I am wounded by love" (5:8) — instead of the possible alternative: "I have been struck by the dart of his desire."

Thus in the divine Scriptures it makes no difference whether it says, "desire" or "love" or "delight," except that God himself is called "love," even as John says: "Beloved, let us love one another, for love is from God, and everyone who loves is born of God and knows God. But anyone who does not love does not know God, for God is love" (1 John 4:7-8). And although it may be the business of another occasion to say something about these words we have cited from John's letter for the sake of an example, yet it does not seem out of place to touch briefly on some points from the passage. "Let us love one another," he says, "for love is from God," and then, after a bit, "God is love." In this he shows both that God himself is love and that the one who is "from God" is also love. And who is "from God" if not the one who says, "I came from the Father and have come into this world" (John 16:28)? If God the Father is love, and the Son is love, while the one love and the other are one thing and differ in no respect, it follows that the Father and the Son are one thing and differ in no respect. It is appropriate, therefore, that just as Christ is called Wisdom and Power and Righteousness and Word and Truth, so too he is called Love. That is why Scripture says: "If love abides in us, God abides in us" (1 John 4:12) — God, that is to say, the Father and the Son, who also come to the person who has been perfected in love in accordance with the word of our Lord and Savior when he said, "I and my Father will come to him and will make our dwelling with him" (John 14:23).

It must be understood, then, that this love that God is, no matter in whom it dwells, esteems nothing earthly, nothing material, nothing corruptible; for it is against its nature to have regard for anything corruptible, seeing that it is itself the fount of incorruption. It is love itself that alone has immortality — if indeed "God is love" (1 John 4:8), who "alone has immortality, dwelling in light inaccessible" (1 Tim. 6:16). Moreover, what is immortality if it is not "eternal life," which God promises he will give to those who believe in "the only true God" and his Son "Jesus Christ, whom he has sent" (John 17:3)?

Hence it is said that first of all and before anything else this is agreeable and pleasing to God: that one love the Lord God with all one's heart and with all one's soul and with all one's strength. And since "God is love," and the Son, who is "from God," is love, he seeks within us something like himself, so that by means of this love that is in Christ Jesus, we may be tied in with God as if by a bond of kinship through the name of love, even as he who was already joined to God said, "Who will separate us from the love of God, which is in Christ Jesus our Lord?" (Rom. 8:35, 39).

This love, moreover, counts every human being as a neighbor. The Lord, after all, censured one man on this very score, a man who held that a righteous soul does not owe the duties of a neighbor to a soul that is entangled in wickedness. For this very reason, moreover, he constructed the parable that tells how a certain man fell among thieves while going down from Jerusalem to Jericho; and he blames the priest and the Levite who passed him by when they saw him lying half-dead, but he approves of the Samaritan who had compassion; and by the response of the man who had asked the question he established that the Samaritan was a neighbor to the victim, and said, "Go, and do thou likewise" (Luke 10:37). For by nature we are neighbors to one another; but by works of love a person who can do good to one who is unable to do so becomes a neighbor. Hence too our Savior became a neighbor to us. He did not pass us by while we were lying half-dead from wounds inflicted by thieves. So it must be understood that love directed to God is always moving toward God, from whom it takes its origin; and it has regard for its neighbor, to whom it is akin as being similarly created in incorruption. Thus, then, take whatever is written concerning love as if it had been said about desire, and do not worry about labels; for the same sense is manifest in both of them.

(2) Gregory the Great

After the human race was expelled from the joys of the Paradise, and it entered upon the pilgrimage of our present life, it was possessed of a heart that was blind to spiritual understanding. If the divine voice said to this blind heart, once for all banished from the Paradise, "Seek God," or "Love God," as is said in the law, the heart would not grasp what was addressed to it because of its cold and listless unbelief. Therefore the divine speech addresses the cold and listless soul in figurative language, and by way of things with which it is acquainted introduces it to a love with which it is not acquainted.

Allegory, after all, devises, for the sake of the soul that is far removed from God, a stratagem that will elevate it to God. When figurative language is interposed, the soul, even while it grasps in the words something on its own level, apprehends in their intelligible sense something that is not on its own level, and by earthly words is separated from what is earthly. For in the simple act of not rejecting what is familiar and known, it apprehends something that is unknown. The divine teachings, after all, are clothed in things that are familiar to us, the things out of which allegories are made; and as we consider the exterior words, we achieve an interior discernment.

Hence it is that in the Song of Songs . . . words are set down that pertain to bodily love, so that the soul, wakened anew out of its listless state by language to which it is accustomed, may heat up and may by the language of a lesser love be aroused to a higher. For in this book kisses are mentioned, breasts are mentioned, cheeks are mentioned, the loins are mentioned; and the holy picture these words paint is not meant for mockery or laughter. Rather ought we to focus our minds upon the greater mercy of God. We must notice how marvelously and mercifully, in making mention of parts of the body and thus summoning us to love, he works with us; for he reaches down to the vocabulary of our sensual love in order to set our heart on fire, aiming to incite us to a holy loving. Indeed, by the act in which he lowers himself in words he also elevates our understanding; for from the words associated with this sensual love we learn how fiercely we are to burn with love for the Divine.

But we must be wise enough to pay close attention to this, lest when we hear the words of an external love we become mentally fixed on things outside of us, and the very stratagem whose aim is to elevate us holds us down instead, so that we are not raised up. For in these corporeal words, these words that are outside us, we ought to look for whatever is more interior and, while speaking about the body, become as it were outside the body. We must come to these sacred nuptials of the Bridegroom and the Bride with the understanding proper to interior love — come, that is, dressed in a wedding garment: lest if we are not attired in a wedding garment, we be cast out of the wedding feast into the outer darkness, the blindness of ignorance. By way of words that express passion we are meant to make the transition to the virtue of impassibility.

For it is the same with the words and meanings of sacred Scripture as it is with the colors and subjects of a painting; and anyone who is so intent upon the colors in the painting that he ignores the real things it portrays is immeasurably silly. For if we embrace the words, which are spoken externally, and disregard their meanings, as if knowing nothing of the things that are portrayed, we are clinging to the mere colors. "The letter kills," it is written, "but the spirit gives life" (2 Cor. 3:6). For the letter covers the spirit in the same way that the husk conceals the grain. The husks, however, are food for beasts of burden; it is the grain that feeds human beings. Whoever, then, makes use of human reason casts away the husks that belong to beasts of burden and hastens to consume the grain of the spirit.

To be sure, it serves a good purpose for mysteries to be hidden by the cloak of the letter, seeing that wisdom that has been sought after and pursued is savored the more for that. That is why it stands written: "The wise conceal a meaning" (Prov. 10:14) — because, to be sure, the spiritual sense is hidden under the covering of the letter. Hence, again, it is said in the same book: "It is the glory of God to conceal a word" (Prov. 25:2). For to the mind that seeks God, God appears the more glorious to the degree that he is searched out more delicately and inwardly — as will become plain. But ought we not hunt down what God has veiled in mysteries? Of course we ought; for the very next words are: "It is the glory of kings to search out what is said." For kings are those who know how to rule and to search out their bodies and the stirrings of their flesh. Therefore, the glory of kings is to "search out what is said," because the praise accorded to those who live well is that they search the hidden depths of God's commandments.

Hence when we attend to words that are employed in human intercourse, we ought to stand as it were outside our humanity, lest, if we take in what is said on the human level, we detect nothing of the divinity that belongs to the things we are meant to hear. It was Paul's desire that his disciples cease, as it were, to be mere humans. He says to them, "For while there is jealousy and strife among you, are you not . . . ordinary men?" (1 Cor. 3:3). The Lord no longer regarded his disciples as ordinary men when he said, "Who do men say that the Son of man is?" (Matt. 16:13). When they had answered him by citing the words of ordinary humans, he instantly added, "But who do you say that I am?" (Matt. 16:15). For since he says "men" in the first instance and then adds "but . . . you," he has made a distinction between men and disciples, plainly enough because he was making the latter more than merely human by implanting in them things divine. The apostle says, "If then anyone is in Christ, there is a new creation; the old things have passed away" (2 Cor. 5:17). And we know that in our resurrection the body will be connected to the Spirit in such wise that everything that had once belonged to passion is taken up in the power of the Spirit. Hence the person who follows God ought to imitate his resurrection daily, so that just as in that day there will be nothing vulnerable in the body, so at the present day nothing susceptible to unruly passions is maintained in the heart — with the result that, as far as the inner self is concerned, there is even now "a new creation," that even now whatever gives off the sound of the old humanity is trodden down, and in the ancient words nothing is sought save the power of the new.

For Scripture is a sort of sacred mountain from which the Lord comes within our hearts to create understanding. This is the mountain of which the prophet says, "God shall come from Lebanon, and the holy one from the dense and overclouded mountain" (Hab. 3:3). This mountain is dense with the thoughts it contains and "overclouded" with allegories. One must be aware, however, that we are instructed, when the voice of the Lord sounds on the mountain, to wash our clothing and to be purified of every fleshly pollution, if we are hurrying to come to the mountain. Indeed, it is written that if a wild beast should touch the mountain, it would be stoned (Heb. 12:20; cf. Exod. 19:12). Now a beast touches the mountain when people given over to irrational urges hasten toward the height of sacred Scripture and do not understand it as they ought, but irrationally bend their understanding of it to the service of their own pleasure. For all who are senseless or sluggish of mind will be stoned to death, as it were, by dreadful judgments, if they should be seen in the vicinity of this mountain. For this mountain is afire since sacred Scripture

9

sets the person whom it fills spiritually on fire with the flame of love. That is why it is written, "Your speech glows with fire" (Ps. 118:140 LXX = 119:140). That is why, when certain individuals who were on a trip heard words of God, they said, "Did not our hearts burn within us . . . , while he opened to us the scriptures?" (Luke 24:32). That is why it is said through Moses: "In his right hand a law that flames" (Deut. 33:2 Vg). At God's left hand, the wicked are received; at God's right hand, the elect are situated. The "law . . . flames," therefore, at the right hand of God; for in the hearts of the elect, who are set at the right hand, the divine commands flame up and are set on fire by the ardor of love. This fire, then, burns up whatever there is in us of outward blemish and the old humanity, so that it may offer up our mind as a burnt offering for the contemplation of God.

*   *   *

It is not inconsistent with the greatness of this mystery that this book of Solomon [i.e., the Song of Songs] is placed third among his writings. The ancients asserted that there are three stages of life, the moral, the natural, and the contemplative, which the Greeks called ethical, physical, and theoretical. In Proverbs, then, the moral life is set forth, where it says, "Hear my wisdom, son, and bend your ear to my knowledge" (Prov. 5:1). On the other hand, it is the natural life that is set forth in Ecclesiastes — since there the tendency of all things to come to an end is made a subject of reflection, when it says, "Vanity of vanities; all things are vanity" (Eccl. 1:2). In the Song of Songs, however, the contemplative life is set forth, even as in it the Lord's coming and his appearance are sought after, when the voice of the bridegroom says, **Come away from Libanus, come** (4:8). The life of the patriarchs — Abraham, that is, and Isaac, and Jacob — provides a sign of these three stages. Abraham surely by his obedience displayed the moral life. Isaac for his part figures the natural life by his well-digging, for to dig deep wells is to look closely into all things here below by natural reflection. Jacob, however, who saw the angels ascending and descending, held to the contemplative life. But since natural reflection does not lead to perfection unless morality is first maintained, Ecclesiastes is rightly placed after Proverbs. Moreover, since contemplation of higher things is not attained until these things here below, passing away as they are, are despised, the Song of Songs is rightly placed after Ecclesiastes. The first task is surely to get one's morals right, and after that to consider all things present as though they were absent, and in the third place to look upon things exalted and interior with the pure apex of the heart. Therefore by this sequence of books he constructs a sort of ladder that leads to contemplation of God. . . .

(3) William of St. Thierry

As we approach the epithalamium, the marriage song, the song of the Bridegroom and the Bride, to read and to weigh your work, we call upon you, O Spirit of holiness. We want you to fill us with your love, O Love, so that we may understand love's song — so that we too may be made in some degree participants in the dialogue of the holy Bridegroom and the Bride; and so that what we read about may come to pass within us. For where it is a question of the soul's affections, one does not easily understand what is said unless one is touched by similar feelings. Turn us then to yourself, O holy Spirit, holy Paraclete, holy Comforter; comfort the poverty of our solitude, which seeks no solace apart from you; illumine and enliven the desire of the suppliant, that it may become delight. Come, that we may love in truth, that whatever we think or say may proceed out of the fount of your love. Let the Song of your love be so read by us that it may set fire to love itself within us; and let love itself be for us the interpreter of your Song.

We will not make it our business to handle those deeper mysteries that our Song contains — those that concern Christ and the Church; but keeping ourselves within ourselves, and measuring ourselves by reference to what we are, we offer a short account of Christ and the Christian soul, proportioned to the poverty of our understanding, confined to that moral sense which is open to anyone and everyone. And we do not seek any other reward of our labor than what is similar to the matter of the Song, that is, love.

So then, this book of King Solomon's is titled "Song of Songs." One reason why this is so is that the nobility of its thoughts and the dignity of its subject matter seem to surpass all the songs of the ancient patriarchs and prophets, in that it treats of Bridegroom and Bride, Christ and the rational soul. Another is that it is sung out jubilantly in a perfect harmony of holy aspirations by the blessed people that knows jubilation and walks in the light of God's countenance, rather than being intoned in a vocal harmony of different notes. For this Song sings of the love of God, the love, that is, by which God is loved, or the love whose name is given to God himself. Whether this is called "desire" or "love" or "delight" makes no difference, save that the word "desire" seems to signify an affect of warmth and fondness on the part of a lover who is reaching out and seeking; while "love" refers to a spiritual affect, to the joy that accompanies possession; and "delight," the natural longing for an object that affords delight. Nevertheless, in the case of the love of Bridegroom and Bride, all of these are worked by one and the self-same Spirit (cf. 1 Cor. 12:11). For the sake of singing the new song, all holy and virtuous impulses are in the service of the love of Bridegroom and Bride — so that if these impulses make progress in due and proper order, they may all undergo transformation and come to their goal and their finish in doing what love does. The other impulses fade away, but "love never ceases" (1 Cor. 13:8).

Or again, it is called "Song of Songs" because it is perceived to contain four songs within itself. It is divided, on this account, into four sections, each of which comes to an end with their lying together, that is, with the Bridegroom's and the Bride's union. Out of reverence for the "great mystery" (cf. Eph. 5:32) that appears in Christ and the Church, it pleased the Holy Spirit to honor this joining with a nobler name — to call it "being together" rather than "copulation"; for the Bride says, **While the King was together with me, my nard gave off its scent** (1:12). Each of these moments of being together is preceded by its epithalamium — its marriage song, by which the Bridegroom and the Bride are, as it were, led to the marriage chamber. It is brought to a conclusion when on the initiative of the Bridegroom himself peace, and the safety of repose, are ordained for the Bride as she lies in his embrace; for he issues a charge and says, **I adjure you, daughters of Jerusalem . . . , not to rouse my beloved or waken her until she herself wishes** (Song 8:4). The fourth section, however, which is also the last, seems to conclude in a different manner, with a deeper mystery. The others seem to give voice to a festal rejoicing for the union of Bridegroom and Bride; but this last section ends when the Bride enjoins flight upon the Bridegroom, as she proclaims, **Flee, my Beloved, and be like the gazelle, and the young of stags upon the mountains of spices** (8:14). What this may mean will be indicated in the proper place, supposing that the Bridegroom himself deigns to reveal it.

Further, this Song is written in the manner of a stage play in the style of comedy, as if its performance were to be carried out by characters and their actions, so that just as there are different characters and different actions involved in the performance of comedies, so too in this Song the characters and their passions seem to work together for the purpose of bringing the love affair — the mystical transaction of divine and human union — to its conclusion. In the Song, there are four characters: the Bridegroom and his companions; the Bride and the chorus of young maidens. The companions of the Bridegroom are the angels, rejoicing with us over the good things that come to us, in this way taking pleasure in the service they render by their apt ministries. For their part, the young maidens are tender and new-sprung souls who have signed up for instruction in and practice of spiritual love, and delight to follow the Bride, that is to say, more advanced souls, by their humble obedience and eager imitation. Nevertheless, the entire business of love making is left to the lovers; and the result is that — since the sharers in their love are silent, and stand still, and hear, and are overjoyed at the words of the Bridegroom and the Bride — in the whole of the Song scarcely a single word is heard or a single speech inserted that does not come from the Bridegroom or the Bride.

As to the subject matter of the play — be it historical, fictional, or symbolic — it involves some such plot as this. King Solomon has taken the daughter of Pharaoh to wife. He has first of all granted her the significant gift — proper to a betrothal — of love and of a kiss. After that, however, when he has shown her a portion of his riches and a part of his glory, he denies her both conjugal union and the pleasure of a kiss until she has put away her Egyptian blackness and stripped herself of the customs of a barbarous nation, and thus has become worthy to be admitted to the King's chamber.

The spiritual sense is this: The soul has turned its face toward God and is to be married to the Word of God. First of all, she is taught to comprehend the riches of prevenient grace, and is permitted to taste how sweet the Lord is (cf. Ps. 33:9 LXX = 34:8). After that, however, she is sent back into the house of her own conscience; there she is to be instructed, purified by the obedience of love, and thoroughly cleansed of vices as well as adorned with virtues, so that she may be admitted to the spiritual gift of devotion to God and to the passion for virtue, which is the Bridegrom's chamber.

It was necessary to take these matters up by way of preface, so as then, with our path cleared, to chase after the fragrance of the Bridegroom (cf. 1:3) — but on the prior condition that if at some point the beauty of the route should render us a bit more curious in our role as its viewers, no offense would be given to our companion on the road.

But one further observation before we undertake this journey. Since all the sections of this Song represent nothing other than different states of those who pray, not to mention the forms, the springs, and the matter of prayers, it seems that we must say something of the various modes of prayer, so that the serious and devout reader, as he makes his way through the text of the Song itself, may always be returning to himself, and, finding these modes of prayer in the holy Song, may recognize them in his own heart.

So then it is plain that there are three states of people who engage in prayer, or, for that matter, of prayers: animal, rational, and spiritual. Every such individual shapes and represents the Lord God for himself in a way that corresponds to his own way of praying; for such as is the one who does the praying, so does the God whom he addresses appear to him. Just as the person who prays faithfully always attempts, in the prayer he makes, to bring to God something genuine and worthy of God, so too does he maintain an anxious and uncertain heart, until he has some picture of the one before whom he places his offering and to whom he entrusts it.

The individual of animal condition prays to God but does not know how to pray properly. He asks something from God that is neither God himself nor something that leads to God; he asks that he may prosper in his social rank, or that he may be found among the more sensible and realistic members of his generation, but not that his conscience may be cleansed of evil deeds and his heart of wicked thoughts. He presents himself to God just as he is, that is, as a person who desires and seeks something other than God himself. He does not seek a God who is different in character from himself, that is, he seeks a God who accords everything he asks except God himself.

And if occasionally he seems to focus his attention on the One to whom he prays, for him it suffices to think — with, as it were, the eyes of his heart closed — of a God who is unthinkable, invisible, and incomprehensible. What satisfies his thought and his apprehension is not God for what God is, but God as he is able to furnish what he is asked for. This individual sometimes prays with the spirit, not with the mind; and it is his spirit, that is, his will, that does the praying, but his "mind is unfruitful" (cf. 1 Cor. 14:14-15). For one cannot fix attention upon God without the mind's being fruitful — not even if one asks for something other than God himself, as long as one asks rationally. But this individual multiplies words in his praying, often without sense, and thoughts without understanding; and he does not seek either awareness of God, or the prick of aspiration toward God. Even if these are spontaneously awakened in him, he turns them into something else, and therefore for him the God to whom he prays is forever in a cloud, as formerly it was for the fleshly Israel.

The Song of love, however, has no place for prayer in this mode. In this book, the Bride, who desires one thing and loves one thing, asks for one thing only, prays for one thing only. There is also an animal sort of prayer that is proper to saintly persons; and sometimes it concerns what is also pleasing to people who work iniquity — such as temporal peace, the fertility of the earth, or bodily health. Nevertheless such prayer does not share the values of persons of that sort; for even though it asks for something other than God, this is not because it is for the sake of anything other than God, or because it seeks anything else but this one thing. The saints present their requests in a manner devout and holy, handing them over without any reservation, and leaving it to the will of the One to whom they pray to decide whether what they ask is to be granted or not.

From time to time, moreover, an individual of this sort sets the Lord and Savior before the eyes of his mind in his human aspect, and as one human being to another invests his prayer with a kind of human, almost corporeal, affection. He pictures in his mind the one to whom he prays, himself as the one who is praying, and in between them, as it were, the thing for which prayer is made. He molds the form of his prayer to the scheme of this picture. This kind of praying is more proper to a faith that is still simple, one that does not yet grasp the things of God, than it is to a listless animality or to a spirit of merely human prudence. The soul, moreover, when in the presence of Jesus, the caring judge, sets forth her concerns faithfully and places herself at his feet, washing them with her tears and anointing them with the spiritual oil of true devotion — and yet imaging all this for herself in thoroughly corporeal terms; at that time, in virtue of the sweetness of these same animal imaginings, she often comes to deserve enlightenment, and the warm glow of desire for spiritual prayer, that is, contemplation. In a way of which she knows nothing, she comes, with the help of these images, to comprehend certain mysteries of the faith. In the simple heart, this comes about more by the action of the One who bestows grace than by the zeal of the one who is praying. For she loves greatly, and therefore much is granted her and forgiven her (cf. Luke 7:47); and what is more, she often merits to gain much of what she requests, even in the case of requests for external things.

There can be no doubt that to approach God, even in this manner, is a work of piety. As Job says, the person who, even in this manner, sees his own image in God, that is, dwells in thought upon his likeness to God, does not sin (cf. Job 5:24); and it is requisite for the God and Lord of all things to be adored and honored, under the masks of a multitude of faces. Nevertheless, even at the present time Jesus says to his disciples, "It is to your advantage that I go away, for if I do not go away, the Counselor will not come to you" (John 16:7). For as long as she who prays is thinking about something corporeal in the one to whom prayer is made, she prays reverently indeed, but not altogether spiritually. After all, "God is spirit," and it is necessary for one who adores him to do so "in spirit and in truth" (John 4:24).

Further, this manner of prayer is ordinarily shaped by the form of the creed or symbol of faith; for, given the reverence that marks Christian belief, what is faithfully believed is truly and simply loved, and imagination of the corporeal forms of the divine works carried through in the Lord Jesus Christ is transmuted into loving attachment.

Hence the person who is rational and is actuated by reason, labors even as reason proposes, and busies himself in works for his own good, until, having conquered himself, he transcends all that of which we have been speaking, and makes his way into the realm of the spirit. Then the good will is transmuted into a good mind; the desire of one who seeks, into the understanding of one who sees and the love of one who experiences delight. The Holy Spirit comes to the aid of human infirmity, and the human *persona* begins to be renewed to the model of God's image. Grace descends upon reason. It takes mind, life, morals, even the very look of the body, and shapes them into a single devout inclination, into a single image of love, into a single manifestation of the God-seeker. At the same time, the individual is touched by a desire to know God, as far as that is permitted to human beings, and to be known by God; to enjoy a revelation of God's gracious countenance, and, for his conscience, of God himself — all this so that, knowing God and known by God, he may pray to him and worship him "in spirit and in truth," as is right.

And here is the Bridegroom, here, the Bride, here, the dialogue between them! For when, in accordance with the Lord's promise, the Deity begins, in his graciousness, to come and to make his dwelling in one who loves him (cf. John 14:23), God is made known to him to some degree; and since no one can see God's face and live (cf. Exod. 33:20), that is, cannot in this life attain a full knowledge of him, God places in the mind of those who love him, and entrusts to their care, a certain imitation or likeness of the knowledge of God — not some made-up phantasm but a devout effect of God's presence; and the human being who is still living in the flesh is able to grasp this likeness and to endure it. These likenesses are the first fruits of the Spirit (cf. 2 Cor. 1:22; 5:5; Eph. 1:13-14), the down payment or dowry, that anticipate the marriage chamber — and they confer an honor and an abundance proportionate to the Bride's readiness for and proximity to the Bridegroom's chamber.

This gift from God the person full of desire entrusts not so much to his own judgment dwelling in his memory as to the grace of God dwelling in his conscience; and when he is about to return to prayer, he fetches it back from there, and, bearing with him both the matter of his prayer and the pledge of God's grace, appears before his Creator with greater assurance. The more often one returns this likeness to its source, and is once again, devoutly and faithfully, sealed by it, the more it becomes worthy of God, as well as more efficacious and sweeter for its possessor. For the ordinary knowledge of which we speak, no matter what it is knowledge of, normally takes the form of having an image of the object known impressed on the mind or on the memory; and the object known is more clearly known to the degree that its image is more expressly delineated within the knower. In the case of human knowledge of God, some great likeness to God, however known, may well be impressed on the mind — and this apart from any picture created by imagination. This is actuated by the purity of an unalloyed longing and of an awareness that springs of enlightened love: the thing that, in the case of the ordinary knowledge of things, seems to be accomplished by their depiction in memory.

The excellence of that [divine] nature, however, creates a vast difference within this relation; for the likeness is inferior to its original to the extent that it resides in an inferior nature, and dissimilar from its original to the extent that it resides in a dissimilar matter — the Creator's likeness, in short, in the creature, God's likeness in the soul. On the other hand, the grace of the knowledge of God — which, as we have said, comes about only in the awareness, that is, the understanding, of enlightened love — is enriching in and of itself and brings blessing to the one who possesses it. It stoops to him and lifts him up to itself. For the person who knows it, it transforms God's awesome and exalted nature into intimate and inviting impressions and experiences of a divine sweetness and goodness; and this comes about precisely to the degree that the blessed one — the poor in spirit, humble and quiet, the one who trembles at God's words, the single-minded, the customary conversation partner of the Holy Spirit — truly and devoutly acknowledges, prior to the reverent reception of this knowledge or understanding itself, the shortcomings of his poverty, humility, and single-mindedness, and bends his mental powers, which are more subtle to the degree that they are more single-minded, to this end, looking not so much to what is written in books as to the power of the Lord and to his righteousness alone.

Here is the "white stone" of the Apocalypse, with a "name written" on it "which no one knows except him who receives it" (Rev. 2:17). Here is the good and pleasurable life, of which it is written in the praise of Wisdom that "she is not found in the land of those who live pleasurably" (Job 28:13). Therefore, this rational and spiritual practitioner of prayer — he is rational while he seeks his goal under the guidance of reason; but after he has attained it, to the extent that he has attained it, he is already spiritual — he possesses, I say, as a gift of *creative grace,* a likeness and an image of God in his mind. He is more like God, closer to the knowledge of God, to the degree that he has a greater receptiveness to things eternal; and he has a greater receptiveness to things eternal to the degree that, as a gift of *illuminating grace,* he is uncontaminated by the transitory things of this world. For as long as one sees God only "by means of a mirror and in an enigma" (1 Cor. 13:12), one is moving toward contemplation of God only by way of an image. Whether that image is a mirror or an enigma, that is to say, whether it is clearer or more obscure, as long as one is living this life here, one is moving in that direction only by way of an image. Nevertheless, the more faithfully the soul has taken into herself the dignity and truth of the image of God, the more faithful and closer to the truth are the images by which she ascends to God. She does not, by an imaginal and superstitious presumption, make up in her own head something unreal in God or in regard to God; no, but by means of the gift given her, the gift that empowers her, the form of that lively impression within her, she draws near to Him who Is.

For to promise, to hope for, the perfected vision and knowledge of God in this life is empty presumption. A person of the sort we have been describing prays to God as God; this is what reason commands, what spiritual progress teaches, what loving aspiration shapes. He conforms himself to God, not God to himself, and hence asks of God nothing whatever save God and what will bring him to God; he is not content with anything save enjoyment of God and in God; he makes use of nothing save inasfar as it leads to God. This individual, as we have said, is rational as long as he is being purified; but once purified, he is already spiritual. But just as it is the business of someone who is in the rational state always to make growth in the direction of the spiritual state, so too it is inevitable that one in the spiritual state will retreat, from time to time, into the rational. In this life it never happens that the spiritual person is always spiritually motivated. The person who belongs to God, however, must always be rational in desiring or spiritual in love's aspiration.

To himself he sometimes seems to vanquish and rise above every cloud of the imaginal faculty, though not without laborious combat and struggle; but sometimes, though solely by reason of the work of grace, the strivings of the good will are neither inhibited by imagination nor smothered by clouds of darkness, and suddenly, unexpectedly, loving aspiration wakens to itself; and if pictures conjured up by imagination arise, instead of getting in the way, they provide useful assistance. For to eyes that are weak, they are not always without use, nor is every employment of imagination's representations, as they intrude themselves, harmful. Made familiar with their corporeal vehicle, as it were, by dependence on sight and on knowledge that concerns bodies and bodily things, the spirit of the person that practices prayer and contemplation is by their means drawn to the place where truth is. So the individual in question attains the home of the truth that draws him; and although it is by means of an image, nevertheless it is by means of an image that thought has dwelt upon.

For this reason, the Holy Spirit, in handing over to human creatures the Song of spiritual love, attires the whole of its interior, spiritual, and divine subject matter in the external garment provided by images of fleshly love — and this precisely in order that, because love alone can fully grasp the things of God, fleshly love, in being introduced to spiritual love and passing over into it, may quickly lay hold on what is like it. Moreover, since it is impossible for genuine love, hungry as it is for what is authentic, to rest in images and be content with them, it will the more quickly make the transition by the way made familiar in its imaginings. And even though the person in question is spiritual, nevertheless the pleasures of the flesh are natural to him in virtue of his sharing in a bodily way of being; but once they have been taken captive by the Holy Spirit, he embraces them as part of his allegiance to spiritual love.

And that is why in this text a woman leaps forth, as if from some hidden place, and wholly without modesty, without saying who she is, or where she comes from, or whom she is talking to, cries, **Let him kiss me with the kiss of his mouth!**

(4) Honorius of Autun

Sacred Scripture is interpreted and understood in four ways: historically, allegorically, tropologically, and anagogically. This is expressed by the table for the presentation of bread in the ark (Exod. 25:29ff.), which is supported by four feet. The ark represents the Church, in which service is rendered to Christ. The table is sacred Scripture, upon which bread is presented, that is, the food of souls. The four feet are the four kinds of meaning, that is to say: history, when the thing referred to is narrated as it happened; allegory, when the thing referred to is expounded with reference to Christ and the Church; tropology, when it is applied to soul and spirit; and anagogy, when it is understood of the celestial life.

In his vision of God when he foresaw the entire future state of the Church, Ezekiel saw, among other things, a wheel in the midst of a wheel. This wheel had four faces, and "the spirit of life was in the wheels" (Ezek. 1:16, 20). This wheel is sacred Scripture. The wheel within the wheel is the new law hidden within the old law. The four faces are the four senses, which is to say, the historical, the allegorical, the tropological, and the anagogical. In history, the thing referred to is indicated, considered as it has taken place. In allegory, on the other hand, the interpretation of words is weighed. In tropology, the analogies between things that have taken place are searched out. In anagogy the likeness of things is pondered.

For example, it is history that Solomon is called peaceable and that he built a temple in seven years. It is allegory that Solomon is called peaceable and that he is Christ. Jerusalem is the vision of peace and is the Church, which Christ made as a temple for himself by the seven gifts of the Holy Spirit. It is a matter of tropology, accordingly, that just as Solomon constructed the temple out of planks and stones, so too each believer makes, in his soul, a temple for God out of good works and the examples of the saints. On the other hand, it is a matter of anagogy that just as Solomon made the temple in Jerusalem out of precious stones, so too Christ establishes a temple in the heavenly Jerusalem out of living stones, that is, out of all the elect.

(5) Origen

The point has now been reached at which we must speak of the title of the Song of Songs. The expression "song of songs" is similar to what are called "Holies of Holies" in the passage about the Tent of Witness (Exod. 30:29 LXX), and to what in the book of Numbers are mentioned as "works of works" (Num. 4:47 LXX), and to what in Paul are called "ages of ages" (Rom. 16:27). . . . Here, however, our first job is to inquire what the **songs** are of which this one is said to be **the song**. My conclusion is that they are the songs that in times past were sung by prophets or by angels. For the law is said to have been "ordained by angels at the hand of a mediator" (Gal. 3:19). Therefore, all the songs that they pronounced were preludes sung by the friends of the Bridegroom. This song, however, is the one song that the Bridegroom himself was to sing as a marriage hymn just as he was about to take his Bride. In it the Bride no longer desires the friends of the Bridegroom to sing to her. Instead she wants to hear the words of the Bridegroom, now present with her, and says, **Let him kiss me with the kisses of his mouth.**

Justifiably, then, is this song ranked above all other songs; for the rest of them, which the Law and the Prophets sang, were sung while the Bride was still a little thing who had not yet entered upon the beginnings of maturity; but this song is sung to her as one already grown up, truly strong, and able to receive a husband's power and the perfect mystery. That is why it is said of her that "My perfect dove is one" (6:9).

(6) Gregory of Nyssa

Let us then come within the Holy of Holies, that is, the Song of Songs. For from this superlative form of this expression we learn that there is a superabundant concentration of holiness within the Holy of Holies; and in the same way the exalted Word promises to teach us mysteries of mysteries by the agency of the Song of Songs. For though there are many songs within the divinely inspired teaching, through which — from the great David, and Isaiah, and Moses, and many others — we are instructed in noble thoughts about God, from this title we learn that the mystery contained in the Song of Songs transcends these songs of the saints by as much as they stand apart from the songs of profane wisdom. Human nature can neither discover nor entertain anything greater than this for purposes of understanding. This is why, moreover, the most intense of pleasurable activities (I mean the passion of erotic love) is set as a figure at the very fore of the guidance that the teachings give: so that we may learn that it is necessary for the soul, fixing itself steadily on the inaccessible beauty of the divine nature, to love that nature as much as the body has a bent for what is akin to it, and to turn passion into impassibility, so that when every bodily disposition has been quelled, our mind within us may boil with love, but only in the Spirit, because it is heated by that "fire" which the Lord came to "cast upon the earth" (Luke 12:49).

Song 1:2-4

1:2 Let him kiss me with the kisses of his
    mouth.
  For your breasts are better than wine,
3   and the fragrance of your
    perfumed unguents is better
    than all spices.
Your name is perfumed ointment
    emptied out;
  that is why young maidens have
    loved you.
4 They have drawn you.
  We will run after you toward the
    fragrance of your perfumes.
  The King has brought me into his
    storehouse.
Let us rejoice and be glad in you.
  We will love your breasts better
    than wine.
  Righteousness has loved you.

1:1 Let him kiss me with the kiss of his
    mouth,
  for your breasts are better than wine,
2   fragrant with the best perfumes.

Your name is oil poured out;

  that is why young maidens have
    loved you.
3 Draw me after you,
  let us run after the fragrance of
    your perfumes.
  The King has brought me into his
    cellars.
We shall exult and rejoice in you.
  Mindful that your breasts surpass
    wine,
  the righteous love you.

One of the problems faced by interpreters of the Song of Songs was that of decid-ing who the speaker is in a particular verse or passage. So central, indeed, was this issue that certain Christian manuscripts of the Septuagint, dating from the 4th century, provided indications of the speakers in the text of the Song itself (for modern reproductions of these, see The Revised English Bible or The New Jerusa-lem Bible). All interpreters, however, have tended to agree that the first speaker is the prospective Bride; and on the hypothesis stated by Origen, that the Bride rep-resents either the Church or a particular believing soul (or both), it seems logical that Song 1:2-4a should represent the betrothed Bride waiting and longing for her lover's arrival — and this in spite of the odd change from "him" to "you" in

1:2b. The passage thus pictures the people of God waiting for the advent — the incarnation — of the Word, or the soul waiting for the "illuminations and visitations of the Word of God," or, in the case of Nicholas of Lyra, the people of Israel waiting for God to demonstrate his care for them by signs and deeds. A significant variant on this identification of the Bride is that provided by Rupert of Deutz, who takes the theme of the Song to be the incarnation of the Word and in the figure of the Bride sees the Virgin Mary. The other speakers in this passage might be the "young maidens" of Song 1:3c, whom ancient commentators saw as a sort of chorus of aspiring souls who accompany — or, better, follow — the Bride; to them most interpreters assigned 1:4b and 1:4d-f, for the good enough reason that they seemed to be the only persons mentioned who could be identified with the "we" and "us" of those lines.

These assignments seemed to entail, among other things, that the breasts mentioned in Song 1:2b should be those of the Bridegroom — a thought that, as the medieval Glossa ordinaria informs us, and Nicholas of Lyra emphasizes, might be considered paradoxical, since males are not commonly thought or spoken of as having breasts. In ancient or medieval times, however, this interpretation may have seemed somewhat less odd for several reasons. One, of course, was that the Word or Son of God, the Bridegroom, was understood to have a feminine identity in his capacity as the divine Wisdom. Another was the association of breasts with milk and feeding, and the habitual use of food as a figure for nourishment of the soul — that is to say, for wisdom and knowledge ("food for thought," as it is said). Inevitably, then, mentions of breasts in the Song made these interpreters think of teaching or "illumination" or proclamation of the word, and of the interior transformation wrought by conformity of the human mind with the divine Word and Wisdom, the "image" of God (2 Cor. 4:4; 3:18). Correspondingly, the Bridegroom's "chamber" (Song 1:4c), where God's people (or the soul) cohabits with the Word of God, is understood by the Septuagint and the Latin Vulgate alike to be a "storeroom" of entrancing and transforming knowledge.

(1) Origen

Let him kiss me with the kisses of his mouth.

In conformity with the genre of a plain narrative, a certain bride is introduced on the stage. From her most noble bridegroom she has received the most fitting of gifts for her dowry and her betrothal. Since, however, the bridegroom has delayed his coming for a long time, she is torn by desire for his love, and worn out with moping at home, and busy doing everything possible to assure that one day she will be able to see her bridegroom and enjoy his kisses. . . . Let us then think of how — "lifting holy hands without anger or quarreling . . . , in decent clothing with modesty and sobriety" (1 Tim. 2:8-9), adorned with the most proper of ornaments . . . , but inflamed by desire for her bridegroom and afflicted with the internal wound of love — she pours out her prayer to God . . . , and thinking of her bridegroom says, **Let him kiss me with the kisses of his mouth.**

These, then, are the things that the plain narrative account contains in its dramatic form. But let us see whether the inner meaning can be adapted in an appropriate way to the same form.

Let it be the Church that desires to be joined with Christ. Notice, however, that "Church" means the assembly of all the saints. This Church is, as it were, a single but collective character that speaks and says, "I have everything; I am filled up with gifts, which I received before my marriage as a dowry and as a mark of my betrothal. For when I was being prepared for marriage with the King's Son and 'the Firstborn of all creation' (Col. 1:15), the holy angels became my servants and ministers, and brought down the law to me as a betrothal gift; for "the law" is said to have been 'ordained by angels at the hand of a mediator' (Gal. 3:19). The prophets also ministered to me. It was they and no others who spoke all the words through which they showed me and informed me about the Son of God, to whom they wanted to betroth me. . . . Further still, in order to set me on fire with love of him and desire for him, they made announcement to me in prophetic utterances concerning his coming, and, filled with the Holy Spirit, they proclaimed his innumerable deeds of wonder and his boundless works. They also portrayed his beauty as well as his attractiveness and gentleness, with the result that I was set on fire with an unbearable love for him. Since, however, the present age has almost come to its close, and his presence has not been accorded me, and all I see are his servants ascending and descending to me — for this reason I beseech you, Father of my spouse, and pour out my prayer, that you will look with pity upon this love of mine and send him, so that now he may not speak to me any longer by way of his ministering angels and his prophets, but may come in his very own person and **kiss me with the kisses of his mouth** — may, that is, pour into my mouth the words of his mouth, that I may hear him speaking and see him teaching."

For the kisses of Christ are those that he bestowed on the Church when in his advent he himself, present in the flesh, spoke to it words of faith and of love and of peace, just as, when sent ahead of time to the bride, Isaiah had promised by saying that "the Lord himself shall save them" (Isa. 33:22), and not a representative or an angel.

As the third point of our exposition, let us introduce the soul. All her zeal is aimed at union and fellowship with the Word of God and at entering upon the mysteries of his wisdom and knowledge — entering, as it were, upon the private chambers of the heavenly Bridegroom. To this soul his gifts have now already been given as its dowry. For just as, where the Church is concerned, the dowry consisted of the books of the Law and the Prophets, so in the case of the soul the law of nature, rational understanding, and freedom of the will are reckoned as its betrothal gifts. Possessed of these gifts as her dowry, the soul may take as her elementary schooling the teaching that derives from her counselors and instructors. But in these she does not find the full and complete satisfaction of her desire and her love. Let her then pray that her pure and virginal mind may be enlightened by the illuminations and visitations of the Word of God. For when, apart from any human or angelic ministry, her mind is filled with divine understandings and thoughts, she has the right to believe that she has received the **kisses of the Word of God.** . . .

(2) Gregory of Nyssa

Let him kiss me with the kisses of his mouth.

The bride Moses loved the Bridegroom in the same way as the virgin in the Song who says, **Let him kiss me with the kisses of his mouth**; and through the face-to-face converse accorded him by God (as the Scripture testifies [cf. Num. 12:8]), he became after these theophanies more intensely desirous of such kisses, praying to see the object of his yearning as if he had never glimpsed him. In the same way, none of the others in whom the divine yearning was deeply lodged ever came to a point of rest in their desire. And even as now the soul that is joined to God is not satiated by her enjoyment of him, so too the more abundantly she is filled up with his beauty, the more vehemently her longings abound. For since the words of the Bridegroom are "spirit and life" (John 6:63), and everyone who is joined to the Spirit becomes spirit, while everyone who is attached to life "passes from death to life" (John 5:24) according to the Lord's word, it follows that the virgin soul longs to approach the fount of the spiritual life. That fount, however, is the mouth of the Bridegroom, whence "the words of eternal life" (John 6:68) as they gush forth fill the mouth that is drawn to it, just as the prophet does when drawing spirit through his mouth (cf. Ps. 118:131 LXX = 119:131). Since then it is necessary for the one who draws drink from the fount to fix mouth to mouth, and the fount is the Lord who says, "If anyone thirst, let him come to me and drink" (John 7:37), it follows that the soul, thirsty as she is, wills to bring her own mouth to the mouth that pours out life, saying, **Let him kiss me with the kisses of his mouth.**

(3) Bernard of Clairvaux

Let him kiss me with the kiss of his mouth.

Now listen closely. Let the mouth that kisses signify the Word who takes on [human nature], and the mouth that is kissed, the flesh that is taken on. The kiss itself, though, consummated as it is by the one that kisses and the one that is kissed, signifies that very person who is framed by the joining of the two — "the mediator between God and humanity, Jesus the human being" (1 Tim. 2:5). This explains why none of the saints presumed to say, "Let him kiss me with his mouth," but only **with the kiss of his mouth** — surely safeguarding, for their part, that privilege of Christ, upon whom the mouth of the Word was once for all uniquely pressed when the fullness of all Deity bestowed itself upon him bodily (cf. Col. 2:9). A fruitful kiss, this, and wonderful for its astounding kindness, which does not press mouth to mouth but unites God to humanity. In the former case, the touching of the lips signifies an embracing of hearts, but in this case a joining of natures in one fits the human together with the divine and brings peace to things on earth and things in heaven. "For he is our peace, who made the two one" (Eph. 2:14). For this kiss every saint of olden times longed; for they perceived ahead of time that "delight and rejoicing" are stored up "with him" (Ecclus. 15:6 Vg), and that "all the treasures of wisdom and knowledge" are hidden in him (Col. 2:3).

(4) Bernard of Clairvaux

Let him kiss me with the kiss of his mouth.

I cannot be at peace, she says, unless he kisses me with the kiss of his mouth. I am grateful for the kiss of the feet, and also for the kiss of the hand; but if he cares for me at all, **Let him kiss me with the kiss of his mouth.** It is not that I am an ingrate, but that I am in love. I have received much more than I deserve — this I confess; but for all that, I have received less than I want. It is not reason that impels me, but desire. Do not, I beg, when it is love that goads me on, charge me with being too bold. Modesty, to be sure, issues its protest, but love overpowers it. I am not unaware that "the king's honor loves righteousness" (Ps. 98:4 = 99:4); but reckless love does not hang about waiting for judgment to be given: it is not moderated by good advice, or constrained by modesty, or subjugated by reason. I beg, I entreat, I plead: **Let him kiss me with the kiss of his mouth!** Look! Already, for all these many years, I have taken care, by his grace, to lead a chaste and sober life. I am assiduous in reading and study, I resist the vices, I exert myself frequently in prayer, I keep watch against temptations, I call to mind the years of my life in bitterness of soul (cf. Isa. 38:15). I reckon that I have, to the best of my ability, lived among the brethren without bickering (cf. Phil. 3:7) — and I have submitted myself to my superiors, governing my comings and goings in accord with the command of an elder. I do not covet things that are not mine; rather have I given to others of my possessions and myself. I eat my bread in the sweat of my face (cf. Gen. 3:19). Yet whatever all this activity amounts to, it is a matter of habit, not of pleasure. What am I, then, save, as the prophet said, "Ephraim, a heifer that has been trained to love the work of threshing" (Hos. 10:11). Yes, and then in the Gospel, the person who does only what he is bound to do is counted a useless servant (cf. Luke 17:10). True it may be that I am fulfilling the commandments in one way or another; but "my soul is like earth without water" (Ps. 142:6 = 143:6). Therefore, if my whole burnt offering is to become worthy, **Let him,** I pray and beseech, **kiss me with the kiss of his mouth.**

(5) Honorius of Autun

Let him kiss me with the kiss of his mouth.

This . . . is the historical sense: the daughter of Pharaoh who is to be married to Solomon (1 Kings 3:1; 11:1), overcome with love, answers his messengers: "I do not want any further greeting through you messengers. Let Solomon himself kiss me with the kiss of his mouth."

On the other hand, it pertains to allegory that Solomon is Christ, and the daughter of Pharaoh is the Church, which answers his messengers, the prophets, by saying, "He who has for a time kissed me by consoling me and promising peace through your mouth — let him himself now **kiss me with the kiss of his mouth** — that is, let him who has promised become incarnate now after all this time and kiss me with his presence, and with his own mouth speak to me the peace that was once lost and is now restored." The word kiss means something like a drink from the mouth. By kiss, then, we understand peace, and by **mouth**, the Word of the Father, that is, the Son. God kissed the Bride as it were by someone else's mouth, when formerly "In many and various ways" he spoke "to our fathers by the prophets" (Heb. 1:1). He kissed her, so to speak, by his own mouth when "in these last days he spoke to them in the Son" (Heb. 1:2), saying, "Peace be with you" (John 20:19). For this means: "You will know the peace and the grace, which you lost in the Paradise by the agency of the Devil, now restored to you by the agency of my Son." It was the first human being, expelled from the Garden on account of his disobedience, who lost for the human race the peace and grace of God. Hence the primitive Church — Abel, I mean, and all the righteous up to Abraham, and then the patriarchs up to Moses, and after him the prophets up to John the Baptist — foresee in the Spirit the restoration of this peace through Christ and want him to become incarnate quickly. Therefore, as soon as he was born, the angels proclaimed the restoration of peace, saying, "Peace to men of good will" (Luke 2:14). For by a kiss flesh is joined to flesh, and spirit companions spirit; and thus Christ is joined to the Church by way of the flesh, and the Church is associated with his divinity through the Spirit. Moreover, by a fleshly touch love of neighbor is conveyed, and by spiritual touch, the love of God, by which Christ is joined to the Church.

The tropological interpretation is as follows. The faithful soul that is the Bride of Christ ponders where it shall have been, where it will be, where it is, where it is not — to wit, that it shall have been in original and actual sin, that it will be in God's terrible judgment, that it is among the vanities of the present age, that it is not in eternal beatitude. Groaning, then, and trembling, she says, **Let him kiss me with the kiss of his mouth** — as if to say, "He who in my flesh sits at the Father's right hand, my Advocate, the just Judge, let him visit me and **kiss me**, who grieve over my sins, and **let him kiss me** in peace with the sign of friendship that he has promised by his own mouth to those who repent."

But the anagogical interpretation goes like this: The Church, sojourning here and longing for her homeland there, says, **Let him kiss me with the kiss of his mouth**. It is as if she should say: "He who speaks daily with me in the Scriptures and promises eternal joy, let him himself appear as the One who presides in the judgment and bestow the joys of peace with his own mouth, saying, 'Come, O blessed of my Father, inherit the Kingdom prepared for you from the foundation of the world'" (Matt. 25:34).

She speaks to him as absent so that a greater love may be conveyed. This book is said to be a drama, which means a love song that is sung by lovers without identities. Hence that song is called "dramatic" in which various individuals are introduced but are not named. In the same way, praises are sung by various individuals without names.

(6) Rupert of Deutz

Let him kiss me with the kiss of his mouth.

What means this cry, so loud, so startling?

An overflowing joy, O blessed Virgin, a powerful love, a rush of delight wholly seized you, wholly captured you. It intoxicated you deep within, so that you perceived "what eye has not seen, nor ear heard, and has not entered into the human heart" (1 Cor. 2:9), and you said, **Let him kiss me with the kiss of his mouth.** For to the angel you said, "Behold, the handmaid of the Lord; be it unto me according to your word" (Luke 1:38). What "word" was that? What had he said to you? "You have found favor," he said, "with the Lord; behold, you shall conceive and bear a son, and you shall call his name Jesus" (Luke 1:30-31). And again, "The Holy Spirit shall come upon you, and the power of the Most High shall overshadow you: and therefore what shall be born of you will be called the holy one, the Son of God" (Luke 1:35).

Was not this word from the angel a word and promise of the kiss of the Lord's mouth as even now at hand? If so, then let the skilled assessor place the two sayings on reason's scales — both this one (**Let him kiss me with the kiss of his mouth**), the word of a soul or heart that is filled with joy; and the other ("Behold, the handmaid of the Lord; be it unto me according to your word"), which was the utterance of an exultant mouth. Is it not the case that their burden is the same? Is not the same meaning conveyed by the differing words or sounds? Just as you heard and believed — just as you said in making the request, "be it unto me" — so it has happened for you. God the Father has kissed you **with the kiss** of his **mouth.**

What eye sees this? What ear hears it? Into whose human heart has it entered? He revealed himself to you, Mary — he who is the one that kisses, the kiss itself, and the mouth of the one that kisses. When some particular soul, being in reception of the highest gift — "the perfect gift that comes down" from the same "Father of lights" (James 1:17) — is in such wise Spirit-filled, can in such wise perceive within herself the touch of the one who kisses, that she does not hesitate to say, "God has revealed [it] to us through the Spirit" (1 Cor. 2:10) — this is a lesser grace by a considerable margin. How much more truly have you, O happy one, in receiving a unique gift as "the Holy Spirit" came "upon you, and the Power of the Most High" overshadowed you, received a revelation of this order! Straightway your soul **melted** (5:6) as the Beloved spoke — which is to say, God the Father, as, in a wondrous and ineffable act of speech, he placed deep within your womb the person of his Word, and together with him, in your mind, that Love which is his Holy Spirit. . . . It would have been enough to have said to the angel, "'Let it be unto me according to your word,' O angel of God," for God to **kiss me with the kiss of his mouth;** but once turned to the beloved God himself, your soul did not cease to speak and rejoice in its experience of unspeakable sweetness; and the summing up of this rejoicing comes in these words: **For your breasts are better than wine.** . . .

(7) Nicholas of Lyra

Let him kiss me with the kiss of his mouth,
for your breasts are better than wine. . . .
We shall exult and rejoice in you.

Let him kiss me with the kiss of his mouth — that is, "Would that God would show him-self favorable to me by signs and deeds, as a bridegroom does to a treasured bride." **For your breasts are better than wine.** The Hebrew text says, "For your loves are better than wine"; the Hebrew noun written here is ambiguous and denotes both loves and breasts. Hebrew interpreters go with the one meaning of the term, while our translation goes with the other. In this instance, however, the Hebrews seem to have the better case: in ac-cord with the idiom of the Hebrew language, the Bride here is addressing the Bride-groom; but it does not seem suitable to speak of breasts in extolling a bridegroom. It is nonetheless possible to assert that in this text what is meant by the breasts of the Bride-groom is the abundance of God's loving-kindness. So, according to Hebrew exegetes, the expression **For your breasts are better than wine** means "your loves are better tasting to the devout mind than any corporeal flavor whatever is to the sense of taste"; and accord-ing to our translation, **Your breasts are better than wine** means "the abundance of your loving-kindness is sweeter to the human mind than wine, very sweet though it be, is to the corporeal sense of taste."

Fragrant — or, according to the Hebrew interpreters, **scented** — **with the best perfumes**, that is: the abundance of your loving-kindness or of your loves refreshes the devout soul more truly than any smell that sense can perceive. **Your name is oil poured out.** By "oil" here is meant an aromatic liquid that flows from aromatic trees in Arabia and in the Land of Promise. It is collected and kept in jars, and when it is poured out on someone for purposes of cooling or of curing, it gives off a sweet smell, by which the Scriptures understand good repute, in accordance with the words of the apostle at 2 Cor. 2: "We are the aroma of Christ," etc. (2 Cor. 2:15). Thus the words **oil poured out** mean that by the marvels that God performed for the children of Israel in Egypt and in the Red Sea the renown of his name and of his goodness was disseminated to other nations, and many were in consequence converted to Judaism. That is why the next words are: **That is why young maidens have loved you,** that is, other nations have been converted to love of you; for many of the Egyptians were converted in this manner and left the land of Egypt in the company of the Israelites, as it says in Exodus 12 (cf. Exod. 12:38). So it was with Jethro and his household when once they heard the wonders that God did for Israel: Exo-dus 18 (cf. Exod. 18:8-12).

Draw me after you, by bringing me out of Egypt with great power. **Let us run** by following you along the path of righteousness. **After the fragrance of your perfumes,** which means: drawn by the works of your goodness. This phrase, however — **after the fragrance of your perfumes** — does not belong in the text because it is not in the He-brew. It was inserted at a later time by some scholar as an interlinear gloss and afterward put into the text through scribal incompetence. **The King** — the heavenly King —

brought me into his cellars, revealing his hidden treasures through Moses, as it says in Exodus 3: "and when he had led his flock into the interior of the desert," etc. (Exod. 3:1 Vg), and then: "The Lord appeared to him," etc. (Exod. 3:2). **We shall exult and rejoice in you** — and this was done when, after the Red Sea was crossed, they said in a mood of rejoicing: "Let us sing gloriously to the Lord," etc., Exodus 15 (Exod. 15:1).

(8) Origen

For your breasts are better than wine.

Let us now, however, inquire what the inner meaning contains. We find that in the divine Scriptures the governing principle of the heart is denoted by a variety of terms, terms that vary in accordance with the character of the things under discussion. For sometimes "heart" is used, as in "Blessed are the pure in heart" (Matt. 5:8) and "with the heart does one believe and attain righteousness" (cf. Rom. 10:10). On the other hand, in the setting of a meal, it is referred to as "bosom" or "chest," depending on the appearance and order of the persons reclining at the table. Thus John in his Gospel relates of "a certain disciple whom Jesus loved" that "he reclined" either "on his bosom" or "upon his chest" — the very one, indeed, to whom "Simon Peter beckoned and said, 'Ask who it is of whom he speaks'" (John 13:23-24). These words make it certain that John is said to have rested upon the governing principle of Jesus' heart and upon the inner meanings of his teaching, seeking and examining "the treasures of wisdom and knowledge" that "had been hidden" (Col. 2:3) in Christ Jesus. . . .

In accordance with what has been said, let us, in the text before us, since plainly it is a drama that concerns love, understand by "breasts" the governing principle of the heart. From this it seems that the meaning of the words is something like the following: "Your heart, O Bridegroom, and mind — which is to say, the teachings that are within you, or the grace of the teaching — surpasses any wine that ordinarily 'gladdens the human heart . . .'" (Ps. 103:13 = 104:15). The Bridegroom's **breasts** are good, then, because in them "the treasures of wisdom and knowledge are hidden." The Bride, moreover, compares these breasts to wine, but in such wise as to prefer them to wine. Now by "wine" we must understand those decrees and teachings that the Bride used to receive at the hands of the Law and the Prophets before the advent of the Bridegroom. Now, however, when she weighs the teaching that flows from the breasts of the Bridegroom, she is struck with wonder and amazed because she sees how superior it is to the teaching that the holy Fathers and Prophets had set before her — teaching in which, before the advent of the Bridegroom, she rejoiced as in spiritual wine. They too "planted vineyards" and cultivated them — like Noah, first of all, and Isaiah (see Gen. 9:20; Isa. 5:1). Thus she sees now that the teachings and knowledge that the Bridegroom possesses are of the highest order and that from him flows a teaching more perfect than that of which the ancients disposed; and so she says, **Your breasts are better than wine** — better than that teaching with which the ancients delighted her.

(9) Gregory the Great

For your breasts are better than wine.

But look! even while she is sighing, even as she seeks [the Bridegroom] as though he were absent, suddenly she perceives him to be present. For the grace of our Creator is such that, when we speak of him while seeking him, we enjoy his presence. Hence it stands written in the Gospel that when Cleopas and someone else were talking about him in the course of a journey, they merited to see him present (Luke 24:13-27). While, then, the holy Church is longing for her spouse to be incarnate when he is as yet absent, suddenly she sees him present, and she adds, **For your breasts are better than wine.** . . . "Wine" refers to knowledge of the Law, knowledge of the Prophets. But in his coming the Lord, because he wanted to make his wisdom known by way of the flesh, causes it to be concealed as it were in breasts of flesh; for the wisdom that we were hardly able to grasp at all in his divinity, we know through the incarnation. Hence it is right to praise his breasts, since what the teaching of the Law was able to accomplish only minimally, the condescension of his preaching effects in our hearts. For the incarnation's preaching nourishes us more than the Law's teaching. Let her therefore say, **Your breasts are better than wine.**

(10) Nilus of Ancyra

For your breasts are better than wine.

It is a not uncommon experience for many folk that when they are conducting a conversation with someone or other in their heads, they progress to the point where they are so carried away that they talk to this person as actually present — just as David in a dream thought that he was in God's company and then woke up with this experience still reverberating in his mind and said: "I awoke, and I am still together with you" (Ps. 138:18 LXX = 139:18). In his case, then, preoccupation with the waking vision of what he sought persisted in memory even when he was sleeping and, by the agency of his imagination, renewed concerns that had engaged his mind during the day. By the same token, the Bride's mental imagining of converse with the Bridegroom was taken for real and was transmuted into affectionate communication — into the marvel of reaching out to touch the breasts of the One she desired.

The addition, therefore, of the word **for** indicated that she was on the verge of explaining why she was surely bound to be greeted by the embraces of the Bridegroom. She kept silent on this matter either, as some suppose, because she saw him appear, or else because, as we have explained, she imagined that he was present. But instead of giving the explanation, what she adds — as though she had touched the Word of life — is **Your breasts are better than wine,** and her meaning is the following: "The introductory and elementary transmission of your teachings — referred to as 'breasts' because breasts contain the nourishment suited to children — stands out as more nourishing and more 'grown up' than the milk that derives from the wisdom of the Greeks, though the latter seems to be mature and to taste like wine." Or else she means that the mere words of Scripture, which contain the "sincere milk" (1 Pet. 2:2) that nourished those who study the sacred letters from their childhood, when compared with the "higher knowledge" of the Greeks, are more profitable and more edifying in pursuing the blameless life. And then **better than all spices** — which is to say, better than the teachings of the Greeks, seeing that they are contrived by human activities of reflection and synthesis. **The fragrance of your perfumed unguents** is sweeter, no doubt because the spices of the Greeks have no fragrance. They are accorded only the name of perfumes but not the character. **The fragrance of your perfumed unguents**, says she, is not better than any fragrance of spices, but **better than all spices**, because in the case of the Greeks spices have no fragrance. If this were not so, she would have said, "**The fragrance of your perfumed unguents** is better than the fragrance of all spices." . . . The perfumes of the Bridegroom are the letter of the divinely inspired Scriptures as it breathes out the sweet scent of contemplation. For the spoken word of the Greeks, which because of the grandiloquence of its diction contains what they consider perfume, that is, grace and correctness in what it says, lacks the fragrance that inheres in contemplation, and the power to nourish contemplation. It is the bundle of stalks that has no power to produce meal (Hos. 8:7). . . .

(11) William of St. Thierry

For your breasts are better than wine,
    fragrant with the best perfumes.
Your name is oil poured out.

And note this too: in requesting the kiss, the highest longing open to a human being in prayer had focused itself upon the light that is proper to the face of God; but repulsed by the brilliance of that love, this longing was turned back to its more elementary occupations and busies itself in them, saying, **Your breasts are better than wine, fragrant with the best perfumes. Your name is oil poured out.** "As soon as I came to you," she says, "you bared for me your sweet breasts, the primary nourishment that your grace affords; and because of the sweetness of your delights as well as of a clear conscience, they are better than any wine of worldly wisdom or any joy of fleshly pleasure, and they are **fragrant with the best perfumes**, the gifts of the sevenfold Spirit. For since these gifts come into me at your initiative in the order of their importance, the first to take hold of me is the fear of you, which with great sternness impels me toward you. Second in order to present itself is devotion to God, which receives me into you. And since, according to Scripture, such devotion is worship of you — "devotion," says Job, "is the worship of God" — in teaching me to worship you, it taught me to say, in the Spirit, "Jesus is Lord" (1 Cor. 12:3). And thereupon, for a sweet fragrance and for a health-giving power, the oil of your Name itself is poured out from you and poured into me, where it softens all my hardness, alleviates my bitterness, and cures all my infirmity. The touch of the oil of your Name has dissolved the yoke of my ancient captivity into dust; but your yoke, O Lord, has become easy for me, and your burden, light (cf. Matt. 11:30). The sound of your Name — whether it be

"Lord" or "Jesus" or "Christ" — has conveyed instant joy and gladness to my ear; for as soon as the Name is heard, the mystery of the Name also shines forth in my heart, as does love among my longings, evoking devout service to the Lord, devotion and love to the Savior (which is what "Jesus" means), and obedience and awe for Christ the King.

(12) The *Glossa ordinaria*

For your breasts are better than wine.

He mentions the **breasts** of the Bridegroom, a thing proper to women, in order that he may make it clear at the beginning of the Song that he is speaking in figures.

(13) Gregory of Nyssa

The fragrance of your perfumed unguents is better than all spices.

This seems to me to point to the following thought. The **spices** we take to be virtues, such as wisdom, temperance, justice, courage, prudence, and the like; and each individual assumes a different scent as he is touched with them in accordance with his own power and choice. One has in him the scent that comes from temperance or wisdom; another, that which comes from justice or courage or some other quality that is reckoned among the virtues; and yet another happens to have in him the scent that comes from the mingling of all these spices. Nevertheless, none of these can be compared with that absolute virtue of which the prophet Habbakuk asserts that it encloses the heaven when he says, "His virtue veiled the heavens" (Hab. 3:3 LXX). This is Wisdom herself, and Justice itself, and Truth herself, and all things severally. Therefore the Bride says, "The smell of your ointments possesses an incomparable grace by comparison with the spices known to us."

(14) Gregory the Great

. . . the fragrance of your perfumed unguents is better than all spices.

She now continues and says, **and the fragrance of your perfumed unguents is better than all spices.** The Lord's **perfumed ointments** are the virtues, [and] the Lord's ointment was the Holy Spirit. It is about this that the prophet says to him, "God, your God, has anointed you with the oil of gladness above your fellows" (Ps. 44:8 LXX = 45:7). He was anointed with this oil when he became incarnate. It is not the case that he first existed as a human being and afterward received the Holy Spirit. On the contrary, since he became incarnate through the mediation of the Holy Spirit, he was anointed with this very same oil when he was made a human being. Therefore, the **fragrance** of his ointment is the warm radiance of the Holy Spirit, who remains in him while proceeding from him. The fragrance of his **perfumed unguents** is the warm radiance of the virtues, which he has produced. . . . But **The fragrance of your perfumed unguents is better than all spices** because the warm radiance of the Bridegroom's virtues, which came about through his incarnation, overmatched the commands of the law, which had been required before by the Bridegroom as down payments. The Church indeed grew in understanding to the same degree as it was deserving of the illumination of a clearer vision. Those **spices** of the law were ministered through angels, but this unguent has been given by way of the presence of the Bridegroom. But since the good things of the law, which were counted sublime, have been surpassed by the glory of his presence, it is rightly said: **The fragrance of your perfumed unguents is better than all spices.**

(15) Origen

Your name is perfumed ointment emptied out.

Surely one can see in these words a prophecy spoken as by the Bride concerning Christ, to the effect that it would come about by the advent of our Lord and Savior that his Name would be so diffused through the earth and the whole cosmos that "in every place" there would come to be "fragrance," just as the apostle says, "For we are the sweet scent of Christ in every place, to some a fragrance from death to death, but to others a fragrance from life to life" (cf. 2 Cor. 2:14-16).

For if it had been "a fragrance from life to life" for everyone, it would surely have said in our text, "All **have loved you** and **have drawn you.**" In fact, however, it says, "When **your name** had been **emptied out as a perfumed ointment, they loved you** — "they" meaning not those decrepit souls that have dressed themselves in the old humanity (cf. Eph. 4:22), nor those that have spots or wrinkles, but **young maidens**, souls that are increasing in age and in beauty, that are always being made new and are "renewed from day to day" (2 Cor. 4:16), because they have "dressed themelves in the new humanity, which has been created according to God's likeness" (Eph. 4:23).

It is, then, for the sake of these young maiden souls that are growing in life and making progress that he who was "in the form of God . . . emptied himself" (Phil. 2:6, 7) in order that his **name** might become a **perfumed ointment emptied out**, in order that he should no longer dwell only "in light inaccessible" (1 Tim. 6:16) and remain "in the form of God," but that the Word should become flesh, so that these **young maidens**, growing and making progress, might not only love him, but **draw him** to themselves. For every soul draws and takes the Word of God to herself in proportion to her capacity and the degree of her faith. When, though, souls have drawn the Word of God to themselves, and have brought him to dwell in their minds and thoughts, and have known for themselves the delights of his sweetness and fragrance; when they have smelled the scent of his perfumed ointments, and have grasped at least the meaning of his advent, the reasons for his redemption and suffering, and the love that brought him, the immortal one, all the way to the death of the cross (cf. Phil. 2:8) for the salvation of all — well, then these **young maidens**, drawn by all these things as if they were fragrances of a divine and ineffable ointment, being souls filled with vigor and eagerness, run after him toward the fragrance of his sweetness, not at an easy pace nor with sluggish steps, but in haste, with all speed and dispatch, just as did the one who said, "I run so that I may obtain" (1 Cor. 9:24).

I am bound to ask: If his **name** alone, by being **a perfumed ointment emptied out**, accomplished so much and stirred up the maidens to the point that they drew him to themselves and, once they had him with them, took in the smell of his ointments and straightway ran after him — if, I say, his name alone brought all this about, what do you suppose the very reality of him will accomplish? What virtue, what vigor, will those maidens receive from it, if by one means or another they become able to attain to the very incomprehensible and ineffable reality of him? It is my judgment that if they ever got to this point, they would not walk or run, but, bound to him by chains of his love, they would adhere to him, and there would be no room in their lives for any further moving on. They would be one spirit with him, and in them what is written would be fulfilled: "As you, Father, in me and I in thee are one, so too may they be one in us" (John 17:21). . . . And this comes about, as we said, when nothing more than the smell of him has been perceived. What do you think they will do when the Word of God becomes the content of their hearing and sight and touch and taste and furnishes to each of their senses the excellences that suit its nature and its competence — so that the eye, if it is able to see "his glory, glory as of the Only begotten of the Father" (John 1:14), has no wish to see anything else, nor the hearing, to hear anything but the Word of life and of salvation?

(16) Gregory of Nyssa

Your name is perfumed ointment emptied out.

Once again, in what comes next, the soul, the Bride, touches on a higher philosophy. When she says **Your name is perfumed ointment emptied out**, she makes it manifest that the divine power is inaccessible and incapable of being contained by human thought-processes; for to me it seems that by this statement there is conveyed something like the following: that the Nature which has no limits cannot be comprehended accurately by means of the meanings of words. On the contrary, all the power of concepts and all the significance of words and names, even if they seem to have about them something grand and worthy of the Divine, cannot attain the nature of the Real itself. On the contrary, it is as if by certain traces and hints that our reason guesses at the Invisible: by way of some analogy based on things it has comprehended, it forms a conjecture about the Incomprehensible. For whatever name we may think up — she says — to make the scent of the Godhead known, the meaning of the things we say does not refer to the perfume itself. Rather does our theological vocabulary refer to a slight remnant of the vapor of the divine fragrance. In the case of vessels from which perfumed ointment is emptied out, the ointment itself that has been emptied is not itself known for what it is in its own nature. We make a guess about the perfume that has been emptied out on the basis of some faint quality of the vapor that has been left behind in the vessel.

Here then is what we learn from these words. The perfumed ointment of the Godhead, whatever it may be in its own essence, is beyond every name and every thought; but the marvels discerned in the universe provide matter for our theological naming. By their help we name God wise, powerful, good, holy, blessed and eternal, and judge and savior. And all of these refer to some slight trace of the divine perfume, which the whole creation, after the manner of a jar for ointments, imitates within itself by the wonders that are seen in it.

(17) Gregory the Great

Your name is perfumed ointment emptied out.

The **ointment** poured out is the Deity incarnate. For if an unguent is in a jar, its odor outside of the jar is not very strong; but if it is poured out, the scent of the unguent spreads around. The name of God, then, is an unguent poured out in that it pours itself out of its divine immensity for the sake of our nature; from being invisible, it renders itself visible. For if it did not pour itself out, it would never become known to us. The unguent poured itself out when it both preserved itself as God and showed itself as a human. Regarding this outpouring, Paul says, "Who, since he was in the form of God, did not think that it was robbery to be equal to God, but emptied himself, taking on the form of a servant" (Phil. 2:6-7). What Paul calls "emptied," Solomon calls "emptied out." Since, then, the Lord was made known to the human race by the humility of the incarnation, it is said to him: **Your name is a perfumed ointment emptied out.**

(18) Ambrose of Milan

Your name is perfumed ointment emptied out.
   That is why young maidens have loved you
   and have drawn you.

So you went down [into the baptismal water]: recall what your answers were! You replied that you believe in the Father, believe in the Son, believe in the Holy Spirit. That does not mean, "I believe in a greater, and a lesser, and a last." You bound yourself, by the same spoken guarantee, to believe in the Son in the same way as you believe in the Father, to believe in the Spirit in the same way as you believe in the Son, with this single exception, that you acknowledge yourself bound to believe that only the Lord Jesus was crucified.

   After all this, you came up to the bishop. Keep in mind what then followed. Was it not what David said: "Like the perfumed ointment upon the head, that comes down upon the beard, upon the beard of Aaron" (Ps. 132:2 LXX = 133:2)? This is the ointment of which Solomon says, **Your name is perfumed ointment emptied out. That is why young maidens have loved you and have drawn you.** How many renewed souls have loved you today, Lord Jesus, and said, as they drew into themselves the fragrance of resurrection: **Draw us after you, let us run after the fragrance of your perfumes!**

(19) Apollinarius of Laodicea

Your name is perfumed ointment emptied out.

By the name of Christ all are purified, cured, washed, and there is made to dwell in us the veritable sweet smell. I mean the Holy Spirit; and the **name** that has been **poured out** brings about the outpouring of the Spirit upon all, in accordance with the saying: "You have been sanctified and justified in the name of our Lord Jesus Christ, and in the Spirit of our God" (1 Cor. 6:11).

(20) Theodoret of Cyrus

The King has brought me into his chamber.
Let us rejoice and be glad in you.
  We will love your breasts better than wine.

[The young maidens] are not jealous or full of envy because they remain outside and are not admitted into the bridal chamber. On the contrary, they rejoice and are glad, and are happy for the honor accorded the Bride, and they are satisfied with the sound of her sweet voice. Hence they add, **We will love your breasts better than wine.** The very thing she herself had said to the Bridegroom (cf. Song 1:2b) is what, imitating the favor of the Bridegroom, they say to the Bride because of the favor and affection they feel for her. For Christ said to his apostles, "The person who receives you receives me" (Matt. 10:40); and "Whoever gives one of these little ones who believe in me a cup of cold water to drink will not, I promise you, lose his reward" (Mark 9:41, 42). Again the young maidens call the Bride's **breasts** founts of teaching that pour forth streams suitable for all ages; and they promise that they shall love the Bride's breasts more than any human delight, for used as a figure, wine refers to that which gladdens the human heart (cf. Ps. 103:15 LXX = 104:15).

Now these things can be known to have come about both in the Old and in the New Covenants, and can be contemplated as they occur day by day. For in the Old Covenant, God revealed the future to the prophets and through them taught people the right way of life. These prophets, moreover, enjoyed the delights of God's inner chambers and hidden things, and when they had emerged, they would convey to human beings what was revealed and manifested. This explains what David said to God: "You have revealed to me the concealed and hidden things of your wisdom" (Ps. 50:8 LXX = 51:6). But those who were gladdened by the streams of divine teaching that stemmed from the prophets clung to them as mediators between God and humanity. The apostles too, however, inspired by God, spent their lives transmitting the message of true religion to all peoples. Moreover, the apostles enjoyed the delights of God's inner chambers, and the apostles' hearers met the flowing apostolic streams as if they were breasts to be valued more highly than any wine and any gladness. In these present days, further, the Church's teachers make the divine streams available to the people, as from certain treasure rooms, and the person who has the benefit of these teachings draws in the spiritual nourishment as if from a pair of breasts and judges it better than any delight of this life. That is why the Bride in the Song says, **The King brought me into his chamber;** but it is the young maidens who respond by saying, **Let us rejoice and be glad in you,** and promising, **We shall love your breasts better than wine.**

(21) Origen

The King has brought me into his chamber.

The Bride had informed the Bridegroom that young women, captivated by his fragrance, were running after him, and that she herself was going to run with them, so that she might provide them an example in every way. Now, having obtained as it were the reward of her labors for running with the runners, she says that she has been brought by her Bridegroom the King **into his chamber,** in order that there she might gaze upon all the royal treasures. In this she rightly rejoices and exults, inasmuch as she has gazed upon the King's hidden and mysterious realm.

This is the plain sense of the narrative, in conformity with the development of the plot of the drama.

Since, however, what is in question is the Church as it comes to Christ or the soul as it clings to the Word of God, what chamber of Christ or storeroom of the Word of God are we to take this to be, into which he introduces either his Church or the soul that clings to him, unless it be the very mind, mysterious and hidden, of Christ? On this subject, Paul himself said, "But we have the mind of Christ, in order that we may know the things that have been given us from God" (1 Cor. 2:16; 2:12). These are those very things which "eye has not seen, nor ear heard, nor have entered into the human heart, which God has prepared for those who love him" (1 Cor. 2:9). When therefore Christ introduces the soul into a comprehension of his mind, she is said to have been brought into the **chamber** of the King, in which are hidden the treasures of his wisdom and knowledge.

It does not seem to me to be a pointless thing that . . . , since she was about to use the word "chamber," she calls it **the chamber of the King** and does not set down any other name, such as might allow the reader to understand a commonplace person. The reason, I think, why "King" is employed here instead is to show thereby that this chamber abounds in treasure, as being royal and filled with an incalculable multitude of riches. To me it seems that the man who said that he had been "seized . . . all the way up into the third heaven," and thence into paradise, and heard "unutterable words, which no human being is permitted to speak" (2 Cor. 12:2-4), was close to this King or following him.

(22) Gregory the Great

The King has brought me into his chamber.

The Church of God is like a house that belongs to a king. This house has a door, it has a flight of stairs, it has a dining room, it has chambers. Everyone in the Church who has faith has already entered the door of this house; for just as the door grants entry to the rest of the house, so in faith is found access to the other virtues. Everyone in the Church who has hope has already come to the stairs of the house; for hope lifts the heart, so that it may desire things above and depart from things below. Everyone in this house who has charity walks about as it were among places for dining; for charity is broad and extends itself to embrace love of enemies. Everyone in the Church who already explores sublime mysteries and already meditates on hidden judgments enters as it were into the chamber. Regarding the door of this house, someone has said, "Open for me the doors of righteousness, and I will enter them and give thanks to the Lord" (Ps. 117:9 LXX = 118:19). About the stair of hope, he said, "He has placed the steps up in his heart" (Ps. 83:6 LXX = 84:5). Regarding the spacious dining places it is said, "Your commandment is exceeding broad" (Ps. 118:96 LXX = 119:96). The person who said, "My secret place is mine" (Isa. 24:16 Vg), and "I heard hidden words, which human beings are not permitted to utter" (cf. 2 Cor. 12:14), was talking about the King's chamber. Thus the first entry to this house is the door of faith, the second is advancement on the stairs of hope, the third is the broadness of love, and the fourth is the perfection of love for knowledge of the hidden things of God.

(23) Gregory of Nyssa

We will love your breasts better than wine.
Righteousness has loved you.

John, who rested on the Lord's bosom, loved the breasts of the Word, and having brought his own heart up to the fount of life as if it were a sponge, he was filled . . . with the mysteries lodged in the Lord's heart; and he offers to us the teat that has been filled up by the Word. He fills us up with the things lodged within him by the fount of goodness as, in a loud voice, he proclaims the eternal Word. For this reason it is fitting that we too turn to him and say, **We will love your breasts better than wine** — if indeed we have become the sort of people who are youthful, neither immature in heart and mind because of childishness yoked with vanity, nor yet shriveled up and wrinkled by sin in an old age that issues in destruction. And the reason why we love the flow of your teaching is that **Righteousness has loved you.** For this is the disciple whom Jesus loved. And Jesus is righteousness. This saying adorns the Lord with a name more lovely and worthy of God than that accorded by the prophet David. For David says, "Righteous is the Lord God" (Ps. 91:16 LXX = Ps. 92:15), while here he is named Righteousness, by which everything that is crooked is made straight. But for us may everything "crooked be . . . made straight, and the rough ways . . . smooth" (Isa. 40:4) by the grace of our Lord Jesus Christ.

Song 1:5-8

SEPTUAGINT	VULGATE

1:5 I am dark and beautiful,
    O daughters of Jerusalem,
as the tents of Kedar,
    as the curtains of Solomon.
6 Do not gaze at me, for I have been
    made dark,
    for the sun has looked askance at me.
The sons of my mother fought in me.
 	
    They set me up to be a guard in
    the vineyards.
    I did not guard my vineyard.
7 Speak to me, you whom my soul
    loves.
    Where do you pasture?
    Where do you take your rest at
    noontide?
Lest I become as one that is veiled
    above the flocks of your
    companions.
8 If you do not know yourself,
    O fair one among women,
go out in the footsteps of the flocks,
 	
    and pasture your kids
    by the shepherds' tents.
	1:4 I am black but beautiful,
	    O daughters of Jerusalem,
	as the tents of Cedar,
	    as the skins of Solomon.
	5 Do not gaze at me because I am dark,
	
	    because the sun has discolored me.
	The sons of my mother fought
	    against me,
	    they set me up to be a guard in
	    the vineyards.
	    I did not guard my vineyard.
	6 Declare to me, you whom my soul
	    loves,
	    where you pasture,
	    where you take your rest at
	    noontide,
	lest I begin to wander
	    after the flocks of your
	    companions.
	7 If you do not know yourself,
	    O fair one among women,
	go out and depart in the footprints of
	    the flocks,
	    and pasture your goats
	    beside the shepherds' tents.

In this segment of Song 1, interpreters found abundant occasion for differing ways of taking individual lines or verses. Some of these differences arose out of their use of different translations of the original.

Thus Origen and those, like Gregory of Nyssa, who followed him read a version that, at 1:6c, could be construed as saying, "The sons of my mother fought within me." This reading of course elicited an interpretation that dwelt on the struggle between good and evil forces within the soul. On the other hand, someone like Apponius reads the text as saying "fought against me," and applies it to false teachers, or to those who persecute the Church.

Similarly, those who used the Septuagint text or (like Augustine) a Latin translation of the Septuagint found themselves trying to understand what might be meant by **veiled above the flocks of your companions**; *while those who employed the Latin Vulgate could ponder the less baffling phrase* **wander after the flocks of your companions.**

In either case, however, the question arose who these **companions** *might be. Augustine's interpretation of this term is idiosyncratic because of a controversy that had raged in North Africa since the beginning of the 4th century. Song 1:7-8 had become an issue in the struggle between the catholic Church and the Donatist party. Donatists (a) took the phrase* **at noontide** *to mean "in [North] Africa" (where it was notoriously sunny); and (b) held that this phrase was also the Bridegroom's answer to the question where he pastured his flock. Hence they concluded that their Church — which they took to be the African Church par excellence — was Christ's own flock, the one true Church. In response, Augustine predictably takes the* **companions** *to represent the Donatists in their capacity as people who had "gone out" from the Church — that is, heretics. A more traditional interpretation had taken them to stand for the angels assigned by God to "shepherd" the Gentile peoples.*

By the same token, Augustine here ignores the traditional interpretation of **know yourself,** *which took this command to be addressed to the human soul and to enjoin recognition of the human self as a creature made after God's image and endowed with freedom. He takes it instead as addressed to a hypothetical catholic Christian who visits North Africa and wonders which of the two conflicting Christian bodies there is the one whom the true Bridegroom pastures. (For the more traditional exegesis, see the next section and Augustine's interpretation of the words there.)*

(1) Origen

I am dark and beautiful,
   O daughters of Jerusalem,
as the tents of Kedar,
   as the curtains of Solomon.

Again in this verse the person of the Bride is introduced and speaks. She does not, however, address those young maidens whose custom it is to run with her, but the daughters of Jerusalem. Because they have disparaged her on the ground that she is ugly, she is seen answering them and saying, "Yes, I am dark" (or "black") "as far as my coloring is concerned, **O daughters of Jerusalem**; but to anyone who looks upon my inward features, I am beautiful. For," says she, "**the tents of Kedar**, which is a great people, are also black, and its very name, **Kedar**, means blackness or darkness. Moreover, **the curtains of Solomon** are black, yet for all that the blackness of his curtains did not appear unseemly to such a king 'in all his glory' (Matt. 6:29). So then, **O daughters of Jerusalem**, do not count me guilty because of my color, since my body lacks neither natural beauty nor that which is sought after by conscious care."

These are the things that happen in the dramatic narrative and are the surface meaning of the tale before us. But let us return to the order of things hidden.

This Bride who is speaking has the role of the Church that has been gathered from among the nations; but the **daughters of Jerusalem** whom she addresses are those souls that are said to be most dear on account of the calling of the patriarchs, but "enemies as regards the gospel" (cf. Rom. 11:28). They are therefore the **daughters of** this earthly **Jerusalem**; and when they see the Church that is drawn from the nations, they despise her — even though she is forgetful of her people and her father's house and comes to Christ — and vilify her for her base descent, on the ground that she is a Church of low birth because she cannot lay claim to high descent from Abraham and Isaac and Jacob.

Now the Bride is aware that the daughters of the earlier people bring this charge against her, and that on this ground she is also called "black," as if she were one who does not possess the bright splendor of the learning that comes from the patriarchs; and she answers this by saying, "Yes, I am black, **O daughters of Jerusalem**, in this respect — that I do not belong to the lineage of illustrious men and have not enjoyed the enlightenment of the law of Moses. Nevertheless I possess a beauty that is properly my own. For in me what is most elemental and deep-seated is that which has been made after the image of God; and now by drawing near to the Word of God I have recovered my beauteous appearance. For though you may compare me to **the tents of Kedar** and **the curtains of Solomon**, nevertheless even Kedar is descended from Ishmael (for he was born as Ishmael's second son [cf. Gen. 25:13]), and Ishmael was not without a blessing from God. But you also compare me to **the curtains of Solomon**, which are nothing other than the curtains of the tabernacle of God; and yet I wonder, **O daughters of Jerusalem**, that you seek to reproach me on account of my black coloring. How can you fail to remember that it is written in your law what Miriam suffered when she disparaged Moses because he had taken a black Ethiopian woman to be his wife (cf. Numbers 12)? How is it possible for you to be ignorant that in me the foreshadowing which that image represents is fulfilled in reality? I am that Ethiopian woman. I am the one who, because of her low status by birth, is **black**, but is **beautiful** because of her faith and her penitence. For I have appropriated the Son of God within myself, I have received the Word made flesh. I have come to him who "is the image of . . . God, the firstborn of all creation" (Col. 1:15), who is "the radiance of [God's] glory and the imprint of his being" (Heb. 1:3), and I have become **beautiful**.

(2) Gregory of Nyssa

I am dark and beautiful,
  O daughters of Jerusalem.

It seems to me that the great Paul, in his letter to the Romans, makes much of a thought that is very close to this. There he establishes the love of God for us on the ground that when we were sinners and **dark**, God made us full of light and lovely by shining upon us with his grace (Rom. 5:8). For just as at night everything, bright though it be by nature, shares the black look of the prevailing darkness, but once the light comes, there remains no trace of darkness in things that had before been obscured by the night: just so when the soul has been transposed from error to truth, the dark form of her life is transformed into radiant beauty.

Paul, moreover, the bride of Christ who was dark and later became bright, says to Timothy the same thing that the Bride says to her maidens. He says that he, who earlier on was a blasphemer and a persecutor and a man of pride and a dark one, was deemed worthy of beauty; and further that Christ came into the world to make dark ones bright, not calling the righteous to himself, but calling sinners to repentance, whom he caused to shine like stars by the laver of rebirth (Tit. 3:5) when he had washed off their dark appearance with water.

Further, the eye of David sees this very thing in the city on high, and makes of his vision something to wonder at. He tells how, in the city of God, of which "glorious things are spoken" (Ps. 86:3 LXX = 87:3), Babylon is domiciled, and Rahab the harlot is named, and there are foreigners within her, and the Tyrian, and the people of the Ethiopians — so that no one may ever reproach that City for being void of inhabitants by asking, "Shall any say to Zion, 'A human being was born within her'" (Ps. 86:5a LXX = 87:5a)? For there strangers become fellow tribesmen of the City, and the Babylonians become Jerusalemites, and the harlot a virgin, and the Ethiopians bright, and Tyre the City on High.

(3) Bernard of Clairvaux

I am . . . beautiful . . .
  as the curtains of Solomon.

What does it mean, then, when she says: I am . . . beautiful . . . as the curtains of Solomon? In my view, it is something great and wonderful — as long as we have in mind here not this Solomon, but the Solomon of whom it is said, "Behold, something greater than Solomon is here" (Matt. 12:42). For this Solomon of mine is so much a Solomon that he is called not only "peaceful" (which is what "Solomon" means) but also "Peace" itself, as Paul asserts in saying, "He is our peace" (Eph. 2:14). I am certain that in this Solomon one can find something that I would not for a moment hesitate to compare with the beauty of the Bride.

Where his **curtains** are concerned, moreover, notice what it says in the psalm: "He spread out the heavens like a curtain" (Ps. 103:3 Vg = 104:2). It is surely not the other Solomon, altogether wise and powerful though he was, who spread out "the heavens like a curtain," but rather the One who is not so much wise as he is Wisdom herself; he is assuredly the One who spread it out and established it. His — and not the other's — is the voice that says, "When he" — which obviously means God the Father — "established the heavens, I was there" (Prov. 8:27). In his Power and his Wisdom he was assuredly present for the One who was establishing the heavens. Nor are you to think, on the ground that he says "I was there" and not "I established," that he stood idly nearby as an onlooker. Have a quick glance below in the text, and you will find him saying explicitly, "I was with him, putting all things in order" (Prov. 8:30). Accordingly he says, "For whatever the Father does, the Son does too" (John 5:19). It was he, then, that spread out "the heaven like a curtain" — an exquisitely fair curtain that covers the entire face of the earth in the manner of some vast tent and delights human eyes with the admirable diversity of sun, moon, and stars. What could be fairer than this curtain? What could be more splendid than the heavens?

Nevertheless the heavens cannot be compared with the glorious beauty of the Bride. For they are corporeal and objects of sense perception, and even the "form" of them "is passing away" (1 Cor. 7:31). "For the things that are seen are temporal, but the things that are not seen are eternal" (2 Cor. 4:18). On the other hand, what is proper to the Bride is a rational form and a spiritual likeness; and this is itself eternal, for it is an image of eternity. Her beauty — for the sake of a word — is love, and, as you read, "Love never ends" (1 Cor. 13:8). Plainly too, her beauty is justice; and "justice," it says, "endures forever" (Ps. 111:3 Vg = 112:3). It is also patience, and yet you read: "The patience of the poor shall not perish forever" (Ps. 9:19 Vg = 9:18). What then of voluntary poverty? What of humility? Does not the one promise an eternal kingdom, and the other, by the same token, an eternal exaltation? Her beauty also involves "the holy fear of the Lord, which endures forever" (Ps. 18:10 Vg = 19:9). The same goes for prudence, for temperance, for courage, and whatever other virtues there may be: what are they but pearls upon the Bride's apparel, gleaming with an undying brilliance? I say "undying" because the virtues are the seat and foundation of everlastingness; for there is no place in the soul for the life everlasting and blessed unless the virtues enter in and mediate it. That is why the prophet says to God, who is himself blessedness, "Justice and judgment are the foundation of your throne" (Ps. 88:15 Vg = 89:14).

Furthermore, the apostle says that "Christ dwells in our hearts," not in any old fashion, but expressly "by faith" (Eph. 3:17). Again, the disciples spread their garments under the Lord as he was about to mount the colt of an ass (Matt. 21:7), and by this act they indicated that the Savior, or salvation, in no wise dwells in the naked soul — to wit, the soul that he does not find attired in the teaching and practice of the apostles. Hence the Church, possessing the promise of future felicity, takes care in the meanwhile to get herself ready, and to adorn herself in advance in cloth of gold, draped about with a diversity of charisms and virtues, in consequence of which she may be found worthy and capable of the fullness of grace.

In any case, I would in no way compare that visible and corporeal heaven — most fair though it be in its own order by reason of the variety of the stars — to this superb spiritual array that the soul received in her first, preliminary clothing with the vesture of her sanctification. But there is a heaven of the heaven, of which the prophet says, "Sing to the Lord, who ascends above the heaven of the heaven, to the east" (Ps. 67:33-34 Vg = 68:32-33). This heaven, moreover, is of the intellectual and spiritual order; and he who made the heavens by his understanding created it and established it for eternity, and dwells within it. And do not for a moment think that the Bride's love stays itself on this side of that heaven, since she knows that her Beloved dwells there; for where her treasure is, there her heart is also. Indeed, she is envious of those who are in the presence of him for whom she sighs and longs; and she studies to become, in the manner of her life, like those in whose vision she cannot join. By her doings more than with her voice she cries out, "Lord, I have loved the beauty of thy house, and the place where your glory dwells" (Ps. 25:8 Vg = 26:8).

(4) William of St. Thierry

I am black but beautiful,
  O daughters of Jerusalem. . . .

But just as, with the departure of the sun, the night inevitably takes its place, so too, with the departure of the Bridegroom and the delay of his return (cf. Matt. 25:5), the Bride begins to lose her former beauty and to be blackened within herself; and all her deeds are deprived of their attractiveness. The result is that the former warmth of her heart is now gone, and her deeds lack color. For just as the light outside us is in a way the queen of all colors, without which nothing possesses the sheen of beauty, and there is no vigor in anything, so illuminating grace is the source of the vigor that informs all the virtues, and the light of good deeds; without it, the virtues cannot be effective, nor can good deeds yield their harvest. Even if the contrary seems to be true, they do not bloom or rejoice, they lack the oil of gladness, the unction that gives instruction, the taste of God's sweetness, the fragrance of eternity, the authenticity of the experience proper to spiritual perception.

Hence it is that the Bride blushes for herself, and also fears for those for whom she has been a habitual object for imitation and admiration: **I am black**, she says, **but beautiful, O daughters of Jerusalem, as the tents of Cedar, as the skins of Solomon** — things that seem to be more useful than they are attractive. It is as if she were saying, "My interior beauty is unimpaired, even though my color has changed; for 'the spirit is willing, but the flesh is weak' (Mark 14:38); my faith stands firm, but my mind is darkened; my will is the same, but my longing has been weakened." She acknowledges that she is black because of the darkness of her troubled conscience, and this even though she does not deny that she is beautiful because of the rectitude of her faith; for she knows, as she was taught in the **cellars** of the King, that to deny the faith is the work not of humility but of impiety. To lack not only faith but also hope and a sound will is to cultivate death; and so too it is criminal to deny the faith when one possesses it. Truly, then, as long as she does not cease to be Bride and keeps herself from ever denying that she is, the Bride always finds herself lovely in respect of the upright beauty of her faith, and the purity of her intention, and the devotion of her will. Yet that is not inconsistent with her humble acknowledgment of the blackness that comes from awareness of past sins and from the assault of the vices.

(5) Bede the Venerable

As the tents of Cedar,
    as the skins of Solomon.

Cedar was the son of Ishmael, of whom it was said: "His hand against every man and every man's hand against him" (Gen. 16:12; cf. 1 Chron. 1:29). The nation of the Saracens, hateful to all, which originated with him, establishes even today the truth of this portent; and the psalmist, set about with troubles, affirms it when he says, "I have lived with those who dwell in Cedar; long has my soul been with those who hate peace. I am peaceful" (Ps. 119:5-7 Vg = 120:5-7). For David is not said to have borne any of the hatred of the Ishmaelites; but he wanted to magnify the evils that he suffered at the hand of Saul or of other adversaries of his, and so he complained that he was injured by the depravity of a people who never took the trouble to be at peace with anyone. On the other hand, Solomon was a man of peace, by name and in practice: "All the kings of the earth sought the presence of Solomon, to hear the wisdom that God had given him in his heart" (2 Chron. 9:23). Hence the statement, **I am black but beautiful, as the tents of Cedar, as the skins of Solomon,** is divided in such wise that the Bride is **black . . . as the tents of Cedar** and **beautiful . . . as the skins of Solomon.** For the holy Church is very often made dark by the sufferings she undergoes at the hands of unbelievers, just as if she were the universal enemy of the entire world, the word of the Lord to her having been fulfilled: "You will be hated by all for my name's sake" (Matt. 10:22). In the same way she is ever lovely in the sight of her Redeemer, just as if she whom the King of Peace himself deigned to visit were truly worthy.

Moreover, it should be noted that **Cedar** — the very name — indicates that which pours darkness forth, or evil men or unclean spirits; just as **Solomon** too — which means peaceful — indicates, by the mystery of the name, the very One of whom it is written: "His sway shall increase, and of peace there shall be no end, over the throne of David and over his kingdom" (Isa. 9:7). And when it is said that the Church is **black . . . as the tents of Cedar,** the term **as** is set down not because it expresses the truth, but because it expresses the appraisal of fools, who think that she provides housing within herself for vices or malevolent spirits; but when she is called **fair . . . as the skins of Solomon,** the term **as** is set down because it expresses the truth of the exemplar. For just as Solomon used to make himself tents out of the skins of dead animals, so too the Lord gathers the Church for himself from those souls that know how to renounce carnal desires. That is why he said to everyone, "If anyone wants to come after me, let him deny himself and take up his cross and follow me" (Matt. 16:24).

(6) Gregory of Nyssa

Do not gaze at me, for I have been made dark.

For she says, "**Do not gaze at me, for I have been made dark.** I did not come to be so at the very first." It did not make sense, moreover, for one who was shaped by the radiant hands of God to have her appearance stained all over with some dark and gloomy color. "So therefore," she says, "that is not what I was but what I became. For it was not because of my nature that I was blackened. Rather did such ugliness come to me from the outside, because the sun changed my appearance from radiant to black." For, she says, **The sun has looked askance at me.**

What then do we learn from these statements? In a parable (Matt. 13:3ff.; Luke 8:5ff.), the Lord said to the crowds that the sower of the Word does not plant solely in the good heart. Even if a heart be stony, even if it be overgrown with thorns, even if it be alongside the path and trodden down, he casts the seed of the Word into them all because of his love of humankind. Furthermore, explaining in his discourse the characteristics of each class, the Lord says that in the case of the stony heart what happens is this: the seed is not deeply rooted, but gives promise of producing an early ear because of its surface shoot. It dries up, though, when the sun has heated up the soil, because there is no moisture beneath for the roots. In his interpretation of the parable (Luke 8:13b) the Lord identifies the sun as "temptation."

I take it, then, that the teaching we gather from the lady who instructs us is this: Human nature came into existence as a copy of the true light, far removed from the marks of darkness and resplendent in its likeness to the beauty of its archetype. But temptation and trial, when they had deceitfully brought on their fiery heat, destroyed the shoot while it was still delicate and rootless. Before it had a firm hold on goodness, and before it had provided depth for its roots to sink in by thoughtful reflection's husbandry, they straightway rendered it dark through disobedience, having dried up its verdant and thriving form with burning heat.

(7) Gregory the Great

Do not gaze at me because I am dark,
  because the sun has discolored me.

The group that had not believed in Christ looked upon the group that had believed as sinful; but the latter says, "**Do not gaze at me because I am dark, because the sun has discolored me.** The sun, the Lord himself, has himself in his coming darkened me." By his precepts he has shown that there was no beauty in the law's precepts. The sun, when it strikes someone directly, darkens that individual. So too the Lord, when he comes, darkens the person whom he has touched closely by his grace; for the closer we draw to grace, the more we know ourselves to be sinners. Let us think of Paul as he comes out of Judea, darkened by the sun: "For if we, seeking to be justified in Christ, are ourselves discovered to be sinners . . ." (Gal. 2:17). The person who discovers himself to be a sinner in Christ finds himself darkened in the sun.

(8) Gregory of Nyssa

The sons of my mother fought in me.
> They set me up as a guard in the vineyards.
> I did not guard my vineyard.

Here, then, is the meaning of the words before us as far as we have grasped it. Humanity came into existence at the beginning lacking not a single one of the divine goods. Its task was simply to "guard" the good things, not to acquire them. But the treachery of the hostile powers stripped humanity of what belonged to it, when it did not guard the good fortune that had been given it by God as a natural endowment.

So here we have the meaning of these statements; but this sense is conveyed by means of enigmas, in the following manner: **The sons of my mother**, she says, **fought in me. They set me up as a guard in the vineyards. I did not guard my vineyard.**

The text gives us many essential teachings in a few words. First of all, there is the great Paul's declaration, that all things are from God, and that "There is one God, the Father, from whom are all things" (1 Cor. 8:6); and also that there is not one of the things that exist that does not have its being both through him and from him: "For all things," it says, "came to be through him, and apart from him nothing came to be" (John 1:3). But since God made all things, they are "very good" (Gen. 1:31), for he made all things by Wisdom. To the rational nature, however, he gave the grace of self-determination and added a capacity to detect what fits one's purposes. In this way space would be made for our responsibility, and the good would not be compelled and involuntary, but come about as the product of choice.

Since the impulse of self-determination unavoidably leads us toward the apparent good, there was found in the order of being one agent who used this power wrongly and, according to the word of the apostle, became the "inventor of mischief" (Rom. 1:30). Because he too came from God, he is our brother; but since he introduced evil by voluntarily shedding his participation in the good and becoming "father of the lie" (John 8:44), he set himself up as an enemy to all whose choice aims at what is better. Since, therefore, through this agent opportunity was afforded the rest of falling away from the good things (which indeed came to pass for the human race), the Bride who once was dark but now is beautiful is right to specify such **sons of** her **mother** as the cause of her dark appearance — teaching us in these words that there is as it were one Mother of all things that belong to the realm of being, the cause of their existence. For this reason, all things that are conceived as beings are brothers and sisters of one another; but difference of choice splits the family up into a friendly and a hostile part. Those who departed from their disposition for the good and because of this departure from what is better lent existence to evil (for evil has no other reality than separation from what is better) turned every effort and thought to make others their companions in this fellowship with evil. That is why she says, "These **sons of my mother**" (for by the use of the plural she indicates the many forms of evil) "set up a warfare within me, not fighting by way of onslaught from without, but making of the soul itself a territory in dispute with its interior enemy. For the battle is within each of us, as the divine apostle explains when he says, 'I see in my members another law which fights against the law of my intellect and makes me a captive to the law of sin which is in my members' (Rom. 7:23). Because this civil war has been generated within me by my brethren, enemies of my salvation, I became dark when defeated by my adversaries and **I did not guard my vineyard.**"

(9) Apponius

They set me up to be a guard in the vineyards.
 I did not guard my vineyard.

Hence the Bride sets out the reason why she was attacked by the sons of her mother, namely, that once she had discovered a better vine she deserted the guardianship of her own vineyard — the vineyard that had been entrusted to her. For by "guard of a vineyard" we understand anyone who, educated in the wise speech of some philosophy or other, or on whom the authority to teach has been conferred, is gladly heard by the people. Further, you will find that in many texts of the divine Scripture "vineyard" means a people or nation — as in the prophet David's words, "You have brought a vine out of Egypt" (Ps. 79:9 LXX = 80:8). So too in Isaiah the prophet we find, "The vineyard of the Lord of hosts is the house of Israel" (Isa. 5:7); and in Jeremiah God brings a reproach against the Hebrew nation: "I planted you as a true vineyard. How have you been turned into the bitterness of a foreign vineyard?" (Jer. 2:21).

In this text, however, the Bride makes a distinction and says that she deserted her own vineyard, not the vineyard of the Lord. The point of this is to show that apart from the teaching of the Lord, which the world received in the prophets, every other body of teaching is someone's property, and that through such a teaching a people comes to belong to a particular teacher; and the reason why a people is figuratively called "vineyard" is that it must necessarily have a teacher, just as a vineyard has a cultivator or a guard. Further, the reason why it is said that the guarding of this vineyard is to be entrusted to the hands of some member of the people who is preeminently wise is this: that this person receives the authority to teach by the judgment of the elders and leaders, and it is by teaching that he guards the vineyard entrusted to him.

From this vine he will receive the fruit of gladness in rejoicing if he lives a holy life and teaches others in the right way. If, however, he should teach what is wrong, he will drink the bitter wine of the impiety of the aforesaid vineyard that is his, when, before the tribunal of the eternal Judge, he shall be condemned for the profanation of all the souls that he has taught wrongly. . . . For just as he "who . . . does" the good first of all and "teaches" others so "will be called great in the kingdom of heaven" (Matt. 5:19), so too the wicked teachers of the nations, those of the heretics, or the masters of the magical arts, or in our days those of the Jews, who by their serpentine speaking and the dialectical conclusions of their syllogisms turn the truth into a lie (cf. Rom. 1:25) — these great teachers of evil things will be summoned to great punishments. And if one of these should desert the vineyard that belongs to him and should join the vineyard of Christ, and then within it, by wholesome speech and the example of a holy life, spend himself upon its cultivation, they will persecute him; the members of this nation will **fight against** him, and at the instigation of the Devil they are roused up to do battle against him with the sharp darts of their words. It is such a one who says, **The sons of my mother fought against me. They set me up to be a guard in the vineyards. I did not guard my vineyard.**

(10) Origen

Tell me, you whom my soul loves.
  Where do you pasture?
  Where do you take your rest at noontide?
Lest I become as one that is veiled
  above the flocks of your companions.

It is still the Bride who is speaking these words, but she speaks them to the Bridegroom and no longer to the daughters of Jerusalem. Thus from the beginning, where she says, **Let him kiss me,** right up to this place, that is, **Above the flocks of your companions,** everything that is said is an utterance of the Bride. What she says, however, is addressed first to God, then, second, to the Bridegroom, and third, to the young maidens — she being a mediator, as it were, between them and the Bridegroom and now (to maintain the form of a stage play) becoming a sort of chorus leader for them, she directs her statements now to them, at another time to the Bridegroom, and at yet another to the daughters of Jerusalem by way of response. These final words of hers, then, she now directs to the Bridegroom. She asks him where he pastures at noontide, where he locates his flock; for she is afraid that while she is seeking him, she may come upon the places where the companions of the Bridegroom have located their flocks at noonday.

From these words it is further apparent that here the Bridegroom is also a shepherd. Earlier on, moreover, we had been told that he is a king as well, for the good reason that he rules over human beings; but he is a shepherd in that he pastures his sheep, and a bridegroom in that he has a bride who shall reign at his side, just as it is written: "The queen stood at his right hand, in attire of gold" (Ps. 44:10 LXX = Ps. 45:9). The order of the drama itself, the narrative, as it were, comprises these matters.

(11) Augustine of Hippo

Tell me, you whom my soul loves . . .
    and pasture your goats
    by the shepherds' tents.

"But people are right to require a word of Christ from you [Donatists] — the voice of Christ, the voice of the Shepherd, the voice that the sheep can hear and follow. You turn up nothing you can say. You do not have the voice of the Shepherd. Hear and follow! Forget the voice of the wolf and follow the voice of the Shepherd — or else convey the voice of the Shepherd to us."

"That is what we are doing," they say.

"Let us hear!"

"We too convey the voice of the Shepherd."

"Well, let us hear!"

"In the Songs of Songs," they say, "the Bride speaks to the Bridegroom, the Church to Christ."

"We know the Songs of Songs: holy songs, love songs, songs of holy love, of holy benevolence, of holy sweetness. Be sure that I want to hear the voice of the Shepherd speaking in those Songs, the voice of that sweetest of Bridegrooms. If you have something, produce it. Let us hear!"

"The Bride," they say, "says to the Bridegroom, **Tell me, you whom my soul loves, where you feed your sheep, where you take your rest.** And the Bridegroom," they say, "answers her: **at noontide.**"

"Now the evidence I offered you was plain. There was no way in which you could make it say something else: 'Ask of me, and I will make the nations your heritage, and the ends of the earth your possession' (Ps. 2:8). 'All the ends of the earth shall remember and turn to the Lord' (Ps. 21:28 LXX = 22:27). But what is this that you produce from the Songs of Songs? Something that you most likely do not understand. For those Songs are composed of enigmas: very few people who are acquainted with them understand them, and their meaning opens itself up to very few of those that come knocking. Hold tightly to the things that are set out there for all to see and cherish them devoutly, in order that the hidden things may be made known to you. How can you look into hidden things if you treat what is perfectly plain with contempt?"

Nevertheless, brethren, let us look into these words to the extent of our ability; the Lord will be here to help you detect a sound meaning in them.

In the first place — and this anyone, including even those who are no experts, can easily conclude — the words are wrongly divided. And now you will hear how this is so — now you will make your judgment.

The actual text of the passage goes like this. The Bride says to the Bridegroom: **Tell me, you whom my soul loves, where you feed your sheep, where you take your rest.** Neither we nor [the Donatists] have any question that the Bride is speaking to the Bridegroom, that the Church is speaking to Christ. But take notice of *all* the words of the Bride. Why are you minded to assign to the Bridegroom words that still belong to the

Bride? Recite *everything* that the Bride says, and *then* the Bridegroom will answer. Pay attention to the distinction I am going to make, and you will not turn up anything clearer.

Tell me, you whom my soul loves, where you feed your sheep, where you take your rest at noontide. It is still the Bride herself that is saying **where you feed your sheep, where you take your rest at noontide.** And notice why this is the case: what comes next is **lest by some chance I become as one that is veiled above the flocks of your companions.** Now I reckon that everyone, educated or not, knows the difference between the masculine gender and the feminine. I ask, then, what the gender of **veiled** is. I ask this question of everyone: Is it masculine or feminine? **Tell me,** she says, **you whom my soul loves. Whom,** when she utters it, is addressed to a male, to the Bridegroom. But that it is a woman who addresses the man is made clear by the words that follow: **Tell me . . . where you feed your sheep, where you take your rest at noontide, lest by some chance I become as one that is veiled above the flocks of your companions.** Note the word **veiled** [*operta*], so that all this may be unveiled [*aperta*] to you. **Tell me, you whom my soul loves, where you feed your sheep, where you sleep at noontide, lest by some chance I become as one that is veiled above the flocks of your companions.**

Thus far the words of the Bride. At this point — manifestly — the Bridegroom begins to speak: **If you do not know yourself,** he says. Notice that **yourself** is plainly a woman: **know yourself, O fair one among women. If you do not know yourself, O fair one among women, go out in the footsteps of the flocks, and pasture your goats in the shepherds' tents** — not in the tent of the Shepherd. See how, at a moment of danger, the Bridegroom uses a threat, how he abstains from compliments, agreeable though he be. But how complimentary she is! "**Tell me, you whom my soul loves, where you feed your sheep, where you take your rest at noontide.** For the middle of the day will come, when shepherds make for the shade, and it may be that **where you feed your sheep** and **where you take your rest** will be hidden from me; and I want you to tell me, lest it happen that I **become as one veiled,** that is, as one hidden from the eye and unrecognized. For I am here to be seen, but I do not want to come upon the flocks of your companions as if I were veiled and hidden away."

Now all heretics are people who have "gone out" from Christ. All those who have become evil shepherds, who keep their own flocks under the name of Christ, were once his **companions;** they shared his company at table. For the word "companions" denotes people who sit at one table. The Latin language speaks of companions as being, at the same time, *eaters*, because they eat together. Hear him, then, in the psalm, as he censures evil companions, that is, people who belong to a group that eats together: "If my enemy had reproached me, I would have borne it; and if he had boasted against me, I would have hidden from him: but you were my soul mate and my friend, my leader, who ate good food with me" (Ps. 54:13-14 LXX = 55:12-14). Therefore many companions who were lacking in gratitude for the Lord's table went out from it. The evil companions made tables of their own for themselves and set up altar against altar. These are the ones the Bride was afraid of wandering into.

And if you think that **noontide** stands for Africa — though I might well be able to show that sections of Egypt are more nearly the **noontide** of the world, not to mention those sunburnt regions where it never rains; for the real **noontide** is where the middle of the day is boiling hot. There the desert is filled with thousands of God's servants.[1] Supposing, then, that we are talking about places that are hot, why does he not rather feed his flock there, and rest there? For it was foretold long ago: "the empty places of the wilderness shall bloom" (Joel 2:22 LXX).

But all right, I agree: let **noontide** stand for Africa. Let Africa be **noontide**. This is where the evil companions are. The Church from overseas, represented by one of its members who is sailing to Africa, is fearful of going wrong, and she calls upon her Bridegroom and says to him, "I hear that heretics abound in Africa; I hear that re-baptizers abound in Africa; but I hear that your people are there, and no less numerous. So I hear this and that, but from you I desire to hear which are yours: **Tell me, you whom my soul loves, where you take your rest at noontide.** In that noontide in which, as I hear, there are two parties, one that belongs to Donatus and the other that sticks together with your universal Church. So you **tell me** where to go, **lest perchance I become as one that is veiled,** that is, unknown, to the flocks of your companions — lest I come upon the flocks of the heretics as they try to set stone upon stone that will be torn down; lest I encounter the re-baptizers. **Tell me!**

Further still, he who presses upon us the singleness of the Shepherd that in this reading says, "I will feed them" (Ezek. 34:14), and who condemns the shepherds that choose to be many and have lost their unity — he, I say, makes a reply. He is as stern in manner as he can be, not pleasant; but his words are suited to the Bride's danger: **If you do not know yourself, O fair one among women. . . .** "You are indeed fair among women, but *recognize yourself* for what you are. Where shall you recognize yourself? Throughout the entire world. For if you are **fair,** unity marks you. Where there is division, there is ugliness, not beauty. **If you do not know yourself. . . .** You have believed in me; recognize yourself. How have you believed in me? In the same way that those evil companions agree that the Word became flesh, was born of the Virgin, rose from the dead, ascended into the heavens: that is the sort of 'me' you have believed in, and that is the sort of 'me' they too speak of. Know yourself and me; know me as in heaven, and know yourself as throughout the entire world."

Christ here is talking to one representative member of the Church *as* the Church. For after all, how can the Church go looking for the Church? I am talking now in the way that [the Donatists] talk. **Tell me, you whom my soul loves, where you feed your sheep, where you take your rest.** What is she looking for? The Church. And he answers — as if he were pointing the Church out — **at noontide.** That is how they want to understand it.

But let them answer my question: How can the Church go looking for the Church? **Tell me, you whom my soul loves. . . .** Who is the speaker? The Church. What does she want to be told? **Where you feed your sheep, where you take your rest,** which is to say, "Where is the Church?" The Church is speaking, and asks where the Church is; and he replies, on their view, **at noontide.** If the Church exists only **at noontide** — in Africa, as they think — how can the Church be asking where she is? On the other hand, a part of the overseas Church can perfectly well inquire about **the noontide,** to see if it is in error. Christ is addressing any member of his Church whatever *as* the Church; and what he says is, **If**

1. Augustine is referring to the monks in the deserts of Egypt.

you do not know yourself, O fair one among women, go out. Now going out is what heretics do. Either know yourself, or go out; for **if you do not know yourself,** you shall go out. Go out where? **In the footsteps of the flocks,** that is, by following after evil flocks. Do not make the mistake of thinking that if you go out you will be following sheep. Hear the very next words: **Go out in the footsteps of the flocks, and pasture your goats** — sheep no longer. You know, brethren, where the goats will be. All who have gone out from the Church will be at Christ's left hand. To Peter, who stays in the Church, it is said, "Feed my sheep" (John 21:17): to the heretic, who goes out from the Church, it is said **Feed your goats.**

(12) Apponius

Where do you pasture your sheep?
   Where do you take your rest at noontide?
Lest I become as one that is veiled
   above the flocks of your companions.

After the assaults and the battles, after the sweat baths of so many labors, she complains that the Christ whom she loves has kept away from her. This is so that we may learn with what great desire and what floods of tears — after the assault of the vices, after the struggles with demons — we ought to seek God by a purer life, so that he may come to our aid by showing us the way to walk in; by what sorts of actions we must be sustained to be able to share the company of those souls whom the Lord himself pastures, whom he himself makes to rest, with whom he is ever present. As I see it, no violence of demonic wolves can any longer harm them; and I am sure that they do not give in to any carnal vice nor suffer harm because of any infection of sin. They are the ones of whom the Lord says in the Gospel: "My sheep hear my voice, and follow me, and I give them good pasture" (John 10:27).

As to who they are, these souls who are so close to him, so fruitful, so lovable, and whom he does not entrust to angels or archangels for pasturing but pastures in his own person, the blessed Paul has told us plainly. When by his commands he was regulating the place to be occupied by individual sheep in the Lord's sheepfold — that is, what the wife owes her husband and the husband his wife, what the father owes to the son and the son to the father, what brother owes to brother, what the slave owes to his Lord and Lord to his slave (cf. Eph. 5:22ff.) — when he has arrived at this class of sheep, those whom he pastures in the clear **noontide** light, he says that nothing has been enjoined him regarding the matter of imposing commands on them. Here are his words: "But regarding virgins, I have no command from the Lord; I merely give advice as one who has received mercy" (1 Cor. 7:25); and elsewhere, on the same subject, he says, "Those who are Christ's have crucified their flesh with its passions and desires" (Gal. 5:24; cf. Col. 2:20). Christ our Lord, then, has souls that have been joined to him by intense love, and these he ever keeps in the clear noontide of his wisdom and his love. These souls, by the innocence and gentleness of their chastity, or by their insightful attentiveness to his testimonies, have bound themselves to him with a burning love. These he not only rules with his own "staff" (cf. Ps. 22:4 LXX =

23:4), but he is shown by the words of the prophets to gather them together with his arm and carry them in his bosom — as, for example, by Isaiah: "The Lord . . . will come with might. Like a shepherd he feeds his flock; he will gather the lambs with his arm and take them up into his bosom, and himself carry the young" (Isa. 40:10a, 11). . . .

Notice, then, the order followed by this Song which the Holy Spirit sings for the Bride at her wedding. In this mystery [i.e., the Song] we are taught that for our attainment of eternal life it is not enough that the filth of our sins has been washed away in baptism; or that our soul receives the **kisses** of Christ in the taste of his body and blood; or that she has been introduced into the **storeroom** of the knowledge of the divine Scripture; or that she preserves unchanged the straight path of the faith as the apostles handed it down — it is not enough, unless she put behind her the good things she has done, and with all her strength stretch herself out ahead (cf. Phil. 3:12-13) — by seeking, by searching, by knocking (cf. Matt. 7:7) — toward that which has not yet been attained. For God has no desire to have something else as a partner that shares the human soul's love. . . .

(13) Nilus of Ancyra

Where do you pasture?
  Where do you take your rest at noontide?
Lest I become as one that is veiled
  above the flocks of your companions.

"I have seen," says she, "the profusion of treasures in your storerooms [cf. Song 1:4c], and I have beheld the exact realization of the coming divine plan of salvation; but I seek also to be taught the reasons that govern providence — reasons in accordance with which, as you give created beings your attention, you demonstrate your providential care for them — and also, perhaps, for your companions, themselves shepherds, the possessors of individual flocks of their own, to whom as angels you have committed the governance of creatures. For you rule the entire cosmos as if it were a great flock."

(14) Origen

. . . veiled above the flocks of your companions.

And first of all consider whether we can say that the Lord, whose "portion" was "Jacob" and "the lot of" whose "inheritance was Israel" (Deut. 32:9), is himself to be understood to be the Bridegroom, while his **companions** are those angels by reference to whose number, "when the Most High divided the nations and scattered the children of Adam, he assigned the boundaries of the nations according to the number" — so the Scripture says — "of the angels of God" (Deut. 32:8). Then perhaps **the flocks** of his **companions** may be those nations, which is to say, all the nations, which like herds have been set under shepherds who are angels. On the other hand, it is those of whom he himself says in the Gospel, "My sheep hear my voice" (John 10:27), who make up the flock of the Bridegroom. For observe — and remark carefully — that he says, "My sheep," as though there were other sheep that are not his. Indeed, he says as much elsewhere: "You are not of my sheep" (John 10:26). And these details can appropriately be fitted into the present deep mystery.

If indeed this is the case, it is also proper that the Bride wanted the flock that belonged to each of the **companions** to be understood as the bride of that companion — and this is the bride she calls **veiled**. But because she was assured that she herself was **above** all these brides, she does not want to appear to be like any of them, seeing that she understood that she must surpass those brides of the companions — whom the Bride calls "veiled" — to the same extent that her own Bridegroom excelled the companions.

(15) Cyril of Alexandria

Tell me, you whom my soul loves,
   where you pasture your flock,
   where you take your rest at noontide?

"He who has the bride is the bridegroom; the friend of the bridegroom, who stands and hears him, rejoices greatly at the bridegroom's voice; therefore this joy of mine is now full" (John 3:29). Once again the text speaks in language familiar to us, but it points the way toward discernment of notions of great subtlety; for things tangible are offprints of things intelligible, and a gross corporeal replica often furnishes a clear pointer to things spiritual.

"Christ," then, [the Baptist] says, "is the Bridegroom who presides over the festivities, while I am the one who issues the invitations and leads the Bride. Mine is the great joy and the conspicuous honor of being ranked among his friends and of hearing the voice of him who gives the marriage feast.

"So then I already possess that which I long for, and the thing I have been most eager for has achieved fulfillment. For I have proclaimed not only that the Christ shall come, but that I have already seen him present, and that I have already heard his voice. You disciples, on the other hand, full of wisdom, see human nature being given in marriage to the Christ and going to him, and you perceive the nature that was deprived of its beauty and has turned away from loving him attaining spiritual intimacy with him through baptism. But do not be distressed," [the Baptist] says, "that it does not find its home with me but runs spontaneously to the spiritual Bridegroom; for this is truly the right and most proper thing. For 'He who has the bride is the bridegroom,' that is to say, 'Do not seek the Bridegroom's crown on my head,' for it is not to me that the psalmist sings: 'Hear, O daughter, consider, and incline your ear, forget your people and your father's house, for the king has desired your beauty' (Ps. 44:11-12 LXX = 45:10-11). Nor is it me after whose chamber the Bride inquires when she says: **Tell me, you whom my soul loves, where you pasture your flock, where you take your rest at noontide**; she is in possession of the heavenly Bridegroom. For my part, I will rejoice that I have surpassed the honor due a slave by having the name and the reality of being a friend.

· 4 ·

Song 1:8-12a

<table>
<tr><td>

SEPTUAGINT

1:8 If you do not know yourself,
    O fair one among women,
    go out in the footsteps of the flocks,

    and pasture your goats
    by the shepherds' tents.
9 I have likened you, my close one,
    to my horse among the chariots
      of Pharaoh.
10 How beautiful your cheeks are, like a
      dove's,
    (and) your neck like circlets!
11 We will make you likenesses of gold
    with studs of silver,
12a until the King is in his bed.

</td><td>

VULGATE

1:7 If you do not know yourself,
    O fair one among women,
    go out and depart in the footprints of
      the flocks,
    and pasture your goats
    beside the shepherds' tents.
8 I have likened you, my beloved,
    to my cavalry among the chariots
      of Pharaoh.
9 Your cheeks are fair like those of a
      dove;
    your neck is like a necklace.
10 We will make you necklaces of gold
    with chasings of silver,
11a while the King is on his couch . . .

</td></tr>
</table>

The ancient advice, "Know yourself," is said in Plato's Philebus *(48C) to have been recorded in an inscription at the shrine of the Delphic Apollo. Here it stands as the Bridegroom's response to the Bride's expressed desire to know where he is to be found (1:7). As much treasured and thought on by Christian writers as by their pagan predecessors, the aphorism was so beloved and valued that no one seems to have noticed that in this passage it does not actually answer the Bride's question. "Know yourself" represents a misunderstanding of the original Hebrew; but it went cheerfully uncorrected, and Origen supplies what was to become its standard interpretation.*

    More trouble for exegetes was occasioned by the comparison of the Bride to "my horse among the chariots of Pharaoh." Readers of the Septuagint thought that "horse" here, which is feminine in gender, referred most likely to a body of horses, that is, cavalry (though of course it could also simply mean "mare"). They could not help noticing, however, that in the story of the Exodus there is no reference to any literal or earthly cavalry that fought for the fleeing Hebrews. The question then became what "horse" could possibly refer to; and an answer was arrived at by examining some of the occurrences of the word "horse" in various books of the Bible, a process nicely illustrated by the observations of Origen and Gregory of Nyssa.

Again, the comparison of the Bride's neck to hormiskoi *("circlets") in the Septuagint led to various speculations. The intended reference of the word is doubtless to chains or necklaces of some sort; but since in the Septuagint the Bride's neck is not said to be adorned by circlets but is rather likened to them, Nilus of Ancyra can see them as symbols of humility (a curved or bent neck).*

It should be noted that the words "until the king is in his bed" (Song 1:12a LXX) belong with the next line of the Song; but they were uniformly read by Christian interpreters as the concluding clause of v. 11.

(1) Origen

If you do not know yourself,
  O fair one among women . . .

There are seven whom tradition among the Greeks celebrates as outstanding for their wisdom, and it is to one of them that people attribute, among others, the admirable saying, "Understand yourself," or "Know yourself." Solomon, however — who, as I said in my Introduction, was ahead of all these sages in time, in wisdom, and in his knowledge of things — addresses the soul as a woman and says, in an admonitory tone: "**If you do not know yourself, O fair one among women,** and recognize that the sources of your beauty derive from your creation 'after the image of God' (Gen. 1:26-27), by reason of which there is a great store of natural beauty lodged within you; and also recognize how fair you were at the beginning, though even now you excel other women and are the only one among them to be called **fair** — nevertheless, **if you do not know yourself** — for I do not want your beauty to look like a good thing in comparison with lesser beauties, but on the basis of your deliberate and even-handed assessment of yourself and your beauty — if, I say, you do not know yourself, then I order you to go out and take your place **in the** very last **footsteps of the flocks, and feed** not sheep nor lambs but **goats** — those who for their perversity and licentiousness will stand at the left hand of the King as he presides in judgment (cf. Matt. 25:33). Moreover, even though I have shown you, when you were brought into the King's chamber, the greatest goods of all, **if you do not know yourself,** I will also show you the greatest evils of all, so that you may benefit from both, that is, both from your fear of evil things and your desire for good things. For if you are in ignorance of yourself, and from ignorance of yourself you fail to cultivate a zeal for knowledge, you will surely have no tent of your own but will run about among **the tents of the shepherds,** and you will **feed goats** — that restless, errant animal, set apart for sins — now in this shepherd's tent, then in another's. You will suffer these things until you understand, in the light of circumstance and of experience, how great an evil it is for the soul to be ignorant of herself and also of her beauty. . . ."

It seems to me, then, that the soul is obliged to secure two sorts of self-knowledge: she is to grasp what she herself is, and how she is motivated, or, in other words, what is proper to her in regard of her very being, and what is proper to her in regard of her acquired dispositions — so that, for example, she may understand whether she is of a good disposition or not, whether her intention is right or not; and if her intention is in fact right, whether, in thought as well as in act, she exercises the same persistence with regard to all the virtues, or only with regard to those that are necessary and those that are easy. . . .

One kind of knowledge that the soul must have of herself, then, is knowledge of her dispositions and actions. Deeper and more difficult, however, is that other sort of self-knowledge that the soul — now already **fair among women** — is commanded to possess. Should she be able to lay hold on it, she can hope for every good thing. If not, let her be aware that she must go forth after the tracks of the flocks and must tend the goats in the tents of shepherds who are foreign to her. Let us then, as far as we are able, look into, and begin a discussion of, this sort of knowledge.

The divine Word says through the prophet: "Make the light of knowledge shine for you" (Hos. 10:12 LXX). Among spiritual gifts, however, there is one that is truly the greatest — the gift that is ministered "through the Holy Spirit, the word of knowledge" (1 Cor. 12:8); and the principal business of this knowledge is that which Matthew's Gospel puts in this way: "No one gets to know the Son except the Father, and no one gets to know the Father except the Son and anyone to whom the Son wants to reveal him" (Matt. 11:27). In Luke, though, it is put in this way: "No one knows who the Son is except the Father, and no one knows who the Father is except the Son and anyone to whom the Son wants to reveal him" (Luke 10:22). In John's Gospel, on the other hand, it is written thus: "[my own shall comprehend me] just as the Father comprehends [knows] me and I grasp the Father" (John 10:14-15). Then in Psalm 45 it says, "Be still, and comprehend [know] that I am God" (Ps. 45:11 LXX = 46:10).

Hence the first and most important work of knowledge is to grasp the Trinity, but then in the second place to comprehend what the Trinity has created, in accordance with the one who said, "For he himself gave me true knowledge of the things that are, the constitution of the cosmos and the working of the elements, the beginning and the term and the middle of the times," and so forth (Wisdom 7:17-18a). Among these things, therefore, will be the soul's grasp of its own self, by means of which she ought to know what her constitution is, whether she is corporeal or incorporeal, and whether she is simple or composed of two or three or many elements. . . .

(2) Augustine of Hippo

If you do not know yourself,
  O fair one among women . . .

"Let his face shine upon us" (Ps. 66:2 LXX = 67:1): this has a twofold meaning, and both meanings are acceptable.

"Let [your] face shine upon us," he says; that is, "show us your face." Now God, as we know, does not let his face shine just occasionally, as if there were times when it is in the dark; so the meaning is, "'shine upon us,' so that what was hidden from us may become apparent to us — so that what was there but had been concealed from us may be manifested 'over us,' that is, brought to light."

Surely too it means, "Shine your image upon us." This signifies, "Shine your face upon us; you have impressed your face upon us, you have made us 'after' your 'image and likeness' (Gen. 1:26), you have made us your coin; but your image ought not to remain in darkness. Send forth the ray of your wisdom, let it drive out our darkness, and let your image gleam within us. Let us know that we are your image, and hear what is said in the Songs of Songs: **If you have not known yourself, O fair one among women. . . .**"

The words **If you have not known yourself** are said to the Church. What does that mean? "Unless you have known that you are made after God's image! O treasured soul of the Church, redeemed by the blood of the unspotted Lamb, be aware how much you are worth, think what has been given in return for you."

Therefore let us say, and let us pray, "Let his face shine upon us." Let us wear his face. In the same way that they speak of the faces of emperors [on their coins], truly there is in God's image a sort of sacred face of his. The wicked, though, do not acknowledge God's image within them. What then ought they to say that the face of God may shine upon them? "You will light my lamp, O Lord; my God, lighten my darkness" (Ps. 17:29 LXX = 18:29), that is, "I am in the darkness of my sins, but let my darkness be dispelled by the ray of your wisdom. Let your face appear — and if through my fault it seem to have been somewhat distorted, let that which you have formed be by you re-formed." So "let his face shine upon us."

(3) Nilus of Ancyra

If you do not know yourself. . . .

"Desire" — says [the Word] — "is a beautiful thing, but its purpose is frustrated, by reason of its still being lowly, childlike, and modest. For one cannot grasp God from the orderly way in which he governs the cosmos, but rather from the soul's purity, since in its own nature it possesses an imitation of my nature, its character of being 'after the image' (Gen. 1:26). Once you have the image purified of any wicked defilement, you have me in your sights when you look upon yourself; for by every excellence that you bring to fulfillment, you are copying my nature. If, then, you have not yet been able to see in this fashion and have not known yourself in your own beauty, **go out in the footsteps of the flocks**, which is to say, 'make your way by following the traces of the things which I have created, and which now rejoice in providential care,' and by this searching you will see me as Creator. For just as the feet of the flock, making tracks in the earth, guide the one who is following them to the place where the shepherd is (for it is essential that the shepherd be with the flock, if it is not to be uncared for and unsupervised, deprived of a good guide) — in exactly the same way a well-directed search among created beings leads to discernment and knowledge of the Creator, to the extent that it affords a conjectural picture of what he is. In just this way David, taking the creation to be a book for contemplation, fixes his mind — a mind more than usually adapted to knowledge and science — upon created things; and looking into the reason that informs them as if it were a text to be read, he said, 'I will meditate on all thy work' (Ps. 76:13 LXX = 77:12). For writings have more of reason about them than footprints when it is a question of the sure grasp of truth.

"But she who imitates me in her own love of humanity, and in her own justice reproduces mine accurately, will no longer contemplate me by way of conjecture but clearly, because she has become by imitation what I am by nature. For to those who desire to know me I have said, 'Be merciful, even as your heavenly Father is merciful' (Luke 6:36), and 'Be compassionate like your Father' (Eph. 4:32), and above all be 'perfect, as your heavenly Father is perfect' (Matt. 5:48). If then you do not already know yourself to be that sort of person, you will not know me either; but you will know yourself when you have been formed by the aforesaid virtues after my likeness. Since, however, as it seems, you are not yet able to know yourself, you should have sought me, not among the flocks, but among the saints, for I am the 'Most High who take my rest among the saints' (Isa. 57:15). **Go out in the footsteps of the flocks, and pasture your goats by the shepherds' tents,** tracking the nature of the things that are by practicing intellectual discernment, and restraining the disorderly motions of the soul by your practice. For once you have in this way cleansed the divine image of all its defilements, it is by reference to that image — and rightly so — that you shall know me as God; for every image is naturally adapted to make its archetype known."

(4) Bernard of Clairvaux

If you do not know yourself,
O fair one among women. . . .

It is my desire, accordingly, that the soul should, before anything else, know herself. This is required at once by utility and by the order of things. It is required by the order of things because the question what we are comes first for us; and it is required by utility because such knowledge does not "puff up" (1 Cor. 8:1) but renders us humble and lays a foundation for building. For a spiritual building cannot stand unless it is set upon the firm foundation of humility. Furthermore, the soul can find nothing that will serve more appropriately or forcefully to render herself humble than the act of discovering the truth about herself. Let her not dissimulate, let her practice no deceit; let her look directly upon herself and refuse to turn her attention away from herself.

(5) Origen

I have likened you, my close one,
to my horse among the chariots of Pharaoh.

But in the revelation of John we read that a horse appeared to him, and sitting upon it one who is "faithful and true," and who "judges in righteousness" and whose name, it says, is "The Word of God." The passage says, then: "And I saw the heaven opened, and behold, a white horse! He who sat upon it is called Faithful and True, and in righteousness he judges and makes war. His eyes are like a flame of fire, and on his head are many diadems; and he has a name inscribed which no one knows but himself. He is clad in a robe dipped in blood, and the name by which he is called is The Word of God. And his host was in heaven, and they followed him on white horses dressed in fine linen, white and pure" (Rev. 19:11-14).

It takes the grace of God, however, to make these statements comprehensible to us, so that we may see what these visions refer to — who the "white horse" is, and who it is that sits on him, whose "name" is "The Word of God."

Now someone will say that the white horse represents the body that the Lord took to himself, and by means of which he who as the Word of God "was in the beginning with God" (John 1:1) was as it were borne about. On the other hand, someone else will prefer to say that it represents the soul that "the firstborn of all creation" (Col. 1:15) took to himself and regarding which he said, "I have power to lay it down, and I have power to take it again" (John 10:18). But another will say that it represents both at once, both body and soul, as if he reckoned that the horse is called white when there is no sin. Yet another, in the fourth place, will say that it represents the Church, which he sanctified for himself "by the washing of water" (Eph. 5:26), as being "without spot or wrinkle" (Eph. 5:27). Further, he will understand each of the matters mentioned in what follows in a way that fits in with this interpretation — that is, "his host . . . in heaven," and the army of the Word of God, and how it is that their individual members, in following the Word of God, sit "on white horses" and are dressed in fine white linen garments that are also pure.

Christ therefore is comparing and likening his Church to this white horse on which the One who is called "the Word of God" is carried, or to this celestial cavalry that follows him on horses that are no less white. Moreover, as to the expression **among the chariots of Pharaoh**, we can also take that to mean two things. Either it says, "You who are **beautiful among women** excel and surpass all other souls that still bear the yoke of Pharaoh and suffer the weight of his horsemen, in the same way that here the Lord's cavalry surpasses and excels the cavalry and **chariots of Pharaoh**; or else it surely says, "**My cavalry**, which, cleansed 'by the washing of water,' has been rendered pure and dazzling white and has earned the right to have the Word of God as its rider, has been brought from among **the chariots of Pharaoh**." For all believers come from there, since "Christ came into" this "world to save sinners" (1 Tim. 1:15). So we can explain the meaning of this expression as follows: "I judge you, my close one, to be like my cavalry, which once was **among the chariots of Pharaoh** and now follows me 'on white horses,' having been purified through the washing of water."

Happy, therefore, are those souls who have bent their backs so as to receive upon themselves the Word of God as their rider, and who submit to his reins so that he may turn them in whatever direction he pleases and guide them with the harness of his precepts; for they no longer march at the behest of their own will, but are led, and led back, by the will of their rider.

Furthermore, it will perhaps be understood, following on this, that the Church is assembled out of a multitude of souls, and that it has received the pattern for its life from Christ. It has not received this model from the very deity of the Word of God, which transcends any actions or passions that ought to be given to human beings to serve as a pattern. On the contrary, the soul that has been assumed by the Word of God and in which there exists the height of perfection — that very soul has been appointed to serve as the pattern. It is this soul herself that he here calls **close one**, and it is her likeness that the Church too must bear, assembled as it is out of a multitude of souls, those souls, I mean, that had formerly been under the yoke and the chariots of Pharaoh and are called the cavalry of the Lord. But you the reader must determine which of the two interpretations seems better to fit the expression in question.

(6) Gregory of Nyssa

I have likened you, my close one,
  to my horse among the chariots of Pharaoh.

From the scriptural narrative (cf. Exod. 14:1-29), we learned of another force that was arrayed against Pharaoh's cavalry: a cloud, and a staff, and a strong wind, and a sea divided into two parts, and a dusty seabed, and walls made of waves, and a dry deep that had been turned into land through the midst of watery walls. By the agency of all these salvation came to the whole host of the Israelites, while Pharaoh with his horses and chariots was covered over by the waves. Since, then, there was no cavalry force arrayed against the Egyptian army, it seems hard to determine what kind of **horse** it was, showing itself in opposition to the Egyptian chariots, to which the Bride is now likened by the text. For it says: **I have likened you, my close one, to my horse** that achieved victory **among the chariots of Pharaoh**.

Surely, though, it is plain that it is not possible for any fleet to be worsted in naval combat unless a fighting force has overcome the troops aboard the ships of its enemy; and by the same token, no one would be worsted in a cavalry battle unless an opposing cavalry force had been arrayed against him. Since, then, the mightiest element in the Egyptian army was the horse, our text uses the word "horse" to refer to the invisible force by which victory was gained over the Egyptians. For those Egyptians also sensed the presence of this Fighter and cried out to each other, "The Lord fights against the Egyptians," and "Let us flee from the face of the Lord!" (Exod. 14:25). Obviously the true General of the Armies outfitted forces of his own to meet the the enemy array. It was therefore some invisible force that worked the destruction of the Egyptians through the marvels at the Sea — and which the text calls "horse."

My surmise is that this cavalry was the angelic host, of which the prophet says, "You will mount upon your horses, and your cavalry is salvation" (Hab. 3:8 LXX). David too mentioned God's chariot: "The chariot of God is ten thousandfold, to which thousands of thriving beasts are yoked" (Ps. 67:18 LXX = 68:17-18). Furthermore, the power that took the prophet Elijah up from the earth to the ethereal realm is called "horses" by Scripture, and the narrative calls the prophet himself "chariot of Israel" and "horseman" (2 Kings 2:11-12). And the prophet Zechariah called those who go about the inhabited world, by whom the earth is settled and pacified, "horses," as they discoursed with the man who stood in the midst of the two mountains (Zech. 1:8-12 LXX).

There is, then, a cavalry that belongs to the One who possesses the universe. On the one hand it takes the prophet up on high, while on the other it colonizes the inhabited earth; then it is yoked to the chariot; and there is one troop that bears God mounted upon it for the salvation of humanity, and another that drowns the forces of the Egyptians. Given, then, that there are significant differences of function among God's cavalries, differences that are marked by their varying activities, the Bride who has come close to God by running the race of virtue is likened to the body of horses that destroyed the Egyptian force. That is why the Word says to her: **I have likened you, my close one, to my horse among the chariots of Pharaoh.**

(7) Apponius

How beautiful your cheeks have become, like a dove's!

After the holy kisses she has received, after all the joys enumerated earlier on, after the fight begun by the aforementioned sons of her mother, after the self-knowledge she has attained of why and by whom and as what she was created, after her virtue has been compared to the Lord's cavalry, in this verse it is taught that the dawning of the Church's beauty starts with her **cheeks** before any other of her members. Those **cheeks**, moreover, are accorded great praise by being compared to those of the turtledove, in order to demonstrate, in an enigmatic way, the progress she has made by distancing herself from the tumultuous confusions of the present age. For this beauty of her cheeks, which adorns the face of the Church with the radiance of chastity and the blush of modesty, is shown to have two antitheses: the thronging of great numbers of people, and the desire for things that belong to the here-and-now, sought to a greater degree than is necessary.

If the slothful person, who represents the very type of the sinner that takes no account of a future life, is, as a mark of censure, sent for instruction to the ant as a tutor (cf. Prov. 6:6), it is nothing to be wondered at if the persons of those who adorn the face of the Church are compared to the turtledove. It alone, more than all other birds, loves to inhabit places that are far removed from the resorts of throngs of humans; and there it builds a nest and raises its young, where its enemy either never comes, or hardly ever. And this very thing the holy soul, which is called **close one** by the Word of God, is known to do — by fleeing the company of the wicked, by refusing whatever is perceived as precious in the present life, she dispatches to heaven the heavenly offspring that are begotten by the word of her teaching and nourished by the example of her life. For the turtledove, of whom we spoke earlier, is said by those who have given accounts of the characteristics of birds to be so chaste that it has only one mate. If one of the two spouses is captured, the second is never joined to another bird but spends its entire life searching, full of desire, for its lost mate. That is why the Church, because of the charm of her chastity and modesty, is aptly compared to the turtledove in respect of the beauty of her cheeks.

Now these things are spoken of at the level of the literal meaning, but in my view there is a more elevated meaning concealed in this comparison; for it seems to me that the Church's cheeks are compared to the beauty of that very turtledove concerning which the prophet speaks in the Eighty-third Psalm: "For the sparrow has found itself a house, and the turtledove a nest for its young" (Ps. 83:4 LXX = 84:3). No knowledgeable person will be unaware that what is referred to here by "dove" is a figure of the Holy Spirit, and by "sparrow," the spotless flesh that the Word assumed. It is when the Church has to some degree taken into herself the likeness of the humanity of Christ that she is praised from both sides, by the good and wicked alike, as beautiful for her cheeks (for they are visible to any and all). It is when the modest appearance of her cheeks is a source of admiration for the impious on account of the splendor of her purity that the whole body of the Church is perceived to be at its loveliest. Her chastity is acknowledged to be a great virtue by her enemies when in their attacks on it they fail of victory. For just as — when they are beautiful — the parts of the human body that are associated with the head compensate for the unseemliness of the rest of its members, which are covered by clothing; so too those who as priests are acknowledged to be parts of the head lend beauty to the unseemly image produced by the people's heedlessness. On the other hand, there is nothing so ugly, so disgraceful in the body of the Church, as scandalous life and reputation in persons of the sort just mentioned.

(8) Theodoret of Cyrus

How beautiful your cheeks have become, like a dove's,
    (and) your neck like circlets!

Let us not understand the cheeks and neck here at the fleshly level, but let us take careful notice that the Holy Scripture often employs names of corporeal things to refer to the soul. So the prophet Jeremiah says somewhere, "I suffer pain in my gut, in my gut"; and indicating that the gut is not what he actually has in mind, he adds, "and in the sense organs of my heart" (Jer. 4:19 LXX). Then too the blessed Paul once says, "Therefore lift your drooping hands and strengthen your weak knees, and make straight paths for your feet, so that what is lame may not be put out of joint but rather be healed" (Heb. 12:12-13).[1] The blessed Paul was not exhorting his readers about their hands or their feet or some visible lameness, but referring by means of these words to the active operations of the soul.

---

1. In the early church Paul was considered the author of the Epistle to the Hebrews.

Let us then understand **Your cheeks have become beautiful, like a dove's, and your neck like circlets** in the very same way. For the Church is composed of large numbers of men and women, and she has some that are named cheeks, others that are called eyes, yet others that are labeled ears, others mouth, or hands, or feet. The Bridegroom, therefore, is praising people who are endowed with gravity and possess the blush of modesty.

More than this, he says, **Your cheeks have become beautiful, like a dove's.** Those who have written about the characteristics of animals say that the dove is not only a lover of the desert, but also chaste. The male is joined to a single female, and the female for her part shares herself with only one male, and after a death occurs she refuses to be joined to any further partner. It is reasonable, then, for the Church to be likened to this bird — the Church that is joined to Christ, that flees sharing herself with any other, and even after his death refuses to desert him, but awaits the resurrection and his anticipated second coming.

Further, he likens her neck to **circlets**. Now this means a necklace and a kind of adornment that lends beauty to the neck. He is rightly praising the Bride as one who takes upon herself the yoke of true religion, regarding which the Bridegroom says in the Gospels, "Take my yoke upon you, for my yoke is easy and my burden is light" (Matt. 11:29-30). The reason why, in the Songs, he marvels at the neck that bears this yoke is this: that it does not require any alien adornment or imported affectation, but has a home-bred comeliness, and so, even though it is naked, it is likened to the **circlets** that adorn the necks of others.

(9) Nilus of Ancyra

Your neck is like circlets.

Because he wishes to commend the Bride's humility of mind as it touches her actions, the Word says this: **Your neck is like circlets.** For just as he calls "the neck" of the arrogant "an iron sinew" (Isa. 48:4) because it is stiff, so too he calls that of the modest person a circlet, designating the form of the virtue by the shape of the neck. For the modest individual is bent down in the manner of a circlet, very tall though he be, whenever he thinks humble thoughts about himself and restrains the vanity that dogs the steps of virtue because of the weakness of human nature. For recollection of the earth and of one's ancient kinship with clay (cf. Gen. 2:7; Job 10:9) is sufficient to cleanse away false pretensions, even if the honor of the image and the outstanding character of one's actions encourage the swellings of vainglory.

Further, however, the Word does not stop at calling the neck of the humble a circlet; for there are some who out of a desire to please make a show of humility for the sake of their reputation in the eyes of others. To such persons the Word says, "If you bend your neck as a ring is bent" (Isa. 58:5 LXX). Wanting to show the difference between such persons and the perfect soul, he has likened the behavior of the former to the ring of iron that those who have been condemned wear as punishment; for in the end virtue contrived for the sake of deception is a punishment. The virtue of the Bride, however, he compares to gold, which by its appearance intimates her state of being, and by the stuff it is made of, her proven worth. For what is more worthy of acceptance than virtue that is perfected for the sake of the good itself and has God, who "sees in secret" (Matt. 6:4), as the one who commends it?

On the other hand, virtue that does not have the quality of truth and reality is of no use, and the Lord made this apparent when he said in the Gospels, "Every tree that does not bear good fruit is cut down and thrown into the fire" (Matt. 7:19). For not only does he not welcome the cultivated tree that bears just any sort of fruit, but he also, in exactly the same terms, condemns those that bear no fruit. For if the person that bears no good fruit is thrown into the fire, and the person who pays no mind to the hungry and thirsty and naked poor goes "into everlasting fire" (cf. Matt. 25:41-42), the identity of their punishment makes it plain what their behavior has in common: the one who pursues no form of virtue is subject to punishment because he bears no fruit at all, and the one who works the good with corrupt intent is guilty because he has come to abound in fruit that is not good. For the timber both of the wild tree and of the tree that is cultivated but not of good stock are alike chopped down with the axe and thrown into the fire, and the reason is that it is entirely unprofitable and unsuitable as food.

For love of moral stardom corrupts the good thing that is coming about by making the action void of reward to the person who performs it — or rather it affords as reward that which the action truly intended; for about people who do what they do for the sake of their reputation among other human beings, the Lord said, "Truly, I say to you, they have received their reward" (Matt. 6:2). The prophet was right to call vainglory a purse with holes in it: "He who earns wages," he says, "earns wages to put them in a bag with holes" (Hag. 1:6) — calling the deed a bag, and the hole, the aim of enjoying a noble reputation. For that achievement of hard work which one reckons to be lasting is entirely destroyed by the deed's intent; no sooner is it accomplished than it is in process of corruption. It does not stay in the purse but runs through it and hastens its way to the exit hole, like water that seeks every chance of running off — which has no notion of how to stop and stand if it encounters even the least opportunity for making its exit.

If the circlet, then, signifies that which is humble, the Bride's neck, being **like circlets** that are accorded praise, manifests the whole mass of the virtues and the humility that touches each of them. For just as the circlet, though forged in the shape of a straight edge, is in the end conformed to the use to which it is put and bent down, so too the person who is perfect in virtue is made humble by submission: being straight in the manner of his life, he is bent down in the disposition of his mind.

(10) William of St. Thierry

Your neck is like a necklace of jewels.

The neck of the Bride represents holy intention, by which the entire body of a work is joined to its Head, which is Christ. Regarding this neck, that same Head of ours says, "If your eye" — that is, the intention of the work — "is unblemished and unalloyed, your whole body will be full of light" (Matt. 6:22). But just as a necklace of jewels ornaments the neck, so the badges of the holy virtues are the ornament of good intention. The **neck** of the Bride, however, is only *like* **a necklace of jewels**; for though it is the business of a necklace to ornament the neck, the neck of the Bride, in contrast, ornaments all its virtues. For unless these jewels are hung upon right intention, they are not shown to possess either the attractiveness or the beauty, or, for that matter, even the name, of virtues. An alternative reading might say that what ornaments the Bride's neck is love of the Bridegroom, apart from which any intention is foul and perverse. But when intention becomes active longing, the neck of the Bride is made like its own necklace.

(11) Origen

We will make you likenesses of gold
with studs of silver,
until the King is in his bed.

At this point the friends or companions of the Bridegroom — who at the mystical level of understanding . . . can be understood as angels or even the prophets or patriarchs — are seen speaking these words to the Bride. . . . These figures, then, were, so to speak, the guardians and overseers designated, along with her custodian, the law, to take care of the Bride when she was a child, until "the time had fully come," and God had sent "his Son, born of a woman, born under the law" (Gal. 4:2-4; 3:23-24), and had brought her, who was under guardians and overseers and the law her custodian, to the point of receiving the kisses of the Word of God himself, that is, his teaching and his words.

Before the time came for these events, therefore, the Bride was being tended in many ways by the ministry of the angels, who in those days appeared to people and spoke whatever was demanded by the time and setting. For it would be wrong to suppose that she is called "Bride" and "Church" only from the time of the Savior's advent in the flesh. No. These titles apply from the beginning of the human species and from the very foundation of the world. Indeed — to take Paul as my guide in seeking out the origin of this deep mystery — they apply even "before the foundation of the world." For thus he says: "even as he chose us in" Christ "before the foundation of the world, that we should be holy and blameless before him," predestining "us for adoption as sons" (Eph. 1:4-5). But it is also written in the Psalms: "Remember thy congregation, O Lord, which thou hast gathered from the beginning" (Ps. 73:2 LXX = 74:2). Truly, then, the first foundations of the congregation that is the Church were laid "from the beginning," which explains why the apostle says that the Church was built not only "on the foundation of the apostles," but also "of the prophets" (Eph. 2:20). . . .

So then the prophets ministered to the Church "from the beginning," and so did the angels. . . . Our aim at this point is to indicate the way in which the holy angels, who before the advent of Christ acted as the Bride's guardians while she was still a child, are the same as the friends and companions of the Bridegroom, who are seen to address her in the words: **We will make you likenesses of gold with studs of silver, until the King is in**

his bed. They point out that it is not gold they are promising to make for the Bride — for they do not possess any such gold as could worthily be offered to the Bride — but likenesses of gold in the place of gold, and not one likeness but many. So too they speak of silver, as though they possessed some of that substance, but only a little, and they promise that they will make her not **likenesses** but **studs of silver.** They do not have silver enough to be able to make a whole object of solid silver out of it, but they intersperse nothing more than **studs** and certain small signs like spots into the object that they were making out of a likeness of gold. These, then, are the ornaments that the friends of the Bridegroom — the ones of whom we spoke above — are making for the Bride. . . .

Now, therefore, let us hasten to discern in what sense . . . the friends of the Bridegroom say that they are making **likenesses of gold** for the Bride together **with studs of silver.**

It seems to me, then, that the law, which "was ordained by angels through an intermediary" (Gal. 3:19), inasmuch as it had "a shadow of the good things to come instead of the true form of these realities" (Heb. 10:1), and whatever things "happened to those" who are mentioned in the law "happened in a figural way" (1 Cor. 10:11) and not in truth, all those things were **likenesses of gold** and not true gold. True gold is discerned in those realities that are incorporeal and invisible and spiritual; but by the likeness of gold, in which there resides not truth itself but a shadow of the truth, is understood things corporeal and visible. Thus that tabernacle "made with hands" (Heb. 9:11) was a likeness of gold — the tabernacle of which the apostle says, "For Jesus has not entered into the holy places made with hands, which are copies of the true, but into heaven itself" (Heb. 9:24). Hence the true things are those that exist incorporeal and invisible in the heavens; but those visible and corporeal things that are on earth are said to be "copies of the true," not the true.

It is the latter, then, that are also called **likenesses of gold.** Among them are the ark of the covenant, and the mercy seat, and the cherubim, and the altar of incense, and the table of presence, and the breads; but also the veil and the pillars and the bars, and the altar of burnt offerings, and the temple itself — and all the things that are written in the law. All of these are **likenesses of gold.** Furthermore, the visible gold itself, to the extent that it was visible, was not the true gold, but was a likeness of that true, invisible gold. Hence it is these **likenesses of gold** that the friends of the Bridegroom — that is, the angels and prophets that acted as mediators in the law and the other mysteries — made for the Bride who is the Church. It was with these things in mind, I judge, that Paul said, "in . . . piety directed to angels" in the things that he sees, "vainly puffed up by the mind of his flesh" (cf. Col. 2:18). Thus Jewish piety and worship as a whole are **likenesses of gold.** . . .

We have spoken of these matters at length because we wanted to show what the friends of the Bridegroom mean when they say to the Bride that they make her **likenesses of gold with studs of silver** — that is to say, the things that are transmitted in written form in the Law and the Prophets by way of figures and images and likenesses and parables. Among these, however, there are also certain small **studs of silver,** by which I mean particular pointers, exceedingly rare and slight, to the spiritual Word and to understanding at the level of reason. For before the advent of the Lord, scarcely at any point did any of the prophets render intelligible the slightest bit of occult discourse. An example of one who did is Isaiah, when he says, "For the vineyard of the Lord of hosts is the house of Israel, and the house of Judah is his beloved new shoot" (Isa. 5:7); and again in another place when he says, "The many waters are the many nations" (cf. Rev. 17:15). Furthermore Ezekiel, when he names the two sisters "Oholah" and "Oholibah," distinguishes the one as meaning Samaria and the other as meaning Judah (Ezek. 23:4) — and wherever such expressions are made intelligible by interpretations provided by the prophets themselves, they are called **studs of silver**.

But when our Lord and Savior Jesus Christ arrived, "upholding the universe by the word of his power" (Heb. 1:3), a sign was given in his passion that things that had been cloaked in obscurities and mysteries would be brought into the light and be made plain; and the sign was provided when "the curtain of the temple," by which the secret and hidden parts of the Holies were veiled, "was torn in two from top to bottom" (Matt. 27:51) — openly announcing that what before had seemed to be concealed within would now be open to everyone.

So then, whatever was mediated through the angels and the prophets was a likeness **of gold with** small and trivial **studs of silver**; but the things that have been transmitted through our Lord Jesus Christ himself are set in true gold and solid silver. For this likeness **of gold with studs of silver** that has been made by the friends of the Bridegroom is not promised to last forever, but they themselves assign it a period of time when they say, **until the King is in his bed.** For when he has lain back and has gone to sleep "like a lion and like a lion's whelp," and after this the Father has wakened him (Gen. 49:9) and he has risen from the dead, if there are people who are conformed to his resurrection, they shall abide no longer in the likeness **of gold**, that is, in the worship of corporeal things, but they will receive the true gold from Christ himself, in hope seeking not "the things that are seen but the things that are not seen" (2 Cor. 4:18), nor the "things that are on earth," but the things that are in the heavens; and they will say, "If we once knew Christ according to the flesh, now we know him so no longer" (2 Cor. 5:16).

(12) Gregory of Nyssa

**We will make you likenesses of gold
  with studs of silver,
until the King is in his bed.**

But it is time to subject the next statement to examination. The text runs: **We will make you likenesses of gold with studs of silver, until the King is in his bed.**

Now to someone who considers how our interpretation has unfolded hitherto, the meaning of this statement seems in some way to fit in and to follow along; but the text runs deep and by its figurative turns of speech makes what its figures convey difficult to understand.

For since the beauty of the soul has earlier been likened to that of the horse — that is, the angelic host — that destroyed the chariots of the Egyptians; and since the good Rider says that for that horse purity serves as rein and bit (which is what he meant by comparing her cheeks to those of a dove), and that the adornment of her neck is the different necklaces that gleam with the virtues; the friends of the Bridegroom also want to contrive some enhancement of this mare's beauty in their own right, by adorning the bosses of her gear with likenesses of gold, into which they etch the purity of silver, so that the beauty that adorns her may shine forth the more intensely when the gleam of silver is mingled with the glitter of gold.

It would serve best, however, to set the figurative expressions in the text to one side and not to divert our thought from the meaning that profits us.

Now the soul that has been purified by the virtues has been compared to that **horse**; but she has not yet come under the control of the Word, nor has she carried upon herself the One who rides upon such horses for salvation (Hab. 3:8). For the horse must first of all be adorned in every way and then, in this state, receive the King as its rider. Whether he — the One who, according to the prophet, mounts himself upon us horses and rides upon us for our salvation — renders the horse docile from above on its back, or whether he comes to be within us as one who at once indwells us and tarries within us and makes his way through to the depths of our soul — this makes no difference to the meaning. The person for whom one of these things happens has the other accomplished for him as well. The individual who has God mounted upon him also has God within him in every sense; and he who receives God within him is beneath the One within. Hence the King will lie down upon this horse. But where the divine power is concerned, sitting and reclining are the same, as we have said; for whichever of the two comes to pass within us, the grace is the same.

Since, then, the King's grooms are readying a horse whose adornments suit it to receive him, and since it is the same thing for God to be within someone and to be mounted on someone, the grooms and attendants deserted the logic of their metaphor and turned the horse into a bed. "For," it says, "we must **make likenesses of gold with studs of silver**, which confer splendor on the horse's appearance, in order that the King may be, not on his seat, but **in his bed**."

So then, the sequence of thought in the wording does indeed have this general drift, as the text indicates; but it is important not to pass over without examination the question why it is that not gold itself but **likenesses of gold** are taken as adornments, and not silver itself but **studs** of that substance that are struck into the **likenesses of gold**.

The underlying meaning that we detect here is this. Though it seems to exhibit an understanding that is noble and worthy of God, all teaching about the ineffable Nature amounts to **likenesses of gold**, and not gold itself. For it is not possible to set out with accuracy the Good that transcends our conception of it. Even though there was a certain Paul who, in Paradise, was initiated into things unspeakable, and even though he heard unutterable words, his intuitions concerning God remain inexpressible; for he asserts that the words for these intuitions cannot be spoken (cf. 2 Cor. 12:3ff.). Hence it is that teachers who provide us with fair thoughts relating to the mysteries are quite unable to articulate what they are with respect to nature. Rather do they say "radiance . . . of glory," "stamp of the substance," "form of God" (Heb. 1:3); "Word in the beginning" (Phil. 2:6); "God the Word" (John 1:1). To us who are unseeing, all these expressions seem like the gold of that treasure; but to those who are able to look up toward the Truth, it is **like-

nesses of gold and not gold that makes itself seen between the delicate studs of silver. Silver means a verbal act of signifying, as when the Scriptures says, "The tongue of a righteous person is silver tried in fire" (Prov. 10:20).

What is conveyed, therefore, by these words is this: that the divine nature transcends the mind's grasp. Our thought concerning it is a likeness or image of what we seek, for it does not manifest the form of that which no one has seen or can see. Rather, it sketches darkly, in a mirror and an enigma, a reflection of what we seek that comes to birth in our souls on the basis of some conjecture. All speech, however, that refers to such intuitions has the function of some indivisible mark, being unable to make clear what the mind intends. Thus all our thinking is inferior to the divine understanding, and every explanatory word of speech seems to be an abbreviated tracery-mark that is unable to embrace the breadth of the act of understanding. Hence Paul says that the soul that is led by such intuitions to awareness of things that cannot be grasped must bring the nature that transcends all intellect within herself by faith alone. And this is what the friends of the Bridegroom say: "We shall make for you, O soul, rightly likened to the horse, certain manifestations and likenesses of truth (for this is the function of the *silver* of words: the things people say seem to be spark-like embers that cannot with accuracy express the intuition they carry); but you, when you have received these likenesses, shall become a dwelling place and a servant by faith in the one who is coming to recline within you by dwelling within you. You shall both be his throne and become his home."

(13) Gregory of Elvira

**We will make you a likeness of gold
   with chasings of silver.**

But what he says here — **We will make you a likeness of gold with chasings of silver** — when it says "gold" is referring to the bright splendor of the Holy Spirit. Thus the Magi presented gold to the Lord in order to declare his kingly majesty. **Silver**, however, denotes the lustrous holiness of virginal flesh. Therefore the Holy Spirit, when joined with pure and unspoiled flesh, constitutes **a likeness of gold with chasings of silver**. And because on the authority of the apostle we have learned that we are members of the body of Christ, which is the Church, so too the martyrs are compared with gold (as it is written: "Like gold in the furnace he will try them" [Wisdom 3:6]), the virgins with silver, and the righteous confessors with precious stones because, by subjecting the neck of the churchly body to the discipline of the gospel yoke, they adorn minds with the fair beauty of their virtues; and this is why he says, **Your neck is like a jeweled necklace; we will make you a likeness of gold with chasings of silver.** He was declaring clearly that there will be spiritual persons in the Church to serve as jewels.

Until, he says, **the King be settled in down-lying.** What does **in down-lying** mean? There is no doubt that the King is Christ; therefore, this King of kings had nowhere, in the synagogue, where he might lay his head, as he himself bears witness in the Gospel when he says, "Foxes have holes, and the birds of the air have nests; but the Son of man has nowhere to lay his head" (Matt. 8:20). He did not say this in reference to houses or cities made with hands. He was talking about the vessels that are human beings, about which the apostle says "that Christ may dwell in the inner self" (Eph. 3:17), because the Devil had so blockaded and besieged everyone's senses that at that time no one was deemed worthy to have Christ the King enter and lay down his head; for prior to the Lord's advent all human beings were vessels of the Devil, since that strong man had not yet been bound by the stronger Lord, nor had his vessels been plundered (cf. Mark 3:27), nor had his vessels been washed in the water of baptism or made a temple of God by the consecrating action of the Holy Spirit.

That is why it says in the Gospel, "All who came before me are thieves and robbers" (John 10:8); for before Christ arrived in this world, there were the night of ignorance and the shadows of error; before Jesus Christ came as life, death reigned among us over all; before faith came, unbelief raged about; before we were made the temple of God, we were the place where demons lodged. These, then, are the "thieves and robbers": ignorance, faithlessness, uncleanness, filth, avarice, fraud, lust, and every diabolical activity. These persisted within everyone before the Word of God "became flesh and dwelt among us" (John 1:14). That is why he says in our text, **until the King be settled in down-lying**. This means that in the synagogue the Lord had nowhere to lie down, until the Church came, in which our King in coming lay down, for which he also "humbled himself and became obedient unto death, even death on a cross" (Phil. 2:8), by which down-lying he is able to enter within her and dwell there, as it is written: "I will live in them and move among them, says the Lord" (2 Cor. 6:16; Lev. 26:12); and, as the apostle says, "You are God's temple, and . . . God's Spirit dwells within you" (1 Cor. 3:16). Let us render thanks to God the Father himself through our Lord Jesus Christ, who is blessed to the ages of ages. Amen.

(14) Philo of Carpasius

We will make you likenesses of gold
   with chasings of silver.

The expression **likenesses of gold**, I take it, refers to nothing other than the holy martyrs, inasmuch as those who have been tested by fire exhibit a more brilliant faith. For Scripture says, "Like gold in the furnace he tried them, and like a sacrificial burnt offering he accepted them" (Wisdom 3:6). And in order that it might be shown from the words that follow that our text is speaking of martyrs, consider what it says: **with chasings of silver**. For **chasings** plainly means the lashings and tortures of those who suffer for the sake of Christ — as Paul too attests when he says, "For I bear on my body the marks of our Lord Jesus Christ" (Gal. 6:17).

Until the King is in his bed. This means: "Until the rebirth that comes in the form of the great marriage feast" — until at that time these **likenesses** of silver are gathered together, that is, those who suffer on account of the faith — not only those who suffer by being tortured in a time of persecution but also those who in a time of peace suffer by walking in the hard and narrow way (cf. Matt. 7:13-14) and imitating the martyrs by their deeds.

Song 1:12b-14

1:12b My nard gave off its scent.

13 My Kinsman is a sachet of myrrh for
me

that shall dwell between my breasts.

14 A cyprus cluster is my Kinsman for
me

among the grapevines [of]
En-gaddi.

1:11b My nard gave off its scent.

12 My Beloved is a sachet of myrrh for
me,

he shall dwell between my breasts.

13 My Beloved is a cyprus plant for me

among the vines of Engaddi.

Modern readers of commentaries on the Septuagint text of the Song need to note Origen's explanation of the word adelphidos, *which is here (1:13a) applied to the Bridegroom for the first of many times. It is a Greek word that, as Origen indicates with his customary care, normally means "nephew." It can also, however, mean, more broadly, "kinsman"; and also, since it is in form a diminutive, "little brother." The latter — a term of affection; compare the English "sweetheart" — is most likely the sense intended by the translators of the Hebrew: it is a rough equivalent of the Latin "beloved." Greek-speaking interpreters, however, including Origen, took it in the sense of "kinsman": the Bridegroom is akin to the Bride in that he shares her humanity through the incarnation. For this reason the present translation of the Septuagint text uniformly renders* adelphidos *as "kinsman" except in the passage just below, where Origen is explaining its meaning.*

Ancient readers had difficulty with Song 1:14, with its mentions of "Engaddi" and of "a cluster of kypros." *The former was generally recognized to be a place name, but it was sometimes taken to mean "in Gad" (the "en" being read as the Greek preposition that means "in"), and was equally often given a fanciful etymological explanation. Where a "cluster of* kypros" *is concerned, Origen wanted to give it the sense of "cluster of grape blossoms," on the ground that the sort of cluster in question is explicitly said in this line of the Song to occur in "vineyards." He recognized, however, that* kypros *could also refer to "a certain sort of bush that comes from foreign parts"; and he intimates that it might sig-*

nify balsam, since En-gaddi "is a sector of the land of Judea that bears more bal-sam trees than it does grapevines." This suggestion was followed up by many later commentators — Apponius, for example, identifies this balsam or balm with the "healing fragrance of Christ" — and it even found its way into the Glossa ordinaria in the Middle Ages, as did many of Origen's other suggestions. The truth seems to be that kypros refers to the henna plant (see the Revised Version of 1885) and not to any sort of balsam or balm.

(1) Origen

My nephew is a sachet of myrrh for me.

But since this is the first time that she names the Bridegroom **nephew**, and since she employs this title frequently throughout the greater part of the text of the book, I think it proper to inquire first of all why this title is used, and then to explain what the word means and where it comes from.

The son of one's brother is called one's **nephew**. Let us then ask in the first place who is the Bride's brother, the one whose son the Bridegroom is taken to be, and see whether we can say that the Bride is the Church that is drawn from the nations, while her brother is the earlier people and so, obviously enough, an elder brother. This being so, "Christ according to the flesh" (2 Cor. 5:16) is born of that people, and hence is called "son of my brother" by the Church that is drawn from the nations. Therefore the statement **My nephew is a sachet of myrrh for me** refers to the mystery of the Word's corporeal birth.

(2) Gregory of Nyssa

My spikenard gave off its scent.

Once the friends of the Bridegroom have lavished these gifts upon the pure and virgin soul (for they must be the "ministering spirits" [Heb. 1:14] sent for the sake of those who were to inherit salvation), the Bride comes a step closer to perfection because of these further graces. And when she has approached the Object of her desire more closely, but before his beauty is manifest to her eyes, she touches the One she seeks through her sense of smell, as if by her power of smell she recognized the distinctive quality of some color; and she says that she recognizes his fragrance by means of the sweetness of a perfume whose name is **spikenard** — saying to the friends of the Bridegroom, **My spikenard gave off its scent.** "For," she says, "just as you confer not the pure gold of the Godhead but, by way of concepts comprehensible to us, **likenesses of gold**; and do not disclose what pertains to it in clear speech but furnish intimations of the Object of our search by means of the laconic tracery of the silver of rational speech — so too I, in the fragrance of my perfume, sense the sweetness of that very One himself."

The meaning that the statement seems to me to bear is as follows. It is an artful and balanced mixture of many different aromas — each with its proper sweetness — that produces this perfume, while, of all those that are blended together, it is one sweet-smelling herb called nard that lends its name to the entire preparation. Further, the purified sensibility perceives what has been put together into one fragrance out of all the particular aromas as the very sweetness of the Bridegroom.

Hence we judge that the words of the text are teaching us this: that, whatever it be in its essence, that which transcends the entire structure and order of Being is unapproachable, impalpable, and incomprehensible; but that, for us, the sweetness that is blended within us by the purity of the virtues takes its place because by its own purity it images that which is by nature the Undefiled — and by its goodness, the Good; and by its incorruptibility, the Incorruptible; and by its unchangeability, the Unchangeable; and by all the things within us that are rightly done in accordance with virtue, the true Virtue, concerning which the prophet Habakkuk says that it embraces all the heavens (cf. Hab. 3:3 LXX). Therefore she who explains to the friends of the Bridegroom, "My **spikenard** gives off **its scent**," seems to me to say, in her philosophic discourse, both these things and the following.

If a person, having gathered every sweet-smelling flower or scent from the various blooms of virtue, and having rendered his whole life a perfume by the fragrance of his daily doings, should become perfect in all respects, he does not have it in him to look intently upon the divine Word itself any more than upon the disk of the sun. Nevertheless he sees the sun within himself as in a mirror. For the rays of that true and divine Virtue shine upon the purified life through the inward peace that flows from them, and they make the Invisible visible for us, and the Incomprehensible comprehensible, because they portray the Sun in the mirror that we are.

(3) Nilus of Ancyra

My nard gave off its scent.
My Kinsman is a sachet of myrrh for me
   that shall dwell between my breasts.

This is what it means: "You [friends of the Bridegroom] reckon that the Bridegroom is still far off, and so, because of my unquenchable desire for my beloved, you try to beguile me with your own words, which are like imitations and shadows of him. I, though, am no longer satisfied with **likenesses**, since now enjoyment of the reality itself is available. For by night a lamp is no doubt requisite for those who employ it, but when day has arrived and the sun with its bright rays is lighting up everything, it is pure folly to rely on the light provided by a lamp. At all events, you see that I breathe in the scent of my nard from right at hand, and that I await the sachet of myrrh that, after not very long, shall dwell between my breasts."

She calls him "nard" because of the working of wonders and good deeds by which he reaches out to all; but she calls him "sachet of myrrh" on account of his suffering and his death and the apparent disgrace that derives from the cross, when he compressed the power of the Godhead, inactive, into his body as into a tiny bag. For to put one's trust in a person who works wonders and is glorified is not the same thing as to put it in one who is crucified and buried and taken for dead. If people who benefit from his good deeds and are persuaded by his many signs confess his Godhead, that is an act that almost anyone might perform; for this work is not so much a matter of the mind's perception and judgment as it is of the compelling character of the miracle. On the other hand, to see him suffering and mocked and enduring the insults of malefactors, and to do this without doubt or uncertainty, but rather to remain of the same mind in every circumstance — this is the work of a very few, or perhaps only of the perfected soul. That explains why she says, **My nard gave off its scent** and does not add "for me," but says **gave off** without any qualification or limit; but **sachet of myrrh** is not said for everyone but **for me**. To herself alone does she ascribe faith directed to him in the moment of despondency, but to all the rest, that which comes about when they are compelled by wonders to believe even if they do not want to. For the latter response is so easy, and the former so rare, that at the time of his wonders even the imperceptive Jews, and the very demons in their state of terminal wickedness, discern God himself and confess the Son of God, while in the face of his cross and his death even the apostles fall into a state of doubt. No doubt this is what the prophet too predicted: "The person who is firmly fixed in a trustworthy place shall be moved" (Isa. 22:25 LXX).

That the Bridegroom dwells **between the breasts** of the Bride is a sign of his condescension from the days of his infancy and his assumption of human afflictions in the form of hunger and thirst, sleep and bodily weariness.

(4) Philo of Carpasius

My spikenard gave off its scent.

While the Bridegroom himself is speaking of the martyrs, she answers by giving him thanks and says, **My spikenard gave off its scent.** That means: "You made a gift of these good things." For by the reference to spikenard, he means the flask of ointment about which the Lord says, "Let be, and do not trouble the woman, for she has done a beautiful thing for me" (Matt. 26:10), and so on. The Bride, then, speaks as one who is giving thanks in her response: "You yourself have given to me the fragrance of the martyrs." For **My spikenard gave off its scent** means: "Your martyrdom and your fragrance spurred the martyrs on to suffer on your behalf, inasmuch as you suffered on our behalf"; but from the line that follows anyone at all can recognize the appropriateness of the words.

A sachet of myrrh is my Kinsman for me. Straight off he puts us in mind of the water and the blood that fell in drops from his side in the passion. **A sachet of myrrh is my Kinsman for me,** that is to say, "On the basis of the water and the blood that fell in drops from his side, he himself became my Bridegroom, and I became his Bride; by the blood from his side I was bought and joined to him; then by the water from his fleshly parts I was washed for him; but by the Spirit who proceeds from his Godhead I have been brought together with him and perfected."

That shall dwell between my breasts. This means: "In the middle between the two covenants the testimony concerning these mysteries shall lie." For the Old Covenant speaks in Isaiah and says, "Like a lamb he was led to the slaughter" (Isa. 53:7), while the New Covenant says the same thing through Philip when, for the benefit of the eunuch, he refers this statement to Christ (cf. Acts 8:32).

(5) Origen

A cyprus cluster is my Kinsman for me
   among the grapevines of En-gaddi.

As far as explication of the literal sense itself is concerned, the meaning of the expression **cyprus cluster** is uncertain. A grape cluster in bloom is called "cyprus," and at the same time there is a certain sort of bush that comes from foreign parts that is called "cyprus," and it too bears a lovely fruit that comes out just like a grape cluster in bloom. In view of the mention of **grape vines of En-gaddi**, however, the word seems more likely to refer to the fruit of the vine. En-gaddi, be it said, is a sector of the land of Judea that bears more balsam trees than it does grapevines.

    The following, then, will be the plain sense of the Bride's words as she speaks to the **young maidens**. She must be understood to say — first of all — "My nard returns to me the scent of my Bridegroom." In the second place she says, "My Kinsman has been made a sachet of myrrh that dwells between my breasts"; and then in the third place, he is "a grape cluster in bloom from the grapevines of En-gaddi" that surpasses everything in the way of fragrances and flowers of sweet scent. . . .

(6) Nilus of Ancyra

A cyprus cluster is my Kinsman for me.

By **cyprus cluster** the Bride means either "grape cluster in bloom" or "grape cluster from Cyprus," a land that no doubt possesses some rare aptitude for the successful cultivation of grapes.

    Of these two alternative possibilities, which one, supposing it to be what the Bride says, coheres with the previous line of thought?

    For if she says that her nephew is a grape cluster in bloom, she is saying something like this: "As long as he is in the midst of difficult circumstances — such as the cross, death, the grave — he is a grape cluster that is in bloom. He does not yet possess the ripeness that belongs to the resurrection. For that reason he does not seem admirable to most people, since a grape cluster that is in bloom is not of great use to the general run of folk, but only to one who, on the basis of hope, looks forward to its maturity. For me, however, it procures, even by its mere blossom, if not the pleasure of eating, then at least the pleasure of its fragrance, and it intimates the joy of the resurrection: by the blossom it hints at the fruit, hidden away, and in the meanwhile, by the fragrance of its blossom, it gives encouragement."

For he is **among the grape vines in En-gaddi,** which means "eye of trial and temptation." For the grape cluster that is in bloom, hanging from its branch, is not an object of desire for everyone because it fails to possess a here-and-now pleasure. After all, people who rejoice in deferred pleasures are scarce indeed. Human beings are somehow naturally disposed to cling to pleasures that are at hand; but pleasures whose usefulness is not immediate but consists in hopes are not even reckoned to be useful. It pertains to the art of the husbandman, however, to recognize, in the present condition of fruit that is not yet ripe, its future usefulness, and in the unripe grape to discern the future, and assured, maturity of the fruit.

In the same way too, the Lord hanging upon the cross — like someone being tried and tested before the eyes of all — evoked an immense despair in the people who saw him. For who would not suffer perplexity — and understandably too — when he saw the One who set the human race free undergoing the ultimate punishment, and the One who worked so many marvels and loosed Lazarus from the toils of death nailed to the cross, his life passing over into death? Thus the condemnation that then fell to his lot, when compared with the opinion regarding him that everyone entertained, induced doubtfulness in those who saw it; every eye, untimely filled with the sight of the suffering by which he was tested, was diverted to another matter and, forgetful of the wonders, took sides with the suffering it could see. For not only the Jews but also the disciples themselves fell into doubt at that point, with the consequence that even after learning that he had been raised from the dead they did not believe in the resurrection. Being aware of this, the Lord, having come to the very moment of his suffering, said to his apostles, "You will all fall away because of me this night" (Matt. 26:31) — using "night" to mean the darkness of perplexity; and to Mary, by the mouth of Simeon, he said, "And a sword will pierce through your own soul also" (Luke 2:35), using "sword" to mean the uncertainty that derives from lack of faith. In the same way the mass of the Jews cried out, "He saved others. Himself he cannot save. If he is the king of Israel, let him come down now from the cross, and we will believe in him" (Matt. 27:42). It was, however, by way of irony that they said, "Let him come down . . . and we will believe."

It is not so, however, with the perfect soul. She keeps her love for him unshaken and is convinced by the prophecies that these things "must come to pass" (cf. Luke 24:26); and she attests the mental calm that is hers alone in so calamitous a storm when she says, **A cyprus cluster is my Kinsman for me.** "For," says she, "even if the things that have occurred jolt and perturb many, nay everyone, and perplexity has caused those who do not consider that these things 'must come to pass' to loose their grip on a right judgment regarding you — nevertheless, none of these things disturbs me or leads me astray into doubtfulness; for I discerned the ripe maturity of the grape cluster that to many appeared, because of the passion, to be in bloom, and considered it to be the mystery of the resurrection. That is why, though all had been led astray by the disquiet that had taken possession of them and were constrained by what had happened to think of you as a mere human being, I alone confessed you to be God Most High: 'I shall make a loud cry to the Lord Most High, the God who has shown his kindness to me' (Ps. 56:3 LXX = 57:2).

And in order to bring those who had been led astray back to a true judgment regarding you, I exclaimed: 'Be exalted, O God, above the heavens!' (Ps. 56:6a LXX = 57:5a) — which I had learned from David, who says, 'Your glory has been uplifted far above the heavens' (Ps. 8:2 LXX = 8:1). For while you abide upon the earth for the sake of the divine scheme of salvation, those who look upon 'the form of a slave' (Phil. 2:7) are diverted from your true worth; but if you have been exalted above the heavens, then 'your glory is over all the earth' (Ps. 56:6b LXX = 57:5b), for the signs that attest your resurrection bring all, by the proof they afford, to the confession of your glory."

For who that sees Paul called from above, and with his eyes blinded in his trial so that he may not see the glory with the same eyes with which he had seen the cross, will still be heedless of the faith? Who that sees the apostles flogged and "rejoicing that they were counted worthy to suffer dishonor for" the crucified One (cf. Acts 5:41) will not run to the proclamation? And as for the marvel of those who were cured of various illnesses, how many did it convert to the truth in the end, even though at the beginning they had rejected the grape cluster in bloom? For this One, pressed upon the cross, has left a sweet drink for those who thirst; and about him Jacob, prophesying, said, "He washes his garments in wine and his vesture in the blood of grapes" (Gen. 49:11). "Wine" means the blood that flowed from his side, while "garments" and "vesture" mean the Lord's body.

(7) Ambrose of Milan

Among the grapevines of En-gaddi.

If what we seek is the location of a certain sector of Judea (i.e., En-gaddi), there is a place of this name in which balsam is produced; but if we want a translation of the word, what it signifies in Latin is "trial."

In those vineyards, there is a wood that produces a perfumed ointment, and this ointment is the wood's product. If the wood is not cut open, it does not give off a fragrance or scent; but when it has been pierced by the hand of its cultivator, then it sheds its tear. So too Christ, crucified upon the wood of trial, wept over the people so that he might wash away our sins, and from the bowels of his mercy he poured out perfumed ointment when he said, "Father, forgive them; for they know not what they do" (Luke 23:34). Hence when he was pierced by the spear, the victim accepted by God, blood and water came out of him, sweeter than any ointment, shedding throughout the entire world the fragrance of sanctification. And just like balsam from a tree, power came out of his body — which is why he says, "I perceive that power has gone forth from me" (Luke 8:46). The more plainly, then, is it called balsam, in that by the piercing of the tree balsam comes forth through the hole made by the incision.

Jesus, then, once pierced, pours out the fragrance of redemption and of sin's remission. For he was fettered, even though he was the Word made man; and he became poor even though he was rich, so that we might be enriched by his poverty (cf. 2 Cor. 8:9). He was powerful, and he allowed himself to be despised; thus Herod scorned him and made sport of him. He moved the earth, and hung upon the wood of the cross. He veiled the heavens in darkness and crucified the world; and he was crucified. He lowered his head, and the Word went forth. He was emptied, and he filled all things; he came down as God, but ascended as a human being. The Word became flesh in order that the Word's flesh might vindicate for itself a throne at God's right hand. He was an incision, and ointment came forth. . . .

(8) Theodoret of Cyrus

A cyprus cluster is my Kinsman for me
   among the grapevines of En-gaddi.

The Bride is at a loss to know what sort of name to apply to the Bridegroom, and she looks about this way and that and, loving him as she does, applies names to him that come from here, there, and everywhere; for she is driven by love to call upon him but cannot find a name worthy of him. That is why she names him a **cyprus cluster**, that is, a cluster that is "blooming," as opposed to "beginning to bloom," for it is in the season of blooming that the vine is fragrant.

But she adds, **among the grapevines of En-gaddi** — a grape cluster of that sort being fragrant. If, then, this refers to an area in Judea that is adorned with grapevines of admirable quality, our text must be understood figuratively to mean, "Your fragrant grape cluster surpasses those vines." On the other hand, if she employs the word **En-gaddi** on account of the connotation of the term itself, which signifies "eye of trial," then it must be understood to mean: "Even when I am in a situation of trial and temptation, and am assaulted on every hand, I apprehend your fragrance; and before the vines that bloom in the present time — which, figuratively understood, exist in the midst of trial, since the life of a human being on this earth is trial — I prefer the fragrance of the grape cluster in bloom." But if the vine that is now in bloom is of such a character, one is bound to inquire what it will be like when it is ripening; and if the ripening vine is superior to the former, one must ponder what the fully mature growth, which is fit for pressing, will be like. For I judge that, relative to the stage of their spiritual growth, the very same vine is blooming for some, for others is still unripe, for yet others is beginning to ripen, for some is mature, but is to be drunk by the perfect. "And thy cup inebriates because it is the very best" (Ps. 22:5 LXX = 23:5).

(9) Apponius

. . . among the vineyards of En-gaddi.

But [Christ] daily ministers the aforesaid spiritual food and drink to those who put their faith in him: to persons, I mean, who are gathered in his presence **among the vineyards of En-gaddi**, that is to say, in the place where the "goats' water spring" is located. This is the place where the peoples of many nations — signified by **vineyards** — possess in their midst, once they have acknowledged their Creator and set up assemblies of Christian believers, the "goats' water spring." This is the font of holy baptism, to which the goats who had been set on the left hand before the judge's tribunal, to be handed over to the fire, come down, and then come up as unspotted lambs, to be awarded the everlasting kingdom. For it is certain that in the whole world there is one font of baptism, and there, once the name of the co-eternal Trinity has been invoked, those who have been bathed in it are sanctified, so that from goats they may be made lambs. Certain it is too that just as the one Jewish people is called "the Lord's vineyard" (cf. Isa. 5:7) by reason of its knowledge of the divine law, so the various peoples that that have been brought to faith in Christ by the apostles' nurturing, that is, their teaching, are called **vineyards** in the plural. And it is in their midst, as we have said, that there sits the font of holy baptism, to which goats come and are made lambs. For the font of baptism has been established on account of sinners, who are called "goats," not on account of the righteous, who have no need of being bathed. . . .

Now these **vineyards** produce not wine but balsam. For En-gaddi is a village by the Dead Sea in the land of Judea — a land that figuratively points to the land of the living — where there are balsam vineyards. Many kings have transplanted baby balsam trees from this village into other places or lands, and they have failed to take root or to live. . . .

It is well worthwhile, moreover, to grasp why these vines grow in no soil other than that of En-gaddi. For it is my opinion that this soil with its vines is thought to embody a type of the one confession of faith. In it the faith of believers is firmly grounded, and in it alone there sprouts up the healing fragrance of Christ that restores life to dead souls. . . . For just as a body cannot survive without food and drink, so too the Church proclaims that there is no life apart from the **cluster**, which represents Christ, eternal life coming down from heaven — and he is found, by those who hunger and thirst after righteousness, nowhere save in the land of promise, that is, in **the vineyards of En-gaddi**. He is found in no assembly of heretics, in no sect of philosophers, in no union of schismatics; and if any individual is transplanted into such groups, he perishes as one deceived, withered up by the hunger that attends his own perversity.

(10) The *Glossa ordinaria*

My Beloved is a cyprus plant to me.

The balsam trees that grow in En-gaddi are called vines because they are cultivated in the way that vines are. The Bridegroom, then, is **among the vines of En-gaddi** because, coming in the flesh and full of the Holy Spirit, he lavishes upon believers the gifts of that same Spirit through the [baptismal] unction of chrism, in the manufacture of which balsam is mixed with oil.

Song 1:15-17

SEPTUAGINT	VULGATE
1:15 Behold, you are beautiful, my close one;	1:14 Behold, you are beautiful, my friend;
behold, you are beautiful.	behold, you are beautiful;
Your eyes are doves.	your eyes are doves' eyes.
16 Behold, you are beautiful, my Kinsman,	15 Behold, you are beautiful, my Beloved,
and fair,	and fair!
thickly shaded at our bed.	Our bed is full of flowers.
17 The beams of our house are cedars,	16 The beams of our house are of cedar;
our paneled ceilings are of cypress.	our paneled ceilings are of cypress.

In these three verses, the Bridegroom speaks to the Bride, presumably as they lie together on the King's bed, and the Bride replies. It is the occurrence of this conversation itself that interests Bernard of Clairvaux, who wonders how the Word of God and the soul communicate. Origen, on the other hand, emphasizes the Bridegroom's explicit praise of the Bride as "beautiful" or "fair," and discerns in it a culmination in his praises of her — a culmination that reflects her own progress in virtue and is expressed not only in the description of her as his "close one," but above all in the comparison of her eyes to doves (or to "doves' eyes") — a comparison that instantly and naturally evokes a reflection on endowment with the Holy Spirit and the effects of such endowment. It is interesting to notice how Apponius — whose interest is elicited more by the reference to eyes than by that to doves, and who dwells here on the Bride's identity as the Church rather than as the individual soul — constructs an exegesis that wants to answer the question, "Who or what are the Church's 'eyes'"?

In interpretations of the Bride's reply, different interests emerge. Following Origen, Gregory of Nyssa focuses first on the statement that the Bridegroom, as the Septuagint would have it, is "thickly shaded" or "in the shadow" by the bed. This is a reference, he thinks, to the incarnation, in which the glory of the Word is "shaded" by the humanity of Christ, with the result that it becomes accessible to the human eye and mind. To Gregory of Elvira, however, the shadow is that of death, and the bed represents "the sepulchre of the Lord's body." Of course there is nothing of this in the Latin translation of the Vulgate, which comes closer to the sense of the original with the words "Our bed is full of flowers." Apponius too sees the union of Bridegroom and Bride in their bed as a symbol of the incarnation, but he also draws on Gregory's idea that the bed represents the Lord's tomb. Now, however, the "shadow's" place has been taken by flowers: he sees in this line an "enigma" of Christ, at one with his body, the Church, in his tomb — but surrounded already with the tokens of the resurrection of his humanity, the flowers and the spices with which his body was anointed.

(1) Origen

Behold, you are beautiful, my close one;
  behold, you are beautiful.
  Your eyes are doves.

Now for the second time the Bridegroom engages in a verbal exchange with the Bride.

The first time he addressed her, he invited her to know herself (cf. 1:8), telling her that she was the **fair one among women**, but that unless she were to know herself, she would suffer certain things. And as if she had progressed quickly toward self-knowledge in awareness and understanding, he compares her to his horses or his cavalry, by which he overcame the chariots of Pharaoh. At the same time, he compares her cheeks to doves and her neck to circlets of jewels because of her signal modesty and the swiftness of her conversion.

Now, however, he pronounces that she is already beautiful — and beautiful not, as previously, only **among women**, but as his **close one**; and he further affirms that she is not only **beautiful** in being **close** to him, but also that she is **beautiful** even if she happens to be away from him; for he indicates this in that, after he had said, **Behold, you are beautiful, my close one**, he then added — unqualifiedly and without adding anything — **Behold, you are beautiful**. In the earlier passage, however, he had no praise for her face because, in my view, she had not yet progressed to the stage of seeing with a spiritual understanding. Here, therefore, he says, **Your eyes are doves**.

This demonstrates the great extent of her progress in that she who previously was merely said to be **beautiful among women** is now called **close one** and **beautiful**. No doubt it is from the Bridegroom himself that she receives her shining loveliness, so that as soon as she has appropriated her beauty from him, she may remain beautiful even if she happens for a short time to suffer the Bridegroom's absence.

As to the comparison of her eyes with doves, surely the explanation of it is that now she does not understand the divine Scriptures after the letter but after the spirit, and in them beholds spiritual mysteries; for the dove is a token of the Holy Spirit. Hence to have the eyes of the dove means to understand the Law and the Prophets with a spiritual sensibility.

And while in this text her eyes are called the eyes of a dove, in the Psalms a soul of this sort desires to be given "the wings of a dove" (Ps. 67:14b LXX = 68:13b) so that she may be able to soar in the understanding of spiritual mysteries and come to rest in the courts of Wisdom. But if a soul can also sleep — that is, be placed and rest — "in the midst of the lots assigned" (Ps. 67:14a LXX = 68:13a), and understand the reason behind the assigned lots and grasp the causes of the divine judgment, it is not only wings of a dove, wherewith to soar among spiritual understandings, that are promised her, but more than that, "wings . . . silvered over" (Ps. 68:13b), which is to say, wings embellished with the marks of reason articulate in speech. Further still, "her back" is said to become "golden in color" (Ps. 68:13c), and this refers to that constancy in the faith and steadfastness in the teachings which is proper to those who are perfect.

Therefore just as Christ is called "the head" (1 Cor. 11:3), there is, as I see it, nothing absurd if the eyes of those who understand and judge spiritually "according to the inner self" (Rom. 7:22) are called the Holy Spirit. . . .

Let these remarks be a sufficient treatment of the words **your eyes are doves** in the text before us; it is the equivalent of saying, "Your eyes are spiritual, perceiving spiritually, understanding spiritually."

As to the words **Behold, you are beautiful, my close one**, which may well adumbrate a still deeper mystery, they can be understood to be spoken with reference to the present age, since here and now the Church is **beautiful** when it is close to Christ and imitates Christ. On the other hand, when he repeats himself and says, **Behold, you are beautiful**, this can refer to the age to come, in which the Bride is lovely and beautiful not only by imitation but by right of her very own perfection, and in that day to say that her **eyes are doves** may mean that the two doves corresponding to her two eyes are understood to be the Son of God and the Holy Spirit. Nor should you wonder if they are both called doves, since each of them equally is called "advocate," even as the Evangelist John declares when he calls the Holy Spirit "paraclete," which means the same as "advocate," and yet for all that speaks in his letter of Jesus Christ and says that Christ himself is the "advocate with the Father" for our sins (see John 14:16-17; 1 John 2:1). For that matter, the "two olive trees" set on the right and the left of the lampstand in the prophet Zechariah (Zech. 4:3) are believed to designate the Only-begotten and the Holy Spirit.

(2) Bernard of Clairvaux

Behold, you are beautiful, my Friend. . . .
    Behold, you are beautiful, my Beloved. . . .

But maybe thoughts are surfacing in your heart, and, more and more doubtful, you are asking yourself: "In what way are the words that the Word speaks to the soul — and, conversely, those that the soul speaks to the Word — conveyed? How does she hear the voice of the One that is talking to her and telling her that she is **beautiful**, and how does she in turn render the same tribute to the One who is praising her? How can this happen? It is not the words that speak; it is we who speak the word. By the same token, the soul has no way of speaking unless her bodily mouth shape the words she speaks."

Well, that is a good question. Consider, though, that it is the Spirit that speaks, and that what is said must be understood spiritually. Accordingly, as often as you hear that Word and soul share speech with each other, and that they look upon each other, do not indulge yourself in the fancy that there are audible sounds running back and forth, any more than there are corporeal images of the partners for the eye to see. No, but hear instead what you are to think about such converse. The Word is spirit, and the soul is spirit as well; and they have their own sort of tongues with which to address each other and show themselves present to each other. The "tongue" of the Word is the goodwill [*favor*] shown in his condescension to us; while that of the soul is the ardor [*fervor*] of her devotion. The soul that fails to possess this ardor has no "tongue" and is speechless. She is without any capacity for converse with the Word. It follows that when the Word employs this "tongue" of his, wanting to speak to the soul, it is impossible for the soul not to be aware of him, for "the Word of God is living and active, sharper than any two-edged sword, piercing to the division of soul and spirit" (Heb. 4:12). Conversely, when the soul employs her tongue, the Word is even less able to hide himself — not only because he is present everywhere, but even more because unless he himself quickens it, her "tongue" — her devotion — is scarcely moved to speak at all.

Thus for the Word to say to the soul, **You are beautiful**, and to call her **Friend**, is to impart that which empowers her to love and to know that she is loved. But for her, in response, to call the Word **Beloved** and to confess that he is **beautiful** is to give him, truthfully and sincerely, the credit for her loving and her being loved. It is to marvel at his kindness and to wonder at his grace. Accordingly, the Bridegroom's beauty is his love: which is all the greater for its being prior to the Bride's. Therefore she cries out — with all her heart and with words of deep feeling — that she must love him, and the more fully and fervently because she realizes that he loved her before he was loved by her. Thus the Word's "speech" is the imparting of a gift, and the soul's response is a rendering of thanks accompanied by wonder. . . .

(3) William of St. Thierry

Behold, you are beautiful, my Friend;
  behold, you are beautiful;
  your eyes are dove's eyes.

Behold — which is to say "discern" in this reverent passion, in this manner of giving praise, in this manifestation of perfection, that is, in the image of God. For the human person has been created after the image of God in this sense, that in being reverently mindful of God for the sake of knowing him; in being humble in knowledge of him for the sake of loving him; in loving him ardently and discerningly, for the sake of being touched with the joy of delight in him — that in these ways, the human person might actualize its character as a rational animal. For this is what is meant by fearing God and keeping his commandments, and that in turn is what it means to be all that a human person is (cf. Eccl. 12:13). Just this is the image and likeness of God in the human person — such as, and to such a degree as, it can exist in so unlike a medium.

Now surely the likeness in question consists in that rationality which distinguishes a human being from a beast. To be mindful of God is not for beasts. To be mindful of God without seeking knowledge of God is proper to "something" midway between beast and human being. To be mindful of God for the sake of knowing God is proper to the human person: to possess knowledge of God that leads to loving him and, in thus loving, to delight in him, is proper to the person of perfected rationality. Take it, then, that reverent mindfulness quickly brightens into a certain sort of knowledge of God, and into a certain kind of rational reflection. Purified knowledge, that is to say, rational reflection on God, straightway heats up into love; but love, by reason of its passionate attachment to what is good, is instantly engaged in decking itself out in the image of the highest Good — such as, and to such a degree as, is suitable to itself. This image is present to memory by the will's consent; to purified understanding by its own acts of reflection; to the passion of love by the delight of possession; to love — that is, to the lover-Bride — by the condition of her awareness; but to others by the desire proper to a good will. For the Bride's memory of the Bridegroom is a seeking of the Bridegroom in simplicity of heart; understanding of him is to think of him in goodness (cf. Wisdom 1:1); love is attachment to him, enjoyment of him — to be, in a word, even as he is.

Finding the Bride in this condition or state of awareness, the Bridegroom says, **Behold, you are beautiful, my Friend; behold, you are beautiful.** For whatever had been stained had been restored by the Sun of Righteousness to the beauty of a Bride; what had lost its heat in his absence had been filled again with warmth in his presence. Moreover, the "substance" of the Bride — of which the apostle says, "Faith is the substance of things to be hoped for" (Heb. 11:1) — possesses the lustrous colors that are proper to it, which are the holy virtues. These, as we have already indicated above, are either discolored or restored according as they have been either abandoned or shined upon by illuminating grace.

Perceiving, then, the restored countenance of the Bride, the Bridegroom is drawn to lift his voice in her praise, and says, **Behold, you are beautiful, my Friend; behold, you are beautiful.** The repetition here signifies corroboration of what has already been said, or else it points to an enhancement of a beauty that is still in the making. Or perhaps he is saying, "You are beautiful in your deeds, beautiful in your affection"; or "Beautiful because attractive, and beautiful because full of color." "Behold, then," he says, "in purifying your memory for me, in teaching your understanding humility, in gracing me with your love, **you are beautiful, my Friend; behold, you are beautiful** — to the degree that you are beautiful."

Since the perfection of contemplation is made up of just these factors, he adds something about that, and says, **Your eyes are dove's eyes.** Contemplation has two eyes: one is reason, and the other is love. In accordance, moreover, with the prophet's saying that "the riches of salvation are wisdom and knowledge" (Isa. 33:6), one of these eyes functions in the manner of ordinary knowing and investigates things human, while the other follows the way of wisdom and investigates things divine. But when grace enlightens them, they are of great assistance to each other; for not only does love give life to reason, but reason clarifies love, and there emerges a dovelike insight, endowed with simplicity for the sake of contemplation and prudence for the sake of caution. Often, moreover, these two eyes become a single eye when they cooperate with each other loyally — when, in contemplation, in which love is the primary force, reason passes over into love and is shaped into a kind of spiritual or divine understanding that overcomes and absorbs all reasoning. This understanding is what the Bride speaks of to the Bridegroom further on when she says, **You have wounded my heart . . . , you have wounded my heart, with one of your eyes and with one curl on your neck.**

(4) Apponius

Your eyes are doves.

After the comeliness of the cheeks and of the neck, it is the beauty of the Bride's eyes that is extolled, and, in the Bridegroom's reiterated word of praise, her whole body as well; and her eyes are compared to the eyes of doves. They are compared to that creature which, for gentleness, for fertility, for sharp-sightedness, for speed in flight, surpasses almost all winged animals.

Now the eyes are the guides of the whole body. Without them the body cannot make its way, or at any rate only clumsily and with difficulty. Among them one must properly reckon bishops, to whom God has committed the holy mysteries. In their faith lies the glory of the Church; and in their spotless life the Church is exalted by repeated praises. The Church is **beautiful** as she presents to God the purest of consciences. She is **beautiful** as she demonstrates, to her enemies and to those who stand outside faith in Christ, her blameless way of life.

There is added a third praise of her beauty, that is, the keenness of her eyes. For in addition to what we have already noted, the nature of doves has been established to possess this characteristic property, that from a distance they perceive, in water, the coming up of an enemy from behind them. Their beauty, then, is surely praised in the bishops' spoken admonition, in which they forewarn the people of the snares of that hawk, the Devil.

(5) Gregory of Elvira

Your eyes are doves.

When he speaks of the eyes of a dove, he is setting before the reader the lamps of spiritual grace by which we perceive things past and present and future. He calls the Church a dove not only on account of her simplicity and innocence, in that she is not steeped in the bile of malice; but also because among the Greeks a dove is called *peristera*, and the letters of this name, reckoning according to the Greek method of counting, add up to a total of eight hundred and one; but one and eight hundred are denoted in Greek by Alpha and Omega. Hence the Lord himself, whose flesh the Church is, says, "I am the Alpha and the Omega" (Rev. 1:8), by which number the name "dove" is signified. Hence too the Spirit, descending as a dove upon Christ in the Jordan, manifests the Trinity of Father, Son, and Holy Spirit: the voice is in the Father, the Son is in Christ, and the Holy Spirit is in the dove.

(6) Apponius

Behold, you are beautiful, my Beloved,
    and fair!
Our bed is full of flowers.

No one can praise the splendor of someone he dislikes, nor can he love someone whose morals he repudiates. This is exactly what the blessed apostle Paul teaches when he says, "No one speaking by the Spirit of God ever says 'Jesus be cursed!' and no one can say 'Jesus is Lord' except by the Holy Spirit" (1 Cor. 12:3). Anyone therefore who can perceive the beauty and the comeliness of the Beloved, the Son of God, and can heap him with praise is one who holds on to the Spirit in his mind by the holiness of his deeds. Hence in the text before us the Church, full of that Spirit of Truth who under the form of a dove came down from heaven upon the man whom the Word took to himself, recognizes both the beauty of his body, without sin as it is, and the glory of that genuine soul which knows no falsehood or guile, and with alternating and redoubled praise says, **Behold, you are beautiful, my Beloved, and fair!**

    Our bed is full of flowers. Although, to be sure, a shining face or precious garb may manifest the Bridegroom to the Bride as he stands at a distance, she is nevertheless ignorant of the glory of the rest of his members until the joining that takes place in the marriage bed; but she knows it after the lawful wedding has been celebrated and the two have been made "one flesh" (Matt. 19:6; cf. Gen. 2:24) in accord with the judgment rendered in the case of the first human being — a mystery that our teacher the apostle Paul avers was made known in Christ and the Church (cf. Eph. 5:31-32). In the same way the aforesaid **close one** loved him by desiring his advent, praised his face and his kisses, up until the time of his burial; but nevertheless it is after the time of his resurrection that the whole of her love, and all the glory of his beauty, have achieved their established end, the outpouring of blood for the sake of his name. For the **bed . . . full of flowers** — that is, with flowers scattered all over it — in which she discerns his glorious beauty in all his members is understood by the Church to signify, by way of enigmas, the Lord's tomb, where together there repose the body of Christ, the Church, and the Word of the Father who fills "all things" (Eph. 4:13) — and is everywhere at every time in his totality — and who had taken a body to himself. For it is solely by reason of the presence of the Word for three days and three nights that his "flesh" did not "see corruption" (Acts 2:31).

    The **bed**, moreover, is rightly called **full of flowers** in that, together with the body of Christ, there were brought into it spices and aloes (cf. John 19:39-40), which are mixed together by the apothecary's art from the saps or flowers of many sorts of plants and trees; and with them, when he was rising, the tomb was besprinkled. In his teaching the Church — that is, the mass of believers — found freedom; in his death, life; in the silence of his tomb, rest from the hard labors that she carried out daily, driven by the scourges of demons. That is where he is known to be truly human, because kept safe by the confinement of his body under the seal of unbelievers; and truly God, because he departed from the sealed tomb with his humanity. That is where the marriage of the Son of God and the Church was celebrated. That is where the Church merited to discover the delicious sleep of the passion and the joy of eternal awakening; for the apostle cries out to her members, "If you died with Christ, seek the things that are above, where Christ is . . . at the right hand of God" (Col. 2:20; 3:1). From his resurrection on, both people's minds and buildings that house congregations of believers are being provided daily for the indwelling of the Holy Spirit, and so both visibly and invisibly, at every point and without cease, homes for the Son of God and the Church are increased in number. . . .

(7) Gregory of Elvira

Behold, you are good, my brother,
and fair indeed.
Our bed is shadowed,
our beams are of cedarwood,
our dwellings are cypresses.

There are two things that she seeks in Christ. There is goodness because he is God (for, as he says, "No one is good but God alone" [Mark 10:18]), and she calls him **good** in order to show that he is God. In the same way, she calls him **fair**, and David says that he is "fairer in aspect than the sons of men" (Ps. 44:3 LXX = 45:2). Surely it is in his resurrection that he is seen to be **fair**, because he, who before his passion was called "a man of sorrows, and acquainted with grief" (Isa. 53:3), had already returned into the glory of his Father. For, says Isaiah, "We saw him, and he had no beauty or comeliness" (Isa. 53:2). Why did he not have "beauty or comeliness"? Because, as the apostle said, "he emptied himself, taking the form of a servant and . . . humbled himself . . . unto death, even death on a cross" (Phil. 2:7-8). That, then, was the time when "he had no beauty or comeliness," but when he was glorified after the resurrection, he ascended into heaven in virtue of that grace — beauty, as it were. That is why she says, **Behold, you are good, my brother, and fair indeed** — in order to make manifest his humanity and his worthiness.

Then she adds: **Our bed is shadowed, our beams are of cedarwood, our dwellings are cypresses.** When mention is made here of a bed, what is meant is the sepulchre of the Lord's body, where the Lord lay put to sleep with the sleep of his passion, covered over by the shadow of death, even as the apostle said, "Although he died because of weakness, he is nevertheless alive in virtue of power" (2 Cor. 13:4). For this reason **the shadowed . . . bed**, covered over with a shadow as I said, clearly refers to the weakness of the body, that is, the sepulchre for the dead flesh.

Our beams, she says, **are of cedarwood.** She was not speaking here of wooden beams, nor of a house made with hands, but when she mentions beams of cedarwood, she is showing that the renowned patriarchs were exalted with great glory in the house of God; therefore, she calls them "cedars," because this sort of tree cannot decay and is immensely high, and so it manifests the undying glory of the patriarchs and the transcendent worth of the promised kingdom.

Our dwellings are cypresses. The cypress is of a higher order than the cedar; indeed, this kind of tree is called the king of all trees. Hence just as she calls the patriarchs cedars, so too she calls the apostles cypresses, which means that our dwellings, that is, the Church, are filled with the food of evangelical teaching. Indeed, even the Savior himself, when he deigned to be born as a human being, was placed in a manger because he was to become, in a fashion, food for us flocks, as he says in the Gospel: "He who eats my body as the bread of life will have eternal life" (cf. John 6:54). These **dwellings**, then, are the precepts of the apostles' teaching, and they are called cypresses on account of the unsurpassed glory of the kingdom of heaven, being full of the food of his sacred body and the drink of his blood, on which the souls and bodies of believers are fattened.

(8) Gregory of Nyssa

. . . thickly shaded at our bed.

Then she adds: **thickly shaded at our bed.** That is, "Human nature knows you, or will know you, as one who became shaded by the divine Economy. For you came," she says, "as the beautiful **Kinsman**, the glorious one, who became present at our couch **thickly shaded.** For if you had not shaded yourself, concealing the pure ray of your Deity by 'the form of a slave' (Phil. 2:7), who could have borne your appearing? For no one shall see 'the face' of the Lord 'and live' (Exod. 33:20). Therefore you, the glorious one, came; but you came in such wise as we are able to receive you. You came with the radiance of Divinity shaded by the garment of a body." For how could a mortal and perishable nature be adapted to live together with the Imperishable and Inaccessible unless the shadow of the body had mediated between the Light and us who live in darkness?

In a figurative turn of speech the Bride uses the word **bed** to mean the mingling of human nature with the Divine, just as the great apostle has the virgin — us — betrothed to Christ, and leads the soul in a bridal procession, and declares that the joining of the two in the communion of one body is the great mystery of the union of Christ with the Church. For when he said "The two shall become one flesh," he added, "This is a great mystery, but I apply it to Christ and the church" (Eph. 5:32). So in view of this mystery the virgin soul gives the name **bed** to communion with the Divine.

(9) The *Glossa ordinaria*

The beams of our houses are of cedar;
  our paneled ceilings are of cypress.

Houses, different throughout the world, [signify] the nations that make up the Church. The **beams**, which customarily serve to hold up the house, are preachers, and by their word and example the structure of the Church is held together so that it does not tumble down. The **paneled ceilings**, which serve to beautify the house, are the simpler members of Christ's household, who hold on to the beams and are held up by them, and embellish the Church not with their teaching but with their virtues.

· 7 ·

Song 2:1-2

SEPTUAGINT	VULGATE

2:1 I am a flower of the field,
    a lily of the hollows.
 2 As a lily among thorns,
        so is my close one among
            the daughters.
	2:1 I am a flower of the field
	    and a lily of the valleys.
	 2 As a lily among thorns,
	        so is my Beloved among
	            the daughters.

The word translated here as "hollows" is in Greek related to a verb that means "scoop out." It does indeed refer to a valley (as tradition has taught us), but not, apparently, to a very green one. Ancient interpreters of the Song almost uniformly took it to connote a place that is low down indeed, gloomy, even rocky — and not just deep, but also, figuratively, low in point of value or esteem or status, a connotation that "valley" certainly does not ordinarily carry in English.

Modern commentators point out further that the Hebrew word rendered "lily" seems in fact to refer to a kind of lotus — and therefore does not carry the connotation of purity and exaltation that ancient commentators discerned in the white-flowered lily, whose long stem elevated it far above the surrounding terrain. Nevertheless, as a result of its use in the Authorized Version's translation of this line, the phrase "lily of the valleys" has been fixed in the English language and even established itself as the name of a flowering herb (Convallaria majalis). The drooping bloom of this plant also lacks the long stem of the lily.

There is a question about who is speaking in 2:1. Origen takes it that the Bridegroom is speaking in both of the above verses, and his view prevailed in many quarters. On this view, Christ, the Word of God, is the "lily of the valleys." Not everyone has assented to this view, however, and Philo of Carpasius below takes the opposite position; he thinks that the Bride speaks in 2:1, and the Bridegroom replies in 2:2.

There are two points at which Nilus of Ancyra's argument in the excerpt quoted below may seem obscure — points that illustrate the difference that could be made for interpretation by the way a text was construed grammatically. Thus in his discussion of a line from Ps. 64:11 in the Septuagint, Nilus argues that "its" in the phrase "its drops" refers to Jesus' side (cf. John 19:34). His (not very persua-sive) reason for this — obscured in translation by the requirements of English grammar — is (a) that the pronoun we render as "its" is feminine in gender, as is the Greek word for "side"; and (b) that in the Greek text of the psalm there is no grammatically feminine word other than "side" to which "its" can clearly refer back.

Similarly, it is a grammarian's point that explains his way of taking Deut. 32:5c-6a, which he cites at the very end of our excerpt. Nilus read a Greek manu-script of the Septuagint which contained no marks of punctuation. He could therefore construe the word "generation" in 32:5c as a vocative (i.e., as meaning "O generation . . ."), and 32:6a as a question put to that same generation. The translators of the RSV obviously thought it necessary to punctuate the Hebrew text otherwise.

(1) Origen

I am a flower of the field,
   a lily of the hollows.
As a lily among thorns,
   so is my close one among the daughters.

These words, it seems, are spoken by the Bridegroom and Word and Wisdom to his friends and companions concerning himself and his Bride. But in accordance with the pattern of exposition we have announced, Christ must be understood to be speaking these words concerning the Church, and to be asserting that he is a **flower of the field**.

Now **field** refers to flat land that farmers tend and cultivate, while **hollows** refers rather to places that are rocky and untilled. For this reason, we are justified in under-standing by **field** the people that was tended by the Law and the Prophets, but by **hollows** the rocky and untilled place of the Gentiles. This Bridegroom, then, was a flower set in the midst of that people; but since the law brings no one to perfection (cf. Heb. 7:19), the Word of God was unable in that setting to progress from the status of a blossom and achieve the perfection of bearing fruit. So it was that he became a **lily** in the vale of the Gentiles.

But what sort of **lily**? No doubt the sort of lily of which he says in the Gospel that your "heavenly Father clothes" it, and that not even "Solomon in all his glory was dressed like one of these" (cf. Matt. 6:30, 29). The Bridegroom accordingly became a **lily** in this hollow because the heavenly Father clothed him in a garment of flesh of a sort that "Solo-mon in all his glory" could not possess. For Solomon did not possess a flesh unspotted by male lust or copulation with a woman and liable to no further sin.

But he seems further to indicate why it is that he who had been **a flower of the field** chose to be **a lily of the hollows**. For even though he had been **a flower of the field** for a long time, he says that no one from the field had come forth to be an imitation and like-ness of himself; but no sooner had he become **a lily of the hollows** than his **close one**, by imitation of him, also became a **lily**. Thus it was the reward of his act of becoming a **lily** that his **close one** too — by which I mean any and every soul that draws near to him and follows his model and example — should become a **lily**.

Hence we take the following words — **As a lily among thorns, so is my close one among the daughters** — to refer to the Church of the Gentiles, either because she has sprouted up out of the midst of the thorns, as it were, of nonbelievers and unbelievers — or because she is said to be set **among thorns** in the sense that she is surrounded by heretics with their barbed clamorings. The latter seems the more plausible because of the words **so is my close one among the daughters**; for he would not have called **daughters** those souls who had never turned to the faith at all. All heretics, though, come to belief first of all, and later turn away from the way of the faith and from the truth of the Church's teachings. Furthermore, this is what the apostle John says in his letter, "They went out from us, but they were not of us; for if they had been of us, they would have continued with us" (1 John 2:19).

We can also take this as referring to the individual soul: I mean the soul that on account of its simplicity and evenness of temper or equanimity can be called **field**, whose **flower** the Word of God becomes and whom he teaches the beginnings of good works. On the other hand, for those who are already seeking deeper truths and peering into the depths of things, down, as it were, in the hollows — for such souls, whether because of their splendid virtue or their shining wisdom, he becomes a **lily**, so that they too may become lilies that spring up out of the midst of the thorns, that is, that flee the thoughts and cares of the present age, which are compared in the Gospel to **thorns** (cf. Mark 4:18-19).

(2) Philo of Carpasius

I am a flower of the field,
  a lily of the hollows.
As a lily among thorns,
  so is my close one among the daughters.

For the delight of her Bridegroom, [the Bride] lingers to continue the same line of thought. It is fitting for her to state that she is **a flower of the field**, for in studying the prophecies she hears the words of Isaiah: "Rejoice, you thirsty desert; be exultant, O desert, and bloom like the lily — and" the ancient desert "shall blossom" (Isa. 35:1-2 LXX). Now, however, she not only gives off the fragrance of flowers. She also abundantly generates sweetness of taste by producing the fruits of righteousness. Hence when she says, **I am a flower of the field**, she is making sense of the prophecies; but when she adds **a lily of the hollows,** she is rejoicing in the evangelical, saving, and fragrant words of her very own Bridegroom when he himself enjoins freedom from care upon his disciples, saying, "Consider the lilies of the field, how they grow; they neither toil nor spin" (Matt. 6:28). Thus when she calls herself **lily of the hollows**, she is thinking of the gospel teachings, while when she calls herself **flower of the field,** she is tacitly referring to the qualities of the prophetic revelations.

Then the Bridegroom responds to her, saying in answer to her words: **As a lily among thorns, so is my close one among the daughters.** The point of this is that she conducts herself in this world as a righteous one among the unrighteous, as a God-fearer among the impious. It is to her that the apostle says, "That you may be . . . children of God without blemish in the midst of a crooked and perverse generation" (Phil. 2:15).

(3) Theodoret of Cyrus

I am a flower of the field,
  a lily of the hollows.

For he says: **I am a flower of the field, a lily of the hollows.** "You have looked upon my human beauty," he says, "for 'No one has ever seen God' (John 1:18). For I became **a flower of the field,** that is to say, I assumed an earthly body and I sprouted up in the earth, even though I existed before the ages, exalted, and more than that, beyond all limit. I did not become a lily of the mountains or the hills, nor simply of the fields, but **of the hollows.** I not only proclaimed good news of salvation to living beings, but also resurrection to the dead, descending into the lowest parts of the earth in order to fill all things" (cf. Eph. 4:10). This explains why he names himself on the one hand **flower of the plain,** and, on the other, **lily of the hollows,** that is, of those who have died, since for the latter he both proclaimed their restoration to life and himself brought it about.

Then, since he has called himself by such names, he says to the Bride, "**As a lily among thorns, so is my close one among the daughters.** For by as much as the lily surpasses thorns, you surpass the beauty of the daughters, who are called so because they have been reckoned worthy of the calling but have deprived themselves of being among the chosen. 'For,' says he, 'many are called, but few are chosen'" (Matt. 20:16; cf. 22:14).

(4) Nilus of Ancyra

I am a flower of the field,
  a lily of the hollows.

In order to understand **hollows** one must set a similar expression alongside it — I mean the following: "The eye that makes mockery of a father or dishonors the old age of a mother — may the ravens of the ravine pluck it out, and the nestlings of eagles devour it" (Prov. 30:17 LXX). In this verse, "eye" denotes a person who has been possessed of the power of insight, but who has made use of this power not for proper ends but for base concerns and for interests unworthy of the nobility of the divine truths that are its objects. Aiming to prevent such a person's remaining preoccupied with these matters, the God who watches over us commits to the Powers close to the earth the task of plucking thoughts occupied with hollow things out of the ravines and giving them as food to the nestlings of eagles as they dart about on high. God's purpose is not that, once consumed, these thoughts may lapse into nonexistence, but that they may come forth, so to speak, out of the bowels of the eagles, tried again in the furnace, in imitation of those with whom Paul was a second time in travail because in their first birthing they had not rightly formed Christ within them (cf. Gal. 4:19).

One must realize that the **hollows** of which the Bride says she is a **lily** resemble these ravines; for because she stands out among the **hollows**, as they are called on account of the base character of their deeds and thoughts, she — brilliantly embellished and radiant in their midst — is a lily; or else it is because in the age to come, even though she has no natural advantage over them, she is going to pass judgment on such souls on the basis of a comparison with her own righteous deeds, just as the Ninevites and the Queen of the South pass judgment on the faithless generation (cf. Matt. 12:41-42).

What is more, since she herself came to be as a **lily** among the **hollows** and nothing sprouted up there before her, it may be that these hollows began to produce fruitful plants out of envy of the loveliness of her blossom, accepting seeds from the Sower who went out to sow (cf. Matt. 13:3-9) — and that they received the Word not like the rock that rejoiced but for a short time in the words; or like the earth bearing thorns whose growth stifles the seeds; or like the road that receives the Word on its surface so that it is right at hand for people who want to tread upon it or for birds who try to plunder it: but on the contrary like good, rich earth that multiplies the seed — just as the prophet says, hinting at their fruitfulness, "the hollows abound in grain" (Ps. 64:14 LXX = 65:13); for the phrase that immediately follows shows that these hollows are rational souls: "they shout and sing," it says.

And she is further said to be **a flower of the field**. Perhaps — if **the hollows**, being low down and uncultivated and spoken of in the plural, denote the Gentiles who have come to knowledge out of the depths of impiety — **the field** denotes Israel made level by the teachings of the Law and the Prophets so as to be ready for cultivation. Moreover, it is right that she is not called their fruit but their **flower**; for as yet the plow of the cross has not opened the earth, the plow to which the Lord affixed the apostles like so many oxen when he sent them out in pairs to cultivate it, nor has it yet been watered by the Lord's blood. For this reason it was fruitless and sterile, with only one flower blooming in the whole field, that is, the Christ, of whom it is written: "a flower shall sprout up from the root" (Isa. 11:1). When, therefore, the tree of the cross was planted, and it received the Lord in his humanity, and his side was pierced by the lance, and the precious blood dripped from his side upon the earth — then the earth bloomed, and righteousness sprang up from the earth (cf. Ps. 84:12 LXX = 85:11), and those who had comprehended the saying of the psalmist say in turn, "She who is rising up shall rejoice in its drops" (Ps. 64:11c LXX = 65:12b). He says "its," but he does not indicate what "it" is; for having said "flooding her furrows, make her fruits burgeon" (Ps. 64:11ab = 65:10), he adds: "she who is rising up shall rejoice in its drops." By failing to specify the source of the drops, he allows us to understand the [Lord's] side; and the same thing is conveyed in the words, "Rejoice, O thirsty desert, and bloom like the lily, and the desert places of the Jordan shall blossom, because the glory of Lebanon has been given her, and the honor of Carmel" (Isa. 35:1-2) — which words seem to point to the calling of the Gentiles and their honor.

This is the very voice of the Bridegroom as it bears witness to the Bride more ample than she had just borne to herself. For when she said that she was a lily and the other souls hollows, she made the comparison without quite guessing at some of the truth. He who has a deeper knowledge of the special qualities of the two states of being determines the proper label for the underlying identities, having assigned names appropriate to the characters in question. For, says he, **As a lily among thorns, so is my close one among the daughters.** He likens her to a lily because she has never entertained care or worry for corporeal things, and because she takes care of her bodily needs as they arise without being obsessed by them. For so he teaches in the Gospels as well, saying, "Why are you anxious about clothing? Consider the lilies of the field, how they grow; they neither toil nor spin" (Matt. 6:28). He is showing that those who have chosen a way of life that is uncalculating and free of compulsive striving because it is focused on the kingdom of heaven are the nearest thing there is to lilies, which effortlessly dress themselves in a natural splendor more interior than that of Solomon's royal robe; and he likens the rest to thorns because they direct all their care upon the things of this present life. It is no longer the case that their inward fixations are called thorns; no, they themselves, because of their intense devotion to things earthly, have shaped themselves after the character of thorns and, starting from the thorns within them as from a worst possible state of mind, have changed themselves into thorns. Perhaps Paul betrothed himself to Christ for the sake of being one with him as "a pure virgin" (cf. 2 Cor. 11:2), a **lily among thorns**, "among whom," he said, "you shine as lights in the world," and "that you may be . . . children of God without blemish in the midst of a crooked and perverse generation" (Phil. 2:15). But what generation is this, that is made crooked by its perversity? Moses makes the answer plain when he says to nonbelievers, "Crooked and perverse generation, do you thus requite the Lord?" (Deut. 32:5-6). But the Bride takes a straight path, and for that reason she is loved by Righteousness (cf. 1:4), that is, by Christ the Bridegroom.

(5) Rupert of Deutz

I am a flower of the field
    and a lily of the valleys.

As you say, my dear one, I am **beautiful . . . and fair**, for **I am a flower of the field and a lily of the valleys** — which is to say, the ornament of the human race and the glory of our humble forebears, the fathers — such as Abraham, Isaac, and Jacob, and David too — that were "poor in spirit" (Matt. 5:3), and all the rest, who, though they stood as high as mountains in virtue of their merits, were **valleys** in their own minds; though rich in esteem, were "poor in spirit." Thus I am their ornament and their beauty — true flower, true lily, because "splendid in form beyond the sons of men" (Ps. 44:3 Vg = 45:2), for there is not one of the sons of men who possesses this form in the way that I do. The lily, be it noted, is a plant whose flower is white like milk; and while its bright show is located in its petals, it nevertheless gleams on the inside with the brilliance of gold. That is the precise way in which I am **a flower of the field** or **lily** — a milk-white flower, the most pure of children: **a flower**, I say, and the **lily** of chastity; but while its flesh or humanity, its outside, is as pure as can be, on the inside the brilliance of its Divinity is incapable of being equaled.

(6) The *Glossa ordinaria*

As a lily among thorns,
   so is my Beloved among the daughters.

In the Church there cannot be bad persons without good ones, or good persons without bad ones. There has never been a good person who could not tolerate the bad ones.

(7) Augustine of Hippo

As a lily among thorns,
   so is my close one among the daughters.

"We have received your mercy, O God, in the midst of your people" (Ps. 47:8 LXX = 48:9). Who is it that "received," and where did they receive it? Was it not your people themselves that received your mercy? And if it was your people that received your mercy, how it is that "We have received your mercy," and "in the midst of your people," as if there were some who received and others in whose midst they received?

This is a great mystery but not an unfamiliar one. And after what is familiar to you has been extracted and dug out of these lines, the result will not be something unheard of, but something very sweet.

Now we may be sure that all who bear God's mysteries are reckoned to be his people, but not all attain to his mercy. Certainly all who take to themselves the mystery of the baptism of Christ are called Christians; but not all live in a manner that is worthy of that mystery, for the apostle describes certain persons as "having the form of true religion, but rejecting its power" (2 Tim. 3:5). Nevertheless, on account of that same appearance of true religion, they are named among the people of God, just as it is not only the wheat but the chaff that belongs on the threshing floor as long as the threshing continues. But does it also have a place in the granary?

In the midst of a wicked people, then, there is a good people that receives the mercy of God. It lives worthily of the mercy of God because it hears and obeys and performs what the apostle enjoins: "We admonish you and beseech you not to receive the grace of God in vain" (2 Cor. 6:1). Those, then, who do not receive the grace of God in vain receive both the mystery and the mercy of God.

And what harm does it do them that they are in the midst of a disobedient people until the threshing floor is winnowed, until the good are separated from the wicked? What harm does it do them to live in the midst of the people? Let them be of the number of those that are called "firm support." Let them be the lily in the midst of thorns. For the thorns themselves belong to the people of God, as you can hear if you wish. That is what the comparison itself says: **As a lily,** it says, **among thorns, so is my close one among the daughters.** It does not say, "among outsiders," does it? Not at all; but "among the daughters." So there are wicked daughters, and in among them is the **lily among thorns.** Therefore, those who have the mysteries and do not have good morals are said both to belong to God and not to belong to God. They are said to be his and the Outsider's: his on account of his very own [baptismal] mystery, and the Outsider's on account of the vice proper to him. So too there are daughters that are outsiders: daughters because of "the form of true religion," and outsiders because of lost virtue. . . .

Song 2:3-7

SEPTUAGINT

2:3 As an apple tree among the trees of
the wood,
    so is my Kinsman among
the sons.
In his shadow I rejoiced and sat
down,
    and his fruit was sweet in my
throat.
4 Bring me into the house of wine.

    Set love in order upon me.
5 Strengthen me with perfumes,
    encompass me with apples,
    for I have been wounded by love.
6 His left hand is under my head,
    and his right hand shall embrace
me.
7 I have charged you, O daughters of
Jerusalem,
    by the powers and virtues of
the field,
    not to rouse or waken love

    as far as it wishes.

VULGATE

2:3 As an apple tree among the trees of
the woods,
    so is my Beloved among the sons.

Under the shadow of him whom I
was desiring I sat down,
    and his fruit was sweet to my
throat.
4 The King has brought me into his
wine cellar;
    he has set love in order within me.
5 Sustain me with flowers,
    surround me with apples,
    for I am fainting with love.
6 His left hand is under my head,
    and his right hand shall embrace
me.
7 I adjure you, daughters of Jerusalem,

    by the gazelles and stags of the field,

    not to rouse my beloved or waken
her
    until she herself wishes.

*In this section, the Bride is apparently addressing the "daughters of Jerusalem"
and in effect responding to her consort's description of her as "my close one
among the daughters." In 2:4, however, the Septuagint mistakenly takes the verb
("bring me . . .") to be a command and thus makes the verse sound as though it
were addressed to the Bridegroom — which of course means that Greek-speaking*

interpreters took it that way. The imperative is correct, however, in 2:5 ("Strengthen me . . ."), where, however, the Bride is plainly speaking not to her Lover but to the chorus of her hearers.

The description of the Bridegroom as an "apple tree" among the uncultivated trees of a wild thicket makes Gregory of Nyssa think again of the incarnation and its transformative power: he pictures the apple tree as somehow sharing and enhancing the existence and the produce ("fruit") of the other trees. In Origen's case, however, the incarnation lurks only in the back of his mind. In this excerpt, he seizes on the reference to the Bridegroom's "shadow" and develops its meaning in the light of a verse from Lamentations and another from Hebrews: to live and to rejoice in the shadow of Christ, as believers now do, is to enjoy both his life-giving power and his protection; but it is also to know him only in a preliminary way, still "shaded" by the here-and-now obscurity of the "letter" of Scripture and of Christ's own existence in the life forms of humanity in "this age."

Inevitably, the reference to the Word's "setting love in order" in or upon the Bride produces in Christian exegetes a series of observations on the double commandment of love for God and neighbor, and on the different kinds of love proper to different human relationships. Among contemporary scholars, on the other hand, there is general agreement that this represents a wrong interpretation of the Hebrew expression rendered "set in order" — though there is less certainty about what a correct rendering might be.

A further difficulty is found in the last line of 2:7, which literally reads, in the LXX, "if you rouse or waken love until it wishes" — a clause that seems to make little or no sense in Greek (or English) in the context of the rest of the verse. It appears, however, that this way of talking represented a kind of abbreviated formula for a curse. The "daughters of Jerusalem" are told that if they do what this conditional clause specifies, things will somehow go ill for them, though this consequence is left unexpressed. Thus Jerome's Latin paraphrases the meaning of the clause properly: it is in effect a prohibition. The daughters are told not to rouse or waken love. Even if one understands this, however, Nilus of Ancyra (who did not understand it) is correct: it is hard to know whose love, or what love, is to be allowed to have its own way.

(1) Gregory of Nyssa

As an apple tree among the trees of the wood,
 so is my Kinsman among the young men.

. . . again the Bride rises above herself and contemplates a mystery by means of the eyes of the dove (i.e., by the Spirit of prophecy).

This is what she sees: **As an apple tree among the trees of the wood, so is my Kinsman among the young men.** What is it, then, that she has seen? As its custom is, the Holy

Scripture assigns the name "wood" to that material life of the human race which is bursting with various sorts of passions — the wood in which destroyer beasts lurk and hide, whose kind accomplishes nothing in the light of the sun but takes its strength from darkness. For after the sun has set, the prophet says, when night has come, "the wild beasts of the wood" (Ps. 103:20 LXX = 104:20) come out of their lairs. The wild boar that feeds in the thicket ravages the beautiful vineyard of human nature — as the prophet says, "The wild boar ravaged it, and the wild pig grazed over it" (Ps. 79:14 LXX = 80:13); and this explains why the **apple tree** is planted in the midst of the thicket. Because it is a tree, it is of the same substance as the stuff of humanity (he was tried "in every way in accordance with his likeness to us, apart from sin" [Heb. 4:15]); but because it bears a fruit by which the perceptive faculties of the soul are touched with sweetness, it differs to a greater degree from the **wood** than the **lily** does from the thorns. The **lily** is pleasing in its appearance and its scent; but the delight afforded by the apple is shared, in a way suited to each, among three senses: it gladdens the eye by the splendor of its appearance; by its scent it gives pleasure to the sense of smell; and as food it provides sweetness to the organs of taste.

The Bride was right, then, to discern a difference between herself and the Lord. He is joy to our eyes when he comes as light, perfume for our sense of smell, and life to those who eat him (for anyone who eats him will live, as the Gospel says somewhere [John 6:51ff.]). On the other hand, human nature, when through virtue it achieves its fulfillment, becomes no more than a flower that does not feed its planter but adorns itself. For he stands in no need of our good things, but we stand in need of his, as the prophet says: "You have no need of my goods" (Ps. 15:2 LXX = 16:2).

Why is it that the soul that has been purified perceives the Bridegroom as **an apple tree** in the midst of the thicket's bushes? So that when he has grafted all the wild branches into himself, he will equip them to abound with fruit like his own. Thus because they are likened to thorns, we understand the **daughters** to be children of the counterfeit Father (cf. John 8:41, 44), but children who, once they have grown alongside the flower and together with it, are themselves changed as time goes on into the beauty of the lily. In the same way, when we hear of persons who resemble the trees of the wood, we presume that what is meant is not the friends but the enemies of the Bridegroom. Yet though they be sons of darkness and children of wrath, he transmutes them into sons of light and sons of peace by their sharing in the fruit he bears. This is the reason why the soul that has trained its organs of sense says, **His fruit was sweet in my throat.** The word **fruit**, certainly, means teaching; for the prophet says, "Thy words are sweet to my throat, sweeter than honey to my mouth" (Ps. 118:103 LXX = 119:103).

(2) Origen

In his shadow I rejoiced and sat down.

But as to that **shadow** under which the Church says that she had desired to sit, I think it is a good idea to call attention to passages in the divine Scriptures that provide a worthier and more elevated understanding of what the **shadow** of this **apple tree** signifies.

In Lamentations, Jeremiah says, "The breath of our face, Christ the Lord,[1] has been caught up in our corruptions, to whom we said, 'We shall live in his shadow among the nations'" (Lam. 4:20). You see, then, how the prophet, moved by the Holy Spirit, says that life is supplied to the nations by the shadow of Christ — and how should his shadow not supply us with life, considering that at the conception of his own body it is said to Mary, "The Holy Spirit will come upon you, and the power of the Most High will overshadow you" (Luke 1:35)?

If, then, at the conception of his body, the overshadowing was that of "the Most High," his shadow shall justly give life to the nations. Justly too, his Bride the Church desires to sit **under the shadow** of the apple tree — no doubt with a view to becoming a participant in the life that is in his shadow. On the other hand, the shadow of the rest of **the trees of the wood** is such that anyone who sits under it might be taken to sit in the region of the shadow of death.

But more than this, in order that the text we are considering may be rendered more clearly, let us inquire what the apostle means when he says, "The law has . . . a shadow of the good things to come" (Heb. 10:1), and relates that everything that is written about feast days or sabbaths or new moons (cf. Col. 2:16) is "a shadow of the good things to come" — with reference, of course, to things done according to the letter; and also what he means by asserting that all the worship of the ancients was "a copy and shadow" (Heb. 8:5) of heavenly things. If this is so, then it is apparent that all those who were under the law and had a shadow rather than the true law sat **under the shadow** of the law.

We, however, are strangers to their shadow, because we are "not under the law but under grace" (Rom. 6:15). But even though we are not **under** the **shadow** cast by the letter of the law, nevertheless we are **under** a better **shadow**. For "in the shadow" of Christ we "live among the nations" (Lam. 4:20 LXX). Furthermore, to come from the shadow of the law to the shadow of Christ is a kind of progress. Thus, since Christ is "the life and the truth and the way" (John 14:6), our first step is to come into the shadow of the way and the shadow of the life and the shadow of the truth, and to understand "in part" and "in a mirror in an enigma" (1 Cor. 13:12), in order that after this, if we make progress in the way that is Christ, we may come to the point of understanding "face to face" (1 Cor. 13:12) the things that we previously saw in a shadow and "in an enigma." For no one can attain the things that are real and perfect unless he has first desired and craved to abide in this shadow.

Job, moreover, says that the life of human beings "on the earth" is "a shadow" (1 Chron. 29:15; cf. Job 7:2) — for the reason, I reckon, that in this life every soul is clouded over by the veil of this dense body.

Hence it is a matter of necessity that all those who are in this present life be in a shadow of one sort or another. Some of them, however, are sitting "in the region" of the "shadow of death" (Matt. 4:16) — those, surely, who do not believe Christ; but the Church trustfully says: **in the shadow** of the Bridegroom **I rejoiced and sat down** — even though there was a time when a person who stayed under the shadow of the law could be defended from the rigors of heat and of tempest. That time, however, has passed away. In

---

1. Origen's text of the Septuagint here reads *Christos Kyrios,* that is, literally, "the Lord anointed."

these times, one must come to the shadow of the apple tree; and though someone may make use of a different shadow, it seems to me that every soul must, for as long as it is in this present life, have a shadow because — in my judgment — of the heat of the sun, which, when it has risen, ceaselessly dries up and destroys the seed that has not put its roots deep down (cf. Matt. 13:6). The shadow of the law wards off this heat with indifferent success; but the "shadow" of Christ in which we now "live . . . among the nations" — that is, faith in his incarnation — turns it away and extinguishes it (for the one who used to burn up those who walked under the shadow of the law was seen, at the time of Christ's suffering, to have fallen "like lightning from heaven" [Luke 10:18]). In any case, the time of this shadow too will be fulfilled at the end of the age because, as we have said, after the consummation of the age we will no longer see the truth "in a mirror" and "in an enigma," but "face to face."

(3) Apponius

Under his shadow I rejoiced and sat down,
   and his fruit was sweet in my throat.
The King has brought me into his wine cellar;
   he has set love in order within me.

Under his shadow, freed from the tossings of sour regret and from every weight of sin, the Church has experienced the rest she had so desired and has fed upon the sweetest fruit of all; and so she tells the youthful souls of the joy that has become hers: **In his shadow I rejoiced and sat down, and his fruit was sweet in my throat.** And so she bears witness that she has been introduced step by step into higher mysteries: The King **brought me into his wine cellar; he set love in order within me.**

Thus she summons the youthful souls, and by her praises charges them to hasten to that sweetness which in his teaching Christ sets out for their enjoyment when he says, "Do a work that does not perish but which endures to eternal life" (cf. John 6:27). This is the work regarding which he says that Mary has chosen a better portion than Martha; and he also says, "Blessed are the eyes that see what you see, and blessed are the ears that hear what you hear" (Luke 10:23 and Matt. 13:16-17). In like terms, the prophet too asserts that those who are engaged in this work are blessed when he says, "Blessed are those who keep his testimonies, who seek him with their whole heart" (Ps. 118:2 LXX = 119:2). For in the law of the Old Testament there are testimonies that show how Christ is coming, has arrived, and will come again in glory.

Let us, then, assert that the divine law is the most spacious of palaces, in which Christ the King dwells, the Word of the almighty Father, and **into** which the souls of the faithful are **brought** to constitute an everlasting military array. There, even though all who are brought in are the soldiery of a single King, nevertheless each one, to the extent that he has given good service, attains a high rank and with great boldness occupies a place at the King's side.

Therefore this queen, whose figure is brought on stage and speaks, sets forth for the young maidens a step-by-step account of the progress she has made in the wisdom of God. First of all, at the start of this Song, as though still anxious or desirous of that food which she describes as **sweet in** her **throat**, she rejoices that she has been brought **into the wine cellar** of the King — which, as we have said, means the multiform wisdom of God. There souls are introduced to knowledge of the one true God, leaving behind the service of a multitude of base deities. Here, however, raised already to a much nobler estate, she sees herself brought, by understanding of the law of the Old Covenant, to reflect on the marvels that God has wrought by the individual patriarchs and prophets up to the point where the virgin gave birth. It is these to which, using a figure, she assigns the name **wine cellar.**

Once **brought into** this place, she has appropriated within herself the way in which love is ordered — the manner in which she must understand how all the things that were solemnly observed in the Old Covenant are spiritually reimaged in the coming of the Christ; and the manner in which the things that the prophets say about God by analogy with human nature are not set forth because of any deficiency in God, but in order that human weakness may, to the extent possible, discern in the ordering of the Trinity the greatness of God — the love of God that, according to the apostle Paul, remains forever.

In this ordering of love, the first thing it is necessary to learn is to believe and to acknowledge that first of all the Father is to be named, in whom the Son ever exists, like the word in the voice; in the second place, the Son, in whom the Father is always present; and in the third place, the Holy Spirit, who is affirmed truly to proceed from the voice and the word, from the Father and the Son. This accords with the opening words of the Decalogue: "You shall love the Lord your God with all your heart"; then in the second place, "with all your soul"; and in the third place, "with all your strength" (Matt. 22:37 and Mark 12:30). After that, love is ordered in the Church by the individual precepts of the law, which indicate in what way or with what kind of affection one's neighbor, or particular individuals, are to be loved.

Once she is **brought in**, she rejoices, not that she has achieved the very height of understanding of the divine law, but that love has been **set in order within her**; for the door that affords entrance to the entire royal palace of which we have spoken is this: to believe in the one true God, unique and everlasting. This is in order that we may learn that anyone can have some sort of love, but not anyone can have love that is **set in order**. The only ones who possess a true, perfect, and ordered love are those who by their love of the divine law have shown themselves worthy of being **brought into** comprehension of the law in which he has taught us that the ordering of love is to be found. For unless one has understood, on the basis of God's commands, what must be hated, what is to be loved with a perfect love — like the one who said to God: "Through your precepts I have gotten understanding; therefore I have hated every false way" (Ps. 118:104 LXX = 119:104) — and to whom the duty of love is owed, as well as the manner and the form of love that is owed, one's love will appear disordered and unacceptable to God.

For there is one order of love in the responsive love that is to be rendered to God — the God who, according to the apostle, first loved us (cf. 1 John 4:19), who is shown to have conferred love in its wholeness upon us in Christ. Another order of love is to be given to our parents, through whose agency we exist when before we did not. Another is that accorded a faithful friend, and yet another is love for a son most dear. Another order of love is directed to a brother, and another to a spouse. Another order is that owed by a servant to a master, and another, that owed by a master to a servant. Of still another order is the love to be paid a fellow citizen, while another is that to be accorded a foreigner. There is an order of love due to great personages, and another due a bishop, and another due relatives or neighbors.

For to bestow necessities upon the needy, or the sick, or the stranger, not for the sake of a display of human praise, but on account of an eternal reward — this is an evidence of ordered love. To bring relief to those who mourn or those beaten down by an unjust judgment, to visit the sick or those in prison is a proof of ordered love. Never, in any cause or business, to favor rank or status in despite of the truth, mercifully to counsel the unwise, truthfully to rebuke the arrogant — in this is manifested the ordering of love. But if someone loves father or mother, or wife or children or brothers, or the riches of the present age, more than God, there is love in such a one, but it is not ordered. Such love, moreover, in time of persecution, does much to hold people back from bearing witness and sometimes even occasions loss of the crown of martyrdom. What demonstrates the presence of ordered love is the suffering of manifold torments for the name of Christ, and the laying down of one's life on behalf of the brethren out of a love of justice.

In order, then, that every child of the Church may know what order of love determines the sort of duty he owes to each person, the Son of God **set love in order** in his Church by saying, "Render . . . to Caesar the things that are Caesar's, and to God the things that are God's" (Matt. 22:21). And through the blessed apostle Paul he says, "Pay all of them their dues, honor to whom honor is due, fear to whom fear is due, tribute to whom tribute is due, revenue to whom revenue is due" (Rom. 13:7). It is not everyone, however, who is called a Christian who is **brought into** this ordering of love, that is, into the aforesaid understanding that he calls a **wine cellar**; but it is the person who shall have been, in however small a way, an imitator of the Paul who said, "I have worked harder than all, in vigils, in fasting, in many labors, in hunger and cold" (cf. 1 Cor. 15:10 and 2 Cor. 6:5; 11:27), and the other things mentioned in his letters; and further, "I count them as refuse, in order that I may gain Christ" (Phil. 3:8).

(4) Theodoret of Cyrus

Bring me into the house of wine.
   Set love in order upon me.
Strengthen me with perfumes,
   encompass me with apples,
   for I have been wounded by love.

It is my view that when she says **house of wine**, what she means is the divine wine presses. Regarding these the prophet says, "How lovely are thy tabernacles, O Lord of hosts! My soul longs, yea, faints, for the courts of the Lord"; for he added these words after he had given the psalm the title "Concerning the wine presses" (Ps. 83:1 LXX = 84:1), and his teaching is that the churches of God are wine presses when the spiritual wine is pressed out in them and — thoroughly trodden, as it were — gives delight to the souls of the faithful in accordance with the saying, "They are drunk on the abundance of thy house, and thou givest them drink from the river of thy delights" (Ps. 35:9 LXX = 36:8).

This is why the Bride wants to enter his **house of wine**, and exhorts the Bridegroom's servants in these words: **Set love in order upon me**, that is to say, teach me the way to love, so that I do not love father or mother above the Bridegroom, or field or vineyards, and so seem unworthy of the Bridegroom. For he himself spoke out and said, "Whoever loves father or mother more than me is not worthy of me; and whoever loves sons or daughters more than me is not worthy of me" (Matt. 10:37). Even the old law that was given to Adam says things like this: "Therefore a man leaves his father and his mother and cleaves to his wife, and they become one flesh" (Gen. 2:24). Therefore, **Set love in order upon me,** that I may be joined to my Bridegroom and value him more highly than father, and mother, and everything else.

Strengthen me with perfumes — that is, "Support me with the fragrance of the Bridegroom, and secure me, so that nothing may shake me, ever showering me with that fragrance, so that I forget not my Bridegroom and wander off after others." But also **encompass me with apples**, which means: "Load me down with my Bridegroom's fruits, in order that, seated under his shadow, and catching the scent of his perfume, and loaded with his fruit, I may keep his memory unfailingly." **For I have been wounded by love,** for he is after all the chosen arrow (Isa. 49:2) that wounds the souls it strikes.

(5) William of St. Thierry

The King has brought me into his wine cellar.

For she who had previously departed from [the King's] **cellars** (cf. 1:4), mature in her devotion, and was worriedly seeking contemplation, has now been tested and approved in all respects, cleansed to the point of being pure, rendered properly humble, and she is beginning to make her entrance into the place of the wondrous tabernacle, all the way to the house of God (cf. Ps. 41:5 Vg = 42:4), so that there she may recline at table and taste the joy she had formerly desired with great impatience when she said, **Declare to me, you whom my soul loves, where you pasture, where you take your rest at noontide** (1:6).

For just as we have already stated above, these are the very riches of which the prophet speaks: "The riches of salvation are wisdom and knowledge" (Isa. 33:6). In knowledge, that is, in the **cellars**, reason and understanding are fed and nurtured. In wisdom, which is the **wine cellar**, love and desire are nourished. The former things are known, the latter are relished. In the one place, the search for exactness and clarity is at work; but in the other there is nothing save the rejoicing that accompanies the experience of fulfillment. Not everyone can participate in the benefits of knowledge; they are imported from without at the cost of hard work on the part of learners. But the pleasures of wisdom are discovered even by simple children of God — any who in their goodness possess awareness of God and who seek God in simplicity of heart; and these pleasures are encountered as if they were inward formations of nature, brought gratuitously to birth, without labor. So then the **wine cellar** is a sort of hiding place for the wisdom of God, the condition of the mind that is wholly drawn to God. Like the temple of God, such a mind is separated from the heavenly realm, the Holy of Holies, solely by an interposed veil, that of the mortal body — though it possesses a sure and intimate communion with the heavenly realm in proportion to the measure of its progress and to the gift of illuminating grace. There too is found the bed that is **full of flowers** (cf. 1:16), the bed full of delights, which the Bride was seeking but a moment before, though she would not receive it under the beams (cf. 1:17) of faith and hope, but only in the fullness of love, which is the **wine cellar**.

For love, or, better, the conscience that is made clear by love's perfection, is the **wine cellar**; while the wine that is in this wine cellar is joy in the Holy Spirit. Hence there is nothing but wine in the wine cellar. Whatever enters it, whatever is brought into it, either is wine or becomes wine; for the fire of divine love takes it over, every bit, and consumes it and, like ordinary fire, changes it into its own nature, since "all things work together for good" for one who loves God (Rom. 8:28).

In that place — by the abundance of wine and the plenty of God's house, by the torrent of delight — love is brought to a boil, it overflows in its elation, it delights in its object, to the point that it may often appear disordered, unless the King restores it to order. Thus Paul chooses to be "accursed and cut off from Christ for the sake of" his "brethren" (Rom. 9:3); and Moses asks that his name be removed from the book of life if the mortal sin of God's people is not forgiven (cf. Exod. 32:32). If the conscience that is clear in its conformity with God should be afflicted as touching matters that have to do with the business of love — if it is seized with sympathy and shares grief; this does not diminish its joy but enhances it. For in the happy consciousness in which it is rooted, the joy of the Lord is not disrupted by any worldly sadness that breaks in, nor is it obscured by any empty delight. It is sustained and held together, steadily and securely, in its uninterrupted course. Always and at every point it is serene, and it does not undergo change even though it gives of itself in a multitude of ways. There the turmoils that mark human affairs have no effect, any more than do the strifes of tongues (cf. Ps. 30:21 LXX = 31:20). Far removed from it are vain delight, every sort of sadness — there, once the old humanity has been done to death, the only thing that is alive is the mind that has tasted the sweetness of the highest good and the desire that motivates piety. Far removed from it are all the things that normally invade the self: empty and pointless merriments, which bring color to the face but do not fill the heart; which moisten the skin but do not reach the inward parts. These are the destructive joys of the present age, which bring with them idle imaginings of amusements, which take away whatever there was of energy or strength in the mind, which disappear and fluctuate, and are more hurtful than any sadness.

(6) Nilus of Ancyra

Bring me into the house of wine.
  Set love in order upon me.

With good reason the Bride finally requests to be brought **into the house of wine**. For she alone believed beforehand in the grape cluster hanging upon the cross — the grape cluster that was despised by everyone because while still in bloom it failed to exhibit the qualities and advantages of wine to everyone; the grape cluster that would manifest its true identity at a later time. The Bride had fixed firmly in her thinking — and before the proper season — a notion of wine that enabled her to discern the wine beforehand in the flowering vine, and to bear witness beforehand to the exalted Deity within the one who hung on a cross, and to picture for herself impassibility within suffering and resurrection within death. She had firmly grasped — as though it had already been spoken — the message, soon to be pressed out, of the grape cluster on the cross; and before the outcome of it all, she experienced what everyone else experienced only after the event. Hence she requests the special privilege proper to such discernment — entrance into **the house of wine**.

But if the Word is wine, then the Father will be **the house of wine**; for in him the Word is found, as he himself says, "I am in the Father and the Father in me" (John 14:11); and again, "Do you not know that I must be [busy] among the things of my Father?" (Luke 2:49). Perhaps it was out of a desire to see **the house of wine** that Philip said to the Lord, "Show us the Father, and we shall be satisfied" (John 14:8).

(7) Augustine of Hippo

Set love in order within me.

Therefore do not take what I have said — "Let him delight you who is the source of whatever delights you" — as referring to sin and say, "Sin surely delights me. Is God then the source of my sin?"

First of all, you must understand that it may not be sin that delights you at all. It may be that when you commit sin, something else delights you. When you love a created thing in a disordered way, when you love it in a way that is contrary to proper practice, contrary to what is licit, contrary to the law and will of the Creator himself, then by your love for a created thing, you sin. You do not love the sin itself, but by wrongly loving what you love, you are entrapped by sin. You grasp after food in a snare, and fill yourself with sin. Then you defend the act this way: If it is sin to drink a great deal, why did God create wine? If it is sin to love gold, I am a lover of gold, not of its Creator. God is the Creator of gold; why did he create what it is wrong to love? So with other things that you love wrongly, things that involve excess and extravagance, when many disgraceful acts are committed: notice, observe, consider that everything created by God is good, and that there is no sin in it, unless you make wrong use of it.

Hear this, then. You say, "Why did God create what he forbids me to love? He might not have created, and then there would be nothing for me to love; he might not have made room for any of the created things that he charges me not to love, and there would be nothing for me to love and be condemned for loving."

If that created thing — the thing that you love wrongly because you do not love yourself either — could speak, it would answer you thus: "You prefer that God should not create me, lest there be something for you to love. So see how unfair you are; and it is by your words themselves that you are discovered most unfair of all. You want God to create you and that which is above you, but you do not want him to create any other good. That which God has made for you is good; but there are other goods, some great, others small, some earthly, others spiritual, and others again temporal. All of them, however, are good things because he who is good made things that are good. That is why, somewhere in the divine Scriptures, it is said: **Set love in order within me.** God made you as a good thing. Under himself — and under you too — he made something of a lower order. You are higher than one thing, and lower than another. Do not desert the higher good and bend yourself down toward the lower. Be upright of heart, so that you may have praise; for "those that are upright of heart shall be praised" (cf. Ps. 31:11 Vg = 32:11). For why do you sin, save that you deal in a disordered way with things that you have received for use? Make correct use of things that are below you, and you will rightly enjoy the higher good.

(8) Origen

Strengthen me with perfumes,
  encompass me with apples,
  for I have been wounded by love.

Thus the Church is encompassed **with apples** and rests on them. Now these apples must be taken to be those souls that "are being renewed . . . after the image of the One who created them" (cf. Col. 3:10). For given that in renewing themselves the children of God are restoring God's image, they themselves are deservedly styled apple trees, since their Bridegroom too has been said above to be like **an apple tree among the trees of the wood** (2:3). And do not marvel if this very same one is called **apple tree** and "tree of life" (Rev. 2:7) and many other things as well, since the same one is named "true bread" (John 6:32) and "true vine" (John 15:1) and "Lamb of God" (John 1:29) and many other things. For the Word of God becomes all of these things to each person, according as the aptitude and the desire of each requires — in just the way that the manna did, which, even though it was a single food, would nevertheless provide for each individual the taste that matched his wants. Thus he not only presents his very self as bread to those who are hungry and as wine to the thirsty, but he also manifests himself as sweet-scented apples to those who covet delights.

For this reason, then, the Bride too — now restored and well nourished — asks that she may be stayed **with apples,** for she knows that for her not only all nourishing food but also all delights reside in the Word; and it is these in particular that she runs through mentally when she feels herself **wounded** by the darts of **love**. If there be anyone anywhere who has ever burned with this unwavering love for the Word of God; if there be anyone who, as the prophet says, has received the sweet wound of this "chosen arrow" (Isa. 49:2 LXX); if there be anyone who has been pierced through and through by the lovable javelin of the knowledge of him, so as to long for him by day and by night, to be unable to speak of anything else, to refuse to hear anything else, to know not how to think anything else, to have no inclination to desire or want or hope for anything else except him — this is the soul that deservedly says, **I have been wounded by love**, and has received the wound from him of whom Isaiah says, "He established me as a chosen arrow, and hid me in his quiver" (Isa. 49:2).

It is right and proper for God to smite souls with a wound like this, to transfix them with spears and darts like these, and to hurt them with these saving wounds, so that, since "God is love" (1 John 4:8), they too may say for themselves, **I have been wounded by love**. And in truth the Bride in this love-story-like drama says that the wounds that she has sustained are those **of love**. Moreover, a soul that in a similar way burns with desire for God's Wisdom — a soul, I mean, that is able to discern the beauty of Wisdom — can say, **I have been wounded by** Wisdom. Further, yet another soul, one that perceives the grandeur of the Word of God and has wondered at his power, can say, **I have been wounded by** Strength — such a soul as her that said, "The Lord is my light and my salvation; whom then shall I fear? The Lord is the strength of my life; of whom then shall I be afraid?" (Ps. 26:1 LXX = 27:1). But again another soul, burning with love of his justice, and perceiving the justice of his dispensations and his providence, surely says, **I have been wounded by** justice. And another, that sees the immeasurable greatness of his goodness and his goodwill, says similar things. What includes all of these, however, is that wound of love by which the Bride proclaims she has been wounded. . . .

His left hand is under my head, and his right hand shall embrace me. This description, which belongs to a love story in the form of a drama, is of a bride who is hastening to consummate her marriage with her bridegroom. But turn yourself swiftly to the "life-giving spirit" (1 Cor. 15:45). Set aside talk of bodily things. Discern clearly what is the **left hand** and what the **right hand** of the Word of God, and also what the **head** of his Bride is, that is to say, of the perfected soul or of the Church; and let not a meaning that refers to things fleshly and passible carry you away.

For in this text the **right hand** and the **left hand** refer to the very things that are said about Wisdom in Proverbs, where it is stated: "Long life is in her right hand; in her left hand are riches and glory" (Prov. 3:16). And just as in this place you will not suppose that Wisdom is being called a woman because she seems to have a feminine appellation, so neither should you understand the **right hand** or **left hand** of the Word of God in a bodily sense merely because he is called "Bridegroom" in the masculine gender, or understand the Bride's embraces in a bodily sense because "bride" has a feminine ending. On the contrary, even though "Word of God" comes out in Greek as masculine in gender, but with us [Latin speakers] as neuter, the realities of which the passage speaks are to be taken as transcending masculine and neuter and feminine, and as transcending absolutely everything that words of this sort refer to; and this is the case not only with the

Word of God, but also with his Church and with the perfect soul who is called his Bride. For so the apostle himself says: in Christ "there is neither male nor female, but we are all one in him" (cf. Gal. 3:28).

For realities of this sort are rendered by the divine Scripture in the manner of human speech for the sake of human readers since they are unable to take such realities in except by way of words they customarily employ. The aim of this is that we may take these realities in by way of familiar and accustomed language, and understand them, in the sense that is worthy of them, as having to do with things divine and incorporeal. For just as someone who says that he is a lover of Wisdom's beauty shows that he has transferred the natural love that is part of him to the quest for Wisdom, so too in the text before us the Bride who is the Church requests that her Bridegroom, the Word of God, will support her **head** with his **left hand**, while with his **right hand** he embraces all the rest of her body and holds it tight.

Now the **left hand** is the one in which Wisdom is said to hold "riches and glory." But what riches does the Church possess, and what glory, if it be not those that she has received from him who "though he was rich became poor, so that by his poverty" the Church "might become rich" (2 Cor. 8:9)? And what is this "glory"? Beyond all doubt it is that of which he says, "Father, glorify your Son" (cf. John 12:28), by these words referring surely to the glory of his passion. It is, then, the Church's faith in the passion of Christ that is her glory and riches, and these are held in his left hand. I take it that the **left hand** of the Word of God should be understood in this way, on the ground that there are in him certain dispensations carried through prior to the incarnation, but there are also others carried through by means of the incarnation. That part of the Word of God which was executed in dispensations prior to the incarnation can be seen as the **right hand**, while the latter, which were carried out through the incarnation, can be assigned to the left hand. That explains why "riches and glory" are said to be in the left hand; for through the incarnation he sought "riches and glory," that is, the salvation of all nations. In the **right hand**, however, there is said to be "long life," by which surely there is indicated that everlastingness of his in virtue of which the Word is God with God from the beginning.

It follows that the Church, whose **head** is Christ, wishes to have this **left hand** under her head, and to have her head secured and supported by her faith in his incarnation, while she is embraced by his **right hand** — that is to say, she knows and is taught about the things that are contained in the mysteries and hidden matters that came about before the time of the dispensation of the flesh. In short, all those things are right-handed that come about where there is nothing of sinners' wretchedness or of weakness's fall to be found, but left-handed, where our wounds are cured and he himself, who for us became sin and was accursed, bore our sins — all of which, even though they support the head and the faith of the Church, are nonetheless called the Word of God's left-handed works. In the number of these there are some that he is stated to have suffered contrary to that nature which is wholly of the right hand, wholly light and splendor and glory.

(9) Bede the Venerable

Sustain me with flowers,
  surround me with apples,
  for I am fainting with love.

The soul that **faints with love** is the soul that truly tastes the love that her Creator directs to her; for when she rouses herself to seek the eternal Light, she grows weary of this love of things temporal, so that the more ardently she rises up to contemplate the joys of the everlasting kingdom, the more she cools toward concern for the age that is passing away.

But let us see upon what couch the soul that burns with such love seeks to recline in her weakened state. **Sustain me**, she says, **with flowers, surround me with apples.** "Flowers" signifies the tender beginnings of the virtues, while "apples" signifies their perfection. Hence the soul that is **fainting with love** entreats the daughters of Jerusalem — that is to say, the souls that have surpassed her in desire for things heavenly — to support the beginning she has made with their good examples, and frequently to summon to memory the start, the way, or the end by which they have followed out the way of the virtues, in order that with the help of what she thus takes in — a supremely pleasing scent, as it were, of flowers and apples — she may rest with greater ease and delight upon the goodwill of her Creator.

(10) Nilus of Ancyra

I have charged you, O daughters of Jerusalem,
  by the powers and by the virtues of the field,
to rouse or waken love
  as far as it wishes.

This verse is exceedingly puzzling. It is nonetheless often right to let the understanding run free in its search for the point of a text — in imitation of people practicing archery, who loose many arrows at the target but can hardly hit it even once. Indeed, those who make the divine Scripture their study are quite like archers: they direct their arts like an arrow at the target of the passage. It is not easy, in this case, to say which of the characters [in the Song] is the proper subject of the act of wakening love — or, to put it better, the act of wakening is plainly assigned to the "daughters of Jerusalem," but it is not at all obvious in whom love is to be wakened, whether in themselves, in the Bridegroom, or in the very one who is speaking. For this reason, we must try to fit the verse to all of these subjects, and whichever arrow, when fired, turns out to come close to love or to the truth must be adjudged the winner.

If, then, the Bride wants love to be awakened in the "daughters of Jerusalem," she can say something on the following order: "You indolent people, unaware of what really counts! How great a gain you overlook because of your inexperience — the gain that accrues, just because of their love, to those who love the Bridegroom! I charge you by the powers of the field who administer the world, and by their virtue, through which the opposing powers are rendered harmless, to rouse up and waken the love for the Bridegroom that slumbers within you, and to know the pleasure that is mine because of my experience of that love." She wants to tell them about the gladness that comes to birth in those who love him, but she is unable to convey this in words; and therefore she summons them to experience the thing for themselves, so that in this way they may grasp what they have been unable to take in through verbal accounts, for she knows well that one comprehends the natures of things better by way of experience than by way of words. So it is with intent to help them and with their welfare in mind that she exhorts them: she wants to see that many are saved by her assistance. Such was Paul's desire when he said, "So we are ambassadors for Christ, God making his appeal through us. We beseech you on behalf of Christ, be reconciled to God" (2 Cor. 5:20). He summons the unheeding and ignorant with powerful supplication and demand. He is quick to mourn over them, and wants them to have as serious a care for their own salvation as do others by their sympathy with them.

On the other hand, if it is the love of the Bridegroom that she wants to be wakened, this is what she says: "I adjure you, **daughters of Jerusalem**, approach the One I love, and tell him of my suffering, how because I have loved him I cannot remain at home: longing drives me out and compels me to explore every street in the hope that by chance I may encounter the One I long for." And this is no small matter for a lover who for reassurance makes do with the shade and the vision that come in the night, when the fullness of the reality is not available. For she may well be in doubt whether she is truly loved even if it appears that she has already met her Bridegroom and has heard from him words that speak of love. Lovers after all suffer something like this: if they see the ones they love turn away from them a bit, they often suppose that they are hated, and then they enlarge their desire beyond what it was when they enjoyed the things they wanted without any hindrance. What is more, the Bridegroom knows this perfectly well. Often he withdraws himself, awakening her love the more, ever training her love to reach youthful heights, and rekindling by his brief absence whatever of her desire is being stifled, lest the unhindered character of her delight be quenched with time when it is not aroused by any of the things that naturally set it afire. Therefore she charges the young maidens — in her doubtfulness and, yes, in her inability to believe that she is loved and that the Bridegroom's attitude toward her has remained unchanged — to meet him and tell him of her love, on the chance that they can awaken him to love her in the same way.

In some manuscripts, the text goes like this: **Do not rouse love nor waken it until it wishes.** Now if the love of the Bridegroom for the Bride is meant, [the Bride is saying:] "I have no need of an intermediary; for I know that once I am worthy, I awaken his will to love of me, since the heavenly love does not use a go-between, but steps in personally, drawn by the soul's beauty and filled with satisfaction by her virtuous deeds, disregarding the rumors that have been circulating." On the other hand, if it is a question of the love of the young maidens, [she is saying:] "Do not rouse up your love for him, for you, since you do not yet possess the constancy requisite for the disposition of lovers, still have need of a time for serving him in fear. Otherwise you may stir up love precipitately and behave wantonly toward him (cf. 1 Tim. 5:11), because without having learned yet to love wisely and well, you may undergo the experience of being unable to take up your love for him at the proper moment, and so stir up that love at an inappropriate time and at the wrong age." For there is a kind of love that is childish and unripe, one that is not impelled by a natural vigor, but through an easy assent of the mind comes about simply by happenstance: it does not last long, or defy the span of time, for it is not regularly and habitually aroused to an affection that is deliberately chosen.

Pharaoh, mad as he was for fame, experienced this after he had played out his unsuitable affair with Sarah, who symbolizes virtue (cf. Gen. 12:14ff.). By reason of the empty reputation accorded him by his people, when he discerned the nobility of the man who cohabited with her legally, a man perfect in his demeanor — and also because he had judged that pleasure would follow his cohabitation with virtue — he suffered great distress. For to the intemperate, self-control occasions no little agony, even as moderation does to the licentious; and when tormented by them, the person who is seized by a love that is out of place sends virtue packing, and being unable to enjoy intimacy with her legitimately because of his corrupt intent, he renounces any further relationship with her from fear of what it might cost him. For the toil associated with virtue brings to the person who undertakes it as a result of deliberate choice delight and much gladness of heart; and he finds consolation for his hard labors in the expected pleasure and enjoyment that attend the nobility of his demeanor. On the other hand, the person who draws near to virtue without intent or awareness is rewarded with distress and unremitting chastisement — until he either desires the good or else acknowledges his defeat and renounces what does not appeal to him, like an athlete who relaxes his ardor and in his frivolity has lost heart through great negligence — who declines a match against a noble and ready adversary and from fear of combat fails to reckon the honor that the prizes will bring him.

Song 2:8-17

SEPTUAGINT	VULGATE

SEPTUAGINT

2:8 The voice of my Kinsman!
  Behold, he comes
leaping upon the mountains,
  bounding upon the hills.
9 My Kinsman is like a gazelle,
  or a young stag
  on the mountains of Bethel.
Behold, he stands
  behind our wall,
leaning through the windows,
  peering through the lattices.
10 My Kinsman answers and says to me,
Rise up, come, my close one,
  my fair one, my dove!

11 For behold, the winter is past,
  the rain is gone; it has departed.

12 The flowers are seen on the earth,
  the time for cutting has come, and
the voice of the dove is heard in our
  land.
13 The fig tree has put forth its summer
  fruit;
the vines blossom;
  they give off fragrance.
Rise up, come, my close one,
  my fair one, my dove.
14 Come of yourself, my dove in the
  shelter of the rock,

VULGATE

2:8 The voice of my Beloved!
  Behold, he comes
leaping upon the mountains,
  jumping over the hills.
9 My Beloved is like a gazelle
  and a young stag.

Behold, he stands
  behind our wall,
looking down through the windows,
  peering through the lattices.
10 And my Beloved speaks to me:
Rise up, hasten, my beloved,
  my dove, my beautiful one, and
  come!

11 For already the winter is past;
  the rain has gone away and
  departed.

12 Flowers have appeared on our earth;
  the time for pruning has come;
the voice of the turtledove is heard
  in our land.
13 The fig tree has put forth its unripe
  fruit;
the vines are blossoming
  and giving off their fragrance.
Rise up, my friend,
  my beauty, and come,
14 my dove, in the openings of the rock,

close by the the wall.	in the hollows of the wall.
Show me your face,	Show me your face,
and let me hear your voice,	let your voice speak in my ears,
for your voice is sweet	for your voice is sweet,
and your countenance, glorious.	and your face is beautiful.
15 Catch us the little foxes	15 Catch us the little foxes
that destroy the vines;	that destroy the vines;
and our vines blossom.	for our vineyard has bloomed.
16 My Kinsman is mine, and I am his:	16 My Beloved is mine, and I am his —
he who shepherds his flocks	he who feeds among the lilies,
among the lilies,	
17 until the day dawns	17 until the day breathes
and the shadows depart.	and the shadows give way.
Turn back, my Kinsman, be made like	Turn back, my Beloved, and be like a
the gazelle	gazelle
or the young hart on the	or a young stag on the mountains
mountains of the plains.	of Bethel.

In this section, the Bride — who is apparently inside a house or other enclosure her consort cannot enter — speaks and in the course of her speaking relates things the Bridegroom has said to her as he urges her to show him her face and to join him. Verse 15 ("Catch us the little foxes . . .") has proved difficult for commentators to account for or to assign with any certainty to either of the principal characters in the poem. The closing verses (2:16-17) are clearly the Bride's again.

In spite of the difficulty of envisaging the situation the passage sketches or presupposes, Christian commentators found much in it to stimulate their imaginations and reflections. Origen, for example, true to his own liveliest concerns, sees in the opening verse of this section, with its contrast between the Bride's hearing the Bridegroom and her seeing him, a sketch of the experience of serious students of the Scriptures, who in their explorations alternately enjoy and are deprived of the presence of the Word. On the other hand, Theodoret's "take" on this verse — and not, it should be said, his alone — turns on the comparison (in 2:9) of the Bridegroom to a gazelle and a stag: the former associated with keenness of vision (the Greek word for a gazelle is etymologically related to a verb for seeing), and the latter with its hostility to snakes and the like.

In general, this section provides good illustrations of the manner in which individual details of a text — the lattices (or, for Ambrose, "nets"), for example, through which the Bridegroom "peers"; the wall that seems somehow to separate Bridegroom and Bride; the eloquent portrayal of springtime; the "little foxes" already mentioned — provide picturesque ways of speaking of human beings relating to God, or with moments in the history of salvation.

(1) Origen

The voice of my Kinsman!
  Behold, he comes
leaping upon the mountains,
  bounding upon the hills.

To begin with, the Church recognizes Christ by his voice alone. For his first step was to send his **voice** ahead of him by the ministry of the prophets, and even if he was not seen, he was nevertheless heard. He was heard by the things that were proclaimed concerning him, and for a long time the Bride — that is, the Church, which was being gathered from the very opening of the age — only heard his voice, until the time when she saw him with her eyes and said, **Behold, he comes leaping upon the mountains, bounding upon the hills.** . . .

Yes, and every single soul, if there be a soul driven by love of the Word of God, that finds herself engaged in a controversy about texts — as anyone knows who has experienced the way in which one finds oneself in the dark and entangled in perplexities about statements and issues: every single soul, I say, if ever the enigmas and obscurities of the Law and the Prophets have her helplessly trussed up, is instantly encouraged and comforted if it happen that the soul becomes aware of the Word's nearness and hears the sound of his voice at a distance; and when he begins to become more and more perceptible to her and to shed light on the obscurities, that is when she sees him **leaping over the mountains . . . and hills.** This means that he suggests high and lofty interpretations to her, so that the soul can deservedly say, **Behold, he is coming, leaping upon the mountains, bounding upon the hills.**

In saying this, we have not forgotten that the Word has already, in previous scenes, spoken with the Bride as present to her; but since, as we have repeatedly said, this little book contains a sort of stage play, things are spoken at one point with regard to a party who is present, and at another with regard to one who is absent. . . . For even though the Bridegroom makes a promise and says to the Bride — that is, to his chosen disciples — "Lo, I am with you always, to the close of the age" (Matt. 28:20), he nevertheless also says in parables that the householder "called his servants," and gave each of them money for purposes of doing business, and "went away" (Matt. 25:14-15). Further, he says that he went away to seek a kingdom (cf. Luke 19:12); and yet again it is said, as though with reference to an absent Bridegroom, that "at midnight there was a cry" (Matt. 25:6) raised by people, saying, "The Bridegroom is coming!"

Thus the Bridegroom is present and teaching at one moment, but at another is said to be absent and longed for. Moreover, each of these situations fits both the Church and the zealous soul. For when he permits the Church to suffer persecution and tribulation, he appears to her to be absent; on the other hand, when she makes progress in peace and flourishes in faith and good works, he is understood to be present to her. So too in the case of the soul. When she is seeking to understand something and desiring to become acquainted with certain obscurities and hidden things, the Word of God is plainly absent from her for as long as she cannot discover what she wants. But when the thing she is seeking appears right under her nose, who doubts that the Word of God is present and is enlightening her mind and supplying her with the light of knowledge? Further, we are aware that he has been withdrawn from us and has again become present in each matter that is open to our understanding or closed to it.

And we undergo this experience up until the time when we are rendered the sort of persons that he judges it right not only to visit frequently but even to abide with: just as when he was asked by one of his disciples, "Lord, how is it that you will manifest yourself to us and not to the world?" he answered, "If a man loves me, he will keep my word, and my Father will love him, and we will come to him and make our home with him" (John 14:22-23). If therefore we too wish to see the Word of God and the soul's Bridegroom **leaping over the mountains** and **bounding over the hills**, let us first hear his voice; and when we have heard his voice in all things, we shall then be able to see him in the same manner as that in which the Bride is described in the verse before us as having seen him. For even she, though she had seen him previously, had nevertheless not seen him **leaping upon the mountains** and **bounding upon the hills**, nor **leaning through** her **windows**, nor **peering through the nets.**

(2) Theodoret of Cyrus

The voice of my Kinsman!
  Behold, he comes
leaping upon the mountains,
  bounding upon the hills.
My Kinsman is like a gazelle,
  or a young stag on the hills of Bethel.

It is well worth asking why the Bride likens him to a **gazelle or a young stag**; and what the hills **of Bethel** are; and what his leaps are, as well as his boundings, and the mountains upon which these take place.

Now they say that the gazelle is so called because of its native sharp-sightedness, and takes its name from its clarity of vision. They also say that stags are destroyers of creeping things and that right along with their herbage they eat snakes and vipers and other such beasts without incurring any harm. Since, then, the Lord Christ in his character as a human being is a "rod" springing "from the root of Jesse, and the Spirit of God" rested "upon him — the Spirit of wisdom and understanding, the Spirit of counsel and strength, the Spirit of knowledge and piety" — and "the Spirit of the fear of God filled him" (Isa. 11:1-3 LXX), the Bride likens him to a gazelle on the ground of his sharp-sightedness, his clear vision, and his foreknowledge of things to come.

At the same time she says that he is like a young stag in that he broke "the heads of the dragons upon the water" and crushed "the heads of the dragon" (Ps. 73:13-14 LXX = 74:13-14) and as with a sword the coiled snake, and slew the dragon that is in the sea. Moreover, he gave his disciples "authority to tread upon snakes and scorpions and over all the power of the enemy" (Luke 10:19). And he "committed no sin" (1 Pet. 2:22), but took away the sins of the world (cf. John 1:29), and slew them like so many snakes. But she likens him to a stag that is young, because he is not only called a man but also "son of man," and not only a lion but the whelp of a lion; for it says: "He lay down and slept like a lion, and like a lion's whelp" (Num. 24:9). And very likely this is suggesting that even when he was very young (in bodily terms), he destroyed the power of the Devil like so many snakes — and as soon as he was born drew the Magi, who spoke for the Devil, to worship him.

According to the law, both the gazelle and the stag are reckoned among the clean animals (Deut. 12:15); but the gazelle is mentioned before the stag because in virtue of its clarity of vision it prefigures faith. For the first thing the person who is drawing near to God does is to "believe that he exists," and that God "rewards those who seek him" (Heb. 11:6). But the Scripture also mentions stags, and the blessed David says in Psalm 17, "God who girded me with strength, and made my way spotless, and established my feet like a stag's" (Ps. 17:33 LXX = 18:32-33); that is, "my way was made spotless once my feet were established to be like a stag's feet." For then I was able to tread "upon snakes and scorpions," and "over all the power of the enemy." Then, too, he says in Psalm 28: "The voice of the Lord readies the stags and unveils the thickets" (Ps. 28:9 LXX = 29:9). Here "stags" names the blessed apostles, whose feet are beautiful because they bring good tidings (cf. Isa. 52:7), because they tread down the murderous serpents that lay snares for human souls. By their work the fruitless thickets have been unveiled, which is to say, the vanity of idols; and that is why everyone gives glory to God in the Lord's temple. Moreover, the blessed prophet Habbakuk says much the same sort of thing: "God, the Lord, is my strength, and he orders my feet like a stag's feet and makes me tread upon high places" (Hab. 3:19).

But it is time to return to the text before us: **Behold, he comes leaping upon the mountains, bounding upon the hills. My Kinsman is like a gazelle and a young stag on the hills of Bethel.** Here the Bride teaches the destruction of idols wrought by the Bridegroom. For **mountains** and **hills** are the names of the groves and precincts of the demons, down on whom he leaps and springs both with the wisdom of his words and with the power of his miracles, and overcomes and abolishes them utterly. Actually, Symmachus translates this better when he says, **Behold, he comes, marching against the mountains, leaping forward against the hills.**

(3) Gregory of Nyssa

Behold, he stands
behind our wall,
leaning through the windows,
peering through the lattices.

The purified and discerning eye of the soul sees these things . . . , and she discourses of the one who is coming in the future as if he were already present, contemplating her hope as something already accomplished, thanks to the trustiness and certainty of the grace she hopes for. For the text says, "He who treads upon the mountains with swift agility and leaps from hill to hill shows himself to us as stationary, standing behind the wall and conversing from behind the lattice work of the windows." That is the point of saying, **Behold, he stands behind our wall, leaning through the windows, peering through the lattices.**

Thus the situation that is literally described in the text is this: the Beloved converses through the windows with the Bride who keeps the house, and, though the wall between them separates the pair, their verbal communication is unimpeded since his head leans through the windows, while his eye peers through the lattice work of the windows upon the interior.

The anagogical sense of the words, however, adheres closely to the line of thought we have already uncovered; for the Word follows a certain path and a certain sequence in adapting human nature to God. First of all, he shines upon it by means of the prophets and the law's injunctions. (This is our interpretation: the windows are the prophets, who bring in the light; while the lattices are the network of the law's injunctions. Through both of them the beam of the true Light steals into the interior.) After that, however, comes the Light's perfect illumination, when, by its mingling with our nature, the true Light shows itself to those who are in darkness and the shadow of death (Luke 1:79). At an earlier stage, then, the beams of the prophetic and legal ideas, which illumine the soul by way of its windows and lattices, as we have understood, evoke a desire to see the sun in the open air — and then, in the way indicated, the Desired steps forward to do his work.

(4) Apponius

Behold, he stands
   behind our wall,
looking through the windows,
   peering through the lattices,
and my Beloved speaks to me.

Behold him who was crucified. Behold him who with the right hand of his deity held the fainting and weary Church, mourning in the persons of the apostles, in his consoling embrace when, in the very flesh in which he has been entombed, he stands risen **behind the wall** of our unbelief, the wall we had constructed in sinning by our squalid deeds. He speaks of these deeds through Isaiah the prophet: "Is my hand without strength to redeem? But your sins have built a wall between yourselves and God" (Isa. 50:2c and 59:2a Vg). The Lord Christ stands behind this wall, and he is waiting to be called upon by the impious; and he summons the sinful soul to repentance.

And even though we do not deserve to look upon him, nevertheless, in virtue of our renunciation of idolatry, we make windows in the aforesaid wall. By their means, in defending us from unclean spirits, Christ looks through, and by bowing the knee to him alone, we make lattices through which he peers by granting remorse to the person who turns to him. But when we have come to the true turning that consists in the aforesaid baptism or repentance, once forgiveness has been granted to those who have been turned, he removes the wall and **he speaks** to us, "Come to me, all you who labor and are heavy laden, and I will give you rest" (Matt. 11:28), and "Come, O blessed of my Father, and inherit the kingdom prepared for you from the foundation of the world" (Matt. 25:34). It is just this that Paul, the teacher of the nations, taught had come about through his advent: "Who removed," says he, "the wall of separation and reconciled us to God by his blood" (Eph. 2:14, 16; Col. 1:20).

(5) Ambrose of Milan

Behold, he stands
   behind the wall,
looking down through the windows,
   peering through the nets.
And my Beloved speaks to me:
"Rise up, come, my close one,
   my fair one, my dove!
For behold, the winter is past. . . ."

So he came, and to begin with he is **behind the wall**, so that the hostility between soul and body may be abolished once the wall is taken away; for it seemed to furnish an obstacle to harmony.

Then he looks **through the windows**, and what they signify you may learn from the prophet, who says: "The windows have been opened from on high" (Isa. 24:18). What this refers to is the prophets, through whom the Lord exercised care for the human race before he descended to earth in his own person. And even today, if a soul seeks him out seriously, she will merit mercy in abundance; for anyone who is earnest in seeking is owed an abundance of good things. If, then, a soul looks for him zealously, she hears his voice from far off, and even though she asks others about him, she hears his voice before the ones of whom she asks.

She sees him come toward her **leaping**, that is, hastening and running and leaping over those who from feebleness of heart are unable to receive his power. Then through her reading of the prophets and by keeping their words, she sees him **looking in** through the enigmas of the prophets — **looking in**, but as through a window and not yet as fully present.

She sees him standing out above the **nets**. What does this mean save perhaps that those **nets** are ours rather than his? There are **nets** because as yet this soul dwells among things that are perceptible and worldly, things that take the human mind captive and have a way of binding it about in their own folds. To one who dwells among the things of this age yet for all that is seeking him, he shows himself **through the nets**; and to the soul of this sort he says at last, **Rise up, come, my close one.** That is to say, "Rise up from the delights of the world, rise up from earthly things and come to me, you who still 'labor and are heavy laden' (Matt. 11:28) because you are anxious about worldly things. Come beyond the world, come to me; for 'I have overcome the world' (John 16:33). Come close, you that are now **fair** with the bloom of eternal life, you that are now a **dove**, that is, gentle and quiet, you that are now wholly a thing of spiritual grace."

By right, then, she ought to have no fear of the **nets** since he who could not be captured by the trials and nets of the world calls the soul to himself. For though as human beings we walk in the midst of snares, and by our need of nourishment we are victims of nets and snares alike, he, placed in a body though he is, does not for a minute fear the **nets** but **stands out over** them — above the trials of the world and the vulnerabilities of the body, that is — and enables others to do the same.

For this reason, wanting to make this soul too firm and secure, he said, "**Rise up, come, my close one**, do not fear the nets. Already **the winter is past**"; that is, the Passover has come, gentleness has come, remission of sins has arrived, temptation has ceased, the rain has gone away, the tempest has passed, and affliction with it. Before the coming of Christ, it is winter; after his coming, there are flowers. Hence it says, **Flowers are seen on the earth.** Where before there were thorns, now there are flowers. Then it says, **The time for cutting has come**: where before there was a desert, there is now a harvest to be gathered. **The voice of the dove is heard in the land**: our prophet rightly adds, almost in wonder, that where before there was immodesty, there is now chastity. **The fig tree has put forth its unripe fruit**: the tree that previously was commanded to be cut down now begins to bear fruit. But why are you puzzled because it says **unripe fruit**? He brings down the earlier fruit so as to introduce better fruit later, just as he rejected the fruit of the synagogue but renews that of the Church.

And even though complete tranquility prevails and the mysteries have reached fulfillment, he nevertheless repeats himself: **Rise up** confident **in the shelter of the rock**, which is to say, the safe protection afforded by my passion and by the rampart of faith; for "they sucked honey from the rock, and oil from the hardest stone" (Deut. 32:13). Invested with this shelter of faith, the souls of the faithful are no longer naked, and for them this is a wall. That is why he says to this soul, **Come, my dove, to the shelter of the rock close by the wall. Show me your face, and let me hear your voice.** He exhorts her to confidence, so that she be not ashamed of the cross of Christ nor of his seal. He exhorts her to confession and wants all crafty calculation to be put away, in order that the good scent of faith may spread abroad, that the day may dawn, that the shadow of unfriendly night may bring no harm, because he who is close to Christ says, "The night is far gone, the day is at hand" (Rom. 13:12).

(6) Gregory of Nyssa

For behold, the winter is past,
    the rain is gone; it has departed. . . .

So then the Word has spoken to her and called her **fair one** because she is close to him, and **dove** because of her beauty. And he continues in the words that follow by saying that the misery of the soul's winter does not triumph because the frost fails to withstand the radiance. **For behold**, he says, **the winter is past, the rain is gone; it has departed.**

He gives many names to evil in accordance with its different workings. **Winter** and **rain** and "drops" are the same: each of the names labels some particular trial in a way that fits its special character. It is called **winter** because that term denotes a plethora of bad things. In the winter, things that have grown up wither away; the splendor that hangs on the trees, which naturally adorn themselves with leaves, drops from their branches and is mingled with the earth. The melody of the songbirds is silenced. The nightingale flees away. The swallow is benumbed. The turtledove is exiled from its nest. All things mimic the misery of death: the blossom is killed, the grass of the field dies. Like bones denuded of flesh, so the branches stripped of their leaves become an ugly sight that contrasts with the splendor given by their blossoms. And what shall one say of the turbulence that winter brings to the sea? Swelling and churning up from the depths, it imitates peaks and mountains, brought by its waters to a standing head. It rushes upon the earth like a foe, throwing itself up and over the sands and shaking the earth with blow upon blow of its waves, like so many volleys of siege engines.

One must understand these afflictions of the winter season, and everything that is like them, by taking them in a transferred, figural sense. What is it that fades and wastes away in the winter? What is it that falls from the bough to the earth? What is the now silent voice of the songbirds? What is the sea that rises up and attacks with its waters? And further: What is the rain, and what the drops of rain, and how does the rain carry itself off? By all these things, the image of a winter like this points, at a deeper level, to the situation of beings that are ensouled and endowed with choice. Even if my discourse does not clarify every individual detail, the sense that shines through in each is clear to anyone who pays close attention. The human race flourished at the beginning, while it was lodged in Paradise, nourished by the water of that spring and flourishing. At that time, its nature was adorned not with leaves but with the blossom of immortality. But the winter of disobedience dried up its root. The blossom was shaken off and fell to the earth; man was stripped of the beauty of immortality, and the green grass of the virtues was dried up as love for God became cold in the face of burgeoning lawlessness. Consequently, the various turbulences, as a result of which the soul's shipwrecks come about, were brought to their peaks within us by the opposing spirits.

But then there came the One who works in us the springtime of souls, the One who, when an evil wind was agitating the sea, said, "Peace! Be still!" (Mark 4:39) — and all became calm and still. Once again our nature began to flourish and to be adorned with its own blossoms. But the blossoms that are proper to our life are the virtues, which put forth flowers now but bear their fruit in their own time. That is why the Word says, **The winter is past, the rain is gone; it has departed. The flowers are seen on the earth, the time for cutting has come.** "You see," he says, "the meadow blooming because of the virtues. You see, that is, self-control, the bright and fragrant lily; you see reverence, the red rose; you see the violet, the sweet smell of Christ. Why then do you not employ these to make wreaths? This is the time at which it is right, the time when the cutting is done, to take pleasure in the plaiting of such wreaths. The **time for** their **cutting has come.** . . .

For since the Word is describing the spiritual springtime to the Bride, and since this season is a halfway house between two others — between wintry desolation and the summer's sharing in the harvest — for just that reason, while he openly proclaims the passing of evil things, he does not yet point to the full fruits of virtue. These, however, he will dispense at the proper season, when the summer is come (and what "summer" means, you know well enough from the words of the Lord: "The harvest is the consummation of the age" [Matt. 13:39]). But now what he manifests is the hopes that come to blossom through the virtues, whose fruit, as the prophet says, is brought forth in due season.

Since, then, our human nature, like the fig tree that is mentioned here, has gathered to itself, during the winter (understood in its spiritual meaning), a great deal of harmful moisture, it is right that he who works in us the springtime of the soul and who cultivates the soil of our humanity by his husbandry should first of all cast out of our nature everything that is earthy and inappropriate, getting rid not of boughs but of transgressions, through the act of confession; and then should proclaim the coming sweetness of the figs as he stamps on our being an impress of the hoped-for happiness by means of a more honorable life — an impress not unlike the early figs. This is what it means to say, **The fig will bring forth its early fruit.**

(7) William of St. Thierry

Rise up, my friend, my beauty,
and come, my dove, in the openings of the rock,
   in the hollows of the wall.
Show me your face,
   let your voice speak in my ears,
for your voice is sweet,
   and your face is beautiful.

And what is said here comes to pass. The Bride carries out the Bridegroom's exhortation. With the disappearance of winter, there is serenity. The Bride exults when the Bridegroom appears. It is a pleasure to start off and, wherever he goes, to follow in the footsteps of the one who promises greater things — out of one's house, out of one's city: which is to say, beyond the limits of the human condition, beyond the limits of the routine affairs of daily life; within the hidden things of the Son of God (which is what is meant by **the openings of the rock**); within the secrets of the law (which are **the hollows of the wall**). For the rock that is Christ is not everywhere closed up; it has openings through which God is manifested. And the wall of the law, which separates two peoples (cf. Eph. 2:12ff.), has hollow places that one can enter with the help of the Word of God, which is more penetrating than any two-edged sword (cf. Heb. 4:12); and in virtue of these openings things that are different and contrary to one another are reconciled. Moreover, this is also the time for pruning; for when useful buds are blooming, there are sure to be useless and harmful buds coming out among them.

Then it says: **Show me your face, let your voice speak in my ears, for your voice is sweet, and your face is beautiful.** The **dove** makes a habit of nesting in **the openings of the rock,** and **in the hollows of the wall;** and she shows her face out of them and makes her voice heard — a charming face and a voice that sighs. What does this represent if not the conscience that is solidly settled in Christ and in her faith in him, that, bringing forth the fruits of the Spirit, raises a voice of praise pleasing to God, and sighs at the delay of the good things she has hoped for? This face the Bride shows the Bridegroom at his request, for the holy conscience loves to appear before her Creator when illumined by the light of his countenance. This voice of the Bride is sweet in the ears of the Bridegroom, for it comes to him in the same way that it comes from her, that is to say, as an expression of her love.

But let us glance back briefly and mentally review the way in which the subject matter unfolds in accordance with the sequence of events and the sense of the text's language. The Bride was sitting, turned in upon herself, awaiting the return of the Bridegroom, in possession of the pledge that he would return speedily, that is, the Spirit. She was praying, weeping, desiring that he would return. Then all of a sudden it seems to her that she hears what she does not see, and perceives with an internal sense what she does not grasp with her mind, that is, the presence of the Deity; and she says, **The voice of my Beloved!** All the senses of the faithful soul are filled with joy. She is rushing to meet him when, after going a short distance, she sees him coming to her — **leaping**, that is hurrying; **jumping** over people of small faith who cannot bear his swift coming, or flying high above every human idea and **jumping** over all rationality. As she sees him coming to her, she pulls herself together so as to receive him, perceiving his approach and standing behind the wall.

Then as she sees him looking through the windows, **peering through the lattices**, and offering himself to the one who desires him, she begins to grasp, in her own experience, the mysteries of God's love — namely, that he frequently withdraws from her aims to assure that she will seek him more ardently; and that he gives himself to his lover from time to time in order to assure that she shall not be overcome by excessive sorrow. And when she rises up to see the one who is calling and cheering her, and hastens forward to hold him, he who appeared quickly disappears, and together with him all that divine and spiritual delight, all those vines and flowers. All his sweetness, all his delights, the joy of the flowers, the scent of the vines, the richness of the fruits — all this follows behind the author of sweetness as he departs. From the **friend** departs the assurance of love; from the **dove**, her beauty of face and sweetness of voice; from the **beauty**, the grace of conformity with the Divine. To the **friend** there is left her solitude, to the **dove** her sighs, and to the **beauty** her own aspect. The **openings of the rock** are shut tight, the hollows of the wall are blocked up; no more do they harbor the dove who has lost her heart.

(8) Origen

Catch us the little foxes
that destroy the vines,
 and our vines will flourish.

There has now been a change in the characters on stage to fit the order of the plot. Now the Bridegroom is not speaking to the Bride but to his companions; and he tells them to

catch . . . the little foxes that skulk among the vines just as they are beginning to bud and do not permit them to flower. He orders that they be caught because he cares about the safety and welfare of the vines.

These matters, however, must be searched out by means of a spiritual interpretation, just as we have been doing from the start. And it is my view that if what you are thinking about is the soul that joins itself to the Word of God, these **foxes** must be taken to mean the hostile powers and demonic depravities that, making use of crooked thoughts and twisted understanding, destroy in the soul the blossom of the virtues and cut off the fruit of faith. In virtue, then, of the promise made by the Word of God, who is the Lord of hosts, he commands "the holy angels, who have been sent for the sake of those who inherit salvation" (cf. Heb. 1:14), that in every such soul they take captive the thoughts inspired by the demons, so that once the latter have been disposed of, the souls may be able to bring forth the blossom of virtue. They take the evil thoughts captive by suggesting to the mind that they do not come from God but derive from the Evil One and by endowing the soul with "the ability to distinguish between spirits" (1 Cor. 12:10), so that she may understand which thought it is that belongs to God and which derives from the Devil. . . .

This is why it is said, **Catch us the little foxes.** And it is plainly right that he orders them to be caught and taken when they are still **little.** As long as an evil thought is still immature, it can easily be cast out of the heart. For if it is frequently repeated and persists for a long while, it brings the soul along to a point of consent; and once that is given and the thought is established in the heart, it is certain to lead to actual sinning. Thus it ought to be caught and cast out while it is still immature and **little**, for otherwise, if it has become mature and deep-seated, it can no longer be gotten rid of. . . .

If, however, we should take all this as applying to Christ and the Church, it will appear that the words are directed to those in the Church who are responsible for teaching, and that they are commanded to take captive the **foxes that destroy vines.** We can then understand the **foxes** to represent teachers of heretical ideas, who by the cunning of their arguments lead the hearts of the innocent astray and destroy the Lord's vine so that it fails to produce the flower of correct belief. So then a charge is given to catholic teachers that while these **foxes** are still **little**, and have not deceived very many souls even though perverse doctrine has gotten a start, they should make haste to censure such people and restrain them — and by opposing them with the word of truth to subdue and **catch** them with statements of the truth. . . .

But in order that what we have said in our two interpretations may be made clearer, let us gather together out of the divine books whatever places there are where mention is made of this animal.

In Psalm 62, then, we find that the impious are spoken of in the following terms: "But in vain shall they seek after my soul, they shall enter into the depths of the earth, they shall be handed over to the sword, they shall be the portions of foxes" (Ps. 62:10-11 LXX = 63:9-10). Then also in Matthew's Gospel, to the "scribe" who had said to him, "Teacher, I will follow you wherever you go" (Matt. 8:19), the Savior replied, "Foxes have their lairs and the birds of the air have nests where they take rest, but the Son of man has nowhere to lay his head" (Matt. 8:20). Likewise also, in the Gospel according to Luke, to people who said to the Lord, "Depart and leave this place, for Herod intends to kill you" (Luke 13:31), Jesus answered, "Go and tell that fox, 'Look, here I am, today and tomorrow, casting out demons and performing healings; and on the third day I shall have completed my work'" (Luke 13:32). In the book of Judges too, Samson, when his wife, who was of the Philistine clan, was taken from him, said to her father, "'This time I will be innocent where the foreigners are concerned, for I am going to do you harm.' And Samson went off and took three hundred foxes, and he took torches, and tied them tail to tail, and placed a single torch between each pair of the foxes' tails. Then he set fire to the torches and sent them out through the standing grain of the foreigners, and their stubble, and their grapevines and their olive groves" (Judg. 15:3-5). Further still, in the Second Book of Esdras, Tobiah the Ammonite, when he was obstructing the construction work of those who had returned from captivity in order to keep them from building the temple and the wall, said to the foreigners, "Will those people ever sacrifice or eat what has been offered in this place? Surely the foxes will climb up and destroy the wall they have built out of stones" (cf. Neh. 4:2-3).

For the moment, these are the texts from the divine Scriptures that we have been able to come across in which mention is made of this animal, so that a perceptive reader can make up his mind whether in what has been said we have given an exposition that fits the words we have to explain, that is, **Catch us the little foxes**. And though it is a toilsome business to interpret the individual points in the sample passages we have mentioned, let us nonetheless touch briefly on them to the extent we can.

And first of all, let us look in Psalm 62 at the place where, because the wicked were persecuting the soul of the righteous man, he sings, "But in vain shall they seek after my soul, they shall enter into the depths of the earth, they shall be handed over to the sword, they shall be the portions of foxes" (Ps. 62:10-11 LXX = 63:9-10). Here it is shown that perverse teachers, seeking as they do to mislead the soul of the righteous by their vain and empty words, are said to "enter into the depths of the earth" — "earth" in that their wisdom is derived from earth, and "the depths" of it in that they descend into a bottomless folly. For it is my belief that those whose manner of life is fleshly are said to be "earth" and to dwell on the earth because the only people they harm are themselves. On the other hand, those who interpret the Scriptures in an earthly and fleshly manner and deceive others by teaching so are said to "enter into the depths of the earth" precisely in their act of spewing out cunning talk and the arguments of a fleshly and earthly wisdom — or, to be sure, because their future punishment will be heavier, in that those who teach earthly wisdom offend more seriously than those who live in an earthly manner; and it is predicted that these same [teachers] will be "handed over to the sword," namely, that "flaming sword which turned every way" (Gen. 3:24).

But how do they become "the portions of foxes"? Every soul is either God's portion, or the portion of some agent that has received power over human beings. For "When the Most High divided the nations and dispersed the sons of Adam, he fixed the bounds of the peoples according to the number of the angels of God, and Jacob became the portion of the Lord" (Deut. 32:8-9). Thus it is a given that every soul belongs to God's portion or to that of some other agent; and it is possible, in virtue of its freedom of choice, for each individual soul to move from one portion to another, either to that of God if she is getting better or, if she is getting worse, to that of the demons. It follows, then, that those who are mentioned in the psalm, those who "shall seek after the soul" of the righteous "in vain," shall be "the portion of foxes," which means: "they shall be the portion" of the worst and most iniquitous demons. Thus the word "foxes" describes any and every wicked and deceitful power, through which the deceits and falsehoods of "false knowledge" have been introduced. Those, moreover, who have been led into such error . . . are the very same as those among whom, as the Gospel would have it, those **foxes** we named above are said to "have their lairs," and among whom "the Son of Man has nowhere to lay his head." Herod too must be thought to have been called a fox on account of his guileful shrewdness.

Where Samson is concerned, though, of whom it is recorded that he "took three hundred foxes, and took torches, and tied them tail to tail," and placed burning torches between the foxes' tails, and sent them through "the standing grain of the foreigners, and their stubble, and their grapevines and their olive groves" — the interpretation of this image or figure strikes me as extremely difficult. Let us make an effort, however, as far as we are able, to hammer something out of it, and stipulate that the **foxes** are guileful and perverse teachers, as the above exposition states. Samson, then, who symbolizes a true and faithful teacher, captures them by means of the word of truth, and ties them "tail to tail"; in other words, he confutes those who oppose each other and whose views and teachings contradict each other. From what they say, he takes statements and inferences and out "into the standing grain of the foreigners" he sends the fire of his conclusion. In this way he reduces their whole harvest to ashes as well as the "vines and olive groves" of this worst of crops. . . .

(9) Gregory of Nyssa

Catch us little foxes
that destroy the vineyards,
   and our vines blossom.

Thus the pure Bridegroom accepts the prayer of the Bride because she is righteous; and meaning to show himself openly, he first of all urges the hunters to chase down the foxes so that they will no longer prevent the vineyard from blooming. "**Catch us . . . foxes**, he says, which, small though they be, destroy vineyards. For the vines will blossom when there is nothing left that harms them. **Catch us little foxes** that destroy vineyards, **and our vines blossom.**"

Can we then fittingly attain the loftiness of these thoughts? How great a display of the majesty of God does this text contain! How great a preeminence of the divine power does the sense of its words evince!

How is he described? — he, I mean, of whom such things as these are said — that he is humanity's slayer (cf. John 8:44), powerful in doing evil, with a tongue like a whetted razor (cf. Ps. 51:3-4 LXX = 52:2)? Of him the prophet says, "The arrows of the Mighty One, sharpened with the coals of the desert" (Ps. 119:4 LXX = 120:4); and, "Like a lion he lies in wait in his lair" (Ps. 9:30 LXX = 10:9). He is the great dragon (cf. Ezek. 29:3), the Apostate, Hades which opens its mouth (cf. Isa. 5:14), the World Ruler of the power of darkness (cf. Eph. 6:12), he who has the power of death (cf. Heb. 2:14). Then prophecy describes him speaking for himself. He is the one who removes the borders of the nations (cf. Isa. 10:13), which he — obviously this refers to the Most High — established according to the number of his angels (Deut. 32:8). He is the one who seizes the inhabited earth as if it were a nest and takes it up like forsaken eggs (cf. Isa. 10:14). He is the one who says that his throne sits above the clouds and that he is like the Most High God (cf. Isa. 14:13-14). Then there are all the fearful and awful things that the Word narrates about him in the book of Job: his ribs, it is said, are of bronze, and his limbs of cast iron (cf. Job 40:18), and his entrails are emery stone (cf. Job 41:7 LXX) — and all such statements in which the scriptural text sketches that fearsome nature. Such he is, then, and so great, the commanding general of the legions of demons.

But how, I say, is this one named by the true and only Power? He is a little fox! And all those who are about him, the army that is under his orders — all are disparagingly named in the same way by the one who urges the hunters to chase them down.

No doubt these hunters would be the angelic powers, those who precede the Lord's advent on the earth, who lead the King of glory's way into this life, and who make plain to the ignorant "Who this King of glory is, the one who is strong and mighty . . . in battle" (Ps. 23:8 LXX = 24:8). By the same token, one might also say "the ministering spirits" (Heb. 1:14), dispatched in the service of those who shall inherit salvation; and no doubt one might say that the hunters are the holy apostles sent forth to chase these wild animals — the apostles to whom the Lord said, "I will make you fishers of men" (Matt. 4:19); for they would not have carried out this fishing for men with the net of their words, catching the souls of the saved, unless they had first of all cast these wild beasts out of their lairs — the **little foxes**, I mean, out of the hearts in which they lay hid — so as to make a place where the Son of God may lay his head because the fox breed is no longer lurking there. Besides, the very ones whom the Word commands to be hunters are taught the greatness and the wonder of the divine power by the things enjoined upon them. For he did not say, "Hunt the wild pig which ravages God's vineyard from its thicket, or 'the wild boar' (cf. Ps. 79:14 LXX = 80:13), or the roaring lion, or the great Leviathan, or the monster of the deep" (though indeed the Word showed the hunters, in such beasts, something of the power of the opposing forces). No: "All these earthly powers," he says, "with whom humans struggle — princes and authorities and world-rulers of darkness, and spirits of wickedness — are **little foxes**, wretched and treacherous, consigned under your power. If you overcome them, then our vineyard, our human nature, will receive the grace proper to it, and will begin the harvest of grapes with the blossom of virtuous conduct." Therefore, **Catch us the little foxes that destroy the vineyards, and our vines blossom.**

(10) Augustine of Hippo

Catch us the little foxes
that destroy the vineyards. . . .

Then there follows: "And Samson was angered because his companion married his wife" (Judg. 14:19-20). This "companion" is the type of all heretics — a vital truth, if veiled, my brethren. For heretics, who have divided the Church of God, desire to marry their Lord's wife and take her away. They have departed from the Church and from the Gospels in committing an act of impious adultery; they attempt to drag the Church, Christ's body, into their own camp — which is why that faithful servant and friend addresses the Lord's bride and says, "I betrothed you to Christ to present you as a pure Bride to her one husband" (2 Cor. 11:2). . . .

And who are these companions, these heretical deserters that seek to take away the Lord's bride? They are Donatus, Arius, Mani, and the other vessels of falsehood and perdition. It is with such persons in mind that the apostle says, "I hear that there are dissensions among you; for one says, 'I belong to Paul,' and another, 'I belong to Cephas'" (1 Cor. 1:11-12).

Let us see, then, what this mystical Samson did when some outsider injured him over his wife. He caught the foxes, that is to say, his adulterous companions, of whom it is said in the Song of Songs: **Catch us the little foxes that destroy the vineyards. . . .** What does **catch** mean here? It means lay hold of them, convince them, refute them, so that they do not lay waste the vineyard, the Church. What does it mean to catch foxes but to subdue them by the authority of God's law and to bind and constrain them by the testimonies of the holy Scriptures as by so many cords? He catches foxes, and when he has tied their tails together he fixes firebrands to them. And what is the significance of the foxes' tails when they have been tied together? What are the tails of foxes except the rear ends of heretics? Their fronts display a deceptive charm, but their rear ends are bound, that is, sentenced, and they drag firebrands behind them, to burn up the fruits and works of those who are seduced by them.

He says to someone, "Do not listen to heretics; do not agree with heretics." The answer comes, "Why not?" Did not this or that other Christian do just as much evil, commit as many adulteries, engage in as much plundering? And what bad things happened to him? It is the way the foxes look from the front that those they have seduced see; and what comes behind that is fire. . . .

(11) Nilus of Ancyra

My Kinsman is mine, and I am his:
  he who tends his flocks among the lilies,
until the day dawns
  and the shadows depart.
Turn back, my Kinsman, be made like the gazelle
  or the young hart
  on the mountains of the plains.

The Bride, alone, dedicates herself to the Bridegroom and once more asserts that the Bridegroom is hers alone; for from Paul, by reason of her close affinity with the righteous attainments [of the Bridegroom], she has learned that in being united with the Lord she is one body with him (cf. 1 Cor. 6:16-17). For since her body is not handed over to adultery but to the Lord, the Lord, once he became a human being, made her body his. So it is, to be sure, that the saints, by their participation in him through virtue, claim a community with him as the Author of creation, and say, "O Lord, my God," and "O God, my God, pay heed to me" (Ps. 21:2 LXX = 22:1), showing that the closeness of their unity with him is due more to their mode of life than to their creation.

She says that he is tending **his flocks among the lilies**, meaning that he is the shepherd who tends souls that are free of anxiety, since those that are drawn away by busyness about bodily concerns stand outside the sphere of his shepherding. About souls of this sort the prophet says: "From mountain to hill they have gone; they have forgotten their fold. All who found them have devoured them" (Jer. 27:6-7 LXX = 50:6-7) — by these words intimating their liability to attack and indicating that, having deserted their shepherd, they do not know the "green pasture" or "the water of refreshment" (22:2 LXX = 23:2), but are still defenseless against wild beasts because of their stubborn willfulness.

It is not forever, then, that he **tends his flocks among the lilies**, but only **until** the coming **day dawns and the shadows** are departed. For since the majority of folk, mentally blinded as they are by the dark cloud of ignorance, think that things that pass and have no fixity are established and endure, they stand in need of the light of day in order that they can see that the **shadows** of worldly phenomena are unstable and have no solid reality. For all things that come and go are shadows (cf. Wisdom 5:9). They find their origin in the good things in the heavens, and they subsist in shadow fashion in virtue of the reality that belongs to the things above. So it is indeed that those for whom the night has advanced and the day has drawn near and bestirred itself, those who have clearly discerned, as if in the light of the sun, the nature of things down here, would say, "Our life on the earth is a shadow" (Job 8:9), and again, "My days have waned like a shadow" (Ps. 101:12 LXX = 102:11), indicating how feeble and quick to vanish is the solidity of the things of this life. The person, moreover, who says, "For although . . . there are many 'gods' and many 'lords,' yet for us there is one God, the Father, from whom are all things and for whom we exist, and one Lord, Jesus Christ, through whom are all things and through whom we exist" (1 Cor. 8:5-6) — that individual can say, **My kinsman is mine, and I am his**; for each text conveys the same thing as the other. For anyone who renounces both "gods" and "lords" lays claim to the one God and Lord, from whom he comes and to whom he returns; for, it says, "for us there is one God . . . from whom are all things and for whom we exist," thus declaring clearly the sense of **he is mine, and I am his.**

Now Symmachus, when instead of **shepherds his flocks among the lilies** he proposed "shepherds the flowers," showed that it is not so much that the Bridegroom shepherds in the place where there are lilies, but that he shepherds the lilies themselves — the souls who are free of care and anxiety . . . , who also pay no mind to earthly things because their minds are truly fixed upon the kingdom of the heavens, and for whom the things that most people worry about pass on their way unnoticed; for, he says, "Seek first his kingdom and his righteousness, and all these things shall be yours as well" (Matt. 6:33); and in saying this he lends support to the idea that we set out earlier when, investigating the statements **The flowers are seen on the earth** and **the time for cutting has come**, we said that **flowers** means the saints that have blossomed within Christianity and **the time for cutting** means the pruning of the Jews. So then it is here that the good shepherd who lays down his life for the sake of the sheep "shepherds the flowers."

As to the expression **the shadows depart**, one is bound to think, in accord with the sense of the previous line, that it refers to the voiding of the works of the law — the shadow that Paul frequently speaks of in some such way as this: "The law has but a shadow of the good things to come instead of the true form of these realities" (Heb. 10:1); or "These are only a shadow of what is to come; but the substance belongs to Christ" (Col. 2:17); and again, "They serve a copy and a shadow of the heavenly realities" (Heb. 8:5), meaning the priests that function under the law. He appears also to make the following point plain: that the shadow of the law, having departed, has come to an end, and that the reality of grace is in control, built as it is upon the rock, against which "the gates of Hades shall not prevail" (Matt. 16:18).

*   *   *

Now the Bride has already said, **My Kinsman is like a gazelle, or a young stag on the mountains of Bethel** (2:9); so how is it that she repeats herself and says, **Turn back, my Kinsman, be made like the gazelle or the young hart**, not **on the mountains of Bethel** but **on the mountains of the plains?** In the one case she speaks as if what she says had already come to pass, while in the other she speaks in the imperative mood, exhorting him to assume this role all over again.

It may be, though, that our puzzle is solved by the difference between the ways in which the mountains on which the Bridegroom is located are described; for in the former case, she said **on the mountains of Bethel**, whereas here she says **on the mountains of the plains**. It may well be, then, that the one signifies a location on the earth, while the other refers to Hades because of the hollowness [that marks plains], so that the text says something like what follows.

For already she says, "You, O Bridegroom, have been like the deer and the **young stag on the mountains of Bethel**; you have conferred benefits on people here, you have subjugated the hostile Powers, and you have given the 'power to tread upon snakes and scorpions'" (Luke 10:19). But there remains this for her to add: "those imprisoned in the place below the earth by all-ruling death also enjoy your benevolence. Go, then, and once more be like **the gazelle or the young hart on the mountains of the plains** and, like a stag who has drawn them out, by your sense of smell overcome the Powers that reign there" — the Powers that Job called gatekeepers of Hades: "At the sight of you the gatekeepers of Hades were terrified" (Job 38:17 LXX). To these Powers, moreover, the angels that form the King's vanguard gave a command: "Lift up your gates, you rulers, and be lifted up, you everlasting gates, and the King of glory shall come in" (Ps. 23:7, 9 LXX = 24:7, 9) — and this in order that your advent may profit the whole human race, and not just a part of it. John the Baptist too says something along these lines: "Are you he who is to come, or shall we look for another?" (Matt. 11:3) — wanting him to bring the good news also to those imprisoned there below. For it is one and the same thing to say "**Turn back . . . be made like the gazelle,**" and to say "Are you he who is to come, or shall we look for another?" Even though the one is spoken as a command and the other as a question, both refer to Christ's descent into Hades, whither he went down to despoil [the Powers] and to liberate from the world the souls held prisoner by this age.

One must further observe that it is everywhere necessary for the Word to rest upon mountains, or at least upon hills. And if he is ever discovered to be in deep valleys or chasms, he is found there by reason of his great condescension and because he seeks, out of his love of humankind, to bring those who are down there to a higher and better state.

(12) Bernard of Clairvaux

My Beloved is mine, and I am his.

It is unquestionable that in this text a love blazes up that is shared between two persons; but surely in this love the highest happiness belongs to one party, while what characterizes the other is a wondrous condescension. For this is not an agreement or a knitting together of equals. In any case, who could pretend to have a clear comprehension of the gift the Bride boasts of on the ground of this token of love, and which she returns, unless it were someone who, by reason of exceptional purity of mind and holiness of body, might deserve to experience the same sort of thing? This is an affair of the feelings. No one attains to it by the exercise of reason, but by likeness. How few there are who can say, "And we all, with unveiled face, beholding the glory of the Lord, are being changed into his likeness from one degree of glory to another, as by the Spirit of the Lord!" (2 Cor. 3:18).

However, in order that these words may receive some sort of rational interpretation, even while the Bride retains her secret (into which for the moment we cannot enter, especially given the sort of people we are), we must surely introduce something that is at once better adapted to what everyone can understand and more familiar — something that orders the words in a coherent way and provides understanding to the simple.

Now it seems to me that it is sufficient for our explanation of the words as well as for the popular understanding if by the words **My Beloved is mine** we understand "inclines," with the result that the meaning is, "My Beloved inclines to me, and I to him." Nor is it the case that I am the only person who has made this judgment — or the first, since before me the prophet said, "I waited patiently for the Lord, and he inclined to me" (Ps. 39:1 Vg = 40:1). There you have, explicitly, the Lord's inclining to the prophet. Moreover, you have the prophet's inclining to the Lord in that he says, "waited patiently." For anyone who waits patiently inclines, and waiting is inclination. In the case of the prophet, the very same meaning is conveyed, and indeed the very words are the same, as in that of the Bride, except that the order is reversed. He puts first what she puts last, and conversely.

Yet the Bride has spoken more correctly. She makes no claim to merit, but gives first place to the favor done her and confesses that the grace of the Beloved has anticipated her. This is right. For "who was first to make a gift to him and it will be repaid to him" (Rom. 11:35 Vg)? Then hear what John thought on this subject in his letter. "Love lies in this," he says, "not as if we have loved God, but that he first loved us" (1 John 4:10). . . .

Later, if I am not mistaken, the Bride admirably employs the very same words, but not in the same order. She herself follows the prophet's order, and says, **I am my beloved's, and he is mine** (6:3; cf. 7:10). Why does she speak in this way? No doubt in order to show that she is more full of grace when she concedes everything to grace, and ascribes to it both beginnings and outcomes. How, after all, can she be full of grace if she has anything about her that does not stem from grace? There is no way for grace to enter, where merit has already moved in. Hence a full acknowledgment of grace points to fullness of grace in the soul of the person who makes the acknowledgment. For if the soul possess anything that is strictly its own, to that extent grace must give place to it. Whatever you assign to your merit you take away from grace. I have no interest in merit that shuts out grace. I shrink from whatever belongs to me in order that I may truly possess myself; unless it be the case that what makes me my own is perhaps more truly mine. Grace restores me to myself as one freely justified and thus freed from slavery to sin. Where the Spirit is, there freedom is.

Song 3:1-5

SEPTUAGINT

3:1 Upon my bed by night,
I sought him whom my soul loves.
I sought him and did not find him.
I called him, and he did not
hearken to me.

2 "I will arise, then, and go around in
the city,
in the markets and in the streets,

and I will seek him whom my soul
loves."
I sought him and did not find
him.

3 The watchmen making their rounds
in the city found me.
"Have you not seen him whom my
soul loves?"

4 It was but a moment after I parted
from them
that I found him whom my
soul loves.
I seized him and did not let him go
until I brought him into my
mother's house,
and into the chamber of her
who conceived me.

5 I have charged you, O daughters of
Jerusalem,
by the powers and the virtues of
the field,

VULGATE

3:1 Upon my bed, night by night,
I sought him whom my soul loves.
I sought him and did not find him.

2 "I will arise and go around the city,

through the streets and the
squares;
I shall seek him whom my soul
loves."
I sought him and did not find
him.

3 The watchmen who guard the city
found me.
"Have you not seen him whom my
soul loves?"

4 Shortly after I had passed them by,

I found him whom my soul loves.

I held him and would not let him go
until I had brought him into my
mother's house,
and into the chamber of her who
bore me.

5 I adjure you, daughters of Jerusalem,

by the gazelles and stags of the fields,

that you [do not] rouse love and	not to rouse my beloved nor
waken it	waken her
until it pleases.	until she herself wishes it.

The opening of Song 3 finds the Bride searching for the one she loves. Not finding him in her bed, she gets up and seeks him throughout "the city" and its streets and squares, asking the watchmen who patrol the city by night whether they have seen him; but she finds him and brings him "into my mother's house" only when she has "parted from them," as the LXX has it.

This picture of course inspired in commentators a series of reflections on the soul's — and the people of God's — search for the divine Word. Much of what they said turned on what they took the poem's city to symbolize. Thus Gregory of Elvira takes it to mean the Scriptures of the Mosaic covenant. Gregory of Nyssa, however, takes it to mean the intelligible world, while Richard of St. Victor thinks that it symbolizes the created order in all its levels; as they see it, it stands for the cosmos, whether in its intelligible dimension or as a whole. A significant departure from this line of interpretation is found in the exegesis of Rupert of Deutz, for whom the passage tells, allegorically, the story of the relation of the Virgin Mary to her son, Jesus.

The mention of "my mother's house" evokes quite different interpretations. For Gregory of Elvira, it seems to echo Gal. 4:26, where Paul identifies "the Jerusalem above," the heavenly Jerusalem, as "our mother." Gregory of Nyssa, by contrast, takes it as a reference to God and thus quietly anticipates what he will later say about "mother" as it occurs in 3:11.

The section closes with a repetition, whose presence is difficult to account for, of the words spoken by the Bride at 2:7. The passage translated here from Gregory of Nyssa reproduces what he had written on that earlier verse in his fourth homily — to which he refers his hearers (and readers) when he comes to the present verse (3:5). He misapprehends the sense of the conditional clause ("If you wake . . .") by construing it as a command rather than a prohibition. Accordingly he uses it to commend, among other things, his belief, based on 1 Tim. 2:4, that God will bring the whole body of humanity to salvation.

(1) Gregory of Nyssa

Upon my bed at night,
  I sought him whom my soul loves. . . .

Now consider in detail, if you will, the speech that presents itself for our study and discernment — but only after you have first understood this, that at the literal level the text describes a bridal chamber and the business of a marriage; and these provide the matter for our inquiry. Philosophical treatment of these matters transposes the surface meaning of the thoughts into the key of the pure and immaterial and sets forth the teachings of the faith; it uses the enigmas provided by the events to arrive at a clear grasp of what is revealed.

Since, then, the text represents the soul as a Bride and designates him whom she loves with her entire "heart and soul . . . and strength" (Mark 12:30) as a Bridegroom, it is logical that she — who in her own mind has attained the highest of her hopes and has already, in her own judgment, been united with the One she desires — calls her more perfect participation in the Good a **bed** and terms the time of her going to bed **night**.

Now the word "night" points to contemplation of things unseen, just as in the case of Moses, who entered into the darkness where God was (cf. Exod. 20:21) — God who, as the prophet says, "Made darkness his hiding place round about him" (Ps. 17:12 LXX = 18:11). And once the soul was there, she learned that she was as far from arriving at perfection as those who had not yet made a beginning. For she says, "Already, like one judged worthy of perfection, I am taking my rest as upon some **bed** of the comprehension of what I have known; but when I have entered into the Invisible, with the world of sense left behind me; when, surrounded by the divine night, I am seeking what is hidden in the darkness — that is when I have indeed laid hold on love for the one I desire, but the object of my love has flown from the net of my thoughts. For I was seeking him **upon my bed by night**, so as to know what his essence is, whence he has his beginning, where he comes to an end, by what means he has existence. But I did not find him. I was calling him by name, as far as I was able to discover names for the Nameless, but there was no name whose sense could attain the one I was seeking."

How, after all, could the One who is above every name be discovered by calling out a name for him? That is why she says, **I called him, but he did not hearken to me.** At that point she knew that there is no limit to his splendor, his glory, and his holiness. Hence she bestirs herself again and in her understanding moves about the intelligible and supracosmic nature (which she calls **the city**), in which are the Rulers and Dominions and the Thrones set over the Powers and the assembly of the heavenly beings (which she calls **the square**) as well as the unnumbered multitude (which she denotes by the word **street**) — to see if she can find the Beloved among these. So she went about, searching every angelic order; and since she did not see the One she sought among the good beings she found, she mused thus within herself: "May it be that the one I love is known to them?" And she said to them, **Have you not seen him whom my soul loves?** But they fell silent in the face of this inquiry and by their silence showed that the One she sought was imperceptible even to them. As, then, she went, in the persistent curiosity of her understanding, through the whole of that supracosmic city and did not see the object of her desire even among intelligible and incorporeal beings — at that point she left behind everything she had already found and in this way recognized the object of her search, whose existence is known only in incomprehension of what it is, in whose case every conceptual trait is an obstacle to its discovery for those who seek it.

So she says, "**No sooner had I passed them by**, having departed from the whole created order and passed by everything in the creation that is intelligible and left behind every conceptual approach, than I found the Beloved by faith; and holding on by faith's grasp to the one I have found, I will not let go until he is within my **chamber**." Now the "chamber" is surely the heart, which at that moment became receptive of his divine indwelling — at the moment, that is, when it returned to that condition in which it was at the beginning when it was formed by the mother who gave it birth. We shall not go wrong to conceive the **mother** as the First Cause of our constitution.

But maybe now it is time once more to set the divine utterances alongside the text itself, so as to conform the words to what the mind has discerned. **Upon my bed by night, I sought him whom my soul loves. I sought him and did not find him. I called him, and he did not hearken to me. I will arise and go around in the city, in the markets and in the streets, and I will seek him whom my soul loves. I sought him and did not find him. The watchmen making their rounds in the city found me.** "Have you not seen the one whom my soul loves?" It was but a moment after I parted from them that I found him whom my soul loves. I seized him and would not let him go until I had brought him into my mother's house, and into the chamber of her who bore me.

(2) Gregory of Elvira

On my bed in the nighttime,
I sought him whom my soul loves . . .

On my bed, that is, in my heart, **in the nighttime**, that is, in the teaching of the wisdom of this age, **I sought him whom my soul loves. I sought him and did not find him.** After she had failed to find him there and failed to hear him when she called upon him in that same place, she addressed herself to another kind of search, so as to seek him in other writings.

I will arise, says she, **and go around in the city, in the forum and in the avenues, and I will seek him whom my soul loves.** What is meant by **I will arise?** Well, she was still lying prostrate, as we have already said above, among the nations, attached to the earth — that is, she was wise in earthly things and in the bed of her heart she meditated on earthly things. But when she could not find the true God there, she said, **I will go about the city, in the forum and in the avenues.** When she speaks of this city, she is referring to the design of the divine Law; for the design of the Law, like a great city, contains a public square and avenues, streets and homes, walls vast and high made strong by their impregnable solidity — that is to say, by the protection that God provides, by which we are all defended and protected — and the turrets of the charisms, whence we are wont to repel the hostile demons; it has streets, that is, the ways along which life moves, and homes, that is, the benefit assured by honest fellowship.

What she says, though, is **I will go about the city**, that is, "I will search through the whole Law." When she says "forum," she is referring to the Law, that is, the Pentateuch, the five books of Moses, in which, as in a forum, there are contained all of divine and human legislation, the foundation of the laws, and the enactments of right conduct: this is the forum of God's Law. She calls the prophetic books "avenues," by which are manifested, to those who frequent them, the correct paths of righteousness that lead to God.

And therefore she says, **in the forum and in the avenues . . . I will seek him.** In the **forum**, doubtless, as I have said, of the Law of Moses, and in the **avenues** of the Prophets, and in all the streets of the divine Scriptures, the Church was promising that she would seek God. Indeed, the Lord himself says, "You search the Scriptures and you see . . . for it is they that speak of me" (cf. John 5:39); and again, "The kingdom of heaven is like a treasure hidden in a field" (Matt. 13:44). The treasure, then, that is, Christ, is hidden in the field of the Scriptures and hence must be sought there.

But, she says, **The guards who keep and guard the city found me.** Who are these **guards** but the scribes and the Pharisees, that is, the leaders of the Jews, who with immense care acted as the guards of this very same city of the ancient law and searched into all its precepts as they went around it? These **guards**, then, and searchers and investigators of the ancient law came across the Church, as something born in the body of Christ, when they themselves answered the Magi who were asking where Christ would be born by saying that Christ was to be born in Bethlehem of Judea; but they did not deserve to keep him.

Finally, she says, **when I passed by them after a short time.** What does this **short time** mean except that with God nothing is very long? Accordingly, she pronounces that the time from his birth to his passion is **short**; for it is at the point when he had risen from the dead after his revered passion that the Church found him whom her soul loved, for the apostles were sent forth starting from the time of the Lord's resurrection to assemble the Church from among the nations. Hence she says, **I found him and would not let him go** by the love that he himself possessed even to the point of shedding his blood — as the apostle said, "Who shall separate us from the love of Christ?" (Rom. 8:35).

But she adds, **until I brought him into my mother's house, and into the chamber of her who conceived me.** This is the voice of the Church. And if the Church is the mother of all, we must inquire who the mother of the Church is — the mother into whose **house** and into whose **chamber** she said she was going to introduce him. I have already shown above what the Church is, that is to say, the body of Christ composed of its mutually adapted members. Therefore the mother of the Church is the holy and heavenly Jerusalem, of which the apostle Paul says, "that heavenly Jerusalem which is above" (cf. Gal. 4:26). She who is mother of the Church, that is, of us who are the Church, sent to us the Christ whom we put on in baptism, as the apostle says, "For as many of you as were baptized into Christ have put on Christ" (Gal. 3:27). Therefore if anyone have Christ within, God enters the chamber of his heart, because Christ remains in the Church and the Church, in Christ; nor can anyone enter that house of the heavenly Jerusalem unless he have Christ within and cling to him with an unbreakable love.

Further she adds, **and into the chamber of her who conceived me.** What is this **chamber** of our mother the heavenly Jerusalem if it be not that of which the apostle says, "what no eye has seen, nor ear heard, nor the heart of man conceived, what God has prepared for those who love him" (1 Cor. 2:9)? So just as the mother of the Church is the heavenly Jerusalem, because the former is the more ancient, while the latter comes afterward on the earth, there is in the former the fullness of the Spirit and the manifestation of reality, while in the latter there is a portion and an earnest of heavenly grace. Now, says the apostle, we receive an earnest of the Spirit (cf. 2 Cor. 1:22; 5:5); then the fullness. Now "we know in part" (1 Cor. 13:9), but then wholly; now we see in an enigma and in a mirror, but then "face to face" (1 Cor. 13:12). The fullness gives birth to this "earnest," and that exalted Jerusalem conceives this "portion." For the heavenly Jerusalem that is our mother gave birth to this Church "by water and the Spirit" (John 3:5) — the Church that in the age to come she will receive into herself.

(3) Rupert of Deutz

Upon my bed, night by night,
   I sought him whom my soul loves.
I sought him and did not find him . . .
   until I brought him . . . into the chamber of her who bore me.

Take these words in, my friends — all of you who possess the Holy Spirit of love, who love the Lord God "with all your heart, with all your mind, and with all your soul" (Matt. 22:37). Take these words in, I say, my friends and daughters of Jerusalem; for within this love there lives a deep desire. The closer your Beloved is, the more intensely you desire him. Those who possess him desire to possess him, and those who see him desire to see him. For the angels see him, and yet, as Scripture bears witness, "they long to look upon" him (1 Pet. 1:12). For my part, I have not in any way possessed or seen him, but I bore him in my womb, and gave birth to him, and as his mother fed him with milk, and diligently watched him. How many sleepless nights do you reckon I have spent watching him and hearing him? For the daytime was not enough to satisfy such a desire, but night by night, on my bed and in my chamber, I would cherish and adore the little one, I would hear and adore him when he had matured — when in the midst of sweet conversations, by his eyes, the eyes of his body, he filled me with the look of his divinity, but so tempering it that I was able to bear him before whom the angels and the powers of heaven tremble, even as you have heard him say in this very book of the Song of Songs, **Turn your eyes away from me, for they cause me to fly away** (6:5).

Thus did I have him **upon my bed,** but then it happened that I did not find him there. For he said, "O woman, what have you to do with me" (John 2:4)? From the time of his baptism by John, I began not to find him on my bed or in my chamber, in that secret place of my habitation. For straightaway "he was led by the Spirit into the wilderness" (Matt. 4:1), and when he had returned he valued the gospel more than his feelings, which is why he said, "O woman, what have you to do with me?" But he also taught other people to do the same thing, namely, to leave father and mother on account of the gospel (cf. Luke 14:26). That is why, with great desire, I sought him and did not find him, wanting to have him entirely to myself alone.

Therefore I said, **I will arise and go around the city, through the streets and the squares; I shall seek him whom my soul loves.** So I said, and so I did; for since he was going around the cities and fortified places, proclaiming the good news of the kingdom of God, I was following and trying to find him. **I sought him and did not find him;** for he was so intent upon his business that he concealed his recognition of me, his mother. In the end there came a day when he was talking to the crowds, and "someone told him, 'Your mother and your brothers are standing outside, seeking you,' and he replied to the one who told him, 'Who is my mother, and who are my brothers?' And stretching out his hand toward his disciples, he said, 'Here are my mother and my brothers! For whoever does the will of my Father in heaven is my brother, and sister, and mother'" (Matt. 12:47-50). In this manner he concealed his recognition of me, his mother; and this is what is meant by my saying, **I sought him and did not find him.**

After this, I stood beside his cross. But did this mean that I had found my Beloved? On the contrary, it meant that I had found a sword that pierced my soul (cf. Luke 2:35). He was buried, and the tomb was closed and sealed. And as for me, with what design was I seeking him? With what sort of desire did I desire him, when I knew that he would be raised from the dead? Consequently **I did not find him. The watchmen who guard the city found me.**

Who were these **watchmen**, and what **city** did they guard? They were his disciples; for it was their determination to guard, indeed to build, the city of the true Jerusalem, concerning which, or to which, the Beloved himself said, "Upon your walls, O Jerusalem, I have set watchmen; all the day and all the night they shall not cease to praise the name of the Lord" (cf. Isa. 62:6). These **watchmen** were already at work then, for they were mourning and weeping and took no sleep. These **watchmen . . . found me.** Also the women who, watching through the entire night, came to the tomb, who bought spices as well so as to anoint him — they found me, as they were enthusiastically carrying the good news that he had risen and that they had seen him. And me, I ask, "You haven't **seen him whom my soul loves,** have you?" "We have seen him," they say, "we have seen the Lord! 'He has risen indeed, and appeared to Simon' (Luke 24:34). Moreover, he was manifested to two disciples on their way to Emmaus; and afterward he stood in our midst and said, 'Peace be with you.' . . . In these and other ways we saw him on the very 'third day' on which he rose."

This is what those watchmen said to me. But I wanted to find him in such a way that no one would scorn me when I said, "I have found him, I have seen him"; and so it was. For **shortly after I had passed them by, I found him whom my soul loves** — and not just anywhere, but I saw him ascending into heaven, and I saw his apostles, once the Holy Spirit had been sent from heaven, proclaiming the glory of the Lord. Such was my finding of him whom my soul loves; and on the basis of this finding of him, **I held him,** so that I might **bring him into my mother's house, and into the chamber of her who bore me,** which is to say, the synagogue. . . .

This beloved one, and most beloved one of all, is an example for all other souls, so that they too may seek the Beloved according to their ability and want to find him. We seek the Beloved **upon the bed** when in the slight repose afforded by this present life we sigh with desire for our Redeemer. We seek him **by night** because, though our mind stays wakeful in the night, our eye is yet, for all that, blinded. But any who do not find their Beloved are patient, so that they may **rise,** may **go around the city** — which is to say, may mentally in their searching run through the Church of the elect; may seek throughout **the streets and the squares** — make their way, that is, through paths both narrow and wide (cf. Matt. 7:13-14), and may look to see whether they are able to find anything in them, seeking for his traces; for there are some, even of those who live the worldly life, who have something of virtue about their doings. As we are seeking, however, the **watchmen who**

guard the city find us. These are the holy fathers, who watch over the state of the Church. They meet us with the good studies to which we apply ourselves so that they may teach us with their word or their writing. When **shortly after** we have **passed them by**, we discover what sort of thing this love of ours is; for our Redeemer, though in virtue of his condescension he was a human among humans, transcended the human condition in virtue of his Deity. So when the **watchmen** have gone by, the Beloved is discovered because, when we see that the prophets and apostles are below him, we understand that he who is divine by nature transcends the human condition. Thus he is sought first of all because he has to be found, so that once he is found he may be the more tightly held. The holy desires of all grow by having their fulfillment delayed, as we said above; and if such delay causes them to fade, they were not desires in the first place.

(4) Richard of St.-Victor

Shortly after I had passed them by,
  I found him whom my soul loves.

God can be sought out and known in the threefold creation: in the cosmos and the things created to adorn it; in humanity; and in the angelic order. The soul that thirsts for God makes the round of these and passes them by one by one, in order that she may find him whom she seeks.

By looking upon the visible aspect of the cosmos, she intuits its Creator. For once viewed, this affords the knowledge that the Lord himself is God, and that God himself made this, and that it did not make itself. But such a seeing is shared by all persons, the evil as well as the good; for all human beings see God in this manner, as we read in Job (cf. Job 26:14); that is, each sees God from afar, because God is seen from outside, and not in himself. This is the manner in which the philosophers have seen him, who, however, find him not by way of love.

From this vision, therefore, she moves on to humanity, which also **passes them by** in virtue of the image, even though it has lost the likeness in which God is contemplated intimately as a friend — the image, I mean, of God in the soul, which it manifests within itself by possession of reason and intellect. She does not, then, shift her attention to any and all human beings, but only to those that are good and spiritual. For she does not turn herself in the direction of those who tread the wide road (cf. Matt. 7:13) that leads to death, but toward those who are practicing virtue for the sake of the kingdom of heaven — those whom above she calls **avenues** and **streets**, by which terms she designates the more imperfect and the more perfect. In these she finds not only the image of God but also God's partial likeness, depending on the degree to which they have progressed in virtue or have mounted toward perfection.

Since, however, she does not find in these the full likeness of God (though she does find a certain degree of likeness), she passes on — in order that she may understand more fully and see more closely — to that which does in fact see more closely, which is to say the angelic creation, in which she looks fully upon the likeness (i.e., the imprint of the

likeness), and in which the imprinted likeness remains and endures from the very beginning. Human beings, however good or holy they may be, nevertheless see **by night**, that
is, obscurely; but the angels see at noontide, that is, in full knowledge. For just as the
blessed Job says, the stars are clouded over by the darkness of this night (cf. Job 3:5, 9), because even folk that glow with virtue and sanctity of life are dimmed and obscured by the
night of human blindness. The angel is bathed with the light of perfect contemplation;
for the angel is the radiance of eternal light and an unspotted mirror of the divine majesty, which, just as it in no way stands apart from God, so too, seeing God perfectly and as
he is, manifests God in itself, because it is a clear and unspotted mirror for people who
turn the eyes of their heart upon it, once they have been more thoroughly cleansed of sins
and vices — and, indeed, even of the images of them. For the vices becloud, and their images also recur, and they impede contemplation and conceal knowledge; anyone, therefore, who looks into this mirror to view the purity of the angels employs the pure eyes of
the heart. In this mirror, the likeness of God shines back to itself. For they are pure even
as he is pure; and they are holy even as the holy Lord is their God.

Finally, from the angel the pure soul passes on to the Author of purity, and from the
holy ones to the Holy of Holies, from those that contemplate to that which is contemplated — and straightway she finds the Beloved. For the angels are so close to him that
there is scarcely a space between him and them, and beyond them there is nothing to be
found save him. Once the Beloved is found, therefore, rejoicing greatly with the angels
and remembering the great gain that has come to her through them, she says, "**Shortly
after I had passed them by, I found him whom my soul loves.** For as soon as I passed by
them, I found my Beloved. I passed by them in order that I might come, and I passed on
with their help in order to find. For by meeting them and by their aid I obtained what I
desired. They evoked and inflamed my desire, and they brought to pass my encounter
with the Beloved." So the "finding" of the Bridegroom is the experience and the revelation of his presence.

For to the soul that seeks and never relaxes her intent he manifests himself and falls
in with her desires. And when he is present, the soul is renewed, and as it were clinging to
him, she becomes sensible of a sweetness in her interior taste, spiritual understanding, illumination of faith, increase of hope, provocation of love, zeal for justice, delight in the
virtues. In prayer she has familiar converse with God, aware that she is heard and heeded
to the highest degree, speaking with God face to face and hearing what the Lord God is
saying within her, constraining God in prayer and from time to time prevailing. Illumined by this grace, she begins to perceive the darkness of her heart, to know herself, to
discern how vices conceal themselves under the appearance of virtues or secretly link
themselves with them. For in her mind a new day dawns after the night of ignorance. . . .

(5) Gregory of Nyssa

I have charged you, O daughters of Jerusalem,
  by the powers and the virtues of the field. . . .

Then the Bride turns and addresses her words to the daughters of the Jerusalem on high. What she utters is an exhortation, stated with an oath, always to increase and multiply love, until "he who wills all to be saved and to come to knowledge of the truth" (1 Tim. 2:4) renders his will operative. This is what she says: **I have charged you, daughters of Jerusalem, by the powers and the virtues of the field, to rouse love and stir it, until it please.**

Now an oath is an utterance that of itself guarantees its truth. The function of an oath, however, is twofold. Either the speaker himself gives a hearer warrant of truth, or else he imposes upon others a compelling necessity to falsify nothing; for example, "The Lord swore truth to David and will not go back on it" (Ps. 131:11 LXX = 132:11). Here the trustworthiness of the promise is ratified by the oath. On the other hand, when Abraham, taking thought about a noble marriage for his only son, orders his own servant not to marry Isaac to one of that Canaanite race who were condemned to slavery (so that a mingling with slave stock would not injure the nobility of his line), but to arrange a marriage for the child from his ancestral homeland and his own kin, he imposes an absolute obligation not to neglect the command by administering an oath to him that he would surely carry out whatever Abraham had sanctioned concerning the child.

Even though, then, the function of an oath is double, in these circumstances the soul that has ascended to a height as great as what we have seen in our previous investigations does not, as she teaches the souls that are her disciples the way to perfection, use an oath to afford her hearers an assurance of what she has attained. Rather does she direct them by her swearing toward the life of virtue — to keep their loving sleepless and wakeful until the time when God's good will achieves its end, that is, until "all are saved and come to the knowledge of the truth" (1 Tim. 2:4).

And just as back then the oath was taken by the patriarch's thigh, so now it is taken **by the powers and by the virtues of the field.** Thus the text says, **I have charged you, daughters of Jerusalem, by the powers and virtues of the field, to rouse love and stir it, until it please.**

So first of all, where these words are concerned, we must try to see what the field is, and then what the "strength" and the "power" of the field are, and whether the latter differ from each other or the same thing is signified by both. In addition to these tasks, we must ask what is meant by "rousing" and "stirring" love. For the expression **until it please** has already been treated in what was said just above.

Well then, it is entirely obvious from the Gospels that by "field" the Master's speech refers to the world. On the other hand, from the lofty words of Ecclesiastes — who counted everything that appears and passes away as vanity — it is evident that "the form of this world is passing away" (1 Cor. 7:31) and that in its unstable nature nothing abiding is discernible. Then what is the "power" of this field that is the world, and what is the "virtue" whose mention makes the order given to the daughters of Jerusalem inviolable because of the oath? For if we look to things that appear as though there were some power in them, Ecclesiastes enters an objection to any such assumption when he labels everything that is brought to light or sought after among appearances as vanity. For what is vain has no reality, and what has no essential reality has no strength.

Maybe, though, it is possible to find a hint at the meaning by attending to the plural form of **power**. For we find in Holy Scripture that there is a distinction made in the case of such terms, to wit: when power is spoken of in the singular, the understanding is referred by this language to the Divine; whereas it is the angelic nature that is present to the mind when the plural form is used. Take the case of Christ as "the power of God and the wisdom of God" (1 Cor. 1:24). Here by the singular form Scripture makes the Divine known. "Praise the Lord, all you powers of his" (Ps. 102:21 LXX = 103:21); in this case, the plurality of the powers indicates a reference to the intelligible nature of the angels. Now the term "virtue," when taken together with "power," puts a strong emphasis on the meaning of the idea conveyed. In this way the Scripture, by repeating words of the same sense, shows more certainly what is intended — as when it says, "O Lord, my strength, the Lord is my stronghold" (Ps. 17:3 LXX = 18:12). For the meaning of each of the words is the same, but the combination of terms of the same sense renders what is signified emphatic.

The plural significance of **powers**, therefore, and the mention of **strengths** in the same mode, seem to point the understanding of the hearers to the angelic nature. Consequently the oath — brought before the disciple-souls to establish the judgments of their teacher — does not appeal to the world that is passing away, but to the eternally abiding nature of the angels. It enjoins looking toward them in order that by their example it may establish the steadfastness and stability of the virtuous life. For since it has been proclaimed that our life after the resurrection will become like the angelic constitution (and he who made the announcement does not lie), it would be appropriate even for our life in the world to be gotten ready for the life we hope for, so that those who live in the flesh and lead an existence in the field of the world do not live according to the flesh and are not conformed to this world, but use their life in the world to practice beforehand the life they are hoping for. This is why the Bride, by an oath, imparts strength to the souls of her disciples — so that, namely, their life, which is being set right in this **field**, may look to the powers, imitating the angelic purity by its impassibility. For when love is thus being roused and wakened — which means being lifted up and always increasing through progress toward what is better — the good will of God is fulfilled, as in heaven, so on the angelic earth and within us, since impassibility is being achieved.

This is what we have understood by the words: **I have charged you, daughters of Jerusalem, by the powers and virtues of the field, to rouse love and stir it, until it please.** But if some other interpretation has been found that comes closer to the truth of what we search for, we shall accept the gracious favor and give thanks to him who reveals the hidden mysteries through the Holy Spirit in Christ Jesus our Lord.

Song 3:6-11

Septuagint

3:6 What woman is this coming up from
the wilderness,
burning like columns of smoke,
myrrh, and frankincense

from all the powders of the
perfumer?

7 Behold Solomon's bed!
Sixty mighty men surround it,
out of the mighty men of Israel.

8 They all bear the sword,
being schooled in war.
Each man has his sword on his thigh
because of fear by night.

9 King Solomon made himself a litter
of the woods of Lebanon.

10 He made the pillars of it silver,
and the back-rest of it gold;
the seat of it was purple,
its interior a mosaic of stones,
love from the daughters of
Jerusalem.

11 Come forth, you daughters of
Jerusalem,
and behold King Solomon
with the crown with which his
mother crowned him,
on the day of his wedding
and on the day of his heart's
gladness.

Vulgate

3:6 What woman is this that is coming
up through the wilderness
like a column of smoke
made of the fragrances of myrrh and
frankincense
and every powder of the perfumer?

7 Behold Solomon's bed!
Sixty mighty men surround it,
out of the mighty men of Israel,

8 all holding swords
and well schooled in war.
Each man's sword is on his thigh
because of nocturnal terrors.

9 King Solomon made himself a litter
of the woods of Lebanon.

10 He made the pillars of it silver,
the back-rest [was] gold,
the step of it, purple.
He strewed the middle of it with love
on account of the daughters of
Jerusalem.

11 Go out, you daughters of Zion,

and see King Solomon
in the crown with which his mother
crowned him,
on the day of his wedding
and on the day of his heart's
gladness.

This passage of the Song seems to picture an elaborate procession in which a bride is brought "up" (to Jerusalem?) from a "wilderness" or "desert" in a royal palanquin. The bride in question is presumably Solomon's. This at any rate is roughly the way ancient commentators understood it. Modern exegetes have wondered whether the mention of Solomon is original, whether in any case it can bear the interpretation thus put upon it — and indeed whether the procession in question might not be, or reflect, a cultic liturgy representing the marriage of a god and goddess. They have also, naturally, wondered whether it is right to see the passage as a literary unity. Such issues, however, did not trouble patristic or medieval interpreters, who maintained their identification of the Bride with the Church or the believing soul, and of Solomon with the Christ, the Word of God — the "prince of peace."

Theodoret's account of the sense of this passage suggests the general shape of patristic interpretation. It is important of course that the "column" to which Bride is compared is composed of the fragrant smoke of incense; for the interpretation of fragrances as moral virtues was a standard device of early Christian allegory. Whereas Ambrose identifies the Bride as an individual soul, and Apponius sees her as the Church of the Gentiles, Theodoret is simply vague about her identity. He is clear, however, about the "bed" and the "litter" of Solomon. The first of these terms signifies the Scriptures (for the Scriptures bear the Word of God, and in that bed the Bride is made morally and intellectually fruitful by her intercourse with the Word). The second represents the apostles, who carry the Word to the nations. Ambrose, on the other hand, prefers to envisage the "bed" as Christ himself, the saints' place of rest, while for Rupert of Deutz some eight centuries later, the bed is the womb of the Virgin. Gregory of Nyssa, for his part, seizes upon the mention of Solomon's — that is, the divine Word's — mother, whom he naturally identifies as God; and this identification leads him into a discussion of the use of masculine and feminine "names" for God.

(1) Theodoret of Cyrus

What woman is this coming up from the desert?

Those who saw the Bridegroom ascending into the heavens after his victory over the Devil and his destruction of death were amazed and said, "Who is this King of glory?" and learned that "He is the Lord strong and mighty, the Lord mighty in battle." Then, wishing to learn more precisely, they ask again, "Who is this King of glory?" and hear their answer: "The Lord of hosts, he is the King of glory" (Ps. 23:8, 10 LXX = 24:8, 10). In the same way here, those who marvel at the beauty of the Bride say, **Who is this woman coming up from the desert?** "Desert" is the name they give to human nature because of the primordial blasphemy. Hence too Isaiah cries aloud, "Be glad, thou thirsty desert; rejoice, desert, and blossom as the lily" (Isa. 35:1 LXX)!

And just as here they are astonished that so much beauty should sprout up out of the wilderness, so too in the prophecy of Isaiah those who see the Bridegroom are amazed and say, "Who is this that comes from Edom? The red of his garments is from Bozrah." Now "Edom" means the earth, while "Bozrah" refers to flesh. And those who are amazed at his beauty cry out, "This one is glorious in his apparel, in strength with might. Why is thy apparel red . . . like grapes trodden in the full wine press" (Isa. 63:1-2)? And they also say, "Being in the body he shines." They are calling his body "apparel," and it possesses a strong beauty, compelling all those who behold it.

Thus in this verse they are amazed not only that the Bride is beautiful, but also that she is mounting up from the desert, that is, that she is coming up from depth to height, and proceeding from lowly things to things on high.

And then it says, **She is like a column of smoke.** The grammatical construction here is not clear; for the Seventy, since they translated the Hebrew literally, did not make the meaning plain. But Aquila and Symmachus made the sense manifest for us when they said, "like a likeness of the smoke of incense." But the smoke of incense frequently looks like a column outlined, as it were, in the air. It is right, moreover, that the Bride is said to be like "the smoke of incense" — that Bride who, according to the blessed Paul, gave her members "as a living sacrifice, holy, acceptable to God" (Rom. 12:1), and "continually" offers up "a sacrifice of praise" (Heb. 13:15), and mortifies "her earthly members" (Col. 3:5), and has been buried with Christ (cf. Rom. 6:4), and presents herself to God as a burnt offering.

They teach us also what sort of incense it is to which she is compared; for they specify **myrrh . . . and frankincense from all the powders of the perfumer.** It is plain from the Mosaic law that **frankincense** is allotted to God, while **myrrh** is ointment for the bodies of the dead. Those, therefore, who marvel at the beauty of the Bride indicate by these words why she is fragrant and why she is likened to the vapor of incense, namely, because she worships both the humanity and the Deity, at once believing in the Bridegroom's death and confessing that he exists from all eternity. **From** among **all the powders of the perfumer,** then, they marvel at her **myrrh** and her **frankincense.** For she possesses the other virtues also, garnered as it were by some **perfumer** from the divine Scriptures; but what stands out in her case are **myrrh** and **frankincense,** which is to say, her understanding of God and of the divine economy of redemption.

Thus those who have marveled at the Bride's beauty tell her about the Bridegroom's riches, and say, **Behold Solomon's bed! Sixty mighty men surround it, out of the mighty men of Israel. They all bear the sword, being instructed in war. Each man has his sword on his thigh because of fear by night.**

To begin with, one must ask why they call the Bridegroom "Solomon." "Solomon" means "peaceful." One can find this in Chronicles; for God said to David when he wanted to build a temple, "Behold, a son shall be born to you; he shall be a man of peace. I will give him peace from all his enemies round about. For his name shall be Solomon, and I will give peace and quiet to Israel in his days. He shall build a house for my name. He shall be my son, and I will be his father, and I will establish his royal throne in Israel for ever" (1 Chron. 22:9-10). Now it is well known that Solomon died after he had lived a relatively short time, and that his dynasty had an end. For that reason, our own peaceful Lord is called "Solomon." Of him the blessed Paul writes: "For he is our peace, who has made both one and has broken down the dividing wall of hostility" (Eph. 2:14).

Hence the blessed David inscribed Psalm 71 "A Psalm for Solomon" and in it related the righteous deeds of our Savior: "He shall judge the cause of the poor among the people, and he shall save the children of the poor, and he shall humble their accusers; he shall live while the sun endures, and before the moon, for generations of generations" (Ps. 71:4-5 LXX = 72:4-5). But Solomon did not live as long as the sun, nor exist "before the moon, for generations of generations." No, but these things befit the one that, considered in his humanity, originated from Solomon, Jesus Christ. He, who existed before the ages, "came down like rain on fleece, and like drops of rain that water the earth" (Ps. 71:6 LXX = 72:6). "Fleece" here denotes the Virgin. For just as rain descends noiselessly upon a fleece, so did that saving offspring come to be without anyone's knowing.

Then David adds, "In his days righteousness shall arise, and peace in plenty, until the moon is done away. And he shall have dominion from sea to sea, and from the rivers to the ends of the inhabited world" (Ps. 71:7 LXX = 72:7) — and everything that follows, which conveys the same meaning; for now is not the time to give an interpretation of the psalm. Solomon, though, did not have dominion "to the ends of the inhabited world," but he who, taken in his humanity, originated from Solomon, Jesus Christ, was called "Solomon" because he was peaceable and gentle and brought peace with him.

Having learned, then, who Solomon is, come and let us undertake our interpretation.

Behold Solomon's bed! We shall take the **bed** of the Bridegroom to be the divine Scriptures. For in the Scriptures the Bride, lying down as it were alongside the Bridegroom and receiving the seeds of his teaching, conceives, carries a child, enters into labor, and gives birth to spiritual profit, so that she cries out with the prophet, "For the fear of you, O Lord, we conceived in the womb, and labored in pain, and gave birth: we brought forth the spirit of your salvation upon the earth" (Isa. 26:17-18).

Sixty mighty men surround it, out of the mighty men of Israel. They all bear swords, being instructed in war. Each man has his sword on his thigh because of fear by night. In my judgment, the number sixty is not placed here to refer to the quantity in question. Rather are the saints who were prominent under the Old Covenant indicated by "sixty." For it is said that ten is the perfect number, but that six befits those under the law. For, it says, "Six days you shall do your work" (Exod. 23:12). Thus the text says that those who have been perfected by the law **surround** the litter — those who are descended from Israel, those who are the mightiest of all, who bear a sword, who have experience of warfare, and who carry other swords on their thighs. **Because of fear by night**, it adds. Symmachus makes this clearer when he says "on account of nocturnal fears." These **mighty men**, it means, make the Bridegroom's litter their concern, protecting the Bride from the attacks of enemies. They carry two swords, one upon the thigh, the other in the hand: the word of reproof, and the hidden and mystical word. The word of reproof is right at hand, while the mystical word is within in a treasure hoard, in its scabbard.

King Solomon made himself a litter of the woods of Lebanon. He made the pillars of it silver, and the back-rest of it gold; the seat of it was purple, its interior a mosaic of stones, love from the daughters of Jerusalem.

Again let us understand this **litter** to be the holy apostles, bearing the Name of the Lord before nations and kings, and before the sons of Israel; for Christ said this very thing to Ananias about the blessed Paul: "Go, for he is a chosen instrument of mine to carry my name before Gentiles and kings and the sons of Israel" (Acts 9:15). Moreover, Paul himself, the holy one, cries out, "Do you seek a proof of the Christ who speaks in me" (2 Cor. 13:3)? Furthermore, the blessed Habakkuk calls the apostles "horses"; for, says he, "You will mount upon your horses, and your horse-riding is salvation" (Hab. 3:8). And again, "You made your horses to march into the sea, stirring up many waters" (Hab. 3:15). He uses the name "sea" for the nations, who were stirred up by the preaching of the apostles. That is why unbelievers said of them: "These men who have turned the world upside down have come here also, and Jason has received them" (Acts 17:6-7). Thus the people whom Habakkuk calls horses, we discover being spoken of in the Song of Songs as a **litter.**

So then **King Solomon made himself a litter of the woods of Lebanon.** The divine Scripture often refers to Jerusalem, and the whole Jewish people, as "Lebanon," and in the introduction to our book we have demonstrated this from the prophetic writings. Since, then, the blessed apostles were descended from them, it makes sense to say that the palanquin was constructed **of the woods of Lebanon.** As to its **pillars,** the text says that they were made of silver; and we find that the apostles were also named **pillars,** for in his Letter to the Galatians, the blessed Paul writes: "Peter and James and John, who were reputed to be pillars, gave me and Barnabas the right hand of fellowship, that we should go to the Gentiles, and they to the circumcised" (Gal. 2:9). It also says that its **back-rest** was golden, and this means the preaching of the gospel, upon which the divine Word reposes. Then **the seat of it was purple;** for it is right for beginners to have a king as their ruler, but it pertains to those who are perfected it to be treated as brides. And **its interior a mosaic of stones.** For the divine oracles are compared to pearls and precious stones, in accord with what the prophet says, "The ordinances of the Lord are true, and righteous altogether. More to be desired are they than gold, and much precious stone" (Ps. 18:10-11 LXX = 19:9-10). And again, "Behold, I have loved your commandments more than gold and topaz" (Ps. 118:127 = 119:127). Further, "The kingdom of heaven," according to the Lord's word, "is like a merchant in search of fine pearls" (Matt. 13:45). And elsewhere he says, "Do not throw your pearls before swine" (Matt. 7:6).

(2) Ambrose of Milan

What woman is this coming up from the wilderness?

Seeing the Bride cleaving to Christ, then, and still ascending with him — for he stoops to meet and assist those who seek him repeatedly, that he may lift them up — the daughters of Jerusalem say, **What woman is this coming up from the wilderness?** This earthly place of ours appears to be an uncultivated wilderness, filled with the brambles and thorns of our sins, and they plainly wonder how a soul, which had earlier been left in that lower place, may cleave to God's Word and ascend after the manner of the shoot of a vine that climbs upward, like smoke that is created by a fire and seeks the heights, and then radiates a delightful fragrance. That fragrance, moreover, gives off the sweet aroma of reverent prayer, which like incense is directed in the sight of God. Further, we read in the Apocalypse that "the smoke of the incense rose with the prayers of the saints" (Rev. 8:4), and this incense — that is, the prayers of the saints — is borne by an angel "upon the golden altar before the throne" (Rev. 8:3) and gives off the sweet perfume, as it were, of reverent prayer, because it is compounded of prayer that asks not for corporeal things, but for things eternal and invisible. More than anything else, however, it gives off the fragrance of myrrh and frankincense because the soul has died to sin and lives to God.

Seeing the Bride ascending, therefore, and not holding back, and delighted by the fragrance of her merits — and what is more, recognizing that she is the Bride of that peace-bearing Solomon — they follow her in an ardent band right up to **Solomon's litter**, because true rest in Christ is owed her. For Christ is the bed of the saints, upon whom the weary hearts of every one of them rest from the struggles of this age. Upon this bed Isaac rested and blessed his younger son with these words: "the elder shall serve the younger" (Gen. 25:23 and 27:20). Reclining upon this bed, Jacob blessed the twelve patriarchs. Reclining upon this bed, the daughter of the ruler of the synagogue rose up from death. Lying on this bed, the departed son of the widow, summoned by the voice of Christ, undid the chains of death.

Once the Bride has been brought to the rest that belongs to the Bridegroom, therefore, they sing a wedding song, and say, **Love from the daughters of Jerusalem. Come forth and behold King Solomon with the crown with which his mother crowned him, on the day of his wedding.** They are singing an epithalamium, and they are calling the rest of the heavenly powers, or the souls, to see the love that Christ has with regard to the daughters of Jerusalem. That is why he deserved to be crowned by his mother as Son of love, even as Paul shows when he says, "He has delivered us from the dominion of darkness and transferred us to the kingdom of his Son of love" (Col. 1:13). Therefore he is Son of love and is himself love, not being accidentally possessed of love, but possessing it forever in what he is, just as he possesses the kingdom of which he said, "For this I was born" (John 18:37). That is why they say, **Come forth**, that is, "come away from the cares and thoughts of this age, come away from bodily constraints, come away from the vanities of the world — and behold what love the peace-bearing King has on the day of his wedding, how glorious he is, because he gives resurrection to bodies and joins souls to himself. This is the victor's crown of the great contest, this is the magnificent wedding-present of Christ, his blood and his suffering. For what more could he give, who did not hold himself back, but offered his death for our benefit?"

(3) Apponius

What woman is this that is coming up through the wilderness
    like a column of smoke. . . ?

I venture, then, that this people that is **coming up through the wilderness** is the one that Paul, the teacher of the Gentiles, gathered together "from Jerusalem all the way to Illyricum" (Rom. 15:19). He anointed it with the fragrant oil of the teaching, and sprinkled it with the perfumes of the mysteries of the heavenly sacraments. He then conducted it all the way to the **litter** of the king that brings peace — just as the next verse says, **Behold Solomon's litter! Sixty mighty men surround it, out of the mighty men of Israel.**

For the Hebrew people, therefore, this is something to wonder at — the Church of the Gentiles coming up through the wilderness to the high point that is knowledge of Christ. For the place where the name of Christ has not been named is truly a **wilderness.** This is the people regarding whom those of the Hebrews who had believed said to Peter, "Therefore God has opened a door of mercy even for the Gentiles" (cf. Acts 14:27; 11:18), when he had consecrated the house of the centurion by baptism. It was at Antioch that the majesty of this great name — a name that for thousands of years had been unknown to the human race — was first confessed. It was there that the royal Church of the Gentiles first glowed with the adornment of precious stones; there that the fragrance of good works — now, compacted into a single mass and ignited by the fire of Deity, a single **column of** the **smoke** of confession — gave off a sweet smell for the sake of the one God Christ and ascended to heaven; for it was at Antioch that, with Paul the friend of Christ as its teacher, the Bride that is the Church, the people of Christ, were first called Christians, as the history of the Acts of the Apostles shows (Acts 11:26).

For just as the nations, on their way to death, marveled at the Church, Israel, **coming up** from Egypt through the **wilderness,** so too the Hebrew people marvels at the Church of the nations, on its way to life, coming up from Egypt by the laborious road of discipline to the mount of knowledge of the Creator, the mount that is Christ, who bears in himself the whole healing art, the pattern of right faith, and the ingredients that constitute the surpassing fragrance of sound teaching. To the young maidens who cleave to him he conveys, from these possessions, both the pattern for the healing of life and the sweetness of his fragrance. For many, and precious, ingredients of surpassing fragrance, when they have been reduced to a single powder, are prepared by the art of the perfumer to serve as a sweet smell for the delight of kings; and because they are many, but brought together into a single mass, they give out, when turned into a vapor by fire, a single **column of smoke** of noble fragrance. In exactly the same way, the confession made by right faith and by prayers to produce a single sweet smell in the sight of God manifests the unanimity of a multitude of peoples. So elsewhere the prophet David prays, "Let my prayer be set forth in thy sight as the incense" (Ps. 140:2 Vg = 141:2).

(4) Rupert of Deutz

Behold Solomon's bed!

For what is the couch of the true, and truly pacific, King Solomon, who made peace between us and God, if not the one in which the divine nature joined human nature to itself? And what couch is that if not your womb, O beloved of the Beloved, your virginal womb? For there the deity of the Word of God, there the Word of God confined himself and inseparably joined to himself, in unity of person, a human nature formed of your flesh; and there is the Bridegroom, that is, God having our flesh together with a rational soul — the Bridegroom, I say, Christ, both God and human being, even as we sing in the psalm: "he himself like a bridegroom coming forth from his chamber" (Ps. 18:6 = 19:5).

(5) Gregory of Nyssa

Come forth, you daughters of Jerusalem,
    and behold King Solomon
with the crown with which his mother crowned him,
    on the day of his wedding.

The next verse contains an exhortation addressed by the Bride to the daughters of Jerusalem. For as the great Paul judges it a loss if he does not share his own good things with all (which is why he said to his hearers, "Become as I am, for I was once as you are" [Gal. 4:12]; and then, "Become imitators of me as I am of Christ" [1 Cor. 11:1]), so too the Bride herself, a lover of humanity who has been made worthy of the divine mysteries of the Bridegroom, when she has seen the litter and has become the palanquin of the King, calls to the young women (who no doubt represent the souls of those who are being saved), saying, "How long will you be shut up in the cavern of this life? Come out, when you have become daughters of Zion, from among the shadows of nature, and behold the wondrous sight. You will see the crown which adorns the head of the King, which his mother placed on his brow in accordance with the word of the prophet, 'You have placed on his brow a crown of precious stone' (Ps. 20:4 = 21:3)."

Now no one who has given thought to the way we talk about God is going to be overly precise about the meaning of the name — that "mother" is mentioned instead of "father"; for he will gather the same meaning from either term. For the Divine is neither male nor female (how after all could any such thing be conceived in the case of Deity, when this condition is not permanent even for us human beings; but when we all become one in Christ, we put off the signs of this difference along with the whole of the old humanity?). For this reason, any name we turn up has an equal capacity for indicating the unutterable Nature, since neither "male" nor "female" defiles the designation of the inviolate Nature. Hence in the Gospel a father is said to give a marriage feast for a son; while the prophet addresses God, saying, "You have put a crown of precious stone on his head," and then asserts that the crown was put on the Bridegroom's head by his mother. So there is one wedding feast, and the Bride is one, and the crown is placed on the head of the Bridegroom by one agent. Hence it makes no difference whether God calls the Only-Begotten "Son of God" or "Son of his love" (Col. 1:13), as Paul has it, since whatever the name is used it is one Power who escorts the Bridegroom to our marriage.

So the Bride says to the young women, "Come out, and become daughters of Zion, so that you will be able to see, from an exalted height (for so 'Zion' is translated), the marvelous sight of the Bridegroom wearing his crown." Now the Church becomes his crown because of the "living stones" with which she encircles his head; and the one that plaits a crown of this sort is Love, whom one may call either "mother" or "love" without risk of error; for according to John's word God is love. Now the Bride says that he rejoices in this crown as he delights in the bridal splendor. For the one who has taken the Church for himself as a partner is joyful when he is crowned with the virtues of those who stand out within her. But it would be more effective to set out the divine words themselves, which go exactly like this: **Come forth, you daughters of Jerusalem, and behold King Solomon with the crown with which his mother crowned him, on the day of his wedding and on the day of his heart's rejoicing.**

(6) Rupert of Deutz

. . . **behold King Solomon**
  with the crown with which his mother crowned him. . . .

. . . **his mother**, namely, the ancient Church of the patriarchs and prophets, to whose faith he was promised, of whose flesh he was born. Before he was born, his mother made him that precious crown with which he was to be crowned and in virtue of which he would be acknowledged as the great and admirable King. And what is the crown? Of a certainty it is the most glorious authority of the truth spoken by the prophets. To this truth there belong as many prophecies as the crown of this Solomon possesses gems and precious stones. [She crowned him] **on the day of his wedding**, the day on which he came forth from my womb, "as a bridegroom . . . from his chamber," **and on the day of his heart's gladness**, the day on which, crowned with a crown of thorns, he brought his work to completion and rejoiced in the triumph of his resurrection, which was to follow.

Song 4:1-8

<SEPTUAGINT>

SEPTUAGINT

4:1 Behold, you are beautiful, my close
one,
  behold, you are beautiful!
Your eyes are doves
  outside your veil.
Your hair is like flocks of goats
  that have been revealed from
  Gilead.
2 Your teeth are like flocks of shorn
  ewes
  that have come up from their
  washing,
all bearing twins,
  and not one of them barren.
3 Your lips are like a scarlet ribbon,
  and your speech is radiant.
Like the skin of a pomegranate is
  your cheek
  outside your veil.
4 Your neck is like a tower of David
  that was built in *thalpioth*.
A thousand shields hang upon it,

  all the weaponry of the mighty
  men.
5 Your two breasts are like two twin
  offspring of a she-goat
  that feed among the lilies,
6 until the day breathes
  and the shadows are moved.

VULGATE

4:1 How fair you are, my beloved,

  how fair you are!
Your eyes are doves' eyes
  outside of what is hidden within.
Your hair is like flocks of goats
  that have ascended from Gilead.

2 Your teeth are like flocks of shorn
  ewes
  that have come up from their bath,

all pregnant with twins,
  and none is sterile among them.
3 Your lips are like a scarlet band,
  and your speech is sweet.
Your cheeks are like a piece of
  pomegranate,
  apart from what hides within.
4 Your neck is like a tower of David
  that was built with battlements.
A thousand shields hang down
  from it,
  all the weaponry of the mighty
  men.
5 Your two breasts are like two twin
  offspring of a she-goat
  that feed among the lilies,
6 until the day breathes
  and the shadows give way.

I will betake myself to the mountain
    of myrrh
    and to the hill of frankincense.
7 You are altogether fair, my close one,
    and there is no flaw in you.
8 Come away from Libanus, my Bride,
    come away from Libanus.
You shall come and be crowned from
    the beginning of faith,
    from the peak of Sanir and
      Hermon,
from the lions' dens,
    from the mountains of the
      leopard.

I will make my way to the mountain
    of myrrh
    and to the hill of frankincense.
7 You are altogether fair, my beloved,
    and there is no spot upon you.
8 Come away from Libanus, my Bride,
    come away from Libanus.
You shall be crowned from the head
    of Amana
    and from the peak of Sanir and
      Hermon,
from the lions' dens,
    from the mountains of the
      leopards.

The sixteen verses of Song 4 are a lengthy declaration of the Bridegroom's passionate love for the Bride, and they open with a series of similes (4:1-5) in which the Bridegroom praises the Bride's beauty as manifested by her eyes, her hair, and the like. Patristic and medieval exegesis of these verses tends to turn on the identification of the Bride as the Church: each part or "member" of the Bride's body is taken to represent in a figurative manner one type of "member" of the Church (cf. 1 Cor. 12:4-12, 27-30) — bishops and teachers, for example, or ascetics.

The passage as we read it in the Septuagint and the Vulgate is beset by problems occasioned by inaccuracies in translation, or simply by the obscurity or uncertainty of the original Hebrew text. Thus the Vulgate translates the word for a veil as "what hides within." Everyone, moreover, had trouble with the verb describing the behavior of goats on Mount Gilead, partly at least because the Hebrew text was uncertain (according to the Septuagint they "are revealed from" Gilead; while the Vulgate has "ascended from," an expression that evoked much exegetical ingenuity). By the same token, the translators of the Septuagint — like many others since — were baffled by the Hebrew word they simply transliterated as "thalpioth" (4:4, of David's tower), and which Jerome, no doubt wrongly, took to mean something like "ramparts" or "battlements." The "shields" and "weaponry" that decorate the tower more likely referred to ornaments of the Bride's neck.

Readers might note further that whatever the phrases "mountain of myrrh" and "hill of frankincense" refer to (the Bride's breasts?), it is not features of the earth's landscape. Again, the problem regularly created by the words libanos *(Greek) and* libanus *(Latin), both of which ambiguously denote (a) frankincense and (b) Lebanon, arises in this passage in an acute form. Finally, the Septuagint translates the Hebrew for "from the peak of Amana" (RSV) by "from the beginning of faith" — which explains the way in which Augustine reads this verse in the excerpt given below.*

Drawing on 4:2, **Your teeth are like flocks of shorn ewes,** *Augustine ob-*

*serves that allegory has pedagogical as well as aesthetic value. It is much more pleasant, he writes, to contemplate spiritual truths through imagery provided by the Scriptures (the beautiful **teeth** of the bride) than to have them presented simply as ideas.*

(1) Ambrose of Milan

Behold, you are beautiful, my close one,
    behold, you are beautiful . . .
from the beginning of faith.

After [the baptism], you dressed in white garments as a sign that you had removed the covering of your sins and put on the chaste robe of innocence. Of this the prophet said, "You will sprinkle me with hyssop, and I shall be clean; you will wash me, and I shall be whiter than snow" (Ps. 50:9 LXX = 51:7). For one who is baptized is cleansed, it seems, in accordance with law and gospel alike, since Moses sprinkled the blood of the lamb with "a bunch of hyssop" (Exod. 12:22), and since Christ's garments were as white as snow when he manifested the glory of his resurrection in the Gospel. Someone whose guilt has been taken away is made "whiter than snow" — which is why the Lord said through Isaiah, "Though your sins are like scarlet, I will make them as white as snow" (Isa. 1:18).

Once the Church is wearing these garments, which she put on by "the washing of regeneration" (Tit. 3:5), she says in the Song, "I am black but beautiful, O daughters of Jerusalem" (1:5) — black because of the frailty of the human condition, beautiful because of grace; black because the offspring of sinners, beautiful because of the sacrament of faith. Seeing these garments, the "daughters of Jerusalem" are struck with wonder and say, "Who is this that comes up all whitened" (8:5)? "She was black, so how is she 'whitened' all of a sudden?"

For the angels themselves were in doubt when Christ rose; the powers of the heavens were in doubt when they saw that flesh was ascending into heaven. That is why they were saying, "Who is this King of glory!" (Ps. 23:8 LXX = 24:8). And while some were saying, "Lift up the gates, you princes! Lift yourselves up, you everlasting gates, and the King of glory shall come in" (Ps. 23:7 LXX = 24:7), others were questioning and saying, "Who is this King of glory?" In Isaiah too you find that the doubtful powers of the heavens said, "Who is this that comes up out of Edom, in crimsoned garments from Bozrah, shining in his white apparel?" (Isa. 63:1).

But when Christ sees his Church in white garments (or else the soul cleansed and washed in the bath of rebirth), the Church for whom he had donned "filthy garments," as it is written in the book of Zechariah (3:3), he says, **Behold, you are beautiful, my close one, behold you are beautiful! Your eyes are doves.** It was in the form of a dove that the Holy Spirit came down from heaven. The eyes are beautiful . . . because he came down like a dove.

And further on it says: **Your teeth are like flocks of shorn goats that have come up from their washing, all bearing twins, and not one of them barren. Your lips are like a scar-**

let ribbon. Now this is no half-hearted praise — and in the first instance because of the nice comparison with shorn goats; for we know that goats graze without danger in high places, and also that they feed safely on steep and rugged terrain, and finally that, when shorn, they are unburdened of superfluities. The Church is compared to a flock of such animals because it has within it the virtues of such souls as are laying aside the superfluity of their sins with the help of the bath of baptism, souls that bring to Christ their faith in the mystery and their well-pleasing mode of life, whose mouth speaks of the cross of the Lord Jesus.

In such souls the Church is beautiful. That is why God says to her, **You are altogether beautiful, my close one, and there is no fault in you** (for her guilt is drowned in the water); **you are here from Lebanon, my bride, you are here from Lebanon. From the beginning of faith you will go through and arrive;** for by renouncing the world, you will pass through the present age and attain to Christ. . . .

(2) Augustine of Hippo

Your teeth are like a flock of shorn ewes
    that have come up from their bath,
all of which have given birth to twins,
    and none is sterile among them.

[a] Why is it, I ask, that if someone should say that there are holy and perfect men and women by whose life and conduct the Church of Christ tears away from their various superstitions those who come to it, and incorporates them into itself by having them imitate the good deeds of the saints; and that there are good and faithful servants of the true God who have cast off the burdens of this age and come to the holy washing of baptism, from which they rise born again with the Holy Spirit and bring forth a double love, that is, love of God and love of the neighbor — why is it, I ask, that it gives more pleasure to the hearer to have the same idea expounded on the basis of that passage in the Song of Songs where it speaks of the Church in language one would use to praise a beautiful woman: **Your teeth are like a flock of shorn ewes that have come up from their bath, all of which have given birth to twins, and none is sterile among them.**

To be sure, one would not learn anything different if the idea were presented without the help of the imagery. And yet, somehow it gives me more pleasure to contemplate the saints when I see them as the teeth of the Church tearing away men from their errors and making them part of its body, breaking down their hardness by biting and chewing. With the greatest of pleasure I visualize the shorn ewes, as though the burdens of this world were cast aside like fleece, coming up from the washing of baptism and giving birth to twins, the two commandments of love, and none failing to produce this holy fruit.

Why this gives me greater pleasure than if no such image was presented by the Holy Scriptures, since the subject matter is the same and the conception is the same, is difficult to say. In any case that is a matter for another occasion. But no one disputes that it is much more pleasant to learn such things through imagery, and much more rewarding to discover meanings that are gained with difficulty.

[b] "For you have smitten all those who are my enemies without a cause, you have shattered the teeth of sinners" (Ps. 3:7); that is to say, in that "you have smitten all those who are my enemies, you have shattered the teeth of sinners." Obviously the punishment of these "enemies" is the act by which their teeth are shattered, that is, by which the words of sinners who tear at the Son of God with their curses are reduced to vanity — even, as it were, to dust. Hence we take "teeth" to mean words of cursing. Regarding these teeth the apostle says, "But if you bite . . . one another, take care that you are not consumed by one another" (Gal. 5:15).

"The teeth of sinners" can also refer to the chieftains of sinners, at whose word each member of the fellowship of those who live rightly is torn to bits and as it were made part of the bodies of those who live wickedly. Opposed to these teeth are the teeth of the Church, by whose teaching believers are cut off from the errors of the nations and of the various schools of thought and are brought over into her who is the body of Christ. . . .

Moreover, it is with these teeth in mind that the Church is told: **Your teeth are like a flock of shorn ewes coming up from the bath, all of whom bear twins, and without a barren one among them.** These are the ones whose precepts are right and who live in accordance with their precepts. They are the ones who act in accordance with the saying, "Let your light so shine before men, that they may . . . give glory to your Father who is in heaven" (Matt. 5:16). Inspired by their authoritative word, people put their faith in the God that speaks and acts through them and become members of the Church, being set apart from the present age, to which they had been conformed. Therefore is it right that those through whom such things are accomplished are referred to as teeth because of their likeness to sheared sheep, on the ground that they have laid down the burden of earthly cares; and then, all of them, as they come up out of the bath — out of the washing away of the filth of this age through the mystery of baptism — give birth to twins. For they observe the two commandments of which it is said, "On these two commandments hang all the Law and the Prophets" (Matt. 22:40). They love God with all their heart, and with all their soul, and with all their mind, and their neighbor as themselves. And among these there is none that is barren, for they return to God fruit of this order. . . .

(3) Apponius

How fair you are, my close one,
  how fair you are!
Your eyes are doves' eyes,
  apart from what is hidden within.

Christ the Lord praises the twofold beauty — of soul and body alike — that belongs to the Church of the Gentiles once the ways of the flesh, that is to say, the ways of all the vices, have been stripped away, and she has been converted from the service of many base deities to the one true God. For the first beauty of the soul is to know her Maker; and the second, to know herself — why she has been created and as what sort of being. After that come the adornments of beauty, which are to desist from evil deeds and to do good ones;

to flee contentions and pursue peace and love; to have her ears bedecked with virtuous hearing; to have her eyes held back by the restraints of modesty from anything shameful — and all this so that those who had, like the hawk, given all their attention to their prey, to lusting after what was not their own, to lewdness, now, once come to knowledge of Christ and set in order by the simplicity **of doves**, may glow with the light of mercy, of gentleness, and of purity.

For among the other members of the Church none is more worthy of the highest praise than those that carry out the function of **eyes**; for among all the members of the body none is more precious than the **eyes**. Such persons, then, whether by their example or by the teaching their speech conveys, in giving guidance to the whole Church by their gentleness, simplicity, and purity, are rightly understood to be called **the eyes** of the Church; and they are compared to the eyes of those birds whose natural aptitude it is to discern the enemy at a long distance as he is approaching. By living watchfully, therefore, and giving no offense to the living, they are compared to **the eyes of doves**. When, however, they present to God **within**, in the mind, the same comely features as they do outwardly to other human beings, this is the very **hidden** thing — whatever sort of good work it was — that is praised by Christ, when he says, **Your eyes are the eyes of doves, apart from what is hidden within.**

(4) Bede the Venerable

Your hairs are like flocks of goats
that climb from Mount Gilead.

By the reference to **eyes**, one can also understand the holy Church's preachers, with whose help she contemplates the hidden heavenly mysteries that the general run of believers cannot grasp. By the reference to **hairs**, one can understand the believers among the populace who — even though they they have not been instructed with a view to their providing for and directing the Church's way ahead — nevertheless accord it, by their obedience, the adornment of their numbers. With people like this in mind, the Lord himself, when, to the disciples he had sent on a preaching mission, he predicted, "You will be hated by all for my name's sake," quickly added by way of consolation, "and not a hair of your head will perish" (Luke 21:17-18). This meant in effect: "Even though the hatred of the persecutors rages fiercely, they are not able to snatch up even the very least of those who belong to me," that is to say, "to your Head."

Now it is appropriate for hair of this sort to be likened to **flocks of goats**; for it is customary to refer to sinners by the word "goats" (cf. Matt. 25:32-33), and since every Church acknowledges — and truthfully — that it is not without sin, all the more should those who belong in the ranks of ordinary believers confess that "we all offend in many ways" (Jas. 3:2). Believers, then, do sin. Nevertheless, in virtue of the daily progress they make through their good works, they are headed for the life in which they will be liberated from all sin.

Hence the text is right to add, with regard to these goats, the words **that have**

climbed from Mount Gilead. For all who have been united to the body of their Redeemer dwell upon the mystical mountain, but the nobler goats — those that seek their pasture in the bosom of the mountain itself — **have climbed** that same mountain. On the other hand, those that are humble and aware of their sins and their weakness are aroused, by anxiety over their infirmity, to seek in Christ the food proper to the heavenly life, and they attempt without ceasing to bring themselves up. Indeed, we read in the books of Numbers and of Chronicles that Mount Gilead has "good and very rich pastures" (1 Chron. 4:40 Vg; cf. Num. 32:1). To this high and very fruitful mountain it is thus appropriate to apply the words that the very city that is established upon it — the holy Church, I mean — habitually speaks, "The Lord shepherds me, and I shall want nothing; he has set me in a place of pasture" (Ps. 22:1 Vg = 23:1). Also appropriate to it is the very name of the mountain that is called "pile of testimony"; for indeed the Lord is the pile of testimony, since in him there is brought together into a unity the multitude of all the saints, the "living stones" (1 Pet. 2:5) who "have been attested by the testimony of their faith" (Heb. 11:39), as the apostle says. Hence the Bride's hair is likened to the **flocks of goats** that, feeding on this mountain, ever strive to climb to its heights. . . .

(5) Rupert of Deutz

Your hair is like flocks of goats
  that have ascended from Mount Gilead.

What **flocks of goats** are these, and when did **flocks of goats** appear **from Mount Gilead?**

Surely what is meant is **flocks of** rational **goats**; and flocks of rational goats appeared when there began to be people of the sort of which the apostle speaks when he says, "They went about in sheepskins and the skins of goats," and the rest, as far as "and in caves of the earth" (Heb. 11:37-38). When did there start to be people of this sort, and from where did people with this sort of lifestyle appear? Surely it was when Jezebel was killing off the prophets of the Lord that they appeared **from Mount Gilead** — that is, from the city of the same name, Gilead. For it is written: "And Elijah the Tishbite, one of the inhabitants of Gilead, said to Ahab, 'As the Lord God of Israel lives, in whose presence I stand, there shall be neither dew nor rain these years, save in accordance with the words of my mouth.' And the word of God came to him, saying, 'Leave this place, and go towards the east, and hide,'" and the rest (1 Kings 17:1-3). These things were said and done by that first instigator and founder of those who have been called "sons of the prophets" — and the authority of the venerable fathers agrees that these were the monks of the Old Covenant. And it is rightly said that they appeared; for the one we have already called their founder, Elijah, is introduced so suddenly there that there is no previous text of Scripture that mentions who he was or where he came from.

(6) Gregory of Nyssa

Your teeth are like flocks of shorn ewes
    that have come up from their washing,
all bearing twins,
    and not one of them barren.

But it is surely time to inquire into the terms of the praise here given the Bride — how the loveliness of her teeth is likened to shorn herds that now, all equally, rejoice in twin offspring as they come up from the washing. . . .

Now if we were to attend to the literal sense of this image, I do not understand how anyone could say that praise is being given her teeth by comparing them with prolific flocks. What is commended in teeth is their hardness, and their appropriate placement, and their being firmly fixed in the gums in an even and consistent arrangement. But as to **flocks** that are coming up from **the washing**, having been scattered over the glens with pairs of offspring — it is not possible to see, on the basis of the obvious meaning of the text, what sort of attractiveness they attribute to the teeth by the example they provide. Teeth stand together in a row, joined to one another harmoniously, while flocks are scattered about, separated because of their need of pasture. Furthermore, it makes no sense to compare something that bears wool to a tooth, which is naturally naked. We are bound, therefore, to inquire how it is that one who lavishes praise on the nice arrangement of teeth can compare their beauty to flocks of ewes that bear twins — flocks whose wool is close-shorn and whose bodily filth has been washed off. What, then, are we to make of this?

Those who grind the divine mysteries up small by interpreting them more lucidly, so that this spiritual nourishment can the more easily be taken in by the body that is the Church — these people carry out the work of **teeth**. They take the thick and compact bread of the Word into their own mouth, and they supply it to the souls of its recipients in edible form by an interpretation that divides it into small bits. Thus — for it is easier to get an idea across by using an illustration — the blessed Paul, simply and without any preparation, sets before us the law's commandment in the form of an indigestible morsel when he says, "You shall not muzzle the ox when it is treading out grain"; but then he goes back and, after tenderizing it by his exegesis, makes the intent of the law easy to appropriate. He says, "Is it for oxen that God is concerned? . . . It was written" entirely "for our sake" (1 Cor. 9:9-10). And he says many other things of the same sort, as, for example, "Abraham had two sons, one of a slave girl, and the other of a free woman" (Gal. 4:22). This is the untouched loaf. But then how does he grind it up to make it edible for those whom he is feeding? He interprets the story as referring to two covenants, one that "bears children for slavery" (Gal. 4:24), while the other liberates from slavery. In the same fashion — lest we waste time on details — he takes the coarsely structured body of the law as a whole and cuts it up into fine pieces by his insightful and discerning treatment of it, rendering it spiritual where it had been corporeal; for he says, "We know that the law is spiritual" (Rom. 7:14).

What we have noted, then, in the case of Paul — how he fulfills the Church's need of teeth by grinding the open truth of the teachings up small — this we also say about anyone who follows his example and clarifies the mysteries for us. Thus the Church has its **teeth** — those who chop up the undigested fodder of the divine oracles for us and chew it as their cud.

Just as the divine apostle, then, describes the lifestyle proper to those who aspire to "the noble task" (1 Tim. 3:1) of the episcopate, specifying point by point what sort of person the recipient of the priesthood ought to be, so as also, along with everything else, to possess the gift of teaching: even so in this text the Word desires those who are assigned to perform the service of **teeth** in the Church first of all to be **shorn** (i.e., stripped of every material burden); and second, in virtue of the **washing** of conscience, to be free of any fleshly or spiritual spot. In addition to this, they are always to be making their way upward in virtue of their progress, and never to be dragged backward, down to perdition — but above all to take pleasure in all the twin descendants of their high-born offspring in respect of every form of virtue, and to be barren in none of the good pursuits. As to the twin offspring, that is an enigma for the esteem that belongs to each of the two things that constitute us: it means that **teeth** of this sort are twin-bearers, giving birth to impassibility for the soul and to "decorum" for the bodily life.

(7) Apponius

Your lips are like a scarlet ribbon,
  and your speech is radiant.
Your cheeks are like a piece of pomegranate,
  apart from what hides within.

The color of the berries of the scarlet oak is that of blood; the **scarlet ribbon** refers to the headband that, fastened together, hung upon the head of Aaron the high priest (cf. Exod. 28:37, 4 Vg), indicating the distinctive regal honor that is attained by confession of the name of Christ, the true king; and this signifies, beyond all doubt, the blood of the martyrs that colors the lips of the Church. For the persons of the confessors and martyrs, acting in the place of lips, afford a great beauty to the Church. These same lips defend the above-mentioned **teeth** from affronts, in order that persons who do not believe the word of the teacher, and blasphemously say that the irreproachable law that promises eternal life after the body's death did not proceed from the almighty God, by the mouth of either prophet or apostle, may believe the testimony of the martyrs.

These martyrs, because of the friendships that have become theirs in virtue of their faith in the one God and the magnitude of their merits, through their prayers defend, by signs and wonders, those who chew upon the Word of God — defend them against the wrongs inflicted by evil men and the attacks of demons, just as lips defend teeth. These teachers also perceive that those who have been killed for the name of Christ are alive, and that they pursue the demons who are the authors of their death with scourgings and blows. For just as, by the compression of teeth and lips, sound that is held back by producing a breath generates the sweetness of a melody from within, so too the Church produces **radiant speech** thanks to the power of the martyrs' marvels and to the interpretation of hidden mysteries by those who act as teeth and rightly expound the Word of God under the inspiration of the Holy Spirit.

Like a piece of Punic apple, so are your cheeks, except for that which is concealed within. By the beauty of the **cheeks** we understand that the modesty of virginity or chastity is signified; for there is nothing in the face of the Church so lovely — so admirable at once to believers and to unbelievers — as the splendor of chastity. For the phrase **like a piece of Punic apple**, that is, pomegranate, demonstrates that virginity imitates the works of Christ our Lord.

It was of him that the Church said earlier on, "Like a pomegranate tree among the forests, so is my Beloved among the sons" (2:3). This tree grows a fruit most beautiful to see and most delightful to taste, and serviceable as a remedy for people who are ill: he who was revealed to the world through the Virgin for the salvation of humanity scattered over the whole world the flowers of integrity and chastity. He shows here that virginity and continence possess a part — that is, a **piece** — of his beauty, and by them the Church's countenance, with the blush of chastity retained, is rendered most beautiful.

But the words **apart from that which hides within** mean that chastity alone, more than all other good works, makes the Church's countenance lovely in those who are ministers of the Christian people, where the chastity that human beings perceive is concerned — **apart from that which hides within**, that is, in the secret places of the mind, which is most beautiful to God but **hides** from human beings.

The noblest of the Church's cheeks, one in the Old Testament and one in the New, are in my view to be identified as the two Marys — the sister of Moses and Aaron, and the blessed mother of the Lord — who by preserving their integrity first began the work of making the Church's cheeks a subject of wonder and astonishment.

(8) Honorius of Autun

Your neck is like a tower of David
   that was built with its ramparts.
A thousand shields hang upon it,
   all the weaponry of the mighty men.

Whenever proper names are mentioned in the Scriptures, one takes account either of the meaning of the name, or of the office to which the person is assigned, or of the significance of something the person has accomplished. For example, these three things are to be considered in the case of Melchizedek: the meaning of his name, which is "king of righteousness"; his kingly and priestly office; and the sacrifice of bread and wine that he offered. He prefigured Christ, who is the king of righteousness and the true priest, and who offered bread and wine in the sacrifice of his body.

Similarly, there are three things to consider in the case of David: the meaning of his name, which is "desirable" or "mighty of hand"; his office, which is that of king and prophet; and the deed he accomplished, that he overcame Goliath in combat. He likewise points to Christ, who is "the King of glory" (Ps. 23:8ff. Vg = 24:8ff.), and in that glory is desirable (for "the angels desired to see" him [cf. 1 Pet. 1:12]); and he is the true prophet since he predicted everything that was to come; and he is mighty of hand in that on the cross he overcame the mighty Devil.

Now the **neck** joins head and body, while a **tower** protects the inhabitants of a city from their enemies. Hence the Church's **neck** are those who are instructed and knowledgeable in the Scriptures — who join the Church to Christ by word and example. Just as David's **tower** is impregnable, that is, just as the primitive Church is like a tower constructed by Christ the true David, the one who is desirable and strong of hand, against persecutors and heresies, and fortified by the gifts of the Holy Spirit, so too these persons are strengthened by Christ with the rampart of the Scriptures, for the purpose of defending the buildings of the faith and repelling the darts of its enemies. Their calling is to protect the ordinary citizens of Jerusalem, untutored as they are, from the citizens of Babylon — heretics, Jews, pagans, and false Christians.

This **tower . . . was built with ramparts** — which means to say that that Church is fortified by the impregnable teachings of the Scriptures, by which she defends herself against her enemies. Or perhaps it means that the apostles were her **ramparts**, in that they fought against the faithless on behalf of the Church with the weapons of patience.

A thousand shields hang upon it: for innumerable rational defenses have been bestowed upon that Church so that by their means she may defend herself against her adversaries. There hangs **all the weaponry of the mighty men,** in that for the purpose of providing examples, there are set forth for her all the works of those who have mightily overcome their vices — as, for example, Joseph did his self-indulgence, and Moses his greed; and by the same token those who constitute the Church's **neck** and **David's tower** because they join the Church to Christ and defend the citizens against their enemies, possess authoritative books as their **ramparts**, have as their **thousand shields** unnumbered defenses drawn from the Scriptures and from rational argument, and have **all the weaponry of the mighty men,** which is to say, all the written passions of the martyrs, and the lives of the saints.

Alternately, the **tower of David** is the holy Scriptures, built by Christ the true King to serve as protection for the Church, his Bride, against her enemies. This **tower** is **built with ramparts,** that is, with authoritative books, in which his prophets and apostles, her champions, fight at her front and defend her. On this **tower** there hang **a thousand shields.** These are all the teachings of the righteous of both the Old and New Covenants, as well as all **the weaponry of the mighty men** — the examples of all the saints, who make other people mighty in their struggle against the vices.

(9) Apponius

Your two breasts are like two twin
   offspring of a she-goat
   that feed among the lilies.

It is my view that the **two breasts** of the Bride who is the Church point to the two sons of Aaron, Eleazar and Phineas. They were the first to serve under the law that regulated the priesthood, and their place is now taken by those who, with wholesome teaching and the example of a holy life, nourish souls that are still babes and sucklings in the faith. Nor does it seem to me absurd to see Aaron himself as the bosom from which the aforesaid breasts grow. Garbed in vestments woven with gold and glittering with a variety of precious stones, Aaron is commanded to enter the Tent of Witness, just as the Bride and Queen, about to marry the King, enters the marriage bed or chamber of the King, with her whole bosom blooming, and radiant with gold and precious stones.

He says **two breasts**, however, because the person who professes to be a teacher and a nourisher of souls is turned into a killer of souls unless he teaches his hearers about the twofold covenant — unless he teaches them, that is, that the Old and the New Covenants have the one Almighty God as their source. For any who sucks at one breast will never so enlarge his strength as to "come to the perfect man, the stature of the fullness of Christ" (Eph. 4:13). But if one accepts, along with the Jew, only the Old Covenant, he will be worn out by marching in waterless places and stand in need of another to carry him; and if he accepts, along with Mani, only the new, he will die swollen up by the damp disease of dropsy.

He says **two breasts . . . like two twin offspring of a she-goat** so that these people who offer themselves to the Church as breasts may learn to present to their hearers . . . in the milk of their doctrine, the equality and similarity of the two covenants — to teach that whatever the Old Covenant asserts in prophetic types will come about for human salvation is achieved in the New Covenant through the incarnation of our Lord. Through him the Trinity, which in the law of Moses shimmered not openly but through an image, now glows like the sun in the face of the whole cosmos by the grace of the Word, as God said through Moses in the first book of Genesis: "In the beginning God made the heaven and the earth" (Gen. 1:1), and then later on: "The Spirit of God was borne about above the waters." Here you have three Persons in one Power: the Beginning, God, and Spirit: the One who made, the One in whom he made, and the One who animated the things that had been made. Further, everywhere in the New Covenant, through the testimony of the blessed evangelist John and the term "Word," the unity of these three Persons is revealed with perfect clarity. He says, "In the beginning was the Word, and the Word was with God, and the Word was God" (John 1:1). Furthermore, the Son himself establishes that the Father made everything in the Son. Asked by the Jews "Who are you?" he answered that he was the Beginning in which Moses attests that heaven and earth were made, by saying "the Beginning, because I also speak to you" (cf. John 8:25). Now "beginning" means "that before which there was nothing," and the point plainly is that before the Beginning, before God the Word, before the Holy Spirit, there was nothing, as the apostle Paul confirms: "All things hold together from him," that is, the Father, "and in him," that is, the Son, "and through him," the Holy Spirit (Rom. 11:36 and Col. 1:17).

This, then, is the likeness and beauty of the "one faith" (Eph. 4:5) proper to the **breasts** that are compared to **twin offspring of a she-goat**. They are praised because they sprang together at the very same time from the one bosom of the Church, the fatness of the Holy Spirit making abundant provision of the milk of teaching by the mouth of orthodox teachers, just as the **twin offspring of a she-goat** are acknowledged to be perfectly like each other.

For the words **that feed among the lilies** are spoken by way of magnifying the Bride's beauty, and at the same time they say that, just as the offspring of she-goats prefer to feed upon plants that stand up straight rather than only upon grasses, so too in the case of those from whom the milk of teaching is fed into the hearts of their hearers, their word and the example of their lives must always be pastured, by way of exhortation, not upon the lowly blossoms of secular literature, but upon the flowers that come from the exalted apostolic mountains. In them the word of exhortation must always sound out to the people on the subjects of modesty, continence, and the preservation of integrity. Further, they are to locate the place where their teaching finds its pasture in the examples of chaste souls — those, I mean, who, amid the thorny forests of shameless wantonness, shine brightly as with the luster of **lilies**, with the perfumes of purity: Elijah, Elisha, Daniel, Jeremiah, Joseph, John, Mary, Thecla, and all those who are like these, whom it would take too long to enumerate.

It is by imitation that the flowers are to be plucked from these **lilies**; it is by teaching that the flowers are to be fed upon; it is by being thought about that the examples are to be chewed over. For then, even though the aforesaid **breasts** are full of the fatness of the Holy Spirit, beauty is added when they are fed upon these **lilies** by imitating the habit of newborn goats. They will be filled as fully as possible with the milk of the teaching when they have fed upon the examples afforded by such flowers for the conduct of life. For where there is love of chastity, there too is the manifold Spirit of God's wisdom; and where the Spirit of God is, there too is freedom to speak; and where there is freedom, there is no slavery of a shamed conscience; and where the conscience is not enslaved, there is found love of abundant teaching.

For this is what the Holy Spirit teaches: that, just as **two twin offspring of a she-goat that feed among the** blooming **lilies** present a delightful appearance, so too a teacher of the people displays in himself a most pleasing gladness, if, among other good things, he has been girt about with the luster of chastity for the whole length of his life, just as the next words say: **until the day breathes and the shadows give way.**

By these words he declares how long God's people hold sound teaching to be a necessity — **until**, that is, that great **day** of judgment **breathes** which is free of darkness, whose breathing turns back the **shadows** of this dark age to their death. For whatever things seem of great consequence in this age are to be reckoned as shadows or dreams: bodily beauty, the wisdom of culture, strength of limb, the symbols of status, the power of rulership. All these are shown to be shadows and dreams by comparison with that eternal day of judgment.

(10) Gregory of Nyssa

I will betake myself to the mountain of myrrh
   and to the hill of frankincense.

Up to this point, the Word has been pronouncing the praise of the Church's individual members. In what follows, he contrives an encomium on her whole body, since "through death he destroyed him who has the power of death" (Heb. 2:14) and was restored again to the glory proper to the Godhead, which he possessed from the beginning, before the cosmos existed. For when he had said, **I will betake myself to the mountain of myrrh and to the hill of frankincense,** indicating by **myrrh** his suffering and by **frankincense** the glory of the Godhead, he added, **You are beautiful through and through, my close one, and there is no flaw within you.** By these words he teaches that no one takes his life from him, but that he has the power to lay it down and to take it up again as he makes his journey **to the mountain of myrrh,** accepting death on behalf of sinners not as a result of any deeds of ours, "lest anyone boast" (Eph. 2:8), but out of his own graciousness; and then that it is not possible for human nature to be purified of its **flaw** unless "the Lamb . . . that takes away the sin of the cosmos" (John 1:29) destroys the evil himself. Therefore the One who says, **You are beautiful through and through, my close one, there is no flaw within you,** and who introduces the mystery of his suffering under the figure of **myrrh** and then makes mention of **frankincense** — this One is instructing us that the person who shares **myrrh** with him will also fully share in his **frankincense;** for the one who suffers with him will be fully glorified with him; and the one who has once for all entered into the divine glory becomes **all beautiful,** having been separated from the inimical **flaw.** May we too be separated from it through the One who died for us and was raised, to whom be glory to the ages of ages. Amen.

(11) Hugh of St. Victor

I will betake myself to the mountain of myrrh,
   and to the hills of frankincense,
and I will speak to my Bride.
You are altogether fair, my Beloved,
   and there is no spot upon you.
Come away from Libanus, my Bride,
   come away from Libanus.
You shall be crowned from the head of Amana
   and from the peak of Sanir and Hermon.

Here a bridegroom is speaking. He has a bride, and he promises that he shall visit her. Note therefore that this bridegroom is not always at home, for he takes great care lest his love be counted of little worth; and since it would become wearisome if he were always present, he sometimes removes himself, sometimes withdraws at an appropriate time, so that while he is being sought in his absence, he may be clutched the more closely when present.

No doubt, moreover, he was absent when he spoke these words. On the other hand, he did not want a longer delay to cause him to be forgotten; and so he made up his mind to return and said, **I will betake myself.** He tells himself what he is going to do, because it is a sweet thing to say what it is a sweet thing to do, and I know not how it is that we never scorn to speak of what we greatly desire. **I will betake myself,** he says. He goes **himself** because a one-to-one love has no place for a sharer in its secret. He goes **himself** because the one who will suffer no partner in his love wants no companion on his journey.

But do you want to know who this bridegroom may be, and who his bride is? The bridegroom is God; the bride is the soul. The bridegroom, furthermore, is at home when he is filling the mind with an interior rejoicing; he goes away when he removes the sweetness of contemplation.

But on the basis of what likeness is the soul called the bride of God? She is a bride because she has been accorded an earnest in the form of the gifts of grace. She is a bride because she is bound to him by a chaste love. She is a bride because by the in-breathing of the Holy Spirit she brings forth the offspring of the virtues.

There is no soul who has not received the earnest of this bridegroom. But there is a gift common to all, and there is another that is special to the individual. The gift common to all is that we are born, that we are aware of things, that we understand things, that we see into things. The special gift is that we have been reborn, that we have received forgiveness of sins, that we have received the charisms of the virtues. Moreover, what each person possesses is, for that person, the earnest. For individuals that are rich, the earnest is the riches by which they are favored, so that the molestation of poverty may not break them up. For the poor, the earnest is the poverty by which they are afflicted, lest by lack of restraint they overflow their banks and stream away. For the strong, the earnest is the strength by which they are supported so that they may empowered for good works. For the infirm, the earnest is the infirmity by which they are broken so that they may accomplish no evil. For the naïve, the earnest is the simplicity that humbles them, lest they fall into pride. And in general, whatever human weakness endures in this life the gracious Creator apportions to the extent that his goodness allows, either for the correction of depravity or for the sake of progress in virtue. So ought we to give thanks in all things, so that while we are aware of God's mercy we may always make progress in love for God.

I will betake myself, he says, **to the mountain of myrrh** and so on. Myrrh, which tastes bitter and preserves the bodies of the dead from decay, signifies the mortification of the flesh. Frankincense, a word that refers to whitening, means purity of the flesh. This then is the route by which the Bridegroom comes to the Bride, **the mountain of myrrh and the hills of frankincense**, because first of all he kills the desires of the flesh by abstinence, and then by purity of heart drives out the mind's unknowing. Finally, as if on the third day, the Bridegroom comes to converse and inflames the soul with desire for him; and therefore it is fitting that he said **mountain of myrrh,** not "hill of myrrh," and **the hills of frankincense,** not "mountain **of frankincense,**" because we have to be steadfast in affliction and humble in the attainment of the virtues. For the loftiness of the mountain signifies greatness of soul, and the moderate height of the hills, the restraint of humility.

Likewise, his use of "mountain" in the singular and "hills" in the plural indicates that in the mortification of outward delights it is but little that we lose; whereas in the inward illumination of the mind, the good we encounter is manifold. Upon **the mountain of myrrh** we receive courage to stand against the lust of the flesh. On the hills of frankincense we receive illumination of mind against unknowing. In the converse of the Bridegroom we receive the gift of love against ill-will and hardness of heart.

Power is said to be proper to the Father, wisdom to the Son, and love to the Holy Spirit. When, then, we sin because of weakness, we sin against the Father, as though against power. When we sin because of unknowing, we sin against the Son as against wisdom. But when we sin out of ill-will, we sin against the Holy Spirit as against love. Therefore if one sins now against the Father and the Son, it is is either forgiven in the future, because someone who sins out of weakness or unknowing, just as he has some excuse for his crime, so too he is owed some relaxation of punishment, whether in this age if he repents, or, if he persists in wrong, in the age to come, so that he may experience a more tolerable punishment. But if there are any who sin out of ill-will, their sin has no excuse, and therefore their punishment is owed no remission; for if they repent in this age, they are to make full satisfaction as their punishment, and if they do not repent, they are to be punished in the coming age by a full condemnation. Therefore people of this sort have no remission, whether in this age or in that to come — not because indulgence is denied to the penitent, but because for unconditional sin unconditional retribution is owed.

I will speak, he says, **to my Bride**. God speaks to the soul in two different ways. He speaks in one way to the soul that has prostituted herself, and in another way to the Bride; in one way to the unsightly, and in another to the beautiful; in one way to the sinner, and in another to one who is justified. The unsightliness of the former he reproves; the beauty of the latter he praises. The former he shakes with fear by his reproof; the latter he incites to love by his praise. He speaks to the former when she shows him her flaws; to the latter he speaks when he recalls to her memory the gifts he has conferred on her. He shines light on the former's darkness, that she may know what she is and weep for what she has done; the latter he touches with an inward feeling of sweetness, that she may reflect on what she has received and not forget the Giver.

I will speak, he says, **to my Bride**. If I am the Bridegroom, if I have spoken to my Bride, know that I am unable to speak anything save love. Therefore after the Bridegroom had said this to himself, he immediately took up his journey; and coming and seeing his Bride he at once burst out with these words, as if her countenance had elicited his wonder: **You are altogether fair, my close one** and so on. Or else this statement is taken with the preceding words, that is, **I will speak to my Bride** — speak, that is, in these words: **You are altogether fair, my close one**, and the rest. But the former is the better way of taking it. "**You are altogether fair, my close one**, and **altogether fair** precisely because you are close. If you were not close, you would not be **altogether fair**."

Notice that he says **altogether**: "You are *altogether* beautiful, my close one." Every soul is either turned away from God or turned toward God. Of those souls that are turned away, however, one is far removed, while another is as far removed as possible. On the other hand, of the souls that are turned toward God, one is close, while another is as close as possible. The one that is turned away is unsightly, but not altogether unsightly.

The one that is as far away as one can get is altogether unsightly. By the same token, the soul that is close is fair but not as yet altogether fair, while the one that is as close as one can get is **altogether fair.**

You are altogether fair, my close one, and there is no spot upon you. "That person is altogether fair in whom no element of beauty is lacking. That person is altogether fair in whom there is no element of moral unsightliness. I am altogether fair because everything beautiful is within me. You are **altogether fair** because there is nothing unsightly within you. **There is no spot upon you.**"

Come to frankincense, fair one. He invites her and summons her; for his motive in coming to her was not that he should remain with her, but that he should draw her to him. **Come to frankincense, come to frankincense, you shall come, you shall be crowned.** Twice he invites her and says, **Come.** Then the third time he adds, by way of affirmation, **You shall come.** But what is this affirmation if not an act of congratulation by which he joins in rejoicing over our good intent? It is as if he were saying, "I praise your obedience, I am not unaware of your intent of being devoted to God. I summon, and you respond; I invite, and you are ready. Therefore **you shall come.**"

But why does he say **come** twice? So that the person who is outside himself may first of all return to himself, and the person who is in himself may rise up beyond himself. First of all he is within us, and he warns transgressors to return to the heart; but then he is above us, that he may invite the justified to come to himself. **Come,** he says, **come!** "Come out inwardly to yourself! Come within, farther within, wholly within, above yourself to me!

Come from frankincense, come to frankincense: come away from frankincense whitened to frankincense not whitened but glistering white. Come from a purified heart to the Purifier of hearts, who is not purified but pure. You shall not come to me if you remain in yourself; rise up above yourself, and you shall find me. **You shall come, and you shall cross over to Seir,** or Sanir. "Seir" means "shaggy" or "hairy"; but "Sanir" means "nocturnal bird" or "stench," and Seir is the same as Edom, that is, Esau. Esau and Jacob were two brothers. Esau was the firstborn, but was supplanted by Jacob the later-born. Esau had been a hunter and a man whose interests were in the countryside. Jacob, a simple man, lived at home. But what do these two brothers designate except two impulses that are in the human person, that is to say, the lust of the flesh and of the spirit? And we know what the apostle says. The spiritual does not come first; it is the carnal that comes first (cf. 1 Cor. 15:46) — which is to say that Esau was the firstborn. But as the lust of the spirit is strengthened, the lust of the flesh wastes away: which is to say that Esau was supplanted by Jacob, the later-born. By the same token, the lust of the flesh, like Esau the hunter, feeds upon things outside him, while the lust of the spirit, like Jacob the man of simplicity, finds its delights inwardly. Seir, then, is a "hairy" impulse of the flesh, unsightly and unseemly. And "hairy" is just right; for just as hair fixes its root in the flesh but goes beyond the flesh by growing out, so too the impulse of the flesh arises from need, but in its growth overflows into gratification. Now hair can be cut without pain but cannot without pain be plucked out; in the same way the desire of the flesh, to the extent that it looks, as it were, outside the range of the flesh's awareness to seek what is superfluous, can be cut off without harm's being done; but to the extent that it looks, as it were, within the flesh to what is needful, it cannot be removed without harm's being done.

So we have said what Seir is; let us now see what **the mount of Seir** is. For Seir has this mountain. It also has a valley — to say yet more, it has a mountain, it has a plain, it has a valley. In the valley, though, it is weak, on the plain it is strong, on the mountain it is invincible. Seir on the mountain is the desire of the flesh in a state of need; Seir on the plain is the desire of the flesh in a state of satisfaction; Seir in the valley is the desire of the flesh in a state of high pleasure. When the flesh takes in sustenance solely for the needs of life, Seir is upon the mountain. When, however, it looks to nourish its strength, Seir is on the plain; and when it demands delights for the sake of licentiousness, Seir is in the valley. Why then is it invincible when on the mountain? Because for people who are still in this mortal state sustenance for the flesh is a necessity. Why is it strong when on the plain? Because a strong flesh is of some use for the progress of the soul. Why is it weak in the valley? Because the pleasure of the flesh is invariably superfluous. In the valley, the desire of the flesh is forbidden. In the field it is allowed. On the mountain it is rewarded. In the valley it acts as a slave, on the plain it is a fighter, on the mountain it reigns. In the valley it is excess, on the field it is temperance, on the mountain it is frugality. In the valley it is easily trodden down with the help of grace, on the field it is conquered with difficulty, on the mountain, lest it be capable of defeat, our very daily needs themselves supply it continuously with strength. The person who prunes superfluities stamps upon Seir down in the valley. But the person who reduces necessities to some extent conquers Seir in the plain; and the one who concedes sustenance only to the necessities of nature complies on the mountain with, as it were, a more correct Seir. . . .

And Hermon. "Hermon" means "his [or "her" or "its"] cursing." But then "cursing *of whom* or *of what*"? That of the cursing itself. It is, then, as though it had been said "the cursing's cursing." We must therefore ask first of all what a cursing is, and then what the cursing's cursing is.

Now "cursing" denotes separation; and "cursing's cursing," the separation of separation. It may be, moreover, that if it is a bad thing to have been separated, then it will be a good thing to have been separated from the state of separation. Further, who can more properly be called "a cursing" than the apostate Angel? By his pride he was the first to separate himself from the society of that City which is on high, as the just desert of his transgression; and after he chose not to be a limb of the Head once he was cut off from the unity of that body, he became the head of all sinners. Moreover, it is well known that every human being is a limb of this head, and belongs to his society, in virtue of its first begetting, by which it was conceived and born in sin. But whoever is reborn in the sacrament of faith and so made a member of Christ is separated from the unity of this body. Who, then, is anathema save the Devil and his members? And who are the anathema's anathema save those who have been separated from the Devil's body and made members of Christ?

Thus we have said what **Hermon** means. Now let us see what **mount of Hermon** means. For just as it was stated above with regard to **Seir**, so too in this case it can be stated with regard to **Hermon** that some are the **mount of Hermon**, others the field of Hermon, and others still the valley of Hermon. Those can be called "valley of Hermon" who have already been separated from the Devil by their faith, but still lie prostrate in dishonorable desires because of their carnal life. "Field of Hermon" are those believers who, occupying a middling status, are neither sunk low because of the pleasures of the flesh nor able to be raised on high by spiritual communion. But **mount of Hermon** are those who are not only separated from the Devil by their faith but also, by the distinction of their virtue and by the constancy of their mind, have been raised up in opposition to the Devil. And without doubt these are the ones that the ancient Enemy most envies — those whom he sees not only to be set apart from him but also to have been raised up to oppose him. These, then, are the ones whom he attempts, by his uninterrupted pursuit, to overthrow — those whom he perceives both to have withdrawn from him and to stand in opposition to him. They therefore are often subject to tribulations that are the greater to the extent that they hold the common enemy of all to be particularly hostile to themselves. Therefore we reckon that nothing is better where the **mount of Seir** is concerned than frugality, or where the **mount of Hermon** is concerned than the patience of the saints.

(12) Augustine of Hippo

You shall come and shall pass through from the beginning of faith.

Many Latin manuscripts, and the Greek manuscripts above all, have these verses (Ps. 68:32-33) divided in such a way that they do not contain one line that says, "The kingdoms of the earth belong *to God*." Instead they place "to God" at the end of the prior verse, with the result that it says, "Ethiopia shall come *to God* ahead of her hands"; and then there follows in the next verse, "Sing to God, O kingdoms of the earth, sing to the Lord!"

By this way of dividing the text — which is surely preferable, given the agreement of so many manuscripts and the authority of the weightier ones — it seems to me that what is being commended is the faith that comes ahead of works; for the ungodly person is justified through faith apart from the merit that attaches to works. It is as the apostle says, "To the one that . . . believes in him who justifies the ungodly, his faith is counted for righteousness" (Rom. 4:5), so that then faith itself may begin to do its work through love. We know that only those deeds are counted good which are done through love for God. But faith must precede such love as this, so that deeds may have their origin in faith and not the contrary; for no one does anything through love for God unless he already believes in God. This is the faith of which it is said, "For in Christ Jesus neither circumcision nor uncircumcision is good for anything, but faith that does its work through love" (Gal. 5:6).

This is the faith that is meant when, in the Song of Songs, it is said to the Church: **You shall come and shall pass through from the beginning of faith.** For she has come like God's chariot in the midst of the rejoicing of thousands, her journey has been prospered, and she is passing through from this world to the Father. In her, then, there has come to pass what the Bridegroom himself says as he passes from this world to the Father: "I desire that they also . . . may be with me where I am" (John 17:24) — but starting **from the beginning of faith.** For faith comes before in order that good works may follow, and indeed there are no good works save those that follow upon a faith that precedes them; and that explains why the words, "Ethiopia shall come to God ahead of her hands," mean nothing other than "Ethiopia shall believe in God." For when it is thus understood, "shall come ahead of her hands" means "ahead of her works." And the "she" in "her works" must be Ethiopia. For in the Greek there is no ambiguity [as to the gender of the word meaning "her"]. . . . The words then mean nothing other than: "Ethiopia shall come to God ahead of her hands" — that is, by having faith in God, she shall come ahead of her works. For the apostle says, "We hold that a person is justified by faith apart from works of the law. Or is God the God of the Jews only? Is he not God of the Gentiles also" (Rom. 3:28-29)? So then Ethiopia, which seems to be the farthest removed of the nations, is justified by faith apart from works of the law.

(13) Richard of St.-Victor

Come away from Libanus, my Bride,
  come away from Libanus.
You shall be crowned from the head of Amana
  and from the peak of Sanir and Hermon,
from the lions' dens,
  from the mountains of the leopards.

"Libanus" is the name of a mountain on which myrrh and frankincense grow. Moreover, Libanus is called "making gleaming *or* white."

Christ, therefore, is calling the Bride away from Libanus in the sense that he is summoning her to a transcendent reward by way of the mortification of sins and of carnality, when she has been purified and made gleaming by devout prayer. Moreover, that he exhorts her to come not merely twice but three times intimates the greatness of his desire and love for her, and the triple reiteration is an attestation of its greatness and unshakability, for a threefold cord is hard to break. By the same token, the multiple repetitions of the summons indicate the pleasure with which he rejoices in her liberation from her present misery. It also indicates how greatly he desires that this may come about swiftly. For the summons repeated again and again expresses the mood of one who is engaged alike in speeding something up and in rejoicing in it. Hence too he summons her many times in order that he may suggest the magnitude of the happiness to which he is calling her — and also in order that the triple summons may point to the delighted enjoyment of the Trinity that she shall receive after her labors, that enjoyment which is eternal happiness.

And when he calls her, he also announces from what she is to be rewarded: **You shall be crowned from the head of Amana, from the peak of Sanir and Hermon.**

"Amana" means "restless" or "agitated." It refers to souls that love the world, who are restless and agitated at the same time.

There is disquiet and weary drudgery in seeking out worldly delights, and when one attains them, one does not find full satisfaction in them. Not possessed, they torment a person; possessed, they do not satisfy. For the more one seeks to satisfy desire with such delights, the more one inflames it. That is why it is said that what cures sins is sickness; for the sinning that enables a person to relieve desire for a time also quickly enough causes them to sicken with a yet greater desire for sinning. Since, then, they have no satisfaction, they exhibit no inner repose. Indeed, the Spirit of God does not abide in the mind that seeks earthly things, since the Spirit rests only upon the humble and tranquil; for that Spirit is not received by the mind that is restless because of earthly desires, and it does not illumine with spiritual light the mind that is full of delight in fleshly things. For where the vessel of the heart is not empty of fleshly things, there the oil of the Spirit cannot rest: the Holy Spirit, after all, cannot come or remain in human beings who are flesh, that is, who are carnal. So it is that when the heart is disturbed by these desires, it becomes agitated as well — that is to say, darkened and perplexed and alienated from the truth. For earthly desires are sources of confusion, and they darken the eyes of the heart, so that the human person fails to know either itself, or its blindness and misery.

The mind, however, refuses to take comfort in the pleasures afforded by these goods, and in this way it merits to enjoy delight and to be illuminated by grace. For the blessed Job condemns and curses the day of fleshly pleasure, and by his sentence he turns it into darkness or night, while he is weighing how much blindness and misery it brings down (cf. Job 3:1ff.). For by means of the night he has observed, the night he observes to follow upon this day, he terminates the day itself, and makes it pass away within himself — and thus arrives at the day of grace. In this way he turns night into day, and after the darkness of the night he condemns, he deservedly hopes for light and receives the illumination of grace.

Amana, therefore, means people whom earthly delight overcomes, that is, the restless and the agitated; and their **head** is the devil, who rules over them by the instrumentality of these pleasures. As long as the dedicated soul resists his suasions and pays them no mind, she celebrates a triumph **in regard of** this **head.**

But Christ promises that this soul is to be crowned not only **from the head of Amana** but also **from the peak of Sanir and Hermon.**

Sanir and Hermon are mountains in Judea in which lions and panthers dwell. These mountains signify individuals that stink of impurity and are separated, because of their fault, from God and from any share in good things; for **Sanir** means "stench," and **Hermon,** "cursing."

As far as concerns those that are **Sanir,** some are polluted by their action, others by their thought, and others still give in to some temptation or weakness, or else fail to escape fault because they do not properly resist uncleanness.

It is plain enough what impurity of action is, and there is no need to say much about it. One sins mortally in thought either by willing to sin or by giving in to a pleasure that occurs in thought and dwelling upon the pleasure. For if you yield to a pleasure that occurs in thought, even if you have no intention of committing the act, you sin mortally, especially if you dwell lengthily upon such a pleasure after reason detects it, and if it gratifies. For if the pleasure itself persists without the consent of reason, or if reason does not pay to it, it is not termed mortal. . . .

The case is the same with one who is full of mad frenzy, or ignorant, or commits a sin of omission. For when persons who are full of frenzy kill in a fit of frenzy, or commit fornication, or perform an act that is reckoned mortal, such persons sin mortally even if at the moment they lack the mental capacity for discerning what they are doing, as long as they fall into the frenzy by their own fault and are in a state of willing to sin mortally, and thus become guilty because of a previous fault. . . . It is the same with those who are ignorant; for even though they do not will to be ignorant of what is right at the moment when such knowledge is requisite, they are nonetheless answerable because earlier, when they were able to know, they disdained to do so. . . .

Sanir, then, means people who give off a foul odor, who have been defiled by the Devil, whether in their doings or their thoughts . . . , while on the other hand **Hermon**, which means "cursing," refers to people who are accursed, that is, separated from God by their own iniquity, and others that are cut off from the fellowship of the Church by a sentence of excommunication on the ground of their manifest sins.

Regarding the first class of these, let us say that they are cut off from God by mortal sins. Every mortal sin is committed by acting contrary to a commandment or by acting contrary to conscience. For if conscience determines something to be death-dealing, anyone who does it contrary to the decree of conscience sins mortally, even if the act is venial; for the apostle says, "Whatever does not proceed from faith," that is, from conscience, "is sin" (Rom. 14:23), and whatever is done contrary to conscience builds for Gehenna. . . .

So then the wrongheaded — that is, those who are restless because they love things earthly — are **Amana**; or else they are **Sanir**, which is to say, those who give off a foul odor by reason of their impure life; or else **Hermon**, that is, those who are accursed by reason of their sin or of a sentence of excommunication. Moreover, their **head** or **peak** is the Devil. He brings them to this condition by tempting them, and through this condition he exercises rule over them, and as long as every devout individual resists his suasion so as not to be entangled in sins, such individuals are **crowned** by their head because they are triumphing over him.

Now the **lions** and the **panthers** are also demons; for in their fury, with unconcealed wickedness, they now lead certain persons astray, now mislead the righteous with enticing counsels and manifold deceits, just as fierce lions and panthers as well are speckled with different colors. The wicked are the dwelling place of these lions or panthers; and as long as good people do not imitate their wrongful morals and their sins, but flee from them, they sometimes turn such folk towards what is good by their example and teaching. By these **mountains** and **dens of lions and panthers** they are crowned and are accorded eternal rewards.

Song 4:9-15

SEPTUAGINT

4:9 You have heartened us, O my sister
Bride,
you have heartened us with one
of your eyes,
by one, with the ornament of
your neck.

10 How beautiful are your breasts, my
sister Bride;
your breasts are more beautiful
than wine,
and the fragrance of your
garments is above all spices.

11 Your lips are a dripping honeycomb,
O Bride;
honey and milk are under
your tongue,
and the fragrance of your garments
is like the fragrance of
frankincense.

12 My sister Bride is a closed garden,
a garden closed, a sealed spring.

13 Your shoots are a paradise of
pomegranate trees,
with the produce of fruit trees,
henna with nard,

14 nard and saffron, calamus and
cinnamon,
with all the frankincense trees,
myrrh and aloe,
with all the finest perfumes.

VULGATE

4:9 You have wounded my heart, O my
sister Bride,
you have wounded my heart
with one of your eyes
and with one of the curls on
your neck.

10 How beautiful are your breasts, my
sister Bride;
your breasts are more beautiful
than wine,
and the fragrance of your
perfumes is above all spices.

11 Your lips are a dripping honeycomb,
O Bride;
honey and milk are under your
tongue,
and the fragrance of your garments is
like the fragrance of
frankincense.

12 My sister Bride is a closed garden,
a garden closed, a sealed spring.

13 Your outsendings are a paradise of
pomegranate trees,
with the produce of apple trees,
henna with nard,

14 nard and saffron, cassia and
cinnamon,
with all the trees of Lebanon,
myrrh and aloe,
with all the primary perfumes.

15 A spring of gardens, a well of living water, that pours forth from Lebanon.	15 The spring of the gardens is a well of living waters that flow swiftly from Lebanon.

In these lines the Bridegroom's eloquent declaration of the manifold charms of his Bride continues. The most obscure — and difficult — of the verses in this section, at least for patristic exegetes, is the very first. For one thing, the Septuagint and the Vulgate differ in their understanding of the verb (whose sense is in any case uncertain; interpreters reasonably construed it to mean "hearten," "ravish the heart," or "wound the heart"). The text, moreover, employs a phrase ("sister Bride") that might on the face of it be taken to intimate an incestuous relationship and that therefore needed careful explanation. Last but not least, in the Septuagint the parallelism between "with one of your eyes" and "by one ornament of your neck" is, to the discerning eye of the grammarian, spoiled because in the case of the second phrase "one" and "ornament" do not agree in grammatical gender. Hence the labored ingenuities of Gregory of Nyssa's exegesis of 4:9. More typical, perhaps, is the brief exposition of Theodoret.

The Bridegroom's praise of the Bride's breasts is treated largely as one might expect; they are sources of nourishment, and especially the nourishment of teaching or doctrine. Richard of St.-Victor follows a slightly different tradition, and develops the idea that they represent the two primary forms of outgoing love. The portrayal of the Bride as a walled and locked garden suggests both her virginity and the delights to be enjoyed in intimacy with her. This picture required no more than a commonplace ingenuity to adapt to the figure of the Church.

(1) Gregory of Nyssa

You have given us heart, O my sister Bride,
  you have given us heart with one of your eyes,
  by one, with the ornament of your neck.

The voice of the Word is always a voice of power. Hence just as in the first creation the light shone forth even as the command was given, and the firmament in its turn came into being simultaneously with the word of command, and all the rest of the creation was in the same way manifested simultaneously with the creative Word — so too now, when the Word commands the soul in her new-found goodness to come to him, she is instantly empowered by the command and comes to be what the Bridegroom willed. She is changed into something more divine, and on account of her happy alteration she is changed from the glory she has already attained to a higher glory, with the result that she becomes a source of wonder to the chorus of angels about the Bridegroom, and propitiously all of them address her with this expression of wonder: **You have given us heart, O Bride our sister.** For the mark of impassibility, which illuminates her just as it does the angels, brings the soul that has achieved impassibility in the flesh into a relation of kinship and sisterhood with incorporeal beings. That is why they say to her, "**You have given us heart, O Bride our sister**; and you are honored with each of these titles in its fullest sense. **Our sister** you are in virtue of our kinship in impassibility, and **Bride** you are in virtue of being joined to the Word."

As to the meaning of **given heart**, we judge it to signify much the same as "enlivened" — as if they were saying to her, "You have put a heart in us."

For the sake of clarity, however, and so that the meaning may become more transparent for us, we will attend to the divine apostle in order to understand these mysteries. For at one point in the Letter to the Ephesians, after he had set out for us the great economy of the theophany that came about in the flesh, Paul stated that it was not to the human race alone that the divine mysteries were taught by this act of grace, but that the manifold wisdom of God was also made known to the heavenly rulers and powers — revealed through the economy that was carried out in Christ among us human beings. These are his words: "That through the Church the multiform wisdom of God might now be made known to the principalities and powers in the heavenly places. This was according to the eternal purpose that he has realized in Christ Jesus our Lord, in whom we have boldness and confidence of access through our faith in him" (Eph. 3:10-12).

For in truth it is through the Church that "the multiform wisdom of God," which has worked its great marvels by the instrumentality of contraries, is made known to the powers above the cosmos: how death came through life, and righteousness through sin, and blessing through curse, and glory through shame, and strength through weakness. In previous times, the powers above the cosmos knew only the simple and undifferentiated Wisdom of God, which brought about wonderful things in agreement with the nature of each; and there was nothing "multiform" among the things that were to be seen — when the divine Nature, powerful as it is, fashioned the entire created order by *fiat*, bringing the system of things into being by a mere act of will, and made all the things that gushed from the fount of goodness "very good" (Gen. 1:31). But they were brought to clear knowledge of this multiformity of Wisdom — which consists in the knitting together of contraries — by the Church: how the Word becomes flesh; how life is mingled with death; how by his own stripe our calamity is healed; how by the weakness of the cross the power of the Adversary was overthrown; how the Invisible was revealed in flesh; how he redeemed the captives, being himself both the purchaser and the price (for he gave himself as a ransom to death on our account); how he died and did not depart from life; how he shared in the condition of a slave and remained in his kingly state. For all of these things, and whatever is like them, are "multiform" and not simple works of wisdom; and learning of them through the Church, the friends of the Bridegroom were **given heart**, grasping in the mystery another mark of the divine Wisdom.

And if it is not too venturesome a thing to say, perhaps those powers marveled at what is invisible and incomprehensible to all beings because they discerned the beauty of the Bridegroom by the agency of the Bride. For the One whom "no one has seen at any time," as John says (John 1:18), whom "no one can see" (1 Tim. 6:16), as Paul bears witness — this One established the Church as his body, and by the addition of those who are being saved builds it up "in love, until we all attain . . . to mature humanity, to the measure of the stature of the fullness of Christ" (Eph. 4:13). If, then, the Church is Christ's body, while Christ is the Head of the body, forming the countenance of the Church with the stamp of his own identity — maybe the reason why the friends of the Bridegroom were **heartened** as they looked upon her was that in her they saw the Invisible more clearly. Just as those who cannot look upon the disk of the sun see it by means of the water's gleaming, so too these powers look upon the Sun of Righteousness as it were in the clear mirror of the Church, grasping it through its manifestation.

That is why it is not just once that the friends tell the Bride, **You have given us heart** (which means: "By your own agency you have worked within us a soul and a mentality that enable comprehension of the light"); no, they use the same expression again, adding to the force of what they say by this repetition. For they repeat the phrase when they say, **You have given us heart with one of your eyes.**

It is this above all that fills the friends with wonder concerning the Bride's state. For the soul's work of seeing is twofold: there is one operation by which it sees the truth, and another that is led astray by attending to things that amount to nothing. And since the Bride's pure eye is open only to the nature of the good, while the other is inactive, the friends for this reason give praise to *one* of her eyes, by whose single means she contemplates the only One — that One, I mean, that is known in its immutable and eternal nature: the true Father, the only-begotten Son, and the Holy Spirit. For that is truly "only" which is contemplated in a single nature, without the introduction of any division or estrangement on the ground that the hypostases are distinct. For there are people who, by making wrong use of different eyes, have a clear vision of what does not exist and divide the One into many natures because of the fantasies conjured by their perverse eyes. These are the so-called "many-seeing": they see nothing because they perceive a multitude of things. And all those who look toward God but are then once more led astray by material imaginings are unworthy of the angels' praise because they waste their time with images of things that have no reality. One the other hand, the person whose vision is acute solely where the Divine is concerned is blind in respect of all those other things on which the vision of the multitude is focused. Hence the Bride inspires wonder in the friends of the Bridegroom by reason of **one** of her eyes. And so too the "many-seeing" person, who looks on empty things with a multitude of eyes, is blind, while the the person who through one eye — that of the soul — looks upon the Good is sharp and clear of sight.

But who does that second **one** refer to, and what is the **ornament** of the Bride's neck? It should not be difficult, on the basis of our investigations up to this point, to come to a conclusion about this, even though there is some uncertainty about the words in relation to their context. Here is the passage: **You have given us heart with one of your eyes, by one, with the ornament of your neck.** Thus the phrase **by one** ties in with the words **with one of your eyes**; and we are going to understand it as an elliptical expression standing for "by one soul."

For in everyone who has been without discipline there are many souls; in such a person the passions, because they have acquired control, occupy the soul's territory, and so the character of the soul is altered to become pain and pleasure, or anger and fear and cowardice and rashness. But the person who looks toward the Word by undeviating practice of the virtuous life is acknowledged to live with only one soul. Hence the text ought to be divided so that the phrase **by one** is construed with what precedes it, since we take it, in accordance with the sense of the passage, to mean either "by one soul" or "by one condition," while the expression **with the ornament of your neck**, which follows, has a different sense. Thus one might restate the whole thing in clearer fashion by saying, "Your eye is one because it looks toward the One; and your soul is one because it is not divided among differing dispositions; and your neck sits perfectly because it bears the divine yoke. . . ."

(2) Theodoret of Cyrus

You have heartened us, O my sister Bride,
  you have heartened us with one of your eyes,
  in one, by the ornament of your neck.

Symmachus renders the words **have heartened** as "you have given us courage." What it means is something like this: "Your two eyes are wondrous and spiritual and appropriately termed 'doves.' But one of them affects me with unbounded wonder; it looks upon things divine, has been taught to speak of God, and contemplates hidden mysteries. Further, I marvel at all the adornments of your neck; these hint at practical virtue, for the neck, which bears the yoke of the divine commandments, attracts and separates the furrows of righteousness. So then I also praise the other ornaments of righteousness that shine on your neck; but I exalt and marvel at one of them. Astounded at the beauty both of the one necklace, and of the eye that contemplates divine realities, I am wounded with love of you."

(3) The *Glossa ordinaria*

How beautiful are your breasts, my sister Bride . . .

Above [1:2], the Bride was praising the breasts of her Beloved. Here the Beloved is praising the breasts of the Bride; and this calls attention to the union of Christ and the Church, for as the apostle says, they are "two" in "one flesh" (Eph. 5:31). That is why each praises the other in the same terms. The teaching belongs to Christ because he gives it and to the Church because she conveys it.

. . . the fragrance of your perfumes

Fragrance — that is, the very sweet renown of the faith as it has been spread throughout the world, more widely than the law of the fathers, which was confined to Judea alone.

(4) Richard of St.-Victor

How beautiful are your breasts, my sister Bride,
    your breasts are more beautiful than wine,
    and the fragrance of your perfumes is above all spices.
Your lips are a dripping honeycomb, O Bride;
    honey and milk are under your tongue,
    and the fragrance of your garments is like the fragrance of frankincense.

The two breasts stand for a twofold compassion, one corporeal and the other spiritual. The soul possesses these when she shares the suffering of those who struggle because of bodily need or some adversity, or when she devotes prayer or consolation to those who find themselves in some sin or temptation. She possesses these breasts when she knows how to rejoice with those who rejoice and weep with those who weep, to be weak with those who are weak, to burn with those who have been made to stumble. Beautiful are the breasts of that soul who shares the suffering of all out of goodwill and is unable, without sorrow of heart, to pass by the sorrows of anyone.

Moreover, with one of her eyes she has a clear spiritual vision of that by which she is also spiritually moved with regard for her neighbors. For the soul that loves God also embraces her neighbor out of charity. Because she has drawn close to goodness, she receives bowels of loyal affection, so that just as she has learned to long for God, so too she is also moved by charity with regard to others. Just as she has a single attitude of care for her own salvation and for God, so too she has a single attitude toward her neighbors, one of loyal affection, not of agitation or rancor.

The soul that has these breasts is deservedly beautiful, and she gives pleasure to Christ as he gazes upon her because she possesses the charity that covers her sins and extends mercy to the sins of others, so that she herself obtains mercy — regarding which it is said in Job, "You shall not sin in visiting your likeness" (Job 5:24 Vg). Our "likeness" is our neighbor, in whom we discern what we are; and when we visit him in this way out of compassion, we do not sin, that is, we are free of sin, because by such loyal affection we are cleansed from sins. Moreover, the soul becomes completely pure of sins when she not only does not elicit sin from her neighbor by an attitude of rancor or hasty judgment and suspicion, but in addition receives forgiveness because she shares the pain of the sin that has been committed.

Deservedly, then, is that soul praised which, through loyal affection, is both cleansed from sin and adorned with merits, and her **breasts** are said to be **more beautiful than wine**. In drinking wine, we can make exactness of justice our own, and this pleases God greatly and adorns the soul; but bowels of mercy commend and adorn the soul yet more. For just as oil floats above other liquids and manifests its luster, so too mercy stands above judgment, is preferred to it, and is more potent. Consequently justice must not exercise any right or judgment until mercy has fulfilled her role, nor is it able to do its work save in regard of matters that mercy relinquishes to it. By rights, then, mercy is so much the superior and nobler that it can carry out its task, given the presence of discernment, without any blame. On the other hand, justice cannot do its job except by the mediation of mercy. It is right, therefore, that the Bride's **breasts** are labeled and commended as beautiful; for she approaches likeness to God — whose property it is to be merciful and to forbear — to exactly the degree that she has a mature knowledge of how to sympathize and to lend aid. . . .

Your lips are a dripping honeycomb, O Bride; honey and milk are under your tongue, and the fragrance of your garments is like the fragrance of frankincense. It is the lips of the dedicated soul that are **a dripping honeycomb,** since they pour out liquid sweetness and produce this for the edification of others. This honey the soul gathers from the manifold flowers of the Scripture. It searches for these flowers, it dwells upon them, from them it extracts and elicits the sweetness of spiritual delight. It disdains and sets aside the knowledge that puffs up; rather, it seeks after edification and chooses ideas for their delightful fragrance, not for their pretentious eloquence. It seeks out the examples provided by the saints and mentally picks them over; for they were flowers and bloomed like the palm tree. Just as their way of life was holy, so too were their words and teachings sweet and pleasant. The soul flies to flowers of this sort, and from them it gathers spiritual honey — but especially from that matchless flower, the flower that sprouted from the rod of Jesse, a flower of the field and not of the garden. The fragrance of this flower is like that of the abundant "field which the Lord has blessed" (Gen. 27:27). Abundant is this field, in which there dwells the "fullness" of Deity (cf. Col. 1:19), in whom are "all the treasures of wisdom and knowledge" (Col. 2:3), in whom all the righteous bloom, and in whom they bear fruit both in the form of a good life and in that of holy knowledge. . . .

To this blooming and abundant field the Bride, like the prudent bee, makes her way. She runs to the fragrance of this flower. She pursues him full of desire. By her love and her faith she attaches herself to him. From him, by the importunity of her prayer, she sucks the honey of grace. From his fullness she receives grace (cf. John 1:16). Charity is shed abroad in her heart by his Spirit (cf. Rom. 5:5), and she receives the teats of loyal affection. Upon her lips, moreover, this grace is diffused, so that she gives off the fragrance of a heavenly sweetness and furnishes it to others.

She also has **honey and milk under** her **tongue,** which is to say, refreshment for the strong, and for the faltering, encouragement: the solid food of the perfect and the milk of the simple teaching that is proper to those who are weak. For she has tasted the delight of the life to come ahead of time — the life in which souls are refreshed by the enjoyment of Christ's divinity and by the milk of his humanity. She has had a preliminary taste of that blessedness inasfar as she is being renewed by the "running brook of honey and curds," with regard to which we read in Job that the shamming hypocrite will not see them (Job 20:5 Vg), that is, will not comprehend or taste them. This double delight, like the current of a river, gives joy to the heavenly city of God; and it visits the little brooks, pilgrims and exiles, to fill them gently and to renew them. . . .

And the fragrance of her **garments is like the fragrance of frankincense.** The garments of the soul are those deeds that are, or come to be, done in charity. Dressed in these, the elect are not found naked before God. The garments are **like the fragrance of frankincense** because good deeds, like dedicated prayer, give off a sweet scent. For if, on account of a useful occupation, someone interrupts his or her praying, the occupation will be counted as taking the place of prayer, since, as the apostle says, the person who is always doing what is good and right is always praying.

(5) Rupert of Deutz

. . . and the fragrance of your perfumes is above all sweet smells.

What then are your perfumes, O my sister, my Bride? Your acts of mercy, which you have performed on my behalf. My friends hear and will hear of a certain woman who poured oil over the head and the feet of your Beloved as he was reclining at table, and they say that "the house was full of the scent of the perfume" (John 12:3), and they understand that woman to represent our Church, which pours her perfumes over my feet and and dispenses their sweet smells as often as she performs acts of mercy for the benefit of our poor. For these are the precious perfumes, the truly sweet smells — to feed any one of my enemies who is hungry, to give drink to one who is thirsty, to take in the stranger or the traveler, to clothe the naked, to visit the sick, and to go to see those who are in prison (cf. Matt. 25:35-36). But **the fragrance of your perfumes is above all** these **sweet smells** — that is to say, the sweetness of your acts of mercy; for you have manifested your unmeasured generosity not merely in my physical members but in my very self.

(6) Honorius of Autun

My sister is a closed garden, my Bride,
   a closed garden.
Your outsendings are a paradise of pomegranate trees,
   with the produce of apple trees,
   henna with nard,
nard and saffron, cassia and cinnamon,
   with all the trees of Lebanon,
myrrh and aloe,
   with all the primary perfumes.
The spring of the gardens is a well of living waters
   that flow swiftly from Lebanon.

. . . In the garden herbal medicines grow, as well as a variety of flowers. The garden is the Church, in which there are the manifold virtues of the saints — the different sorts of herbs that provide cures for the different wounds of sinners. In this garden are a variety of flowers, which represent the different orders of the elect: martyrs, like roses; confessors, like violets; virgins, like lilies; and other believers, like other flowers. The gardener in this garden is Christ. He is also the Bridegroom, who when he plants by grace also irrigates by teaching. This **garden** is **closed** for the benefit of contemplatives — which means fortified against the attack of demons by an angelic guard. It is also **closed** for the benefit of those who lead the active life, for it is walled about by the defense that its teachers provide against heretics. In this garden the herbs and flowers are the individual believers, blooming with faith and good works.

   The comparison here is with the garden of Paradise, which is said to be closed off on every side by a wall of fire and protected by angelic guards (cf. Gen. 3:24), in order that the fire may keep human beings out of it, and the angels may keep the demons away. Thus the Church is the garden of God, surrounded by God's assistance and a fiery wall, and defended by an angelic guard, so that neither demons nor evil humans may be strong enough to harm her. This is said in order that, given the many protectors that safeguard her, their attack may not be feared in the spiritual combat.

In this garden there is a **spring**, to wit, Holy Scripture, by whose stream the Church is watered. In this case the **spring** is **sealed**, because the meaning of Holy Scripture is sealed up in the letter, like a writing that is under a seal, lest the hidden truth that the Bride possesses be apparent to unworthy persons. In this garden there is also the **spring** of baptism, in which the wounds of sins are washed, and this spring is sealed, that is to say, consecrated by the holy cross or the Word of God, closed up for the heathen, opened and revealed for catechumens.

Otherwise understood, the **spring** washes away filth, quenches thirst, restores the image. This **spring** is Christ, who is the spring of life, from whom there flow streams of "living water" (John 4:10, 14), that is to say, the gifts of the Holy Spirit, with which he waters the garden of the Church, so that it may bring forth the breaths of life that are flowers. He washes away the filthy deeds of sinners, he quenches the thirst of those who "thirst for righteousness" (cf. Matt. 5:6) with the fullness of the vision of himself, and he restores to souls the image of God they have lost. He was sealed up in that he was veiled with flesh as with a stamp. Now he is sealed up in that he is concealed from us by the glory of the Father. . . .

But the Church herself is also a **spring**; for she overflows with grace and wisdom, from which there flow streams full of teaching with which she waters the plants in her garden so that they may produce an abundance of **outsendings. Outsendings** are shoots that sprout from trees or plants. Of these he adds: **Your outsendings are a paradise of pomegranate trees, with the produce of apple trees.** The garden of the Church, watered from the **spring** of Scripture, puts forth so many shoots that from them a paradise grows up.

Now a garden is a place where plants or vegetables grow, while a paradise is a place where trees grow. The "paradise of delights" (cf. Gen. 2:8 Vg), understood at the level of the letter, is a place located in the East, which is full of all corporeal delights. In it our first parents lived, and from it they were excluded on account of their disobedience. In it was the **spring** from which Paradise was watered, itself divided into four rivers. In it was also the Tree of Life — that is, a tree such that if a person should have eaten from it, he would never be subjected to corporeal death. Hence it is written, after the occurrence of the sin, "See to it that he does not . . . take of the Tree of Life . . . and live forever" (Gen. 3:22). There too was the Tree of the Knowledge of Good and Evil, a tree such that if they ate from it they would know good and evil. Before he ate of the fruit of this tree, Adam knew good and evil, the good by experience, but evil only by intellectual grasp — just as a doctor knows the pain of a wound by intellectual grasp and not by experience. After his sin, however, Adam knew evil — that is, hunger, thirst, and other disagreeable things — by experience, but the good only by intellectual grasp; and this not because of the nature of the tree but because of the human act of disobedience. The people who live around Paradise say that flowers and fruits from it are sent them by way of the streams that come out of it, and the populace lives on them.

Understood as an allegory, the Church is the garden, filled with every spiritual delight. For Paradise is called a garden of delights, and in the Church are the delights of every sort that are proper to the Scriptures, to the various arts, to the numerous virtues. In this paradise there is a **spring**, that is, baptism or Christ, through whose streams, which are spiritual charisms, such a paradise is watered. The four rivers that come from this spring are the four Gospels. The Tree of Life is the holy cross, whose fruit is the body of Christ, a body such that anyone who eats of it worthily shall not die the death of the soul forever. The **fruit-bearing trees** are the saints. The fruits of these trees are the works of the saints. The Tree of the Knowledge of Good and Evil represents freedom of choice.

In this spiritual paradise different sorts of trees grow, meaning the different orders of the elect. Pomegranates grow there — which are African trees that produce the Carthaginian or red-hued apples that are called "many-seeded," that is, full of seeds; and these are the martyrs, full of red-hued blood and of good works, like seeds. That garden produces these trees, watered by the spring, while the holy Church, bathed by baptism, produces martyrs along **with the produce of apple trees**, that is, the examples of good works.

There the **henna** tree also grows. This is an aromatic tree found in Egypt that has a seed similar to coriander in that it has a white, slightly shiny, fragrant grain, which is cooked in oil and as a result gives off a juice that is called "henna." From this is made "the royal ointment," so called because the royal disease [jaundice] is cured by it. Henna the aromatic tree, which is abundant in Egypt, represents the way of life of spiritual persons, which originally flowered in Egypt, or, on another interpretation, in the darkness of this world, which is called "Egypt." Its seed is similar to manna (cf. Exod. 16:31), which possessed every delight and a fully sweet taste; for the life of the righteous possesses every spiritual delight and the full taste of sanctity. Its seed is white, shiny, and fragrant because the way of life of the righteous is white for its chastity; shining for its doings; fragrant for its love. Its juice is cooked together with oil and is turned into the royal ointment because their life is tested like gold by the flames of temptation, and because the royal disease — the leprosy of the soul — is cured by its ointment. In the house of Simon the leper, Mary brought this ointment to the Lord (cf. Matt. 26:6-7 and Mark 14:3); for the Church offers it to the Lord when by her example she cures heretics of leprosy of the soul, that is to say, heresy.

Nard, which is an aromatic tree, that is, a tree that is good for making spices, also grows in the garden. It is small, with a pleasing smell, and full of warmth. From it is made a most excellent ointment; and this represents the humble and innocent saints, who in the presence of their neighbors make themselves small, that is, contemptible, and with the fragrance and warmth of their love anoint people who have been wounded by their sins.

Saffron also grows in the garden. It is a ruddy flower — its color is gold — and represents those endowed with wisdom, who glow with a divine wisdom. "Fistula" also grows there, a small aromatic tree called **cassia**. It has a hard skin and is reddish in color. It is good for the cure of internal ailments, and because of its low height is reckoned by some among the aromatic plants. It stands for those who suffer with Christ and are ready to lay down their lives for their brethren.

Furthermore, **cinnamon** grows there: a short tree, but fragrant and sweet. It is of the color of ashes, and duplicates the curative function of cassia. It represents the penitents, who count themselves weak and, as they carry out their penance in ashes, furnish the Church with a sweet fragrance. The cinnamon tree has three skins: the outer is called "fistula," the middle one, "cinnamon," and the third, "amomum." The middle skin is sweeter than the others; but the others, separated by someone out of great ardor, are removed from the tree; and they stand for the monks, who separate themselves from the world out of love for Christ. These trees grow in that paradise along **with all the trees of Lebanon,** that is, the cedars and other fragrant trees; and these represent all the faithful, whose faith and works are incorruptible and fragrant.

There also do **myrrh and aloe, with all the primary perfumes,** grow. **Myrrh** is a tree whose sap is an oil called "stacté," which preserves flesh from worms and decay. It represents the hermits or those who practice chastity, doing their vices to death and preserving their flesh from the decay occasioned by lust. **Aloe** too is a tree of pleasant fragrance, so much so that it is burned to honor altars in place of frankincense; but it has an exceedingly bitter sap that resists decay. It represents those who practice continence and suppress the wantonness of the flesh by the severity of their life.

The primary perfumes are those that are more precious, those that are made from the first flowers of the more expensive species of plants — like that precious ointment of Mary in the Gospel. These stand for prelates and others who are full of the primary charisms of the Holy Spirit, that is to say, the primary gifts given to believers, and who, when they blaze forth in word and example, heal the sores, as it were, of sluggish souls.

One must observe that these species of trees or plants, from which perfumed ointments are made, are introduced because they signify the orders of the elect, like the different cohorts of soldiers in the king's camp, whose wounds are healed by ointments. That is why he compares the Bride to a garden, to a spring, and to a paradise, as if he were openly saying to her: "Do not be afraid to fight against the formations of Amana, for you have fighters in your army by whose steadiness and weaponry you shall certainly overcome your foes, and you will be crowned as victor by me. Moreover, with your herbs you will heal the wounded, for you are a **garden** of medicinal plants; and with your streams you will revivify the weary, for you are a **spring** of spiritual waters; and you will satiate the victors with your fruits, for you are a **paradise,** a garden of fruit trees, of spiritual meals."

(7) The *Glossa ordinaria*

The spring of the gardens is a well of living waters
  that flow swiftly from Lebanon.

In the Lord's **closed garden** there is born, among other things, a **spring of gardens;** for from the primitive Church there went forth into the world a heavenly teaching that gave birth to many churches — that is to say, gardens. With regard to this garden the text aptly adds, **a well of living waters;** for this same teaching of the Church is both a **spring of gar-**

dens in that it bears spiritual fruit in the people it instructs, and **a well** on account of the hidden mysteries that are opened only to the saints by revelation of the Holy Spirit. The **waters** are **living** by reason of the divine and moving utterance that proceeds from the invisible treasure houses of divine grace and leads to eternal life. **From Lebanon** means "from that same Church which is white because of the purity of her faith and exalted because of the splendor of her virtues."

• 14 •

Song 4:16–5:1

Septuagint

4:16 Awake, O north wind;
and come, O south wind!
Blow upon my garden,
and let its fragrance be
wafted abroad.
Let my Beloved come to his garden
and eat its choicest fruits.
5:1 I came into my garden, my sister, my
Bride;
I gathered my myrrh with
my spices,
I ate my honeycomb
with my honey,
I drank my wine with my milk.

Eat, O friends, and drink,
and be drunk, brethren!

Vulgate

4:16 Arise, O north wind;
and come, O south wind!
Blow through my garden,
and let its fragrances flow.

Let my Beloved come into his garden
and eat the fruit of his fruit trees.
5:1 I have come into my garden, my
sister, my Bride;
I have mixed my myrrh with
my spices,
I have eaten my honeycomb
with its honey,
I have drunk my wine with
my milk.
Eat, O friends, and drink,
and become drunk, dearest ones!

These two verses contain a dialogue in which the Bridegroom speaks first ("Awake . . ."), the Bride answers briefly, and the Bridegroom speaks of his entrance into his "garden." Presumably the reference is to the Bridegroom's delight in the Bride's intimacy. Both the Septuagint and the Vulgate assume (in 5:1) that the four verbs ("came . . . , gathered . . . , ate . . . , drank") refer to past time; but in the Hebrew this is uncertain. The verbs might actually be taken to refer to future or even present time — though it is unlikely that patristic or medieval interpreters would have been aware of this.

The tendency of interpreters was to take "north wind" and "south wind" as symbols respectively of the chill of evil and the nurturing warmth of goodness — or, more generally, as things attractive and things unattractive. Nowhere is this more obvious than in the passage from Gregory of Nyssa, where "north wind" represents the Devil ("the opposing Power") and "south wind," the Holy Spirit. So attached is Gregory to this interpretation (in which he is in effect followed by Rupert of Deutz) that he refuses the normal sense of the Greek verb that means "waken" or "rouse yourself up" (exegertheti) and takes it in effect to signify something like "up and away with you!" Bede is perhaps more plausible when he takes the two winds to stand for different sorts of trial that the Church (the garden) undergoes in, and at the hands of, the world, and which stimulate it to bring forth the fragrances of virtue. They stand, respectively, for the world's "repellent harshness" and its "deceptive charm."

(1) Theodoret of Cyrus

Up and out with you, O north wind;
   and come, O south wind!
Blow upon my garden,
   and let my fragrances be wafted abroad.
Let my Kinsman come down into his garden
   and eat the fruit of his fruit trees.

The north wind belongs in the category of things that Holy Scripture denounces, and that is why God says through the prophet Jeremiah, "Evils shall be kindled from the north" (Jer. 1:14). Then again, "And I shall banish from you what comes from the north" (Jer. 10:22). And elsewhere, "Behold, evils are coming from the north, and great distress" (Jer. 4:6). Hence the Bride exhorts the north wind to rise up and go away, in order that the south wind may blow through the garden and diffuse its fragrances, and her Kinsman may find delight in its fruits.

   Now the south wind is easy to identify because it blows from the region of the bright noonday, and it is called "south" because it is humid and fills bodies with moisture when it blows; besides, light streams from the noonday region. This is why, moreover, Habakkuk predicts that the Lord will come from the bright noonday region; for he says, "God will come from Teman" (Hab. 3:3), for "Teman" signifies this in the tongue of the Hebrews and Syrians.

   Therefore, she enjoins the opposing Spirit to depart, while she enjoins the divine grace to blow so that her Kinsman may garner the fully matured fruits of her fragrances, with none of them wind-blighted or fallen before the right time.

I have come into my garden, my sister, my Bride; I have gathered my myrrh with my spices, I have eaten its honeycomb with my honey, I have drunk my wine with my milk. Eat, my close one, and drink, and get drunk, my kinsmen.

   "For **I have come into my garden**," he says, "the one that you have presented to me, and **I have gathered** my first crop of myrrh, that is, the myrrh that I planted within you. For I first of all underwent death for your sake, and after that you desired thus to die and to be buried along with me. For you "were buried along with me through baptism into death" (Rom. 6:4), and you "mortified" your "earthly members" (Col. 3:5). Thus did I gather **my myrrh with my spices**," he says, "and I plucked and appropriated the other virtues that you were taught of me; I also ate my bread with my honey — the sweet and solid food that is found among the perfect."

I drank my wine. It is entirely right that he employs the pronoun *my*; for he is the true vine (cf. John 15:1) from which this wine is harvested. **I drank my wine with my milk.** For he does not reject those who are young in the faith and, as it were, sucking at the breast and nourished on milk. On the contrary, he takes from them the fruit that is suitable for them; and since he is good, he also summons his friends to the feast and says, **Eat, you that are close to me, and drink, and be drunken, my brethren.** Those who are close to him are the ones who have been on the way to perfection, the ones who are sure of their kinship with him, the ones who have kept the image uncorrupted. He commands these persons not merely to drink, but to be drunken; for there is a drunkenness that works temperance and not delirium — one that does not enfeeble the limbs but lends them strength. For "His cup inebriates as powerfully as can be" (Ps. 22:5 LXX = 23:5). Elsewhere too the blessed David writes: "They are made drunk by the abundance of your house, and you give them to drink from the torrent of your delight" (Ps. 35:9 LXX = 36:8).

(2) Gregory of Nyssa

Up and out with you, O north wind;
  and come, O south wind!
Blow through my garden,
  and let its fragrance be wafted abroad.

But let us attend to the Queen [i.e., the Bride of the Song], and hear how she sends the north wind away from her, turning its blast backward. For she does not order it to be silent as, in the storm at sea, the Lord quieted the great storm by commanding the waves to be silent (cf. Luke 8:23-24). Rather, by saying to the north wind, **Up and out with you!** she enjoins it to retire and flee, so that the south wind may blow uninhibited, with no contrary blast to impede its course.

But what is the reason for this wind's dismissal? "The north is a harsh wind," says the book of Proverbs, "and its name is called 'On the Right Hand'" (Prov. 27:16). But the north wind is not to the right of anyone unless it is someone whose back is to the east and who is heading to the west. So now you grasp the concealed meaning of the saying: that he who has departed from the east (for so Christ is named in the prophecy [cf. Zech. 6:12 LXX]) and impels himself toward the setting sun, where the power of darkness resides, has the north wind at his right hand to welcome him by providing the evil things he needs for his journey toward darkness. Thus the intemperate person finds the north wind at his right hand gusting in unison with his ignoble passion. In the same way this wicked wind comes to the right hand of the greedy individual and heaps up about him the matter for his greed, like so much sand or dust. In the same way, the north wind is at hand to bestow its cooperation freely in every sin or fault; and for those to whom it comes, since it is "harsh" by nature, it cloaks its repellent character with pleasures.

For this reason, she who is restraining the power of the passions banishes the north wind from her realm, saying, **Up and out with you, O north wind!** As to the reason why the opposing Power is referred to by this title, that must be obvious to everyone who has an understanding of the nature of things. Who does not know how the sun moves, how, starting from the east, it inclines toward the west, making its way through the south? Now since the earth is shaped like a sphere, as the experts in such matters tell us, it is strictly necessary that the side of the earth opposite to that illumined by the sun should be in darkness, cast into shadow by the interposed mass. Since, then, that place is without light and remains forever cold, neither lit nor warmed by the sun's rays, the scriptural text gives the names **north wind** and "harsh" to the Prince of the power of darkness. He hardens the malleable nature of souls by freezing them like water, thus rendering them "harsh." He is the one who contrives the gloom of winter — that winter, I mean, in which, as the Gospel says, flight from danger is impossible (cf. Matt. 24:20; Mark 13:18). In that winter, the splendor of virtue's flowers withers away.

So it is a good thing that the voice of the Queen should send him packing, while summoning to her presence the warm and ever bright noontide wind. This wind, which makes the pleasant streams of the springtime thaw flow forth, she calls **south,** and she says, "**Come, O south wind! Blow through my garden, and let its fragrance be wafted abroad**, so that with that "mighty blast" (Acts 2:2) — just as we hear it happened for the disciples — you may fall upon the ensouled plants, and move God's plantings to bring forth fragances, and and prepare them, as you pour out the sweet savor of the teachings, to let sweet-smelling prophecy and the saving teachings of the faith flow from their mouths freely in every sort of language. In this way the hundred and twenty disciples who have been planted in the house of God will put forth, by the help of the "blast" of such a south wind, the blossom of articulate instruction.

Here then is the reason why the Bride says to such a south wind, **Blow through my garden**. It is because the voice of the Bridegroom, her Creator, constituted her mother of the gardens, as is conveyed by the expression **fountain of gardens** (4:15). Hence she wants her garden, which is the Church burgeoning with living trees, to have the wind blow through it so that its fragrances may flow out. The prophet says, after all, "He makes his wind blow, and the waters flow" (Ps. 147:7 LXX = 148:8); while the Bride for her part, resplendent with a royal opulence, makes the streams of fragrances ever greater, creating by the power of the wind veritable rivers flowing out from the trees of the garden.

(3) Bede the Venerable

Arise, O north wind;
  and come, O south wind!
Blow through my garden,
  and let its fragrances flow.

By **north wind** or **south wind** he indicates the tempestuous blasts of the repeated temptations by which the Church was to be struck in order that she might learn that the degree of spiritual grace within her would correspond to that of her interior virtue. But if we think that there is a significant difference between the meaning of **north wind** and that of **south wind**, of which the one is known to be a chill wind and the other hot, one can without absurdity take **north wind** to mean the world's repellent harshness and **south wind**, its deceptive charm; for the Lord himself shows that his garden is tested by this twofold assault when he says, explaining the parable of the good seed: "As for what was sown on rocky ground, this is he who hears the word and immediately receives it with joy; yet he has no root in himself, but endures for a while, and when tribulation or persecution arises on account of the word, he immediately stumbles. As for what was sown among thorns, this is he who hears the word, but the cares of the world and the delight in riches choke the word, and it proves unfruitful" (Matt. 13:20-22).

If the Lord appears to speak in the imperative mood when he says, **Arise, O north wind; and come, O south wind! Blow on my garden**, that is not because he is commanding the reprobates to do what is wrong. He is allowing them to use their free choice as they will. He, after all, is himself able to make of their evildoings such good things as he wills, and by a strict judgment to requite them with the punishments they deserve for the wrongs they do. Accordingly, "the Lord hardened the heart of Pharaoh" (Exod. 10:20) so that he afflicted God's people; but shortly thereafter, once those who were being afflicted were liberated, he punished their persecutor for all eternity.

(4) Rupert of Deutz

Arise, O north wind;
and come, O south wind!
Blow through my garden,
and let its fragrances flow.

Who is this **north wind**? Surely it is the one who said, "I will sit on the mount of the covenant on the flanks of the north" (Isa. 14:13) — the one of whom the prophet says, "Out of the north evil shall spread out over the whole earth" (Jer. 1:14); in short, "that ancient serpent, who is called the Devil and Satan" (Rev. 12:9).

Whence does such a **north wind** arise? In what way does he arise? He arises out of a concealed ambush, where he formerly lay and slithered about in the form of a slimy snake when he led the first woman astray, as she herself said, "The serpent deceived me, and I ate" (Gen. 3:13). He did not rise up to attack her, but he slithered about and hissed in order to deceive her. Plainly he lacked strength until the woman, whom God had created innocent, gave him her voluntary consent.

Between him and you, O sister Bride, God established hostility (cf. Gen. 3:15); and for that reason he had no hope whatever regarding you. On the contrary, where you are concerned he had no hope at all that he might deceive you with his lie, with his guileful arts.

That is the reason why I say to him, **Arise, O north wind!** Why are you lying on the earth? Why are you lying in wait for our heel (cf. Gen. 3:15)? You will achieve nothing by lying in wait. You will do better to **rise up**, to make use of your powers, and to rage with all the force of your malice. There was a time when you behaved like a snake. Act now as a great dragon, a red dragon with seven heads (cf. Rev. 12:3). I am not giving you an order; I speak as one who gives a permission. For you began to rise up a long time ago, and what I am saying is no different from "Do what you are doing; rise up, you who are rising up; you who are raging, rage away!" For when did you start your rising up? Surely it was before this other woman appeared, against whom your deceptions could accomplish nothing. You rose up just as soon as you heard the word of promise to Abraham that is even now being fulfilled: "In your seed all nations shall be blessed" (Gen. 22:18); for you sensed the presence of the aforesaid hostility between her seed and your seed.

You rose up, you then raised your head, first of all as the head that is the kingdom of the Egyptians. For it was you that spoke in Pharaoh, "Whatever shall be born of the male sex you are to kill and throw into the river; whatever is of the female sex you are to save" (Exod. 1:22), and so on in the same vein, until the time when, as you were pursuing them in their flight, you said, "I will draw my sword, my hand shall destroy them" (Exod. 15:9). Thus you who had been a snake practicing cunning became a dragon engaged in persecution, a great dragon, a red — that is, a bloody — dragon.

After this first head of yours, you raised a second head by killing, by the hand of Jezebel and her line, the proclaimers of this mystery, the heralds of this sacrament, the prophets of the Lord.

Then you raised a third head in Nebuchadrezzar, king of Babylon; and a fourth in the reign of the Persians and the Medes with Haman, who wanted to destroy our nation, so that there would be no one of whom I could be born. Then you raised your fifth head in the reign of the Greeks in the person of Antiochus Epiphanes; and thus, O **north wind**, you have already risen up at five different times. Now we have the sixth head, which is the reign of the Romans. The seventh is yet to come, to wit, the reign of the Antichrist.

Therefore, **Arise, O north wind**, that is, stir up what you are stirring up. For I do not instruct you to stir up evil, which you shall never do; but I permit you to rise up because you wish it. Raise this sixth head of yours, bring it about that this seed of woman is betrayed into the hands of the Romans. **Arise** in this manner, **O north wind, and come**, you Holy Spirit, opponent of the Devil, the **north wind, blow through my garden, and let its fragrances flow**, and let what I said before come to pass: **Your outsendings are a paradise** (4:13) — which has never happened before. For never before, O **south wind**, have you come out against the north wind, so that by blowing through my new garden you may make a new Paradise spring forth, that is, make the new Church of the nations to spread and increase.

(5) Cyril of Alexandria

Let my Kinsman come down into his garden
  and eat the fruit of his trees.

Those who have made mindless perversity their regular companion shall be the food of the grasshopper, the locust, and the caterpillar (cf. Joel 1:4). They shall be forever devoid of all beauty, and within them there shall be nothing that blooms. By contrast, the wise and God-loving soul — the soul that is richly adorned with the teachings of the truth, that all but overflows with fruits for righteousness and has a heart that flowers richly on every hand — will doubtless speak with perfect boldness as does the Bride known to us in the Song of Songs, **Let my Kinsman come down into his garden and eat the fruit of his trees.** For the fruits of true religion and the trees of a correct love of knowledge are sweet — sweet indeed — to Christ the Savior of us all, who is also our kinsman inasmuch as he was born of the holy Virgin our sister.

Song 5:2-8

SEPTUAGINT	VULGATE

5:2 I sleep, and my heart is awake.
The voice of my Kinsman! He knocks
    at the door:
"Open to me, my sister, my close one,
    my dove, my perfect one;
for my head is covered with dew,
    and my locks with the drops of
      the night."
	5:2 I sleep, and my heart is awake.
	The voice of my beloved knocking:
	
	"Open to me, my sister, my friend,
	    my dove, my immaculate one;
	for my head is full of dew,
	    and my locks with the drops
	      of the night."

3 I removed my tunic.
    How shall I put it on?
I washed my feet.
    How shall I soil them?
	3 I have removed my tunic.
	    How may I put it on?
	I have washed my feet.
	    How shall I defile them?

4 My Kinsman has put his hand
    through the opening,
    and my belly has cried out for
      him.
	4 My Beloved has put his hand through
	    the opening,
	    and my belly trembled at his
	      touch.

5 I arose to open to my Kinsman,
    and my hands dropped myrrh,
my fingers choice myrrh,
    upon the handles of the bolt.
	5 I arose to open to my Beloved.
	    My hands dripped myrrh,
	my fingers were full of the choicest
	    myrrh.

6 I opened to my Kinsman;
 	
my Kinsman passed on by.
 	
My soul went out at his word.
 	
    I sought him and I did not find
      him;
    I called him, but he did not
      answer me.
	6 I opened the bolt of the door to my
	    Beloved,
	    but he had turned aside and
	      gone by.
	My soul melted when the Beloved
	    spoke.
	    I sought and did not find him;
	
	    I called, and he did not
	      answer me.

7 The guards that go their rounds in
   the city found me;
   they beat me, they wounded me.
   The guard of the walls took my veil
   away from me.
8 I have adjured you, O daughters of
   Jerusalem,
   by the powers and the strengths
   of the field,
   if you should find my Kinsman,
what will you report to him?
   That I am wounded by love.

7 The guards that go their rounds in
   the city found me;
   they beat me and wounded me.
   The guards of the walls took my
   cloak away from me.
8 I adjure you, O daughters of
   Jerusalem,

   if you should find my Kinsman,
   to report to him
   that I am languishing with love.

The Bride is speaking as this section opens, and she explains that in her (light) sleep she heard the Bridegroom knocking at her door and seeking entrance. She relates how she hesitated to answer, being unclothed and barefoot, but nevertheless — perhaps after anointing herself with myrrh — went to admit her Beloved, only to find him gone. She further acknowledges how her soul sank at his disappearance, how she sought him in vain, and how she was brutally treated by the guards who policed the city and its walls. Her account ended, she turns to the "daughters of Jerusalem" to ask that they tell her Lover, should they meet him, how much she longs for him.

Interpretations of these verses differed, but the general theme that runs through the various readings is much the same: the Bridegroom's calling, the Bride's initial reluctance to answer, the mention of myrrh — all conspired to lead Christian exegetes to see the scene as one in which divine call is answered by human repentance. Gregory of Nyssa, indeed, sees in the Bride's mention of the putting off of her tunic and her shoes an allusion to baptism, in which believers divest themselves of the "old humanity" (Col. 3:9) and "put on" Christ (Gal. 3:27). He also sees the expression, "My soul went out at his word," as pointing to the soul's pilgrimage to the knowledge of God in unknowing. The ingenuity of exegetes was most clearly tested by the Bride's account of the way the guards treated her, which seemed somehow out of place in this context.

(1) Theodoret of Cyrus

I sleep and my heart is awake.
   The voice of my Kinsman! He knocks at the door.

"**I sleep, but my heart is awake:** for even though nature compels me to shut my eyes and go to sleep, I am wide awake in my mind, and I do not allow myself the sleep of the sluggard while I am waiting for the arrival of the Bridegroom. For this reason too I sense his knocking"; for it says, **The voice of my Kinsman knocks at the door.**

To this it seems right to add the words of the Good Shepherd in the divine Gospels; for he says, "My sheep hear my voice"; and again, "A stranger they will not follow, for they do not know the voice of strangers" (John 10:27, 10:5). Blessed, then, is the one who is pastured and who hears the voice of the Shepherd. Blessed is the one that escorts the Bride and knows how to tell the difference between the voice of the Bridegroom and that of the casual lover. Blessed is the one that says, "I will not give sleep to my eyes or slumber to my eyelids" (Ps. 131:4 LXX = 132:4), but keeps watch and looks for the Bridegroom in accordance with the counsel of the Lord himself, who says, "Watch, therefore, for you do not know at what time your Lord is coming" (Matt. 24:42). The blessed Paul, moreover, gives the same advice when he says, "Be watchful, stand firm in your faith, be courageous, be strong. Let all that you do be done in love" (1 Cor. 16:13, 12c). Hence the Bride in her watchfulness delights in the voice of the Bridegroom even though she is sleeping a corporeal sleep, and she hears his knockings at her door. But what are the soul's "doors" if not the bodily perceptions by whose means the Bride admits the Bridegroom not only as he knocks but also as he exhorts her to open the door for him: **Open to me, my sister, my close one, my dove, my perfect one; for my head is covered with dew, and my locks with the drops of the night.**

Now by **night** he signifies the nocturnal rising of the Jews against him (cf. John 13:30; 18:3), while by **dew** and **drops**, he means the three-day death, which touched the hairs of his head, and not him himself. "Since, then," he says, "I underwent death for your sake, and suffered these things on your account, open to me and let me in; for I love your spiritual beauty and your perfection in virtue. Hence I also call you **my sister**, and **my close one**, and **my dove**, and **my perfect one. Perfect**, because you have fulfilled the commandment I enjoined upon you; for I said, 'Be perfect, as your heavenly Father is perfect' (Matt. 5:48). And again, 'If you wish to be perfect, sell your possessions and give to the poor, and you will have treasure in heaven, and take up your cross and follow me' (Matt. 19:21). I call you **my dove**, however, because you have become spiritual, have 'stripped off the old humanity with its passions and lusts' (cf. Col. 3:9 and Gal. 5:24), and are able to see spiritually. I call you **my close one** because you walk in my footsteps and because you desire to come close to me; for it is I who said, 'Draw near to me, and I will draw near to you' (Jas. 4:8). Finally, I call you **sister**, not only because we are akin in virtue of the nature I assumed, but also because of the reverence and love for God that we share."

(2) Apponius

The voice of my Kinsman knocks at the door:
"Open to me, my sister, my friend,
   my dove, my spotless one;
for my head is covered with dew,
   and my locks with the drops of the night."

In our introduction to this Song we say that the nuptial song for the veiled Bride, the Church of Christ, which comes from the Holy Spirit by the mouth of Solomon, has been set forth figurally, in mysteries. Into those souls who, once made spotless by good works, prepare a dwelling place for God in the house of their mind and deny entrance to evil works all the way up to the day of judgment — into such souls, this Church, generation by generation, introduces the person of Christ, who comes to her in virtue of good works and withdraws in the face of evil deeds.

For when the soul is not stimulated by tribulations, she does not seek to know whether the Bridegroom is near or whether he has departed because repelled by her sad lack of interest. When, however, that incorrigible lover of souls, the Lord Christ, sees her untroubled, occupied with the pleasures of the flesh, through which entrance into the heart is accorded to that thief the Devil, he nevertheless — even though he has been rejected and gone sadly away for a time — returns in the darkness of the night (i.e., by way of hidden remorse) when he sees her walled about by the devices of the Enemy, and he **knocks** at the gate of her mind, so that, roused from her deadly sleep, she may see that she is surrounded with dangers and may pray her Helper to come in to her — the Helper in whose presence all the troops of demons are compelled to flee. She, moreover, though she lies there stripped of the garment that the grace of Christ bestowed on her, though her feet are are bare and washed when they had been "shod" by the hope of attaining blessedness "with the equipment of the gospel of peace" (Eph. 6:15), does not blush to rise up from the bed of evil custom, and by repentance to open the door of her mind to the Christ who knocks.

But if, by deferring the time from day to day, she delays opening the door, he passes such a one by in anger and turns away. Furthermore, he explains in the verse before us what justifications he has for his anger and his turning away: how he has summoned her from her sleep of inertia by charming her with a fourfold love, when he says, **Open to me, my sister, my friend, my dove, my spotless one.** Thus he accords her the honor of being his sister in respect of the flesh he has assumed; that of being his friend through the washing of reconciliation, where from being enemies, people are made the friends of God; that of a dove through the restoration of his image, which is restored through fellowship with the Holy Spirit, who descended in the form of a dove upon Christ, the Church's head, in the Jordan; but spotless, in that he re-forms his likeness within her through her repudiation of idolatry in confession of the most sound Rule of Faith in the Trinity — to which gift she could not have attained save by the shedding of his blood.

Here then are the honors, and this the number of blessings, with which he exalts the soul that has come to him to a share in his kingdom and to the glory of being his sister. And he enumerates them in order that, mindful of them, she may **open** the portal of her heart to him, and to none other, as soon as he **knocks**, before her offense is prolonged — so that if, by the preemptive craftiness of demons, her sin has shut God out, she may at any rate quickly, by her repentance, open to the One that knocks. And in these lines, though the soul's power of choice is attested, nevertheless she is admonished not to ascribe to herself anything, whether in deed or in word of wisdom, on the basis of her own power apart from the Word of God, her helper. For just as a city, even though it stands walled about with fortifications, even though it is crammed with people, is overthrown unless it has within it soldiers who are strong and good at their business; so too a soul, even if she be potent in signs and wonders and filled with all knowledge, is overthrown by the great power of the demons and despoiled, unless she has within her the Spirit of truth, who is one with Christ.

"If," says he, "you want to do something in the way of a good work, O **spotless** soul, do not stand behind a closed door, trusting in your own strength, and be used up in fruitless exertions, but rather **open** to me the door of your mind by calling upon me in truth, by seeking me with your whole heart. Put your will in my hands, so that through you I may triumph over your adversary. Give me the trumpet of your voice, so that my words may be heard in your mouth. Give me your tongue as my pen, so that you may praise the revealed truths and hidden mysteries of the law, written down by my finger. **Open**," he says, "**to me, my sister, my friend, my dove, my spotless one; for my head is full of dew, and my locks with the drops of the night. My head is full**," he says, "**of the dew** of wisdom, the dew of prudence, the dew of knowledge, of which you stand in need when you radiate self-assurance. Therefore, **open to me** by living chastely and piously, so that with my coming there may descend into you that One the conduit of whose dew makes fountains and rivers flow from your heart; through whom the patriarchs, prophets, and apostles wrote righteousness; in the absence of whom philosophers and heretics have written unrighteousness — people from whose minds there have issued not the rivers that water souls that thirst for eternal life but, at the instigation of the Devil, bitter and poisonous streams that to this very day infect the ignorant. These folk had the entrance of their heart shut tight by a proud spirit. They were always seated, acting in the role of teachers, without opening their minds to the One who conveys knowledge to humankind. Since, moreover, in the rapid flow of their speech, they spun resounding words about God but without God, they set down blasphemies against God in place of the honor brought by praise.

The voice, then, is that of the Lord Christ. He addresses the soul, saying, **Open to me; for my head is full of dew, and my locks with the drops of the night.** As to what the "head" of Christ means, Paul, the teacher of the Gentiles, shows us in his instruction: "The head of a woman," he says, "is her husband, and the head of the husband is Christ, but the head of Christ is God" (cf. 1 Cor. 11:3). God himself it is that is **full of** the aforesaid **dew** of wisdom, prudence, and knowledge. But by the "locks" of this head we understand his ministers — angels, archangels, powers, thrones, dominions — who are close to him, who do his will. These **locks** are full of the **drops** of hidden wisdom for the benefit of humankind, and they distill the drops that have descended upon them into the members of the Church by announcing things that will come to pass, by revealing arcane mysteries, by carrying God's commands to the prophets. Thus Daniel reports that he has been instructed by Gabriel in a vision (Dan. 8:16ff.); and Zechariah in the same way writes: "And I said to the angel who was speaking to me, "Who are these black, white, red, and vari-colored horses" (Zech. 1:8-9)? — and so too Manoah was taught by an angel about the birth of Samson (Judg. 13:3). . . .

Regarding this **dew** the prophet Isaiah cries out, "The dew that comes from you is healing for them" (Isa. 26:19); and in Hebrew manuscripts, "Your dew is a dew of light" (Isa. 26:19). Plainly he taught in these words that the **dew** of which he spoke is constituted as the light of wisdom and as healing for souls, that is to say, the teaching of wisdom and truth, apart from which the soul is weak and blind. And this we know to come down from the good **head**, God the Father, to the assumed humanity, Christ, and from Christ to the Church. And just as **dew**, though it is a singular noun, imparts nourishment to many green things and fruits of the earth, so too wisdom — with which, under the name **dew**, Christ asserts that his head is full — imparts the gifts of many charisms.

(4) Gregory of Nyssa

I have removed my tunic,
  how shall I put it on?
I have washed my feet.
  How shall I soil them?

But let us further see how obedient the Bride is to the Word — how she opens a door for the Bridegroom. **I have removed my tunic,** she says; **How shall I put it on? I have washed my feet. How shall I soil them?** Rightly did she hear the One who had commanded her to become **sister** and **close one** and **dove** and **perfect**, in order that truth might in this way take up residence in her soul; for she did what she had heard. She stripped off the tunic of skin that she had put on after the sin (cf. Gen. 3:21), and from her feet she washed the earthy stuff that covered them after she returned to the earth from her sojourn in the Garden, when she heard the words "Earth thou art, and to earth thou shalt return" (Gen. 3:19).

These are the ways in which she opened a way into her soul for the Word, having rent the veil of her heart, which is to say, the flesh. When I say "flesh," what I mean is "the old humanity" (Col. 3:9), which the divine apostle commands to be stripped off and set aside by those who are about to wash off the filth of the soul's feet in the bath of the Word. So whoever has stripped off "the old humanity" and rent the veil of the heart has made an entrance for the Word. And when the Word has entered her, the soul makes him her garment in accordance with the apostle's instruction; for he commands the person who has taken off the rags of the old humanity "to put on the new" tunic "which has been created after the likeness of God in holiness and righteousness" (Eph. 4:24); and this garment, he says, is Jesus (cf. Rom. 13:14).

As to the Bride's confession that she will never again take up the tunic she has put off but will be content, in accord with the command given the disciples (cf. Matt. 10:10), with the one tunic that she put on when she was renewed through the rebirth from above — this confession, I say, confirms the Lord's word, which commands that those who have once for all been dressed up in the divine garment shall never again put on sin's tunic, nor possess two tunics, but only the one, lest there be two conflicting garments on one person. For what does the garment of mourning have in common with the garment that is full of light and immaterial?

The law, however, does not merely say that one must not have two tunics, but also that one must not sew new cloth on an old cloak; otherwise the shabby look of the person who wears it becomes even worse when the patch fails to hold, and the old garment suffers a tear that is worse and all but impossible to mend. For he says, "The new patch will tear away from the old cloth, and the result will be a worse tear" (Mark 2:21), and everyone will be able to see the unseemly result. That is why the Bride says, **I have removed my tunic. How shall I put it on?** For who is there who sees himself garbed in the Lord's glistering tunic — woven of purity and incorruptibility as he displayed it in his transfiguration on the Mount — and then allows himself to put on the poor, ragged garment in which "the drunkard and whoremonger," as Proverbs (23:21) says, attires himself?

Moreover, she whose feet have been washed never again contracts, in her walking, the defilement of things earthly. For, says she, **I have washed my feet. How shall I soil them?** Furthermore, it is related that Moses, after, at God's command, he had liberated his feet from their dead clothing of skins when he entered the holy and luminous ground (cf. Exod. 3:5ff.), did not put those shoes back on. And when he had made the priestly garment after the pattern shown him on the mountain — mixing the gleaming colors of "gold and purple and scarlet and linen" (cf. Exod. 28:5, 8, 15) in the robe, so that it was refulgent with a beauty made up of these — he made nothing to adorn the feet. No, the adornment of the priest's foot was its nakedness and its freedom from any covering; for the priest must ever walk on holy ground, and it is not right to enter holy ground wearing dead skins. Hence too the Lord forbade his disciples to wear sandals when he ordered them not to travel "the way of the Gentiles" (Matt. 10:9, 5), but to take the holy way.

And you are in no wise unacquainted with this holy way by which he orders his disciples to go; for you have heard about it from him who said, "I am the way" (John 14:6) — the way upon which no one can set a foot unless he has removed the garment of our dead humanity. Since, then, the Bride finds herself on this very road on which the Lord washes with water the feet of those who walk it and dries them with the towel that girds his waist (and the belt that girds the Lord's waist has the power to cleanse away sin; for it says, "The Lord is robed, he is girded with power" [Ps. 92:1 LXX = 93:1]), for this reason, I say, once her feet are cleansed, she keeps herself on the royal road. She does not stray to the left or to the right, lest she step off the way on either hand and defile her foot with mud.

You perceive clearly, then, what these words convey: that she who has once and for all, through baptism, taken off her sandals (for it is the proper business of a baptizer to loose the thongs of those who are wearing sandals — just as John testified that he was unable to do in the single case of the Lord [cf. Luke 3:16]; for how could he loose one who had never been bound by the thong of sin?) — she has had her feet washed and has shed, with her sandals, all earthy filth. Therefore she keeps her undefiled feet to the paved road, just as David did when he washed off the slimy clay and fixed his feet on the rock, as he says, "He drew me up from the pit of distress, out of the miry bog, and set my feet upon a rock, and made my steps straight" (Ps. 39:3 LXX = 40:2). The rock we understand to be the Lord, who is light and truth and incorruption and righteousness; and with these qualities the spiritual road is paved. The soul that does not turn aside in either direction keeps her feet clean and pure, entirely unsullied by the mire of pleasure.

(4) Richard of St.-Victor

**My Beloved has put his hand through the opening,
and my belly quivered at his touch.**

She calls this visitation of grace the putting of his hand **through the opening**. He pours grace in as it were through a chink, since he does not bathe the entire soul but brings to bear a certain measure of grace; and he does not fully illuminate her to whom he thus ministers in part. This working and gift of grace can be taken to be the Beloved's **hand**. But the **belly** means the mind itself, in which the thoughts boil up, like food in the belly. Further, the Beloved puts **his hand through the opening,** in that he confers these benefits on the soul — providing them through the Holy Spirit — because he has redeemed her by his death, because he has accorded her the gifts of his grace, because he preserves these same gifts by guarding them. For he imparts life and mercy to her, and his coming to her safeguards her spirit. He imparts life to her by dying for her, mercy, by washing her, and his coming to her guards her from any fall into sin by keeping her unharmed.

I arose to open to my Beloved. My hands dripped myrrh, my fingers were full of the choicest myrrh. She arises to open to her Beloved, for once she has received grace, she is further aroused to take possession of it for herself, to love more warmly, to set more earnestly about the care and well-being of her neighbors; for she who had opened to her Beloved beforehand is more fully inflamed for him and sets herself to the works of love.

At that point she employs herself in the love of God, or contemplation, and she devotes herself to profiting her neighbors as their need demands and the time requires. She prays for others, she relieves others, she gives others saving counsel. She also prepares to undertake the work of direction or to engage in the business of preaching should the occasion require it, as long as she is visited by grace and strives to respond to it and to be conformed to it.

She is also set on fire to subdue whatever she detects in herself that is carnal. But to whatever extent she has done her sins and vices to death, nevertheless, because of the more abundant grace she has received, she . . . is quicker to discern that which grace repairs. The more she has been enlightened, the more she recognizes her shortcomings; and the more she has improved, the more she becomes worthless to herself. At that point she condemns the little shortcomings that she has previously put up with, and she understands that she has committed many sins, both in word and in thought, that she used to reckon as less than serious. While she devotes herself to this labor and work of mortification, her hands drip myrrh; for by "hands" is meant this labor, and by "myrrh" this mortification is signified; and **her fingers are full of the choicest myrrh** because she does everything with discrimination and with a pure intention. For **fingers** denotes this action of discrimination, in which she rightly divides what she rightly offers, that is to say, she differentiates what she appropriately aims at. But by **choicest myrrh** we understand a pure intent in the work of mortification. She seeks God in such a way that she mortifies empty glory and disdains praises that come from others, and her eye, that is, her intention, ever fixes itself upon God and upon the true delight that is yet to come. . . .

I opened the bolt of the door to my Beloved, but he had turned away and passed

by. The Bride reflects upon the way in which, if she is to delight in the presence of her Beloved, she must guard against the least degree of negligence, which could occasion his displeasure — by speech that is useless and superfluous, that is, or by thoughts, by bodily ease, or by flighty freedom — all of which can be denoted by a **bolt**, that is to say, by a "bar." For a bar, though it be small and narrow, nevertheless keeps an entire wide door shut, so that unless it is drawn back, the door cannot stand open. Thus unless these minor defects are repudiated, the Beloved does not deign to come to the soul in such wise as to enter her fully and fill her with grace entire. Little acts of heedlessness darken the soul and create an obstacle to fuller grace.

Since she knows this, the Bride guards her heart's eyes against the dust of such deeds in order that she may be able to see the Beloved contemplatively, and receive him more fully. She undertakes, then, a more thorough purification of her heart, so that her Beloved may enter her more fully, and (so to speak) through the door — the door that had occasioned her to realize that his earlier visit had been less than complete, amounting, so to speak, to a touch through an opening. But he turns away and passes her by, not leaving her but stepping off to one side. For he is there at her right hand, lest she be shaken loose from the good thing she had begun, yet his face does not appear to her; for the Lord "is near to all those who call upon him" (Ps. 144:18 Vg = 145:18).

She desires to contemplate him, and to speak with him face to face, in the same way that one converses with a friend. He hides his face, however, while remaining with her and within her even though his presence is less felt. It is in this way that, even though he visits her, he turns aside and passes by, lest she be proud and attribute it to her own merits if her enjoyment of him matches her desire. When, therefore, she has shown herself more worthy of his acceptance, he does not accord her his presence as she wishes, but turns away from her, so that he may keep her humble, and raise her desire to a higher pitch and fulfill it more completely. . . . He is said to turn away when he does not allow his presence to be felt, though he is nevertheless present to her. In that circumstance, the soul experiences as burdensome what before she had performed with delight. By such labors, she is strengthened spiritually, and as long as she does her work vigorously, her heart is strengthened so that she bears up courageously and waits patiently for the Lord, when he either afflicts her with adversities or withdraws his consolation. . . . At the time of contemplation, then, ardent desire for God is created, and when this has come about, what she does meets approval and her virtue is exercised — or else she laments that the Beloved has turned away from her because he who has been partially comprehended is understood to be yet more unfathomable, as the psalmist says, "A man shall rise up to a high heart, and God will be exalted" (cf. Ps. 60:3 Vg); and also Solomon, "I sought wisdom, and she retired far from me" (Eccl. 7:24 Vg = 7:23). For the more a person rises up toward God, the more he finds him exalted and unfathomable. That is why Job says, "And he will not be searched out when his voice has been heard" (Job 37:4 Vg). She also complains of his turning away, because her mind thirsts for the One it has tasted and desires him; and the more she becomes acquainted with his sweetness, the less does what she has known of him satisfy her. . . . All of her melts for love of him whose in-breathing she has received, and this is what she says next.

My soul melted as my Beloved spoke. When the Beloved speaks in the mind, things

unyielding become yielding, and things that used to seem hard in the face of earthly pleasure become easy and full of delight after the soul has melted and thus warmed up —
even as it is written: "The things that my soul refused to touch at first are my food in the
face of adversity" (Job 7:6 Vg). Bitter things then become sweet, because she is so melted
by love that she scarcely feels whatever cross the body may bear. Confronted by the magnitude of his love, she dissolves in tears, and as long as it is not granted her to see her God,
"tears become her bread night and day" (Ps. 41:4 LXX = 42:3).

Hence it is that she resumes her complaint and says, **I sought him and I did not
find him; I called him, and he did not anwer me.** She does not find the one she has
sought in a way that corresponds to her wish, nor does he respond to her in a way that
meets her every request or desire. Thus what she hears does not answer to what she has
asked, nor does she tell him that she had heard him. She does not, then, hear him as she
had wished; but in the meanwhile she hears in a way that profits her more. And though
she thinks she has not heard his voice, she is hearkening to him more fully than before in
that she acknowledges her awareness that this is better for her. When Paul requested that
the "thorn in" his "flesh" be removed (2 Cor. 12:7ff.), God heard him better even though
he did not remove it; for if he had removed it, Paul would not have been saved. Thus he
answers more truly when he is thought not to answer — indeed, it is he that forms in her
soul the words and desires with which she answers. For it is he himself that makes the request, that is, he brings about her entreaty, and it is he that is answering, when she admits
what is expedient for her. . . .

(5) Gregory of Nyssa

I opened to my Kinsman;
    my Kinsman passed on by.
My soul went out at his word. . . .

When, therefore, the Bride had like Moses come to hope that the face of the One she desired would be manifested to her and she might know him, at that very instant the One
she sought escaped her apprehension. For she says, **My Kinsman passed on by** — not de-
serting the soul that followed him, but drawing her to himself; for she continues, **My soul
went out at his word.**

What a happy exodus is this which the soul makes that follows the Word! "The
Lord will keep your exodus and your entrance" (Ps. 120:8 LXX = 121:8), says the prophet.
This is truly at one and the same time the exodus and the entrance that God keeps for
those who are worthy, since the exodus from our present state becomes an entrance upon
the good things that lie beyond. This, then, is the exodus that the soul makes when it
takes the Word as its God — the Word who says "I am the way" (John 14:6), and "the
door," and "whoever enters by way of me . . . will both come in and go out" (John 10:9).
That soul neither leaves off coming in nor ceases going out, but is always entering into
what lies beyond in virtue of the progress she makes, and always taking leave of what she
has already apprehended.

In just this way did the face of the Lord for which Moses longed once pass him by, and just so did the soul of that Lawgiver ever and again take leave of the place she was in as she followed the Word who went on ahead of her. Who does not observe the upward steps that Moses climbed — Moses who was ever in process of growing (cf. Heb. 11:24) and never ceased from growth toward the better? He increased at the beginning, when he preferred the reproach of Christ to the kingdom of the Egyptians, "choosing rather to share ill-treatment with the people of God than to enjoy the fleeting pleasures of sin" (Heb. 11:25). He increased again when, because an Egyptian was maltreating a Hebrew, he fought for the Israelite and killed the foreigner. The manner of his growth in these events you understand fully by shifting the narrative to the level of figurative interpretation. Yet again he became greater than himself when he kept his life tranquil for a long space by living the philosophical life in the wilderness. Then he was enlightened by the fire that played over the bush. After that his hearing too was illumined by the beams of light through the agency of the Word. Further, he strips his feet of their dead covering; he destroys the Egyptian snake with his staff; he frees his people from the tyrant Pharaoh; he is guided by a cloud; he divides the sea; he drowns the tyrant; he makes Marah sweet; he smites the rock; he is filled with angels' food; he hears the trumpet; he dares the burning mountain; he attains its pinnacle; the cloud comes down; he enters the darkness where God dwells; he receives the covenant; he becomes a sun, flashing unapproachable light from his countenance upon those who draw near him.

All these upward steps, not to mention the varied theophanies he experienced — how can words tell them? Yet for all that, it is such and so great a person as this, one whose life was so full of sublime experiences through which he was raised up toward God, who still possesses an insatiable desire for something greater and prays that he may see God face to face — even though the Scriptures had already attested that he was judged worthy of speaking to God face to face (cf. Num. 12:8). Yet even though he addressed God as friend to friend and had intimate conversation with God, he did not cease to desire higher things. On the contrary, his word is: "If I have found grace in your sight, manifest yourself to me in such wise that I may know you!" (Exod. 33:13). And the One who had promised to confer the asked-for gift, the One who said "You have I known above all others" (Exod. 33:17), passes Moses by as he is stationed upon the rock at the holy place and shielded by the divine hand, so that he can scarcely see God's back after God has passed by. By this, as I judge the matter, Scripture teaches that a person who desires to see God catches sight of the One he seeks by always following after him; and that the contemplation of God's face is an unceasing journey toward God that is brought to fulfillment by following the Word.

(6) Ambrose of Milan

The guards that go their rounds in the city found me;
  they beat me, they wounded me.
The guards of the walls took my veil away from me.

Since she was to meet her Bridegroom, she came, quite properly, as a bride, with a mantle veiling her head. Just as Rebecca, who, once she understood that Isaac was coming to meet her, got down from her camel (cf. Gen. 24:64-65) and covered herself with her mantle, so too this soul displays the badges of nuptial attire so that she will not be sent away because she lacks the wedding garment — or else in order to veil her head because of the angels (cf. 1 Cor. 11:10). They, however, beat her, so that she might be tried and tested the more; for souls are trained by temptations. **They took** her **mantle away from** her, trying to see whether she brought with her the true beauty of naked virtue; or else because one is bound to enter that heavenly city bare, without bringing along any clothing to disguise oneself. Then there are people who require that the soul under no circumstances bear with her the remnants of carnal allurements and bodily desire. She is divested of her mantle when her conscience lies open to view. On the other hand, there is the soul that strips herself bare and is right to do so, a soul whom it is allowable to imitate as she says, "For the Prince of this world came, and found nothing in me" (John 14:30); for it is a sure thing that the only one in whom nothing is found is the one who has committed no sin. Blessed too is she in whom he finds no grave sins or numerous sins, but finds in her the mantle of faith and the teaching of wisdom.

So she bears no loss, for even if someone wants to, he cannot carry off true wisdom. Even if the Adversary rages against her, the true integrity of a spotless way of life shines through in such a person. So without loss she passed through the guards and, having joined the daughters of that heavenly city, she seeks the Word, and by her seeking arouses his love for her, and she knows where she may seek the Word. She knows that he tarries among the prayers of the saints and cleaves to them, and she understands well that he pastures his Church — the souls of his righteous ones — among the lilies. The Lord showed you this mystery when he led his disciples through fields of grain. Moses led the Jewish people through the desert, but Christ leads the souls of the righteous through fields of grain and through lilies; for by his suffering, the desert blossoms like a lily. Let us follow him, therefore, so that on the day of Sabbath, the day of that Great Sabbath in which there is great rest, we may gather the fruits.

(7) Honorius of Autun

My soul melted when the Beloved spoke.
  I sought and did not find him;
  I called, and he did not answer me. . . .

Opening the door and failing to find her Beloved, the Bride comes to the chorus of the **daughters of Jerusalem,** who had accompanied her, and in a tone of lament reports to them that she did not open to the Beloved when he knocked, that she did not find him when later she looked for him, that indeed he did not answer when called, that the **guards** of the city had struck her, wounded her, and removed her garment. Further, she anxiously requests that if they find him, they inform him of what she had suffered for love of him. The analogy is that of the lover who anxiously seeks her beloved in the night, incautiously encounters the guards, loses her clothing, receives a beating, and afterward, in her grief, reports these events to her circle of friends.

By the Bride in this passage is meant the Church of the penitent, those who by penitence and confession seek the Beloved whom they have lost by their own fault, and in their confession, speaking in groans, declare this to the daughters of Jerusalem — that is, to the spiritual and the religious: "My soul, which when the north wind was blowing was hardened in wickedness, **is melted** when the south wind blows, as the Beloved speaks the words, '**Open to me, my sister,** whom I have made my fellow-heir by my blood.' My soul, pricked in conscience by these words to exhibit the image of the Bridegroom, is melted like wax."

Next the spirit, that is, the higher power of the soul, speaks here: "In my thought **I sought** the riches of his forbearance, by which he upholds me, obstinate sinner that I am, even though I provoke him at length; and **I did not find** the boundless mercy that spares sinners. **I called** out with a heartfelt cry, desiring to know his hidden judgments: why he preserves evildoers for long life, but punishes the good; why he sometimes chooses evildoers on the ground that they are repentant, but rejects the good on account of a fault; why he converts one individual and forsakes another, though their faults are equivalent: and **he did not answer me.**" This means: "He did not show me by way of the Scriptures to place my trust not in my own works but in his mercy. He came after me himself when he departed from the heavenly chorus of angels and sought me like a sheep wandering lost in the world. He called when he said, "Be turned to me, O returning children, and I will make you over" (Jer. 3:14). I for my part despised this summons. Therefore, the Lord does not hear me when I cry out in my distress.

"The **guards** — which is to say, the leaders of the Church, the guardians, by teaching and example, of God's law — **that go their rounds in the city** — that is, keep the Church secure by use of the Scriptures — found me as I was thus seeking and calling, full of sins and abominations. **They struck me** with fear of judgment and of sins; **they wounded me** with remorse and penitence; **they** — the guards of the walls, that is, the teachers of the books by which the Church, the City of God, is encircled as by a wall — **took away** my mantle, that is to say, the multitude of sins in which I was wrapped, by means of the penitence they enjoined." Another interpretation: "They took away the mantle, that is, the veil of ignorance, as they explained the hidden judgments of God to me. Therefore, to the **guards of the city** or **the guards of the walls**, who found me in such a state and treated me as they did — to them I said, groaning:

"**I adjure you, O daughters of Jerusalem, if you find my Beloved, announce to him that I am sick with love.**" It is as if she said, "O you spiritual souls of the heavenly Jerusalem, daughters in virtue of the sacrament of faith, I require you, if you discover my Beloved in the Scriptures (i.e., if by reading you understand the doings of my Beloved; for surely the one who 'discovers' another is the one who knows his life and his ways), that you announce to him through me (i.e., that you teach me to make this announcement by giving thanks and by preaching to others; for the one who announces something is the one who teaches another to make the announcement) — announce, I say, that I am weak and sick with love." This means: "Because of my love of him I am sick and tired of things earthly and desire only things heavenly."

"And these are the doings of the Beloved: namely, that the Most High hates sinners and is merciful to the penitent; and that "All the ways of the Lord are mercy and truth" (Ps. 24:10 Vg = 25:10) — mercy with regard to the penitent, truth with regard to those who sin. Through me you will announce that he is to be loved because in his mercy he spares those who by their penitence open the way into their heart, and justly punishes those who bar the gate of their heart by evil living."

Notice: in that he performed six works of mercy in the six ages or the six days, he lays down for the sorrowful soul six principles by which she may achieve a sixfold perfection: namely, that at the voice of God, the soul melts with remorse; that she seeks him with anxious repentance; that she calls upon him with moanings; that from desire for him she is daily, that is, at every time, afflicted by adversities, wounded by sorrows, deprived of necessities.

The reason, moreover, why this lament finds a place in this song of love is that the faithful soul, the Bride of Christ, is joined to him by penitence; and "There will be joy among the angels of God over one sinner who does penance" (Luke 15:10). This lament belongs more to the tropological than to the allegorical sense, because in it the Church exhorts the penitent to good morals. Hence the allegorical sense is missing in this passage.

If it be taken in the anagogical sense, the pilgrim Church is sleeping with her **heart . . . awake**, when she is insensible to things earthly and transitory and aspires solely to things heavenly. The voice of the Beloved hammers upon her when he summons her to her heavenly fatherland by bodily ills and the approach of death. She quickly opens to him because she gratefully accepts his calling. For she is brought into the Lord's inheritance as his **sister**; she is admitted into heavenly mysteries as his **friend**; she is enlightened by the Holy Spirit as a **dove**; and as one who is **spotless** she is established in the bedchamber of the Bridegroom. She removes her **mantle** when she lays down the body. She bathes her **feet** when, by her final act of penance, she washes off the fine dust of distracting thoughts. The Beloved puts out his **hand** when he touches her with the pangs of death. But her **belly** trembles at his touch because by her slightest sins, which she committed through the frailty of the flesh, she has merited the judge's sentence. Nevertheless she rises up to open to him because she wishes to have the vision of him who dwells on high. His hands drip with **myrrh** because it stands for the works by which she has mortified herself here in order that for them she may receive eternal rewards.

Song 5:9-16

5:9   What is your Kinsman from a
       Kinsman,
      O fair one among women?
    What is your Kinsman from
      a Kinsman,
    that you have charged us so?

10   My Kinsman is shining white and
      ruddy,
    set apart out of thousands.

11   His head is golden and *phaz;*
    his locks are tall firs,

    black like a raven.

12   His eyes are like doves
      by full pools of waters,
    washed in milk,
      seated by full pools of waters.

13   His cheeks are like bowls of spice
      producing perfumes.
    His lips are lilies,
      dripping abundant myrrh.

14   His hands are finely worked, golden,
    full *tharsis.*
    His belly is an ivory tablet
      upon stone of lapis lazuli.

15   His legs are like marble pillars
      resting upon golden feet.

5:9   What sort is your Beloved from the
       Beloved,
      O fairest of women?
  Of what sort is your Beloved from
      the Beloved,
    that you have charged us in this
      way?

10   My Beloved is shining white and
      ruddy,
    chosen out of thousands.

11   His head is the finest gold;
    his locks are like the buddings of
      palm trees,
    black like a raven.

12   His eyes are like doves
      above rivulets of waters,
  which have been washed in milk
      by overflowing streams.

13   His cheeks are like beds of spices
      planted by makers of perfumes.
    His lips are lilies,
      dripping the choicest myrrh.

14   His hands are golden,
      turned on a lathe, full of hyacinth.
    His belly is ivory
      adorned with sapphires.

15   His legs are marble columns
      that have been set on golden
        pedestals.

His appearance is like Lebanon,
    chosen like cedars.
16 His throat is sweetness
    and wholly desire.
And this is my close one,

    O daughters of Jerusalem.

His form is like Lebanon's,
    chosen like cedars.
16 His throat is perfectly sweet,
    and he is wholly desirable.
Such is my Beloved, and this is my
    friend,
    O daughters of Jerusalem.

The Bride is asked, in effect, what is so special about her Beloved; and this question, which a reader might think was put by the "daughters of Jerusalem," evokes a description of the Bridegroom's physical charms.

In the first line of the passage, the phrase "your Kinsman from a Kinsman," represents the Septuagint's literal translation of the Hebrew (which itself makes no obvious sense). The phrase has commonly been taken to intend a comparison: "How is your Lover better than any other?" The Vulgate too renders the Hebrew literally; but most commentators on the Vulgate text do not take the phrase as expressing a comparison. Rather, they have tended to take "Beloved from the Beloved" to point to the relation of Father and Son in the Trinity.

This passage further contains two verses in which the Septuagint has simply transliterated a word in the Hebrew text without attempting to translate it into Greek — no doubt because the translators were uncertain of its meaning: see phaz *in vs. 11a, and* tharsis *in 14a. A commentator like Theodoret will then refer to alternative Greek versions — most likely those provided by Origen, who in his famous Hexapla had set six different versions in parallel columns — to get the meaning straight.*

Confusion was also caused — as the Glossa ordinaria *notes in the fifth excerpt below — by v. 11b, where the word* elatae *(in the Vulgate's Latin) parallels* elatai *(in the Septuagint's Greek), both words being intended to refer to a characteristic of the Bridegroom's hair. The Latin term can be either an adjective (meaning "lifted up," "high," "exalted") or a noun transliterated directly from the Greek. The noun in question means, in both languages, a type of fir tree (or perhaps the bud of a palm tree!). The standard meaning of the noun may fit the context better, but Apponius below takes the Latin word as an adjective meaning "high" or "lofty."*

(1) Richard of St.-Victor

What is your Beloved from the Beloved like,
    O fairest of women?
What is your Beloved from the Beloved like,
    that you have so charged us?
My Beloved is shining white and ruddy,
    chosen out of thousands.

Beloved from the Beloved means the Son of God from the Father, and anyone who loves the Son loves the Father too, just as anyone who sees the Son also sees the Father.

The devout souls, thus aflame with wonder and with desire for him, again seek the Beloved and name him; they themselves also wish to be taught by the Bride and to be renewed by that sweetness of the Beloved which they have gathered from her. They call her **fairest** because they judge her to possess beauty of mind and to be adorned most surely with the virtues. It is, furthermore, commonplace among good persons to think better of others than of themselves, and to hear with great delight whatever is spoken with knowledge, that is, whatever is proposed on the basis of inward experience. Then too lovers speak out gladly about the one whom they desire. For the devout, when they come together to talk about God, and by shared conversation to be yet more set on fire for God, are accustomed, on the basis of the trust they have, to convey openly to each other what they think or understand about God. Moreover, God is accustomed to be in their midst, and to increase grace in those who are gathered because of him and assembled to speak about him.

Hence it is that the Bride, more fired up to answer the questions about her Beloved, begins to explain how he appears and to tell of the benefits that have come to her from him, saying, **My Beloved is shining white and ruddy, chosen out of thousands.** He is **shining white** because he is the radiance of eternal light and "light from light." He is **shining white** because he is free of all sin, because he has done no sin, nor has "guile" been found "in his mouth" (Isa. 53:9). Moreover, he is **ruddy** because in his passion, in which there was "no form or comeliness" (Isa. 53:2), he was bathed in his blood so that he might make me comely, and his blood might adorn the cheeks of my soul, and he might reform my deformity. That is why my Beloved is truly mine, because in suffering those things for me, he also made these things mine.

He is also **chosen out of thousands** because not one member of the whole human race has been without sin except him. For among the lawgivers there is none like him, nor yet among the thousands of thousands or ten times a hundred thousands of those who serve the Lord of majesty or attend him. For neither gold nor glass measures up to him, by which I mean the community of the citizens of heaven, whose hearts flash their brilliance back and forth to each other and are transparent to purity. And this is because he is not only a human but God.

Hence we next hear: **His head is the finest gold.** His head is his Deity, because God is the head of Christ (1 Cor. 11:3). This head is **the finest gold** because the goodness of the Deity, that is, the gold of the land of the living, surpasses all things that have been made by him, and the gold of that land is the finest. For he is so brilliant that he cannot be seen by human eyes or by those who live in the flesh. For no one shall "see" God "and live" (cf. Exod. 33:20). Hence he is my Beloved because God is his Head, God, his Origin, the sublime One that cannot be seen. I am going to see him when that life appears, for then I shall be "like him," and I "shall see him as he is" (1 John 3:2). He shall furnish me with this double happiness — that he shall conform my "lowly body" to "his glorious body" (Phil. 3:21), and my soul to the likeness of his Deity.

(2) Theodoret of Cyrus

My Kinsman is shining white and ruddy,
   set apart out of thousands.
His head is golden and *phaz*.

To the young maidens who have questioned her the Bride explains how to recognize her Kinsman, and says, **My Kinsman is shining white and ruddy.** First she says **shining white;** second, **ruddy.** For he was ever God, but a human being he became (cf. John 1:14), without relinquishing his original identity, or turning into a human being, but putting on human nature. Hence it is as God that he is **shining white;** for what is more radiant than light? And he is "the true light," as the Gospel asserts: "For," it says, "the true light that enlightens every human being was coming into the world" (John 1:9).

However, he is not only **shining white** but **ruddy** — he is not only God but a human being. For the word "ruddy" indicates what is earthly. Hence it is that in Isaiah the divine Powers ask to see him rising up from the earth into heaven: "Who is this that comes from Edom, in crimsoned garment from Bozrah — he that is glorious in his apparel, in might with strength" (Isa. 63:1)? More than this, they marvel at his bodily beauty, which they call his "garment"; for it is as human that he is "splendid in beauty by comparison with the sons of men" (Ps. 44:3 LXX = 45:2); his Deity represents an unattainable beauty and so is beyond any comparison.

But they question him and say, "Why is your apparel red, as if taken from a wine press all trodden down" (Isa. 63:2)? He then teaches those who want to learn the reason for this redness when he replies, "I have trodden the wine press alone, and from the peoples no one was with me . . . ; for it was no representative, no angel, but the Lord himself who saved us" (Isa. 63:3, 9), according to Isaiah's prophecy. "And I trod them in my anger, and trampled them in my wrath" (Isa. 63:6) — meaning the demons that are enemies of the human race, and their host. "And my garments were besprinkled with their blood" (Isa. 63:3); for in the victory over them and in the destruction of their power, I acquired drops of blood on my garments, that is to say, on my body. For the divine nature is impassible, but the body is susceptible to suffering. It is true that the divine Logos, united to the body as he is, brings it with him, but he does not take over suffering from it since the Divine is beyond suffering by nature.

This explains why the Bride says, **My Kinsman is shining white and ruddy, set apart out of myriads.** For the first fruits are nobler than the whole of the species. For "he committed no sin, neither was guile found in his mouth" (Isa. 53:9), and therefore he offered a spotless sacrifice on behalf of the entire race. This is the reason why the God of the universe, speaking through the prophet Isaiah, addresses him in these terms: "Behold, my servant, whom I uphold, my chosen, in whom my soul delights; I shall put my Spirit upon him, he will bring forth judgment for the nations" (Isa. 42:1).

Rightly, then, does the Bride say, **My Kinsman is shining white and ruddy, set apart out of myriads.** For it was appropriate for the one who bore our sins, which were as red as crimson and as purple, to become **ruddy** and to be spoken of as follows: **His head is golden and *phaz*.** In the version of Symmachus, this means "like a precious stone"; but according to the fifth translation[1] it means "stamped with gold." She uses the expression "his head" allegorically, to mean the Divine, which earlier she called "shining white." Thus she likens him to gold and to a jewel, the material goods that people value most; for she found no other name more appropriate.

(3) John of Ford

My Beloved is shining bright and ruddy . . .

So when you ask what my **Beloved from the Beloved** is like, I [the Bride is speaking] have an answer right on the tip of my tongue: just as the Father is supremely beautiful and supremely desirable, so too, in every respect, is his Only-Begotten: **shining bright** from the **shining bright**, **ruddy** from the **ruddy**. True it is that my Beloved, being fire as he is, shines and burns surpassingly; but the Father, who loves him and is also loved by him in turn with an equal love, is the Source of light and warmth for his Only-Begotten, his Beloved and his Lover. In consequence the two together are one light and one warmth — light in being wisdom, in being truth, in being holiness, in being benevolence; wisdom as the artificer of everything and the One who has knowledge of everything; truth as the One who by his illumination overcomes the shadows of falsehood and the subterfuges of deceit; holiness as intolerant of all corruption and impurity; benevolence as freely imparting himself to the unworthy.

So, then, consider the analogues of all this in that visible light with reference to which the Light we are speaking of said, "Let there be light, and there was light" (Gen. 1:3). For this too, in its own way, gives light to the blind and teaches the human creature knowledge — lifting him from the darkness of blindness and ignorance in which the night had covered him and wrapped him up. It too, by the unexpected gleaming of its light, at once dissolves the darkness, reveals it, and shows it up for what it is. "Therefore nothing defiled gains entrance into her" (Wisdom 7:25), but she keeps herself unspotted. And so the light rises upon the good and the bad indifferently and bestows itself upon both spontaneously and for nothing.

So then, O light most beautiful, O radiance of light eternal, this is what you were from the very beginning, this is what you were, O ancient loveliness, in your ancient days,

---

1. Theodoret is referring to an anonymous translation of the Septuagint.

in the years of your eternity. This is what you were, O Lord Jesus — wise, true, holy, benevolent; but this you were at once for yourself and for your Father, your Beloved who loves you. "Your Source was with you on the day of your power" (Ps. 109:3), and you were with him. You were the fullness of joy for him, as he was for you.

Since, however, you were not only Light's Light but also the fountainhead of light, you suddenly shone in those that you decree to be sharers in so great a good — and this in order that this same good might be manifested to your creation and shared by it. You summoned the stars, and they said, "Here we are." And for you they delighted to give light, eternally rejoicing in you, their incommunicable good, and shimmering perpetually and passionately in the presence of you, their Source.

Where we are concerned, however, whom you created to delight in you, but who withdrew from you and wanted to keep our strength for ourselves — we walked headlong into the darkness of ignorance and weakness. This was a deep darkness indeed, so deep that we had recollection neither of you nor of the state from which we had fallen at the beginning, nor indeed of the direction in which this fall was taking us. Nor for that matter did we have any awareness that we were fallen or that we were continuing to go head over heels downward. Even then, O true light, you were shining in the midst of this darkness of ours; but our darkness did not comprehend you (cf. John 1:5). You who are never absent were near us, but we were far from you; we were exiled in a realm far from your light, in a realm of darkness, in the realm of "the shadow of death" (Ps. 22:4 Vg = 23:4). So you were, for us, inaccessible; for it is useless to rise up to meet you before the light dawns, and any striving on the part of virtue to reach you, however great it be, is pointless and vain apart from the prevenient light of your grace.

Therefore, you — the dawning splendor of eternal Light — by that same free and unoriginate benevolence with which, begotten before the day star from the womb of the Father, you wondrously flash and gleam in the primordial brilliance of the holy ones, mercifully drew near to us, who were incapable of drawing near to you. And because as Wisdom you were the artificer of all things, you dispensed, with a marvelous and astute ingenuity, a salvation of the sort that fitted creatures who were blind and sickly. For since, in the invisible light of your wisdom, the world did not know you by wisdom (cf. 1 Cor. 1:21), it was your gracious pleasure to enlighten the blind and to cure the sickly by means of a sort of folly (cf. 1 Cor. 1:18). You were a great light concealed in the bosom of the Father, but you came out of your refuge into our public domain. You became the great Light of the great, and the modest lamp of the little ones; you became not only a lamp that our eyes could see but also one that our hands could touch. Thus you brought news of the Light to your friend, saying that it might be something for him to possess and that he might rise up to it. You burst forth from the bright womb of the Virgin, O brightest of lights, and there you really did set "your tabernacle in the sun" (Ps. 18:6 Vg = 19:6), which, however, you had fashioned for yourself, being the fountainhead of light.

Therefore, O blessed Light, because you were Wisdom, you wisely adapted yourself to the state of those who lacked wisdom. Furthermore, because you were Truth, you broke up the night of our ignorance by flashing forth in the darkness, and you showed the works of darkness up; for out of the cloud of your flesh, you thundered the threat of judgment and the news of the kingdom. You shimmered with signs and wonders, and you showed that you are our true and unique salvation by taking away our sins.

Nevertheless, it would have been fruitless for you to show us these things on the outside unless you also shone within us. So because you were also Holiness, you count it a matter of first importance to accord us your mercy by setting fear of you within us, and in this way you make us holy, turning us away from our own darkness and mercifully drawing us to you, the true Light.

Finally, because you were also benevolence, and in order that you might attire in splendor those who had garbed themselves in faith's confession, and thus we might "walk becomingly as in the day" (Rom. 13:13 Vg = 14:13), you covered us with the light of your righteousness. You conferred benevolence on us by infusing the Spirit of your grace, and "our earth brought forth its fruit" (Ps. 84:13 Vg = 85:12).

(4) John of Ford

His head is the finest gold.

The Father, then, who is the ultimate height from which love flows and the clearest channel of living waters, loves God his Son with all his heart, that is, with all his reason, understanding, and wisdom; he loves him with all his soul, that is, with his entire will, goodness, and benevolence; and with all his strength, that is, with all his righteousness, power, and determination; he loves him with all his mind, that is, with all his memory, eternity, and changelessness.

Now that "neighbor" of his, whom he loves as himself, is the very same one who is also our neighbor — his neighbor in virtue of delight, and ours in virtue of compassion. The Son is neighbor by nature to both, and that is why he has also been made the Mediator between the two, being the only one fitted for the work of this covenant in that he comes as already allied to each of the parties to it.

Hence the Father delighted in his Son from the very beginning with all his wisdom; and to him, in the act of begetting and loving him, he communicated the status of being himself the whole of wisdom. The Father delighted in him with all his goodness, and nevertheless, in the same manner, constituted him as his own entire goodness. He also delighted in him with all his strength and righteousness, and constituted him his "holy right arm" (Ps. 97:1 Vg = 98:1) and the entire fullness of his righteousness. He delighted in him too with the entire remembrance of his eternity, and made him his eternal and unchangeable Only-Begotten. In a word, he gave himself wholly to his Son, in every bit of whom he delighted with all that he is.

In consequence, the Only-Begotten Son is in the whole Father as a whole. He occupies the heart that is God's wisdom; he fills the soul that is God's goodness; he pervades the inward parts that are God's strength; and he inhabits the entirety of the womb that is God's eternity. He is in the heart of the Father, where he peers into the depths of the riches of his wisdom and knowledge. He is in the soul of the Father, where he searches out the treasures of goodness and benevolence. He is in the holy place of God's righteousness, penetrating all the depths of his judgments and the secrets of his decrees. He is in his memory, where he grasps fully and truly the very same simple and unchangeable reality through which he is also the first principle of absolutely everything.

Finally, so that our usage may be consistent with the language of the Bride's praise, the Bridegroom's **head is the finest gold** in the sense that, as the apostle testifies, "the head of Christ is God" (1 Cor. 10:3 Vg = 11:3); but then, as John testifies, "God is love" (1 John 4:8). And in truth God *is* love, and the very finest love, for he communicates himself as a whole to his Only-Begotten as a whole, and of all the things that are his, of all that he is, he holds back nothing that he does not confer wholly on his Son. . . .

Therefore "the head of Christ is God," the God who is the finest love, because the wisest, the most benevolent, the most righteous and powerful, the unchangeable and eternal. The Bridegroom, the Father's Only-Begotten, is indeed loved by his Father as an only Son, is loved as co-equal, is loved as consubstantial. These ways of loving are, I think, what the Evangelist was talking about when he said, "In the beginning was the Word, and the Word was with God, and the Word was God" (John 1:1).

When he says, "In the beginning was the Word," focus your attention on the unsearchable secret and the incomprehensible sweetness of a love interior to God — a sweetness that none save the Father knows or can know, as the Only-Begotten himself says, "No one knows the Son save the Father" (Matt. 11:27).

When he says, "The Word was with God," understand the equality in every respect of the Son with the Father. Moreover, it is a crime of utter blasphemy to think or to say that the Son is inferior to the Father; and in the eyes of the Father, anyone that sets him above his Son in any way whatever will be accounted guilty of an offense against the majesty of God. It follows that the Father will rise up to take vengeance by his own hand for every honor that is ascribed to the Father but not to the Son, as if it were an injury to Father and Only-Begotten alike.

Further, when "the Word was God" is added, focus your attention on the idea that the Son is consubstantial with the Father. To be sure, there is but one God, since Moses says to Israel, "The Lord your God is one" (cf. Deut. 6:4); but since the Word is God, he is bound to be God truly, the same God as the Father; and he who receives the essence of divinity from the Father undoubtedly receives the same substance as the Father. So it is apparent how great, and how incalculable, is the overflowing love of the Father for the Son, and how sweet and strong is the attraction of the fount of sweetness for the fountain. The Father's gift to the Son is that he may dwell within him as his closest intimate, as the one most dear to him, as the one most like him. His gift is that he may be with the Father as his co-equal in majesty, in power, and in eternity — and also that he may be altogether of the same nature and substance.

Furthermore, just as the Father stands to the Son as the latter's source, so too the Son stands to the Holy Spirit as his source. Just as the Spirit proceeds from the Father, so also he proceeds from the Son. For the Spirit is love in and of himself and the fountain of love that springs from both; and he is called the love of the Father and of the Son on the ground that by the single will and the equal love of both he who is love proceeds from both.

So you see how wonderful and abundant is the fullness of love in that blessed

Threefoldness, and how great is the flood of delight out of whose fullness the Father utters his entire self for the Son (cf. Ps. 44:2 Vg = 45:2), and the Son together with the Father utters the whole of himself for the Spirit. The consequence is that these three are one fount of love, and the love of unity never falters because there the unity of love is regnant.

Further still, even though in the undivided unity of the most holy Trinity there is nothing that is not superlatively wonderful and worshipful, it is not a thing to be marveled at if, in this its noblest fount, love should have a place of priority and privilege. Surely [since there is] One who is able to bring it about that "he who is united to the Lord is one spirit with him" (1 Cor. 6:17), it is nothing strange if, in the power and truth of this same "spirit," Father and Son and Holy Spirit, each of whom taken individually is love, should also be one love, love of a single essence and essence of a single love.

As it is, we see, in the confines of our present life, far removed as that is from this fount, how love is busily at work everywhere in proportion to the degree of its sovereignty, and strives to be sovereign in accordance with its kinds and species, whether good among the good or evil among the evil. It has the capacity, naturally implanted in itself, to compel those whom it gets in its grasp to seek after unity — the more strongly the sweeter it is, and the more sweetly the closer it is to unity. Thus all the bonds created by human relationships are in the service of love — whether that of parents to children or of children to parents; or, what is stronger and closer, that of bridegroom to bride and of bride to bridegroom; or whatever other partnerships there are that occur in the many types of human association. At love's behest, these all move toward the simple principle of unity, or strive to reach it. Further, they follow the guidance of love, to good effect if that guidance is good, and evil if it is evil. Nonetheless, every love of any sort exhibits a significant likeness to that true and eternal love, if there is anyone who bothers to notice it.

Nor is this the case merely in the rational creation, but also among those creatures who are driven by appetite alone, as we are unceasingly taught by familiar examples, even though their very frequency diminishes their effect. Yet here, there, and everywhere on the earth the Wisdom of God plays in the presence of her Father (cf. Prov. 8:30-31), and also in that of people who have learned to join in Wisdom's play through their joy and admiration; and to our eyes she affords evident signs and likenesses of this sublime love.

In order that we may use the example to which God's Wisdom likens herself (cf. Matt. 23:37), we consider the way in which the hen is attached to her chicks, how tenderly and frequently she draws them close while giving birth over and over. The sweeter she becomes in her affection for them, the hoarser her cry becomes; and — wonder of wonders — the more hoarsely she cries, the sweeter her attachment to them becomes. What sense does it make that as she passes into a state that looks like one of love, she shows herself not only hoarse of voice, but with her feathers all ruffled up, her body wilting, her motions restless and disturbed — dedicated in her service, sleepless in her watchfulness, extravagant in her devotion? . . .

Now maybe you will call things of this sort forms of play — and you will be right. But since it is the Wisdom of God that does the playing, the spectator at these games will be seeing serious play. Otherwise he may make mockery of the one who is playing and hear the words: "We piped to you, and you did not dance" (Matt. 11:17). Let this spectator rather join the game and dance and caper before the ark of the Lord in the company of God the Father's Wisdom, who from the highest summit of love, by way of the mirror of the visible creation, sends forth gleaming rays of light into this darkness of ours. For truly there is, in the whole creation, rational and nonrational, nothing that does not speak, nothing that does not have a tongue; and all that exists interprets for us the ineffable mystery of eternal love by way of the instinctive motions of natural desire — if there is anyone who is concerned to take notice. Otherwise, all these creatures are dumb for us, and we are deaf to them.

(5) The *Glossa Ordinaria*

His locks are like shoots *(elatae)* of palm trees. . . .

Another translation says, "His locks are fir trees." In Greek the fir tree is called *elatēs,* so that in this line *elatae* seems not to be a Latin word but a Greek word.

(6) Apponius

His locks are like the lofty <parts> of palm trees,
    black like a raven.

By the word **locks** are indicated the heavenly Powers, Thrones, and Dominations, since, as was said above, just as **locks** beautify the head, so the aforesaid powers are the ornament, the terror and power, of Majesty. But when he said **lofty** like **the locks . . . of palm trees**, he taught that the aforesaid ministers are never brought down from their power and their office, but remain on high **like the locks . . . of palm trees**. The latter always maintain the strength of their green color and are exalted on high, and they are never altered by any sickness stemming from decay. And just as **the head** is known to hold and to bear its **locks**, so too it is taught that God, who, according to the apostle, is the Head of all things, "upholds the universe by his word of power" (Heb. 1:3).

    By saying **black like a raven**, she points to the hiding place of veiled mysteries and to the ministries of the angels, concealed by great darkness, through whom just judgments are carried out — as the prophet David said, "Clouds and thick darkness are round about him" (Ps. 96:2 LXX = 97:2); and then, "He made darkness his hiding place" (Ps. 17:12 LXX = 18:11); and also, "Thy judgments are like the great deep" (Ps. 35:7 LXX = 36:6). Since, then, the mystery of the divine law is darkened, **his tresses** [are] **black like a raven** for those who have the eyes of their hearts blinded and do not see that the friends of God are honored by the ministries of the angels, and his enemies tormented. Even so does the Scripture bear witness in the case of the Egyptians: "He let loose on them his fierce wrath . . . , a company of evil angels" (Ps. 77:49 LXX = 78:49). It is not that those who fulfill the will of God are evil by nature, but that to those who are worthy of punishment they appear evil and full of gloom.

For it is the same ministry of angels that is carried out for those who are avenged and for those who undergo retribution: for those who obtain retribution, the angels are the **locks of palm trees**; but for those that suffer retribution, they are **black like** ravens. The text of Exodus relates that this occurred in Egypt. When the firstborn of the Egyptians were smitten or the individual plagues occurred, the day is said to grow dark amid lamentation; but for the children of Israel, a radiant joy in the retribution wrought by **the lofty <parts> of palm trees** resounded. This accords, moreover, with the words of the prophet Zephaniah to the effect that the day of judgment glows with the greatest splendor for the righteous, but for the impious it turns gloomy with a massive darkness; for he says, "To what end do the impious await the day of the Lord? It is a day of weeping and war, a day of tribulation and misery, a day of cloud and deep darkness, a day of whirlwind and darkness is that day" (Zeph. 1:14-15)!

(7) Gregory of Nyssa

His eyes are like doves
   by full pools of waters,
washed in milk,
   seated by full pools of waters.

But let us move on in order and consider what is said about the Bridegroom's eyes. Here is the text: **His eyes are like doves by full pools of waters, washed in milk, sitting by full pools of waters.** The meaning of these statements is loftier than our understanding can reach (for we realize that what we understand of them will fall short of the truth), but to us as we examined the text the sense seemed to be something like the following.

The divine apostle observes somewhere in his letters that "the eye cannot say to the hand, 'I have no need of you'" (1 Cor. 12:21). In these words he formulates a basic teaching, that it is the business of the body that is the Church to do well at two sorts of activity — to combine discernment of the truth with action. For contemplation does not of itself bring the soul to perfection unless it makes room for works that further the practice of the moral life — any more than practical wisdom is profitable in its own right unless true and reverent belief guide what comes to pass.

If, then, this cooperation of eyes and hand is necessary, it may be that this text is leading us, first of all, to a grasp of what **eyes** refers to, and then to a discerning comprehension of the praise that is accorded them. As to what is said about **hands**, we postpone that to its proper occasion.

Now the distinctive natural function of eyes is seeing. Hence they are located above all the other organs of perception, positioned by nature to provide guidance for the whole body. Therefore, when we hear the teachers of truth named in this way by the divine Scriptures — one of whom is called "the looker" (1 Sam. 9:9), another, "the seer" (Amos 7:12), and yet another, "watchman" (Ezek. 3:17; 33:7) because God called him this in the prophetic corpus — we are led to think that in the text before us it is those who are ordained to oversee, to inspect, and to supervise who are called **eyes**.

We are taught, however, that amazement at the eyes arises out of a similarity and the comparison it suggests. Their beauty is portrayed by comparison with something nobler; for it says, **His eyes are like doves**. Truly the fairest commendation of such eyes as these is innocence, which those persons attain who are no longer polluted by the life of the flesh but live by, and walk in, the Spirit. What sets the spiritual and nonmaterial life apart, after all, is the form of the dove, since the Holy Spirit itself was seen by John in this form, flying down from heaven upon the water.

Hence the person to whom God assigns the place of an eye in the body that is the Church must wash away all the teary haze of vice with water if he is to supervise, oversee, and inspect in purity. There is not, however, one water that flushes the eyes clean. No, our text says that there are many **pools of** such **waters**; for we are bound to think that there are as many wellsprings of purifying waters — by whose means the eyes are becoming ever clearer — as there are virtues. Thus one might say that temperance is one wellspring of purifying waters; others are humility, truth and justice, and courage, and desire for the good, and alienation from evil. These and similar waters derive from a single wellspring, and they are gathered together into a single pool in different streams, and through them the eyes are cleansed of every haze of passion.

Well, then, the eyes — likened as they are to doves by reason of their integrity and innocence — are located **by full pools of waters**, but it says that what washes them is milk, for so the text states: **washed in milk**. Fitting is the praise accorded such eyes as these — praise proclaiming that such a dove is made beautiful by being washed in milk. For it is truly observed of milk that of all fluids it alone has the peculiarity that in it no image or likeness appears. Things that are naturally liquid, as we know, behave like mirrors in that, because of their smooth surfaces, they cause the likenesses of those who look into them to be reflected back; only milk has no such capacity for imaging. Hence the highest praise of the Church's eyes is this — that they do not mistakenly image anything unreal and counterfeit and empty that is contrary to what truly is, but look upon what "is" in the full and proper sense of that word. They do not take in the deceitful sights and fantasies of the present life. For this reason, the perfect soul judges that it is the bath in milk that most surely purifies the eyes.

The next phrase, however, is, for those who read and understand, a law that dictates what it is that the eyes must make it their business to attend to; for it says, **seated by pools of waters**. This expression, as it praises the pure eyes, enjoins unremitting assiduity in attending to the divine teachings. It teaches how, in sitting right up by pools of waters, we can restore the eyes' beauty — seeing that the majority of those who are assigned the place of eyes have given up watching by such waters as these and have seated themselves by the rivers of Babylon, justifying the indictment God has brought against such persons: "They have deserted me, the wellspring of living waters, and they have dug themselves broken cisterns that cannot hold water" (Jer. 2:13).

We are taught, then, how the eye may become beautiful when suited and adapted to the golden Head: it will, on the one hand, be pure after the manner of the dove, inerrant and undeceived like milk, not confusedly forming images of the unreal for itself; and, on the other, it will, by persistence and assiduity, take its seat by the pools of divine waters — just like the tree that has been planted by the streams of waters and has not been moved (cf. Ps. 1:3). For in this way it will bring forth its fruit in due season, and its shoot, decked out in the fine color of its leaves, will be kept ever blooming.

(8) Theodoret of Cyrus

His cheeks are like bowls of spice
   producing perfumes.
His lips are lilies,
   dripping abundant myrrh.

She . . . uses the names **cheeks** and **lips** for doctrine; for both **lips** and **cheeks** are instruments of rational speech, in that by their motions articulate utterance is shaped. The cheeks she calls **bowls of spice** because the teaching is fragrant; but she also adds that they produce **perfumes**; for from them the teachers of the Church take the elements of the teaching and become, so to speak, perfume blenders of the scents of the gospel message, and create the fragrance of edification. On the other hand, **his lips**, she says, are similar to lilies; for the divine words shine, having nothing about them of the merely human; for the Lord teaches that lilies neither spin nor weave, but the heavenly Father clothes them. Since, then, the divine words have been stripped of all human wisdom, and possess only a divine beauty, it is right for her to say, **His lips are lilies, dripping abundant myrrh** — which is to say, enjoining mortification in the present life. For such are the Lord's teachings: "He who does not leave father and mother and wife and fields and vineyards for my sake is not worthy of me" (Matt. 6:28-29); and then, "Whoever does not take up his cross and follow me is not worthy of me" (Matt. 10:37-38 par. Luke 14:26-27); and also, "If you want to be perfect, sell your possessions and give to the poor and take up your cross and follow me" (Matt. 19:21): all this explains why **his lips** drip **abundant myrrh**.

(9) Ambrose of Milan

His hands are beautifully wrought, golden,
   full of hyacinth.

See what hands they are that fashioned humanity — and see what a humanity they fashioned! Without doubt it is the humanity that we have put on in accord with Christ, "putting off the old humanity with its practices, and putting on the new, which is being renewed in knowledge after the image of its creator" (Col. 3:9-10), in which there is "neither slave nor free" (Gal. 3:28), but Christ is all in all. We put on Christ, then, even as it is said elsewhere, "You have put on Christ" (Gal. 3:27). We have received the Holy Spirit, who not only puts our sins away but also makes us his priests to put away the sins of others. Thus the prophet says, "You have shaped me and have laid your hand upon me" (Ps. 138:5 LXX = 139:5): "shaped" by the use of clay, "laid" his "hand" by conferring spiritual grace — even though many take this psalm to have been spoken as by Christ. Hear how the Lord's hand is also called "spirit." Job exclaims, "The divine Spirit who made me" (Job 33:4). These, then, are the hands that fashioned humanity — Christ and the Spirit.

The Lord Jesus, then, is also the maker of our body. He it was who first made the human being after the image and later fashioned it of clay, and willed to rescue what he had made, to save what he had shaped. . . . This the Church specifically teaches, that not only the soul but also the flesh is saved — the soul by knowing God, the flesh by resurrection.

(10) Honorius of Autun

His cheeks are like beds of spices
    planted by makers of perfumes,
His lips are lilies,
    dripping the choicest myrrh.
His hands are golden,
    turned on a lathe, full of hyacinth.
His belly is ivory
    adorned with sapphires.
His legs are marble columns
    that have been set on golden pedestals.
His form is like Lebanon's,
    chosen like cedars.
His throat is perfectly sweet,
    and he is wholly desirable.
Such is my Beloved, and this is my friend,
    O daughters of Jerusalem.

His cheeks are like beds of spices: that is, modesty and love toward God, which shone in Christ with a special brightness, delighted those who were present with the sweetness of the teachings, and attracted those who were absent. Like **beds of spices** they delight those who see them by their appearance and by the beauty of their fragrance. These **beds** are **planted by makers of perfumes**, that is, by physicians, and in particular the apostles and prophets, physicians of souls, who not only gave an account of the sayings of Christ with harmonious voice but also, according to custom, wrote them down on the sacred pages.

His lips drip **the choicest myrrh**, that is to say, the words of his teaching — which to those who bear heavy burdens promise the glory of a heavenly kingdom — proclaim **the choicest myrrh**, that is, contempt of the world and of pleasures. **His hands are . . . turned on a lathe**, which means that his doings are polished and finished like the work of a turner. For what he taught by word he fulfilled by deed, so that by his works he might encourage those who marveled at his teaching. And these hands are **golden** because the glory of his divinity brought to perfection the virtues he cultivated in his humanity, and they incite us to hope for, and to love of, things heavenly. **Full of hyacinth**: hyacinth is a plant with a purple flower that expels fevers by the sweetness of its fragrance, and it stands for the passion of Christ, which expels the disease of faithlessness. His hands were full of hyacinth because on the cross they were pierced by nails and were besprinkled with a color like purple thanks to the crimson of his blood.

His belly is ivory, which is to say that the frailty of his humanity is bright with the gleam of chastity, and exempt from all sin. Moreover, this belly is **adorned with sapphires,** which is a stone that looks like a serene sky, signifying the sublimity of things celestial; for here is understood in part human frailty, known in hunger, temptation, weariness, and death; and in part divine majesty, known in miracles, resurrection, and ascension.

His legs are pillars of marble, that is, the ways followed by his incarnation are straight and enduring, because whatever he has done has been determined by God before all time. These **pillars . . . are set on golden pedestals,** which means the prophets (cf. Eph. 2:20), shining with wisdom, because he has been manifest in the flesh even as foretold by them under the divine dispensation. **His form is like Lebanon's,** which means: his beauty is the splendor of all the saints, even as Lebanon is the splendor of all mountains. He is **chosen like cedars,** which means that just as cedars stand higher than all trees, so Christ surpasses all the saints. For Lebanon stands out by reason of its height and its bulk, and in the very same way Christ shines out among all who have been born of the earth. And just as that mountain is rich in noble trees, so too he raises up and preserves all the saints that are rooted in him. Moreover, just as the cedar surpasses all the splendor of forests in beauty, strength, height, and fragrance, so the Beloved is exceptional in form as compared with the children of men; for he did not receive the Godhead by measure, but in its totality, and "of his fullness we have all received" (John 1:16).

His throat is perfectly sweet: that is, the savor and delight of his words when relished internally — of which few enjoy a taste — are most sweet; and those who do taste of them become yet more hungry. Again the **throat** is the hidden disposition of his goodness, by which it comes about that he speaks to us outwardly. **And wholly desirable,** that is, as God and as a human being; for not only in his divinity but also in his humanity — from the very beginning of his conception until the triumph of his passion, resurrection, and ascension — he is in all respects **desirable.**

Such is my Beloved, and he himself is my friend, O daughters of Jerusalem. It is as if she were saying, "You Churches, or faithful souls, daughters of Jerusalem, if you want to love Christ and be loved by him, it is necessary that you understand him to be such as I have said."

This allegorical interpretation is particularly suited to Christ. The tropological interpretation that follows is more nearly suited to his members.

Christ is the Head of the Church because just as all the members are ruled by the head, so all the elect are ruled by Christ. **His head is the finest gold,** that is, pure gold; for just as, in virtue of that gold, other metals, when gilded, take on the gleam of gold, so all who after Christ are called Christians will "shine as the sun" in his kingdom (Matt. 13:43). **His locks are the lofty <parts> of palm trees.** The palm is called "victory," and the palm is a tree that is narrow toward its bottom and broad at the top; it signifies the life of the righteous, who by taking the hard and narrow way (Matt. 7:14), that is, by fasting and vigils and other bodily adversities, make their way to the wideness of love, so as to attain victory in the battle. **The lofty ‹parts› of palm trees** are the same as the leaves, that is, the longer branches, which always make their way upward, which never lose their greenness as long as they are in the palm, but quickly dry up when cut off. His **tresses**, therefore, are the faithful who make their way toward things heavenly by the triumph of the virtues, who never lose the greenness of their faith, as long as they proceed by the narrow road. Once they depart from this, they soon lose life and wither. (There are some who say that **the lofty ‹parts› of palm trees** are a species of aromatic tree that Latin speakers call "silver fir" or "spathe." For in Greek "silver fir" is called *elatē*, and it signifies saints bending their course toward exalted things.)

And these **tresses** are **black** like a raven, which means that the righteous are despised in this world just as Christ was. **Raven** refers to sinners. The reason why Christ is called "raven" is that he was reckoned among sinners by those who said, "We know that this man is a sinner" (John 9:24); and then again, "If this man were not an evildoer, we would not have handed him over" (John 18:30). **Tresses** are **black**, as in the case of this raven, because the faithful are despised by the wicked in the same way as Christ was by the Jews, by whom it was said, "These are evildoers and seducers." Further, the raven does not feed chicks that are not like him, and Christ rejects Christians who are not like him.

His eyes are like doves over streams of waters. This refers to the wise, who contemplate him with their heart, and through whom others contemplate him. These people are, like doves, plain and modest, dependent upon the Scriptures, and flowing with the divine Spirit. These **doves . . . have been washed in milk**, which is to say that by sweet teaching they are cleansed of things earthly, and they live close to **overflowing streams**, that is, they abide close to the ever-abounding gifts of the Holy Spirit. The rivers are the Scriptures of the Old Testament, **overflowing streams**, copious and abounding with the teaching of the gospel. Doves have the habit of living close to **streams**, so that they may observe the flight of birds by watching their shadows on the water and thus avoid their talons; in the same way the saints perceive in the Scriptures the deceits of the demons, and the deceit they notice, like a shadow on water, enables them to recognize their enemy. These **streams** are called **overflowing** because no matter from which stream scriptural counsel is sought, it is found there to the fullest degree.

His cheeks are like beds of spices. By this is meant prelates of real modesty, who are ashamed to hear anything unseemly, much less to do it: these have within themselves the seeds of many virtues. And these **beds** are **planted by makers of perfumes**; that is to say, the writings that tell of the virtues have been written by the apostles or by one or another of the fathers of earlier times.

His lips are lilies, dripping the choicest myrrh. Choicest myrrh means the best myrrh, and it is understood to refer to the death of Christ, which is "best" because it is the redemption of the entire world. The **lips** of Christ are those who publish his will, and like **lilies** they gleam with the virtues; and these **lilies** drip with **the choicest myrrh**, that is, they are people who by word and example convey the bitter hardness of Christ's death.

His hands are golden, turned on a lathe, which means that they perform good deeds and are blameless in other people's eyes, like shining gold; and these hands are **full of hyacinth** because they do their work solely out of hope and desire for things heavenly. Hyacinth is in fact a stone of the color of the heavens, or green, and is alternated with gold; and the saints are green with the virtues, they seek things heavenly, and they change their manner of life to suit times and occasions.

His belly is ivory, adorned with sapphires. The **belly** of Christ is those who have wives as though they did not have them, maintaining for their spouses the truth of chastity. For the elephant, whose bone is ivory, is a chaste animal, and of so frigid a nature that if a garment of thin linen is placed on top of his bone, that is, his ivory, and then a coal is placed on top of the linen, the coal is extinguished and the linen is unhurt. Moreover, a continuous bone encloses his body, which is why he is called invulnerable. He symbolizes those saintly and chaste folk who are invulnerable to the Devil's weapons. As to the **sapphire**, it is a stone that has the appearance of a serene heaven. Thus the **belly** of Christ is **adorned with sapphires** when those joined in marriage satisfy themselves with heavenly exercises.

His legs are pillars of marble. This refers to those who support the religious[2] with their possessions. Like **pillars of marble** they are upright in knowledge and unshakable by vices. They are **set**, moreover, **on golden pedestals**, that is, upon the faith of the Apostles and Prophets, a faith that shines with the works of chastity.

His form is like Lebanon's. Here we have the virgins, white with purity of life, gleaming with chastity, fragrant like the cedar with good works. **His throat is most sweet**: which is to say that those who are sweetest of all to the taste are the people who convey words of teaching. Further, he is **wholly desirable**, that is, lovable in himself and in all his members. **Such**, as I have said, **is my Beloved**, in himself and in his members; and **this is my friend**, for I love him alone, and love comes from him; and do you also love him, **O daughters of Jerusalem**, that is to say, the peace of the Church as it shall be seen in the heavens.

(11) Richard of St.-Victor

His throat is most sweet,
    and wholly desirable.

The Bridegroom's **throat** is the inward savoring of him and the spiritual consolation that sweetly touch those who have tasted and experienced them. For if by taking thought you comprehend the goodness of God, and reach out for his savor, you will join with the Bride to proclaim the sweetness of this throat. The taste of his love, moreover, is so sweet that it not only restores the mind but also occasions forgetfulness of bodily food. Further, should you focus your attention on things spiritual and mystical, you will acknowledge that whatever you are able to grasp regarding him is sweet and full of delight — to the point where you will count everything beside him as hardly sweet at all, indeed as nothing beside him, but will conclude that he himself is the sole good, the one thing to be embraced and loved. But then, should you make a mental transition to dwelling on heavenly matters, it will be sweet to reflect what it is like to see God and to be filled to the brim with the vision of him, for him to be within us and us to be within him and at one with

---

2. Members of religious orders.

him, to be free of all distress, and to rejoice with him without end. The inward savoring of these things is the throat of the Bridegroom.

It is necessary, however, for the heart that would experience this sweetness to be cleansed of vicious passions; for if the vessel of the heart be not pure, it experiences less, or else obstructs this spiritual sweetness because until now it has drawn near from out of the foul depths of carnality. That is why it refuses to find consolation anywhere but in God: let it be mindful of God, let it delight in him, and let it be preoccupied with this delight, so that the spirit, that is to say, its own will, may be freed and despise whatever delight there may be apart from God. It will be able to delight in God to the extent that it despises outward pleasures. Let it put away delight in worldly things, let it leave the world (i.e., worldly things), let it approach the lonely desert place of the mind, let it sit alone and raise itself above itself, raise the body above the body, so as to transcend bodily affairs, and grasp heavenly and spiritual things.

Everything that is in the world is false desire of the flesh, or false desire of the eyes, or pride of life. He who shall despise these things by overcoming carnal desire, by turning back from outward things to things inward and invisible, by treading down pride and practicing humility, quickly departs this world and comes to the lonely place of the desert, and so is able to take in the knowledge and savor of spiritual things.

This is the Egypt from which the people of God depart, and this is the desert place toward which it must proceed. From this empty wilderness messengers are sent out and bring back word of the fruits of the land of promise. These messengers are spiritual meditations and holy desires. They are sent out by the dedicated soul with a view to inspecting this land. They enter this land by searching into it, they bring news of its abundance and its delights, and they carry back with them a sample of its fruit. This fruit is a taste of that sweetness, a foretaste of that delight, a fruit that is sweet to the throat of the dedicated soul that tastes it and experiences its sweetness. The one who tastes sees him, that is, he knows how sweet is the most sweet throat of the Bridegroom, which not only excels all other sweetness, but even drives it away. The more one experiences its sweetness, the more one desires it. In this life he has hunger, not satisfaction, refreshment, not fullness. For it is so pleasing that it is always desired, so boundless that it is never fully grasped; and if anyone is moved to say that he is satisfied and entirely full, I do not know whether he has drawn refreshment from the Bridegroom's throat or from a counterfeit and lying messenger: "Those who eat me will hunger for more," says the Wisdom of God, "and those who drink me will thirst for more" (Ecclus. 24:21). Here God's goodness is a slight taste; fullness lies in the future, for we shall be filled to the brim when his glory is revealed and we shall be full of the good things of the Lord's house.

One can tell the true savor from the false in this way: the true is not agitated or violent, it does not titillate the flesh but curbs the motions of the flesh and calms them. It is modest, tranquil, easy, sweet, and peaceful. It strengthens the spirit and weakens the flesh; it rouses up the mind and illumines it; it does not exalt but humbles. For its sweetness awakens desire, and in fueling grander hopes it renders one humble with regard to one's progress. For since what a soul possesses is but little, she always thinks humbly of herself just as she always reckons herself needy. An imperfect or fraudulent savor shows us to ourselves as rich, because it does not reach as far as knowledge of the riches of the divine goodness.

Song 6:1-3

SEPTUAGINT	VULGATE
6:1 Where has your Kinsman gone,	5:17 Where has your Beloved gone,
O beautiful among women?	O fairest of women?
Where has your Kinsman turned his regard,	Where has your Beloved turned away,
and we shall seek him with you?	and we shall seek him with you?
2 My Kinsman has descended into his garden,	6:1 My Kinsman has descended into his garden,
into bowls of spice,	to a bed of spices,
to graze his flock among gardens	so as to graze his flock among the gardens
and to gather lilies.	and gather lilies.
3 I am for my Kinsman, and my Kinsman is for me;	2 I am for my Beloved, and my Beloved for me,
he grazes his flock among the lilies.	who grazes his flock among the lilies.

In this brief passage the Bride answers a second question, as Gregory of Nyssa points out. The previous question (5:9) had asked in effect what her Lover was like. This one inquires where he is and in what direction he fixes his gaze. Gregory takes it that both questions come from the same source, that is, from the Bride's companions, the "young maidens" or "young girls" that constitute her chorus and her disciples, who are to be distinguished from the "daughters of Jerusalem." Gregory offers a self-consistent interpretation of the whole passage; Honorius, in the excerpt printed here, concerns himself with the single question what it can mean to ask of God, the Second Person of the Trinity, "where" he is.

(1) Gregory of Nyssa

Where has your Kinsman gone,
  O beautiful among women?
Where has your Kinsman turned his regard,
  and we shall seek him with you?
My Kinsman has descended into his garden,
  into bowls of spice. . . .
  He grazes his flock among the lilies.

Just as Andrew was led to the Lamb by the voice of John, and just as Nathanael came within the true light when he had been introduced into the light by Philip and freed from the shadow of the law that enveloped him, so too the young maidens make use of their guide, the soul who has been brought to perfection by her comeliness, to help them find the Good that had been announced to them. So they say to her, **Where has your Kinsman gone, O beautiful among women? Where has your Kinsman turned his regard, and we shall seek him with you?**

In bringing this question before their teacher, the virgin souls are following a logical order. In the first instance, in the question they posed before this one, they took up the matter of his "what" and asked, **What is your Kinsman, O beautiful among women?** Taught their answer by the clues stated above — that he is white and red, and so on — in which the appearance of the One they sought was described, they now ask about his "where." The reason why they ask, **Where has your Kinsman gone?** or **Where has your Kinsman turned his regard?** is so that they may, once they have learned where he is, make obeisance toward the place where his feet have stood (cf. Ps. 131:7 LXX = 132:7) and, once they have been taught where he turns his regard, may so station themselves that his glory may be revealed to them as well — that glory whose epiphany is the salvation of those who behold it, even as the prophet says, "Show us your face, and we shall be saved" (Ps. 79:4 LXX = 80:3).

Then, like Philip, who said, "Come and see" (John 1:46), the teacher leads the virgins toward a comprehension of the One they seek. She does not say, "See," but she points out the place where the One sought for is, and what he is looking at; for she says, **My Kinsman has descended into his garden, into bowls of spice.** Up to this point the text is indicating where he is located; but from this point on the teacher's language shows what he sees and where he is looking, since she says, "He pastures his flock **among gardens and gathers lilies.**" This, then, is the outward and literal guidance with which the text provides the maidens; from it they learn both where he is and where he is looking.

It is also strictly necessary, however, to descry, by spiritual inquiry and discernment, what is profitable for us in this inspired Scripture-passage. Hence when we hear, **My Kinsman has descended into his garden,** the words are teaching us the mystery of the gospel, since each of these terms illuminates the mystical meaning of the passage.

Because he rose up out of Judah, and brought light to nations that dwelt in darkness and the shadow of death, it is right and appropriate that God-manifest-in-flesh be assigned the title **Kinsman** by the one who has been betrothed to him for the sake of an everlasting union, since she is herself a "kinswoman" who stems from Judah. As to the expression **has descended**, it reveals that he himself, for the sake of the man who "descended from Jerusalem to Jericho" (Luke 10:30) and found himself among thieves, did indeed accompany the descent of the man who fell among foes; and these things signify his coming down from unutterable majesty to the lowliness of our nature.

From the enigma of the garden, on the other hand, we learn that the field that the true Husbandman plants is we human beings (for, according to Paul's statement, we are his field [1 Cor. 3:9]). Now he is the one who in Paradise at the beginning tended the human garden that the heavenly Father had planted. That is why, once the wild boar had ravaged the garden — which is to say, us — and ruined the divine field, he **descended** in order once again to make the desert, which is being beautified by the implanting of the virtues, a garden; and by the Word he channeled the pure and divine spring-waters of the teaching in order to foster such plants.

As to the **bowls of spice**, they were used in the description of the Bridegroom's beauty (5:13) to praise his jaws, by which spiritual foodstuffs are ground fine for those who are fed on them. In the present passage, however, our text declares that they represent the place, the dwelling place, of the Bridegroom; and what we learn is this — that the Bridegroom does not lodge in a soul that lacks the virtues; and further still, that if someone should become, in the sense required by the earlier text, a bowl of spice that produces fragrant ointments, such a person has become a mixing bowl of Wisdom (cf. Prov. 9:2) and receives within himself the divine and unadulterated wine that brings gladness to its recipient.

The text that follows this, however, teaches us on what pasturage the Good Shepherd's flocks are fattened. For he does not drive his sheep into desert places to feed on grass where the thornbushes grow. Rather are spices from the gardens set before them to feed on, and in place of grass comes the lily, which, it says, is gathered by the shepherd as sustenance for his sheep.

In these words, the text philosophizes for us to the effect that the Nature that contains whatever exists and the Power that encompasses all things takes as its place and its proper lodging the purity of those who receive it — those in whom the garden that is richly and variously cultivated by the virtues undulates with the blossoms of lilies and burgeons with the fruitfulness of spices. For the lilies represent, in the manner of an enigma, the mind's radiance and purity, and the sweet scent of the spices stands for estrangement from all the rank stench of sin. It is in such souls, then, that the Overseer of the flocks is said to dwell, grazing in the gardens while cutting and gathering lilies for the sustenance of the sheep — lilies that he puts before the sheep by the hand of the great Paul, who sets out for us the sustenance of lilies taken from the storehouse of God. These are "whatever is true, whatever is honorable, whatever is just, whatever is pure, whatever is lovely, whatever is gracious, if there is any virtue, if there is any praise" (Phil. 4:8). According to my reckoning, these are the lilies with which the Good Shepherd and teacher feeds his flocks.

The next line, though, which the pure and spotless Bride speaks when she says, **I am for my Kinsman, and my Kinsman is for me**, is the norm and definition of perfection in virtue. For through these words we learn that the purified soul is to have nothing within her save God and is to look upon nothing else. Rather must she so cleanse herself of every material concern and thought that she is entirely, in her whole being, transposed into the intelligible and immaterial realm and makes of herself a supremely vivid image of the prototypical Beauty.

Thus the person who sees on the flat surface of a board a sketch that closely approximates the form of a particular prototype declares that the form of the two is the same: he will say both that the beauty of the image is that of the prototype and that the original is palpably discerned in its copy. In the same way, she who says, **I am for my Kinsman, and my Kinsman is for me**, asserts that she is conformed to Christ — that she has recovered her very own beauty, the primordial blessedness of the human race, that is, to be arrayed in a beauty that conforms to the image and likeness of the first, the sole, and the true Beauty.

The same thing comes about with a mirror when — granted that it is put together with skill and in conformity with its function — it displays in itself on its clear surface the exact imprint of the face it reflects. In just this way, the soul, when she has put herself together in a way suited to her business and cast off every material defilement, has graven into herself the pure look of the inviolate Beauty. Hence the life-endued and choice-endowed mirror has this word to say: "Since I focus upon the face of my Kinsman with my entire being, the entire beauty of his form is seen in me." Paul openly echoes these words when he says that he, who has died to the world, lives to God, and that Christ alone lives in him. For one who says, "To me, to live is Christ" (Phil. 1:21), by this statement affirms for all the world to hear that in him none of the human and material passions is alive — not pleasure or grief, not anger or fear or cowardice or agitation or vanity or rashness; not vengefulness or envy, nor yet a vindictive disposition or love of money, of glory, or of honors, or anything else that stains the soul by means of some attachment. "But he alone is mine who is none of these things. I have scraped off everything that is discerned as alien to that nature of his, and I have in me nothing such as is not found in him. For that reason, 'To me, to live is Christ'" — or, in the words of the Bride, **I am for my Kinsman, and my Kinsman is for me**: he who is sanctification, and purity, and incorruptibility, and light, and truth, and all the like.

(2) Honorius of Autun

Where has your Beloved gone,
  O most beautiful of women?

The comparison here is with close companions, who eagerly seek the Beloved together with their friend. "Daughters of Jerusalem" refers to the Churches or souls of the imperfect, while "Jerusalem" means the Church of those who have been perfected. Churches are said to be mothers because they bear spiritual children. The beautiful one is she who is unstained by heresy, the more beautiful is she who blooms with zeal for good deeds, and the most beautiful is she who shines with urgency in proclamation.

Thus the imperfect say to the perfected, the carnal to the spiritual, the active to the contemplative, the lower to the higher, the uninstructed to the instructed, **Where has your Beloved gone, O most beautiful of women?** "O Church of the spiritual in faith and in deed, you that produce spiritual offspring, teach us how it is that you are looking for someone as if he were absent, when you proclaim him to be everywhere present. Teach us also how, if he be present, he is to be seen; and how, if he be absent, he is to be found, **and we shall seek him with you**, faithfully and devotedly."

It is one thing to go away, and another thing to turn away. A person goes away who proceeds to a distant place; a person turns away who avoids the sun's heat and retires into a nearby place, into the shade. Christ went away, corporeally speaking, when in the sight of his disciples he ascended into heaven; but he turned away, spiritually speaking, when from the synagogue he came into the Church by grace. He is to be seen by faith, sought by prayer, and found by righteous living, for it is written: "I fill heaven and earth" (Jer. 23:24).

People ask in what way God is said to be absent or present. One must grasp that there are three kinds of motion. One is spatial and temporal and is proper to the body, which is moved from place to place in time. Another is temporal and nonspatial. This is proper to the mind, which moves in time but not in space, by thinking of things past and future. The third is neither spatial nor temporal but eternal, and is proper to God; for it occurs by God's willing to accomplish that which from all eternity he has determined is to come about. Hence God is said to be absent when he takes grace away from those who are not worthy of it. He is said to be present when his grace is lavished upon those whom, by his grace, he has rendered worthy. And in that case there is no alteration of place or time.

Likewise people ask in what way, since God is everywhere in his totality, he is said to be somewhere in particular in his totality; for if something is somewhere as a whole, no part of it is elsewhere. Everything, most certainly, that is contained in a place is extended in three dimensions in space, that is to say, in length, width, and height; and further it is delimited by six factors, which are up and down, left and right, before and behind. But all dimensions and delimitations are foreign to God, who is portrayed as being spirit.

But further it must be understood that "to be" is said in three modes. Everything that is, is either locally in a place, or nonlocally in a place, or nonlocally apart from place. Body is locally in a place because it occupies space by its bulk, and it does not allow something else to be where it is at the same time; for example, wine occupies the entire interior space of a wineskin, and vinegar cannot be poured into it unless the wine is poured out. On the other hand, the soul in its body is nonlocally in a place, and it does not occupy space there; but it vivifies the body and lends it the capacity for sense perception nonlocally, and has no need to retire and provide space for the entrance of food or drink. God, however, is nonlocally apart from place. He contains all places within himself, and embraces all times in the mode of the present. For that reason God is everywhere in his totality. . . .

Song 6:4-9

<table>
<tr><td>

SEPTUAGINT

6:4 You are beautiful, my close one, like
    good favor,
  lovely, like Jerusalem,
  a terrible wonder, like ranks
    drawn up in order.
5 Turn your eyes away from before me,
  for they have given me wings.
Your hair is like flocks of goats
  that have appeared from the
    direction of Gilead.
6 Your teeth are like flocks of shorn
    ewes
  that have come up from the bath,
all of them bearing twins,
  and without a barren one
    among them.
7 Your lips are like a scarlet cord,
  and your speech is seasonable.
Your cheek is like the skin of a
    pomegranate
  outside your veil.

8 There are sixty queens and eighty
    concubines,
  and young maidens without
    number.
9 One is my dove, my perfect one;
  one is she for her mother;
  she is a chosen one for the
    woman who bore her.

</td><td>

VULGATE

6:3 You are fair, my friend,

  and lovely like Jerusalem,
  fearsome, like an ordered
    formation of troops.
4 Turn your eyes away from me,
  for they cause me to fly away.
Your hair is like a flock of goats
  that have appeared from the
    direction of Gilead.
5 Your teeth are like a flock of ewes

  that have come up from the bath,
all of them with twin offspring,
  and not one of them is barren.

6

Like the skin of a pomegranate are
  your cheeks,
  apart from the things that are
    hidden.

7 There are sixty queens and eighty
    concubines,
  and of the young maidens there
    is no number.
8 There is one dove, my perfect one,
  one born of her mother,
  chosen of the woman who bore
    her.

</td></tr>
</table>

The daughters saw her, and they bless her; the queens and concubines praise her.	The daughters saw her, and they pronounce her most blessed. The queens and the concubines praised her.

This passage — which contains, among other things, a word-for-word repetition of 4:1-3 — shows the Bridegroom again praising the good qualities of the Bride; and the exegetical comments on it show at least two points of special interest.

For one thing, the mention of "sixty queens and eighty concubines" inevitably evoked efforts to explain the significance of the numbers "sixty" and "eighty" — inevitably, because ancient and medieval thinkers habitually attached symbolic significance to numbers. They held, for example, that "ten" is the "perfect number" because it is the sum of its first four parts (i.e., 1 + 2 + 3 + 4 = 10); that "leftness" corresponds to odd numbers, and "rightness," to the even; and that even is "better" than odd. These ideas are reflected in Theodoret's exegesis of 6:8 below — which is relatively unelaborated and straightforward when compared to many other such efforts.

Another focus of attention in this passage is the mention of the "one . . . dove, my perfect one"; for it raises the question who this "perfect one" is. Few were content to think that it referred to the Bride of these poems. Bede, to be sure, applies the description to the Church, but to the catholic Church conceived as a universal communion. Apponius, on the other hand, rather startlingly thinks that this phrase designates the soul of Jesus — the soul to which, in becoming incarnate, the eternal Word of God joined himself. Moreover, from this point on in his commentary Apponius understands the Song to be referring to this human soul of Jesus in its references to the Bride.

(1) Theodoret of Cyrus

You are beautiful, my close one, like good favor,
   lovely, like Jerusalem,
a terrible wonder, like ranks drawn up in order.

He gives her, for her name, the name of the response she has evoked. For since "the Lord showed good favor to his land, and turned the captivity of Jacob, and forgave the iniquities of his people, and covered all their sins" (Ps. 84:1-3 LXX = 85:1-2), it is right that he calls the Bride **good favor**; and just as, above, she called him **desire** (assigning the name on the basis of her own feeling for him; for, desiring him continually as she does, she calls him **desire**), so too he himself, favoring her and wishing to betroth her and marry her, styles her **good favor**. "For," says he, "you are beautiful in that you have evoked **favor** and love from me. You are not merely **beautiful**, though, but **lovely**, and not simply **lovely**, but lovely in the way that **Jerusalem** is." This is not the Jerusalem below, but the Jerusalem above, about which the blessed Paul says, "But the Jerusalem above is free, and she is the mother of us all" (Gal. 4:26). "You are like her, O my close one, for you imitate the angelic way of life. Living on earth, you habituate yourself to things heavenly; and walking 'in the flesh,' you do not wage 'war in a fleshly manner' (2 Cor. 10:3), and you 'press on toward the goal of the upward call' (Phil. 3:14), and you seek 'the things that are above, where' I am 'seated at the right hand of God'" (Col. 3:1).

"On this account **you are lovely like Jerusalem**, and not only lovely but one who inspires **terrible wonder** in those who see you; for all who see your **order** are amazed and astounded; for with you there is nothing out of order, nothing unclear or muddled, but everything is set in order and regulated. Moreover, you have an exact knowledge of the order in which things come: you have learned to value the Bridegroom more than anything else, and, after him, to value those who have grown close to him."

To this he adds, **Turn your eyes away from before me, for they have given me wings.** What he means is something of this sort: "The beauty of your eyes, and the contemplation of your keen-sightedness, and the acuteness of your thinking have drawn me to love of you; but do not fix your sight on me beyond measure, lest you take harm from doing so; for I am beyond reach and incomprehensible and transcend all comprehension, not merely human, but angelic as well. Though you may wish to bypass the limits and waste your time on what is beyond your power, not only will you find nothing, but you will also dim your vision and render it faint. For this is the nature of light: just as it illumines the eye, so too, by the damage it does, it punishes the eye's immoderate desire. So **Turn your eyes away from before me**: do not look into matters too difficult for you, or seek out things that are mightier than you. Occupy your mind with the commandments you have been given."

(2) Ambrose of Milan

Turn your eyes away from me,
  for they have lifted me up.

He says to her, as though to one made perfect, **Turn your eyes away from me**, or **do not direct your gaze contrarily to me**. By her inordinate devotion and her faith she has overstepped the bounds of what is possible for her own nature and condition; for to gaze directly upon "light inaccessible" (1 Tim. 6:16) is a serious business. **Turn your eyes away from me**, he says, on the ground that she cannot bear the fullness of his Deity and the brilliance of the true Light.

It is possible, however, to take **Turn your eyes away from me** in the following sense. "Although you have been perfected, there are other souls that I must redeem, other souls that I must strengthen and sustain; for by seeing me, you lift me up, but I have come down in order to exalt all souls. Even though I have risen and have the Father's throne, I shall not for all that desert you as though you were orphans, deprived of paternal care; on the contrary, I shall strengthen you by my presence. In the Gospel it is written: 'Behold, I am with you right up until the consummation of the world' (Matt. 28:20). Therefore, **Turn your eyes away from me, for you are lifting me up**," since the more someone looks intently upon the Lord, the more he lifts the Lord up, and he is himself lifted up." That explains how it is said: "I will exalt you, O Lord, because you have held me up" (Ps. 29:2 LXX = 30:1). For the holy person exalts the Lord, while the sinner bring him down.

So he wants her to turn her eyes away, lest, by giving attention to her who is already able to pursue higher things, he should be lifted up and desert the other souls. That is also why, in the Gospel, he revealed his glory not to all his disciples, but to the more perfect of their number.

Now picture some teacher who wants to explain an obscure matter to his hearers. Even though he is an able speaker and knowledgeable, let him nevertheless come down to the level of the ignorance of those who do not understand, and let him employ plain, distinct, familiar language in order that he may be understood. Therefore, anyone in his audience who has a livelier intelligence, who can easily follow what is said, lifts him up and questions him. When he sees someone like this, the teacher restrains him, so that he may rather allow the teacher to devote himself to people who are lower down and more ordinary and they may be able to follow what is said.

(3) Theodoret of Cyrus

Your hair is like flocks of goats
    that have appeared from the direction of Gilead.
Your teeth are like flocks of shorn sheep
    that have come up from the bath,
all of them bearing twins,
    and without a barren one among them.
Your lips are are like a scarlet cord,
    and your speech is seasonable.
Your cheek is like the skin of a pomegranate
    outside your veil.
There are sixty queens and eighty concubines,
    and young maidens without number.
One is my dove, my perfect one;
    unique is she for her mother;
    she is a chosen one for the woman who bore her.
The daughters saw her, and they bless her;
    the queens and concubines praise her.

These words we have already explained above [on 4:1c-3] and judge that it is superfluous to explain them twice; for if anyone has forgotten the interpretation, it is possible for him to go back to that passage and find the clarification. But it is not out of stupidity or chance that the Bridegroom applies the same compliments to the Bride twice, but an act in which he reminds her of her proper beauty, and exhorts her to keep it intact and to permit no blemish upon it. "For," he says, "look at the sort of thing you were as contrasted with what I have made of you, and the sort of splendor I lavished upon you and what a high degree of beauty I conferred upon you. For my sake, preserve this unsullied to the end. For I am always together with you, and I inspect your limbs, and take pains that no harm come upon them."

The Bridegroom also says what follows to the maidens, as he urges the Bride to maintain her beauty: **There are sixty queens and eighty concubines, and young maidens without number. One is my dove, my perfect one; unique is she for her mother; she is a chosen one for the woman who bore her. The daughters saw her, and they bless her; the queens and concubines praise her.**

We have been taught that there are many and differing orders of devout and holy persons; indeed, the Lord himself taught this when he said, "In my Father's house are many places to stay" (John 14:2). Further, in the distribution of the talents, each of them did not receive five, but "to one . . . five . . . , to another two, to another one, to each according to his ability" (Matt. 25:15). And in the parable of the seed he says, "but others fell on good earth and produced fruit, some thirtyfold, some sixtyfold, some a hundred. Let anyone who has ears hear" (Matt. 13:8); and he calls all the earth good, not only that which produced a hundredfold, but also that which produced sixty and that which produced thirty, for the number "thirty" belongs in the category of those that are praised since it contains tens brought together with the number "three." The number "sixty," however, owns twice the praise, since sixty is produced by doubling thirty. One hundred, on the other hand, is the most perfect number both because it stands apart from the left hand while containing the principle of the right hand, and also because it is achieved by taking ten ten times. Those skilled in these matters call this a "square." But all the same, even if one hundred is perfect, sixty and thirty also belong in the category of those that are praised; for the Lord calls them all "good earth" (Matt. 13:8).

Let us understand, therefore, that the Bride stands for those souls that have been perfected in all philosophy and virtue, those that undergo the hard work of practicing virtue solely for love of the Bridegroom, and choose both to do and to bear all things. Such a one was the blessed Paul, who said, "For I am sure that neither death, nor life, nor angels, nor principalities, nor things present, nor things to come, nor powers, nor height, nor depth, nor anything else in all creation, will be able to separate us from the love of God in Christ Jesus our Lord" (Rom. 8:38-39). For he teaches us here that he does not long for Christ for the sake of the reign of heaven, but that he would choose rather to be deprived of the reign, and to fall into Gehenna while loving Christ, than to reign while destitute of that love. Hence it is souls of this sort, souls that are possessed only by a longing for Christ, that fill the role and rank of the Bride.

But there are some, on the order of hirelings, who set themselves to bear the toil of the practice of virtue because of their desire for good things to come; these I reckon to be the ones that are named **queens** in this text, on the ground that they desire the reign and for its sake choose to bear the burden of the practice of holiness.

There are others, however, who have not yet been judged worthy of liberty, but still choose to serve as slaves and fulfill the divine laws out of fear of Gehenna. In my opinion, these are the ones who are named **concubines**. For the Bridegroom comes to assist even these, having become "all things to all" (1 Cor. 9:22).

And there are yet others who pass their lives in a state of easy indifference. They are not moved by the Bridegroom's love, nor drawn by a longing to reign, nor touched by fear of Gehenna, but govern their lives without deep concern. They keep the faith unaltered, they preserve the teachings of true religion whole, and they repudiate every alien and heretical teaching; but they live carelessly: at one time they care for themselves, at yet another they wallow in indifference, at another they commit sin, and at another they pour out tears of repentance. Here the Bridegroom addresses such souls as **young maidens**; and because such souls are more numerous than queens or concubines, he says, **and young maidens without number.** It is not only on account of their multitude that they cannot be numbered, he says, but also because they are not worthy of having a number; for even "the hairs" of those who are worthy "are numbered" (Matt. 10:30) by the Father. Nevertheless, the Bridegroom comes to assist even these souls, seeking to remove their indifference, guiding them toward perfection, and working in every way for their salvation.

Let us inquire, however, why the Bridegroom says that there are **sixty queens** but **eighty concubines.** The number "sixty" contains six sets of ten, and the number "ten" signifies perfection, while the "six" comprises the number of the process by which the cosmos was created; for in six days the God of the universe formed the entire creation. Consequently, he names the souls that are perfected in virtue in this cosmos and long for the reign **sixty queens**; for the Bride has her citizenship beyond this cosmos, and lives outside it, and flies above it. She belongs wholly to the Bridegroom, and has him ceaselessly before her mind. The **queens**, though, are citizens of this cosmos, and setting their sights on possession of the reign, they seek the perfection of virtue to the extent of their ability.

On the other hand, those who fulfill the laws out of fear are reasonably given the style **eighty**, for the Holy Scripture assigns the number "eight" to the time of judgment. Thus the blessed David, when in the Psalms he was giving an account of the judgment, titled it "Concerning the Eighth," and said in the opening line, "O Lord, rebuke me not in thine anger, nor chasten me in thy wrath" (Ps. 6:1); and then a bit later, "For in death there is no remembrance of thee; in Sheol who can give thee praise?" (Ps. 6:5). His point is that at the time of judgment absolutely no opportunity for change of mind shall be given sinners who have not repented. Since, then, they have felt dread at this prospect and they have kept the divine laws not out of desire for the reign nor out of love for the Bridegroom, they are rightly said to be **eighty**; for the number "eight" signifies eighth, whereas the number "ten" signifies perfection.

But he says that the Bride is superior to these, both to the **sixty** and to the **eighty.** For **One is my dove, my perfect one**, once again calling her "spiritual" and "one." For beyond the **sixty** and the **eighty, one is she for her mother**; and as her mother she has the sacred font, the "Jerusalem above" (Gal. 4:26).

And **She is a chosen one for the woman who bore her.** For the former were indeed born of her, but out of all of them she esteems this one most highly, and possesses her as her **chosen one**; whence **the daughters saw her, and they bless her**, that is to say, the young maidens. Not only they, however, but the **queens** and the **concubines** also praise her. For she has risen above them because she follows in the way of lofty philosophy — not for the sake of reward, nor out of fear, but out of desire for the Bridegroom.

And may it come to pass for us, with the help of God's grace, that we attain to the perfection of the Bride — but if we are too weak for that, let us be reckoned among the queens; and if we fail of that, let us not be far from the concubines; and if we seem unworthy even of them, let us be reckoned in with the young maidens, and maintain the confession of true religion, and not be entirely deprived of the fellowship of the Bridegroom, but by his grace rejoice in his splendor; for his is glory to the ages of ages. Amen.

(4) Augustine of Hippo

Your teeth are like a flock of shorn ewes
    that have come up from the bath,
all of them bearing twins,
    and without a barren one among them.

[This verse is a repetition of 4:2. For comment see section 12.2.]

(5) Cyprian of Carthage

One is my dove, my perfect one;
    she is the only one for her mother,
    the chosen of the one who bore her.

The Lord is speaking to Peter. "I say to you," he states, "that you are Peter, and on this rock I will build my church, and the gates of hell will not overcome it. And to you I will give the keys of the kingdom of heaven; and what you bind on earth will be bound in heaven, and what you loose on earth will be loosed in heaven" (Matt. 16:18-19). It is on one person that he builds the Church. To be sure, after his resurrection he concedes an equal power to all the apostles when he says, "As the Father sent me, so I send you. Receive the Holy Spirit. If you remit anyone's sins, they are remitted; if you retain them, they are retained" (John 20:21-23). Nevertheless, in order to make the unity evident, by his own authority he fixed a starting point for that unity in one person. No doubt the other apostles were everything that Peter was. They were furnished with an equal share of honor and of power. Yet the start comes from him alone, that the Church of Christ may be shown to be a single thing. Speaking in the person of the Lord, the Holy Spirit also refers to this one Church in the Song of Songs. The Spirit says, **One is my dove, my perfect dove; she is the only one for her mother, the chosen of the one who bore her.** Can those who do not hold to this oneness of the Church believe that they hold to the faith? If people resist and oppose the Church, can they be sure that they are within the Church — when the blessed apostle Paul teaches the very same thing and calls attention to the mystery of unity: "There is one body and one Spirit, one hope of your calling, one Lord, one faith, one baptism, one God" (Eph. 4:4-5)?

(6) Apponius

One is my dove, my perfect one;
    one is she for her mother;
she is a chosen one for the woman who bore her.

This King of ours, the Lord God — among the thousands of thousands of souls that rejoice in him and glorify him, and whom he created for his praise, and regarding whom he spoke by Isaiah, "This people that I created for my praise shall declare my glory" (Isa. 43:21) — found, in the entire mass of souls, **one** unstained, **one perfect dove**, who is queen of all the queens and lord of all the lords. This soul, standing firm at the level of her fashioning by her own free choice, never opened the portals of her mind to the enemy, the Devil. She received the gift of her will from the Creator and enlarged the gift by performing the works of his will. Thus she filled up the storehouse of her heart and with great watchfulness, once it was full, kept it closed and sealed, lest the prince of this world have a place into which he could by persuasion introduce something of his own. She would despise the vain display of all present realities. She would never in any way accommodate to the conspiracy of corporeal delights. She would direct the eye of her mind unchangeably to the good things of the future. All her desire she would focus, not in any way on the acclaim of the present age, or on things that perish, or on worldly doings, but only on love of the Word of God.

Alone upon earth, she is recognized by foreknowledge to be humbler and more perfect than all other souls, just as the one God in heaven is accepted to be Lord over all the powers of dominations, thrones, chairs, angels, or any of the mighty ones, as well as our Creator. As the head of all holy souls, united to the Word of God not adoptively or temporarily but bodily (cf. Col. 2:9), because she abides as matter made one with him, shunning all the works of sinners, free of any ill-will, she is called **dove** and **perfect**.

Through her, the Word of God the Father "condemned sin in the flesh" (Rom. 8:3); he redeemed the world from the sentence that had cursed it. Rage though the Devil might, he overcame him not by force but by reason, so that he might restore humanity, loosed from Satan's hands, to its primordial liberty. Through her, though he shone with a triple glory, he could as flesh born from flesh possess a visible judge. Through her, the souls that were to be redeemed could rejoice in a Redeemer of their own kind, in whom there is real flesh and a real soul. By rising from the dead she could raise up the flesh and at the same time gather the souls to judgment; and as true God he could confer the glory of his kingdom upon those who believe in him.

This beyond any doubt is the **one** soul, the queen of queens, whom the Word of God is known to have assumed and borne; by whose agency he devastated the underworld and unlocked it for the souls imprisoned there, and by his rising brought them back from the lower regions with himself, bodies restored. Because of this soul, and in it, and against nature, human frailty marvelously entered into the heavens. Because of her, once the Devil was ejected, the nature of flesh was made into the temple of Deity. For he, who was the Word made flesh by union with the flesh that he drew from our nature out of the womb of the Virgin, dwelt among us — even as the Evangelist teaches when he says, "And the Word was made flesh and dwelt among us" (John 1:14); and he united indissolubly to himself this **one** soul from our kind of souls, that is, by the fellowship of the Holy Spirit, who descended bodily upon her in the Jordan, to remain with her forever.

By this union, this soul is shown to be **perfect** and **dove: dove** because she is identified with the powers of the Holy Spirit together with his working in all things; and **perfect** because in all things she possesses the omnipotence of God the Father. She — she only and uniquely — by uniting herself to the Word of God like malleable matter to fire manifests one Redeemer, a single judge, a unique Son of the Father as a gift for the ages. The Holy Spirit, foreseeing that among the holy souls she outshines all as the only one without a start or a terminus of sin, says by the mouth of Solomon: **One is my dove, my perfect one; unique is she for her mother, a chosen one for the woman who bore her.**

Plainly it is **for her mother** the synagogue that **she is unique,** for the Hebrew people, who produced, according to the flesh, the one whose soul never proffered a willing right hand to sin; this soul alone, though she possessed everything proper to humanity, assuredly lacked this one thing. **A chosen one for the woman who bore her** — beyond doubt for that Power of the Most High who begets all souls, and who says through the prophet Isaiah, "From me proceeds the spirit, and I have made every breath" (Isa. 57:16); and then through Joel, "My great power will do these things" (cf. Joel 2:25 LXX). This Power by its overshadowing filled the Virgin Mary in her conceiving, as the Evangelist tells us the angel said to her: "The Holy Spirit will come upon you, and the power of the Most High will overshadow you. Therefore what is born in you will be called holy, the Son of God" (Luke 1:35).

(7) Bede the Venerable

There is one dove, my perfect one.

So **there are sixty queens** because throughout the world there are faithful souls in abundance who communicate the knowledge of the Word they have received in order to multiply the Church's progeny with a view to obtaining the kingdom of heaven. There are also **eighty concubines** because there is no lack even of souls that in their attention to earthly things continue in the teaching and, though they themselves give in to the allurements of the flesh, nevertheless by what they say beget spiritual offspring for God. There are also the **young maidens,** whose number is not stated because there are unnumbered crowds of Christian people who, even though they are not yet ready for promotion to the task of ruling and teaching, yet do willingly and faithfully manifest their devotedness in belief and in deeds for the sake of their allegiance to the Church, the Bride, that is, of Christ. But the universal Church herself by right excels all of these, that is, the members of the Church, real and imitation. She it is who in these same believing members praises the name of the Lord "from the rising of the sun to its setting" (Ps. 112:3 Vg = 113:3), "from the north and from the south" (Ps. 106:3 Vg = 107:3), from the beginning to the consummation of the age. In praise of her he says most beautifully:

One is my dove, my perfect one. For she is **one** because she does not allow of the division that schism brings. She is **one** because she has not been gathered as one body before the law, another under the law, and yet another under grace, as one body drawn from the circumcised and another from the uncircumcised; but just as there is "one Lord, one faith, one baptism, one God and Father of all" (Eph. 4:5-6), so there is one catholic multitude of all the elect, which throughout all the world's places and times is subject to one God and Father. Luke teaches us why she is called "catholic" when he says, "So all the churches built up throughout all Judea and Galilee and Samaria enjoyed peace, and walking in the fear of the Lord, they were filled with the comfort of the Holy Spirit" (Acts 9:31); for the Latin expression here is, in Greek, *kath' holēs*. And from this it is patent that the Church is called catholic because in every part of the world she is built up in one peace in one fear of the Lord, and is filled with the one comfort of the Holy Spirit. On the basis of this unity of the Spirit, she is also — and rightly — called **dove**; for the Spirit came down upon the Lord in the form of a dove so that by appearing in this form he might manifest both his own simplicity and that of the Lord upon whom he came down. Since the Lord made his Church a sharer in this simplicity and this Spirit, it is right that he name her his **dove** and call her **perfect**, not only because she herself, out of all the peoples, is constituted one society of the righteous but also because she is perfect by her reception of all the virtues and divine charisms.

Song 6:10–7:1

SEPTUAGINT

6:10 Who is this that looks out like the
 dawn,
  beautiful like the moon, chosen
   like the sun,
  an object of terror, like battle
   lines marshalled up?
11 I went down into the nut orchard,
  to look among the products of
   the valley,
 to see whether the vineyard had
  blossomed,
  whether the pomegranates had
   bloomed.
 There I will give you my breasts.
12 My soul did not know:
  Aminadab set me up to be
   chariots.

7:1 Return, return, O Sulamite!
  Return, return, and we shall look
   within you.
 What should we look upon in the
  Sulamite,
  who comes like choruses
   composed of platoons of
   soldiers?

VULGATE

6:9 Who is this that comes up like the
 dawn rising,
  beautiful like the moon, chosen
   like the sun,
  fearsome like an ordered
   formation from the camp?
10 I went down to the garden of nuts
  in order to see the apples of the
   valleys,
 and to see whether the vines had
  blossomed,
  and the pomegranates had
   budded.

11 I did not know:
  my soul threw me into confusion
   on account of the four-wheeled
   chariot of Aminadab.
12 Return, return, O Sunamite!
  Return, return, that we may
   look upon you.
7:1 What will you see in the Sunamite

  but bands from the camp?

This segment of the Song was — and is — hard to make coherent sense of: its bits do not hang together well. One symptom of this is the unusual difficulty of identifying the speaker in any given verse, and, for that matter, the equal difficulty of deciding, in certain of the statements, who is being talked about. Who, in the opening question, is the individual that "looks out like the dawn"? Who "went down into the nut orchard"? Who are the "we" that want to "look upon" the "Sulamite"? And for that matter, who is this Sulamite? Is it the same individual who is described earlier (6:10) as looking — peering — "out like the dawn"?

Thus the Glossa ordinaria *assumes that the speaker in the opening verse is "the synagogue," that is, the original people of God, who here marvel at the accomplishments of "the Church," the Gentile people of God. Neither of these two identifications was widely accepted, however. Theodoret agrees that the one spoken of is the (Gentile) Church, but defines the speaker as the Bridegroom's attendants. Ambrose might well have agreed with this position; certainly he sees the Church as the one who is spoken of. He even works it out that the Church was so embarrassed by the praises just lavished upon her by the Bridegroom (6:4-8) that she had retired out of modesty, and 6:10 therefore records her re-emergence "like the dawn." But even if Ambrose agrees with Theodoret on this score, Apponius and Honorius do not. Apponius pursues his own thesis, that in this part of the Song the Bride represents the human soul of Christ himself, the "perfect one" (6:9).*

Honorius has yet a third interpretation: as he sees it, the subject in 6:10 is a newcomer — not the Gentile Church but the Jewish people, now, in a vision of the future presented by the Song, turning to Christ. This entails (a) that the speaker in 6:10 is the Gentile Church herself, as represented by the maidens, the concubines, and the queens of the previous section; and (b) that it is the Bridegroom, the Word of God, who says, "I went down into the nut orchard. . . ." It also fits in with Honorius's identification of this "new Bride" with the Sulamite woman of 7:1 (= 6:12 Vg).

Apart from these general differences of interpretation, exegetes had problems focused on particular words. Thus Ambrose understands the Greek word translated above by "valley" (Song 6:11b) in another of its meanings, that is, to denote a river in full spate ("torrent"). Again, Honorius (and all users of the Vg) speaks of the "Sunamite" rather than of the "Sulamite" woman, since the Scriptures know of a Sunamite woman with whom Elisha had dealings (2 Kings 4:8-17; cf. 1 Kings 1:1-4, 15); but "Sulamite" occurs only here in the whole of the Bible. Nicholas of Lyra alludes to this problem in the excerpt from his Postilla *below.*

Another puzzle, of course, is that provided by the reference to Aminadab and his "chariot" (6:12) — a puzzle occasioned by a singularly obscure Hebrew text whose meaning is uncertain. One thing that is fairly certain is that it contains no reference to an "Aminadab" — and maybe not even to a chariot. The reference to Aminadab in the Septuagint and the Vulgate (a name that occurs about a dozen times in the Old Testament) is the product of an effort to make some sense of the Hebrew sentence.

(1) Theodoret of Cyrus

Who is this that looks out like the dawn,
  beautiful like the moon, chosen like the sun,
  an object of terror, like battle lines drawn up?

In the lines before this one, the Bridegroom's words were portraying the Bride's beauty. He extolled each of her members individually, and then in turn accorded them a common praise; and seeing that his praise of her was artfully set out, he also contrived a comparison by setting the Bride alongside young maidens and concubines and queens. . . . So much greater, he said, was the beauty of her form that she was not envied by those with whom she was matched; they acknowledged their beauty inferior to hers and declared her blessed and thrice blessed.

In this verse, however, the Bridegroom's attendants — once they had learned from him the Bride's beauty and decorum and comeliness — were impelled to become more closely acquainted with her (for as yet the beauty of her soul was concealed by the veil of the body); and so they cry out with great delight, **Who is this that looks out like the dawn?** For her light was seen partially for a moment, obscured by this mortal body; and just as dawn marks the border between night and day, and is pronounced to be the end of the one and the beginning of the other, and signals the coming of the day, so too in the present life souls that have been perfected in true piety and in all wisdom — those that Scripture names "Church" and "bride" — give off slight gleams of the virtue that is proper to them. "But when," as the blessed Paul says, "this corruptible shall put on incorruptibility, and this mortal shall put on immortality" (1 Cor. 15:54), their entire light will be seen in its naked glory.

What is more, the Bridegroom's attendants, foreseeing all this, not only liken her to the dawn but also say that she is beautiful like the moon, the chosen, and like the sun, which strikes terror into those that dare to fix their sight upon it. They add the word **chosen**, thereby not only indicating how she differs from the stars but also making the perfection of the moon itself apparent, as if to say that she shines like the full moon — not the crescent moon or the half-moon or the gibbous moon, but the entire moon in its perfect fullness, without any imperfection, and showing its whole disk full of light. So it is that he says, **beautiful like the moon chosen.**

Now those who are experts in these matters say that the moon derives its light from the rays of the sun and that when a small portion of her surface looks upon the sun, she takes in a small amount of its light. When, contrariwise, all of her looks upon the sun, and like some sort of mirror she reflects the whole of its disk, she is illumined as a whole, and no bit of her body is left without light. In this way, accordingly, the Church of Christ, which is the company of souls that have been perfected in virtue, "with unveiled face," as the blessed Paul says, "beholding as in a mirror the glory of the Lord, is transformed into the same image from glory to glory as from the Lord the Spirit" (2 Cor. 3:18) — and this Church takes on the very character of light, so as to be likened to the moon, and indeed to the moon *as chosen,* that is, to the full, the fulfilled, moon.

Yet it is not only the moon to which she is likened, but to the sun as well — and the sun as it strikes **terror** into those who look upon it. Nor do I judge that this passage bears only one sense; for nothing is spoken at random by the divine Spirit. On the contrary, since, according to the blessed Paul, this present life is a nighttime (for he says, "the night is far gone, the day is at hand" [Rom. 13:12]), it follows that the Church is a kind of moon that lights the path for travelers and indicates the straight road. She is also like the **dawn** in that the time that comes after the Lord's advent is a kind of dawn that points to the state of affairs that is yet to come, like the arrival of a kind of day. "We shall find him," it says, "at hand like the dawn" (Hos. 6:3). When that great day of the Lord arrives, all manifest in accord with the prophet's word — the day of which the blessed Paul says, "the day is at hand" — then she will no longer shine like the moon, but like the sun that strikes terror not only into unbelievers but also into the **young maidens**, the **concubines**, and the **queens**, and into the incorporeal Powers themselves. Moreover, the Lord himself attests this when he says, "Then the righteous will shine like the sun" (Matt. 13:43). . . .

(2) Apponius

Who is this that comes up like the dawn,
  beautiful like the moon, elect like the sun,
  an object of terror, like battle lines marshalled up?

The one that **comes up** is, to be sure, that most blessed soul aforesaid [i.e., the human soul of Christ]. She does so **like the moon** in order, by her self-manifestation to Israel, to illumine the night of ignorance and of sins; and to summon those "who sit in the darkness of the shadow of death" (Luke 1:79) to the journey of good works, by glittering with wondrous deeds from earliest childhood; and after the night of ignorance, she rises with the morning light **like the dawn**, coming to sacred baptism in the Jordan. Then, through the arrival of the Holy Spirit from heaven in the shape of a dove, she shines among mortals **like the dawn**. Then, like wayfarers stirred by the **dawn** already **rising**, believers in the God of heaven are reminded to take up their journey now that sleep has been dissolved from the eyes of their mind. Then, as if to say, "Behold, dawn is breaking," John speaks thus: "Behold, the Lamb of God, who takes away the sin of the world" (John 1:29), that dawn of which the Evangelist said, "This is the true light that enlightens everyone coming into the world" (John 1:9), and "The light shines in the darkness, and the darkness has not overcome it" (John 1:5).

Thus she is shown to be **beautiful like the moon** by her signs and deeds of power, either the ones she performed in the world by living in human company, or those that she allowed the apostles to perform. For she "increased in wisdom and" bodily "stature" (Luke 2:52) in the life of this age for as many years as the **the moon** takes days to wax and to wane. In its going down, or in the vicinity of its renewal, the heavenly elements, hidden by black clouds, are often altered; in the very same way, at the end, as it is thought, of her thirtieth year, this soul manifested her beauty through the deeds of power that are her signs by changing water into wine when the marriage feast was darkened by clouds of sadness (cf. John 2:1-11). As the **moon** brings joy to wayfarers by rising and showing herself in the darkness of the night, so too this soul brought the brightness of joy to light when the marriage feast was saddened by a failure of wine. Through this first sign of power, **like** that of **the moon**, her glory is revealed to those among the first believers whose minds had been darkened. In her setting — at the time of her passion — a violent earthquake shook not only the heavenly bodies but the whole world, and, with the disappearance of the light-givers, produced darkness, to make sure that so towering a sin might not seem to be worthy of attention. And when she fell into the darkness of the lower world, resurrection, like the renewal of the moon, succored her, and bolstered the shaky faith of the great apostles, by whom the world was lifted out of the pit of unbelief.

But she is **elect like the sun**: after the fulfilled glory of the resurrection, she is proclaimed to stand forever as one full of the Father's splendor. She manifested a small bit of this glory to the apostles at the peak of the mountain when she was transfigured; and there, together with the election of her humanity, she also revealed her fearsome majesty, to the confusion of the apostles.

Therefore, these three grades of distinction, replete with praise — that is, beauty, election, and fearsomeness — can be comprehended by reference to the order in which she appears in the future judgment to three particular types, in proportion to their merits: to righteous persons she is said to appear in the beauty of the moon; to the heavenly powers, refulgent in majesty **like the sun**; but to the wicked who are assigned to eternal fire, as **an object of terror, like battle lines marshalled up.**

(3) The *Glossa ordinaria*

Who is this that comes up like the dawn rising. . . ?

The Church of the Gentiles is thus firmly established. She is spread abroad everywhere by reason of her manifold character. She has been brought down to these latest times by her stages and successions. Now in these latest times the synagogue looks upon this Church, which has done its business well in the past and is doing it still, which is spread abroad; it looks upon so large a number of wise persons following one faith without schism, not to mention many miracles of the living as well as of the dead, and many other evidences of Christian faith. Now convinced, penitent, and full of remorse, it says, in a mood of wonder, **Who is this . . . , etc.?**

(4) Ambrose of Milan

I went down into the nut orchard,
 to look among the products of the torrent,
to see whether the vineyard had blossomed,
 whether the pomegranates had bloomed.
There I will give you my breasts.
My soul did not know:
 Aminadab set me up to be chariots.

In the course of being praised by the Bridegroom, she modestly flees from being praised while present with him, but then, brought back by the Bridegroom's love, she says, **I went down into the nut orchard, to see the products of the torrent.** For where is the Church if not where the priestly staff and priestly grace are flowering (cf. Num. 17:23 LXX = 17:18)? She is there frequently, that she may be tested by bitter hardships and temptations. By **nut** we think that bitter hardships are meant, and by **torrent,** temptations — but they are bearable, for it is written, "Our soul passed through the torrent" (Ps. 123:5 LXX = 124:5). She descended, then, into a place of bitterness, where the vine flowers, and also a varied and manifold fruit with the look of pomegranates, which is kept safe by faith and charity as though by a hard skin that covers the whole body.

 In the midst of such bitterness, the soul **did not know** herself; for "a corruptible body weighs down the soul," and her "earthly dwelling place" (Wisdom 9:15) quickly collapses. Yet it is her business always to know herself. But Peter too was tempted, and even Peter failed to know himself; for if he had known himself, he would never have denied his Creator. But Christ knew him: he knew him for sure, for he looked upon him (Luke 22:61) — and the Lord knows those who belong to him (2 Tim. 2:19) — and like a good rider he summoned Peter back from his sin with, as we might say, the reins of his mercy. That is why our rider and governor is Christ.

 Hence too the soul says, **Aminadab set me up to be a chariot.** The soul is a chariot that supports the good rider. If the soul is a chariot, it has horses, either good or bad. The good horses are the soul's virtues, and the bad horses are the bodily passions. Hence the good rider reins in the bad horses and summons them back but urges the good ones on. The good horses are four in number: prudence, temperance, fortitude, and justice. The bad horses are anger, lust, fear, and injustice. Occasionally these horses will themselves be at odds with each other, and either anger or fear will pull out ahead, and they will get in each other's way and delay the journey. By contrast, the good horses fly upward: they lift themselves up from the earth to higher realms, and they exalt the soul, and especially if they enjoy the easy yoke and the light burden of the One who says, "Take my yoke upon you, . . . for my yoke is easy, and my burden is light" (Matt. 11:19-20). It is the rider himself who knows how to rule his own horses so that all run at the same pace. If prudence is swifter and justice slower, he cautions the more sluggish horse with his whip. If temperance is gentler and fortitude rougher, he knows how to unite the discordant so that they do not wreck the chariot. Thus the mind's vision is allowed to see each soul being swept up to heaven in a great contest, with the horses racing ahead, to see which may first reach the prize that is Christ, so that the palm wreath may be set on their necks first. These horses bear the yoke of faith, are kept together by the chain of love, the reins of justice, and the halter of moderation.

It is rightly, then, that she says, **Aminadab set me up to be a chariot**, "Aminadab" meaning "father of the people." Moreover, the very one that is father of the people is identical with the father of Nahshon (cf. Num. 1:7; 2:3), that is to say, "of a serpent." At this point, recollect who it was that hung like a serpent upon the cross for the salvation of everyone (cf. John 3:14 and Num. 21:9), and understand that the soul whom God the Father protects and Christ drives is peaceable; for it stands written in the Scriptures: "Father, father, the driver of Israel!" (2 Kings 2:12). This is the driver, then, who says, **Return, return, O Sulamite, return**; and "Sulamite" means peaceable. For the soul that is peaceable swiftly turns and corrects herself, even if she sinned earlier; and Christ by preference deigns to mount and to drive her. To him it is said: "Mount upon your horses, and your cavalry is salvation" (Hab. 3:5 LXX), and again: "I have sent thy horses into the sea" (Hab. 3:15 LXX). These are Christ's horses. Therefore Christ mounts his horses, and the Word of God mounts pious souls.

(5) Honorius of Autun

I went down into the garden of nuts in order
   to see the apples of the valleys,
   and to see whether the vines had blossomed,
And the pomegranates had budded.
I did not know:
   my soul threw me into confusion on account of the four-wheeled chariot
    of Aminadab.
Return, return, O Sunamite.
   Return, return, that we may look upon you.

Previously it was said that the Queen of the South waged three wars for her crown. One was against **Amana** (4:8), another against the **north wind** (4:16), and the third against the **drops of the night** (5:2). Then she came, victorious, to the coronation of the King, and in her company she had **sixty queens** and **eighty concubines** and **young maidens without number**; and the king received her favorably. From her camps, she led forth ordered battle arrays. She herself came forth with her entire company to her triumph. Up front the banner of the dawn, in the color of blood, preceded the array of the martyrs, which entered upon the struggle against the army of the persecutors, whose leader was **Amana**. The banner of the moon, however, in all its shining splendor, went before the array of the confessors, which had armed itself against the army of the heretics, whose leader was the **north wind**. But the banner of the sun with its fiery gleam heralded the array of the sages, who took up arms against the army of false brethren, who are the **drops of the night**.

But the following account reports that a new Bride has arrived from the West, and that the King has received her sumptuously. For as the Queen of the South was triumphing and dancing with the King, behold! here come the bridesmen, Elijah and Enoch, leading the Sunamite in the chariot of Aminadab together with many thousands of people. The **queens** and the **concubines** and the **young maidens** together with their Queen all receive her with loud applause, and with great rejoicing take her down to the King in the **garden of nuts**. The King is very merry at her arrival, and he sings this song for her.

    I went down into the garden of nuts to see the apples of the valleys. For after "the fullness of the Gentiles" (Rom. 11:25) has entered upon the faith of Christ at the end of the world, the synagogue too will accept the faith of Christ through the preaching of Elijah and Enoch, and the King himself will receive it with these words of praise: **I went down into the garden of nuts** — that is, "I have taken up 'the form of a slave' (Phil. 2:7) and come into the world **to see the apples of the valleys**," that is, to reward the deeds of the humble and lowly. It is as though, to the synagogue as it comes to the faith, he should say, "Deservedly you come to me, the one who before came to you, when I came down from heaven into Judea, which was the **garden of nuts**, that is, the dwelling place of believers" — because outwardly they suffer the bitterness of tribulation, but inwardly experience delight through their hope of reward. In a nut, there are three things: the external rind, which is bitter, the inner shell, which is hard, and the kernel, which is sweet. The rind stands for those who have bitter vices. The shell stands for those who subdue the body with fasts and vigils. The kernel, however, stands for spiritual men. "Furthermore, **I went down into the garden of nuts**, that is, into Judea, **to see the apples of the valleys**, that is, the works of the people that dwelt in Jerusalem, which was called 'valley' because it had been set among the empires of the Gentiles as if among mountains; **and to see whether the vines had blossomed**, that is, whether the synagogue, which is called the Lord's vineyard, would bring forth fruit in faith — the synagogue that the Lord himself brought forth out of Egypt and planted in Judea. And also to see whether **the pomegranates had budded**, that is, whether through faith some would choose to be sprinkled with their own blood. And if I did not see these things there, I would teach them to do such things; but they for their part rejected me, and more than that, slew me after subjecting me to abuse."

    To these words the troubled synagogue responds, "**I did not know**, that is, these things of which you speak; and that is why I acted as I did. When I saw you moving as a human person among human beings, I did not know that you were God. When I saw you hanging between thieves, I did not know that you were the Savior. For had I known that you were "the King of glory" (Ps. 23:7, 8 LXX = 24:7, 8), I should never have crucified you. But you blinded me, in order that through me you might work the salvation of the human race; and **I did not know** what I did because **my soul threw me into confusion on account of the four-wheeled chariot of Aminadab**, which means, 'My soul-nature made me anxious on account of the teaching of the gospel, which forbade me the circumcision given by God and the ceremonies of the law, and inculcated baptism and other novel practices.'"

    There are three elements in a human person: flesh, soul-nature, and spirit. Flesh is a burden and a trouble; soul-nature is the inclination of the flesh in accordance with which we live without knowing anything of the truth; the spirit is that which justifies. The people of Ashdod fought against the children of Israel, and when the Israelites were defeated they seized from them the ark of the Lord. Because of this they were later struck by divine vengeance; and when they had consulted the gods, the answer said that they could not be freed from that affliction unless they returned the ark, which then, set upon a carriage with a team of four horses, was brought back to the home of Aminadab the priest (cf. 1 Sam. 5:1–7:1). Christ's carriage is the gospel. Its four wheels are the four Gospels, which run through the whole world on their way to the world's end. The ark is the humanity of Christ; the manna in the ark is the divinity of Christ. The ark was drawn in among foreign peoples, and Christ has been drawn to the nations by the apostles. The ark was brought back into Judea, and Christ at the end of the world will be brought back by the Gospels into the synagogue. From the house of Aminadab the ark was brought back by David into Jerusalem. Now **Aminadab** means "a willing one of my people," and Christ was willingly offered for the sins of the people whose home was Jerusalem, from which the Father transported him into the heavenly Jerusalem. As I have said, the carriage of this Aminadab is the four Gospels, on account of which the soul of the synagogue has been troubled; for the mind of its soul-nature began to be greatly troubled when it heard the gospel of Christ being preached throughout the world. But it travels in that carriage when it is brought by the teaching of the gospel to faith in Christ.

Hence the new Bride was not able to bear the presence of the King, whom, after many shameful afflictions, she condemned to the most ignoble of deaths; and therefore she began to depart from his face, but the chorus of queens and daughters of Jerusalem called her back: **Return, return, O Sunamite! Return, return, that we may look upon you.**

This means that after the synagogue had killed Christ the King she was ashamed to be under his rule; but the voice of the preachers summons her back, saying, **Return, return, O Sunamite.** Sunem is the city in which Elisha raised a dead boy (2 Kings 4:18-37), and it stands for the world in which Christ raised the human race. "Sunem" likewise means bondage; hence the Sunamite is in bondage and is understood to stand for the synagogue taken captive by the Devil's treachery. The Sunamite also means "scarlet" because she has been redeemed by the blood of Christ. To her the preachers of the gospel say **return** four times — that is, from the four plagues of the world: to turn from the error of betrayal to faith in Christ, or to **return** to your Redeemer who calls you and wants to receive you by believing in him; to **return** to him by loving him; to **return** to him by keeping his precepts; to **return** to him by hoping for the life that he has promised, **that we may look upon you,** that is, that we may imitate you. Or else: **return** by way of the four Gospels, **return** by way of the four virtues, so that by looking upon your way of life we may give praise to the Lord; for the Jews, converted at the end of the world, shall evince such a way of life that the Church will be seized with wonder and follow their example. For they shall be converted by Elijah and Enoch at the world's vespers, and will suffer a famine of the word of God like dogs, and will circle around the Church, the city of God, to hear the word of the Lord, and will live by the same practices as the Church formerly did under the apostles. In response to the voice of this calling, the Sunamite has returned to the King and is by him received into grace. . . .

19. Song 6:10–7:1

(6) Nicholas of Lyra

Return, return, O Sunamite,
  Return, return. . . .

Return: the next thing to be touched upon — but briefly and briskly — is the condition of the people [of Israel] from the time of their return from captivity in Babylon to that of Christ; and in this connection it is said, **Return, return,** that is to say, from your captivity.

Sunamite: so the Bride is called here, after the city named Suna, in which Elisha was frequently a guest, as it is related in 4 Kingdoms 4 (2 Kings 4:8; cf. 1 Kings 1:3). In the Hebrew it says, **Return, return, Sulamite;** and if this were put into proper Latin, we would have "Sulamitis," which is to say, "whole" or "perfect." What it means to say is, "Return to your original condition of perfection"; or better still, "Return to the original wholeness of your faith" — for after its return from the Babylonian captivity, the people of Israel was always a subject nation, belonging first of all to the Persians, second to the Greeks, and third to the Romans; but it stood fast in the service of the one true God up to the time of Christ.

The word **return** is spoken four times because the first ones to return came from Babylon under the leadership of Zerubbabel; then a second group with Ezra the priest (Ezra 7:1-8); a third group with Nehemiah; and a fourth in the days of Judas Maccabeus, who on account of the persecution under Antiochus fled into the wilderness, and afterward, when he had defeated Antiochus's generals, returned to the cities of his own homeland, as it is related in 1 Maccabees.

That we may look upon you — that is, as you are serving God in the land of Judah. Since, however, in those days the people of Israel was harassed by other peoples, and thus had frequently to engage in warfare, the passage adds: **What will you see in the Sunamite** [or **Sulamite,** according to the Hebrew text] **but bands from the camp?,** that is, groups of men readied for combat; for in the time of Nehemiah, while the city was being rebuilt, the workers did their jobs with one hand while holding a sword in the other, and half of the people were armed in order the better to resist their adversaries (Neh. 4:15-18). Afterward, in the time of the Maccabees, the people of Israel was all but constantly at war, as is apparent from account given in 1 and 2 Maccabees.

(7) Theodoret of Cyrus

What should we look upon in the Sulamite,
  who comes like choruses composed of platoons of soldiers?

"What," says he, "do you expect to see in the peace bringer? Do not suppose that you are going to see good things that are cheaply bought and imperfect; for, you see, she **comes like choruses composed of platoons of soldiers.**" Now it seems to me that the terms here are in some way contrary to each other; for **choruses** do not fit in with **platoons of soldiers.** The former are festive, whereas the latter are warlike; and festivity is the contrary of war. On the other hand, this Bride — who is made up of many holy persons — is like **platoons of soldiers** at once in her courage, in the nobility of her resolve, and in her warlike harness. She is also a **chorus** in that her mouth carries the praises of God. The blessed David too makes this point when he says, "The voice of exultation and of salvation in the tents of the righteous" (Ps. 117:15 LXX = 118:15); and again, "Equip the festal crowd with wreaths, right up to the horns of the altar" (Ps. 117:27 LXX = 118:27). But the blessed Paul refers to the **platoons of soldiers** when he says, "Our weapons . . . are not fleshly, but have divine power to destroy strongholds, as we destroy arguments and every height that lifts itself up against the knowledge of God, and take every thought captive for the sake of obedience to Christ" (2 Cor. 10:4-5). Again he says, "Therefore take the armor of God, so that you may be able to withstand in the evil day, and having done all, to stand" (Eph. 6:13). Nor does he say "platoons of soldiers composed of choruses," but **choruses composed of platoons of soldiers**; for the choruses are made up of companies of soldiers, and the athletes of virtue, once they have been victorious in their military companies, return singing paeans, and in their chorus they sing the hymn of victory.

Song 7:2-10

SEPTUAGINT

7:2 How lovely are your steps in sandals,
    O daughter of Nadab!
  The proportions of your thighs are
    like bracelets,
    the work of an artisan's hands.
3 Your navel is like a finely wrought
    bowl
    that never lacks mixed wine.

  Your belly is a heap of grain
    fenced in by lilies.
4 Your two breasts are like two fawns,
    twins of a gazelle.
5 Your neck is like an ivory tower.
  Your eyes are like pools in Heshbon,

    in the gates of the daughter of a
     multitude.
  Your nose is like a tower of Lebanon,
    looking upon the face of
     Damascus.
6 Your head sits upon you like Carmel,
    and the plaited hair of your
     head is like scarlet,
    a king tied up in its runnings.
7 How you have become fair and
    pleasing,
    O dearest among delights!
8 Your stature is like that of a
    palm tree,

VULGATE

7:1 How lovely are your steps in sandals,
    O daughter of the prince!
  The join of your thighs is like jewels

    made by the hands of an artisan.
2 Your navel is a finely turned bowl

    that never lacks something to
     drink.
  Your belly is like a heap of wheat
    walled about by lilies.
3 Your two breasts are like two fawns,
    twins of a gazelle.
4 Your neck is like an ivory tower.
  Your eyes are like fishpools in
    Heshbon,
    which are in the gate of the
     daughter of a multitude.
  Your nose is like a tower of Lebanon,
    which looks toward Damascus.

5 Your head is like Carmel,
    and the hairs of your head are
     like a king's purple,
    joined by channels.
6 How beautiful you are,
    and how lovely in delights,
     O dearest one!
7 Your height has been likened to a
    palm tree,

and your breasts are like clusters of fruit.	and your breasts to grapes.
9 I said, I will mount the palm tree, I will get hold of its branches, and your breasts shall be like clusters of grapes on the vine, and the scent of your skin like apples,	8 I said, I will mount the palm tree and I will grasp its fruits, and your breasts will be like grapes on the vine, and the scent of your mouth like that of apples.
10 and your throat like good wine, worthy for my Beloved to drink, and for his lips and teeth to chew over.	9 Your throat is like the finest wine, worthy for my Beloved to drink, and for his lips and teeth to chew over.

Here the reader of the Song meets another listing of the Bride's attractions, a series of praises spoken by the Bridegroom. Naturally enough, therefore, interpreters tended to compare it to other such encomia, especially that in chap. 4, with its partial repetition in chap. 6. The general themes of the exegesis here are, as might be expected, very similar. Only Nicholas of Lyra is an exception to the general trend of interpretation. For him the passage is of absolutely central importance because it marks the point at which the subject matter of the Song shifts from the history of the Church as established in the exodus from Egypt and the giving of the law at Sinai to its history as a people renewed in Christ.

Problems for interpretation occur — for example, that reflected in the different identifications of Nadab, otherwise known as "the prince." For Theodoret this "prince" is the Holy Spirit; for Apponius he is "the prince of this world." A further difficulty was occasioned by the last two lines of the passage. They have to be taken as words of the Bride, it would seem; yet they are connected grammatically with the last words of the Bridegroom. Bede solves the difficulty by suggesting that the Bride suddenly interrupts her Lover with an exclamation.

(1) Nicholas of Lyra

How lovely are your steps . . .
  worthy for my Beloved to drink.

After the love of Bridegroom and Bride under the institutions of the Old Covenant has been described, the same love will now be described under those of the New Covenant. The description is divided into three parts: first, there is set down the beginnings of this order; second, the diffusion of what had been begun (at the point where it says, **Come, my beloved** [7:11]); and third, in the next chapter, the secure settling-in of what had been spread abroad.

Where the first of these parts is concerned, the Bride is (a) initially characterized in general terms, and then (b) where it says, **I said, I will mount**, in more specific terms, with special reference to the perfected. Under head (a), the Bride is portrayed by means of the parable of an attractive wife, but differently than above in chap. 4; for there the Bride's beauty is sketched by beginning with her higher members and moving downward to the lower, whereas here the description moves in the opposite direction. It begins with the lower members and reaches toward the higher. The reason for this is that in the time of the Old Covenant she moves, as it were, away from God and departs from him; while in that of the New Covenant, she is brought back to God, from things earthly to things heavenly.

First, then, comes the parable of the beautiful wife, and then the parable is explained. . . .

How lovely are your steps, in that they go in the way of the evangelical counsels. **In sandals:** sandals are made of animal skins and are a reminder of the death of Christ and of the martyrs, a death that equips the feet of the Bride to walk undeviatingly in the way of the evangelical counsels. **O daughter of the prince,** which means the Church that is called the daughter and Bride of Christ, who is Prince "of the kings of the earth"; see Apocalypse 1 (Rev. 1:5). **The join of your thighs:** this means the joining together of Jews and Gentiles in the one Church of Christ. Moreover, this **join** is **made by the hands of an artisan,** that is, by the hand of Christ, who "made the two one"; see Ephesians 2 (Eph. 2:14).

Your navel, etc. By the **navel** beneath which the fetus is conceived, and by the womb in which it is nourished before its birth, is meant the Church's fruitfulness in bearing sons to Christ himself. Further, these are not born carnally but spiritually (see John 1 [John 1:13]: "Who are born not of blood nor of the will of the flesh . . ."); and therefore that womb is said to be **walled about with lilies,** that is, with chastity.

Your two breasts, that is, the two Covenants from which is sucked the milk from which sons begotten in Christ are nurtured and make increase. See 1 Peter 2: "Like newborn babes, long for the pure spiritual milk, that by it you may grow up to salvation" (1 Pet. 2:2).

Your neck — meaning faith shaped by love (cf. Gal. 5:6), which joins the body of the Bride to Christ her Head. See Ephesians 1: "He made him head over the whole Church" (cf. Eph. 1:22). Moreover, the **nose** of this head refers to that discriminating judgment by which, in the present age, he disinguishes believers from unbelievers, just as the nose discriminates between sweet and foul smells. The **eyes,** on the other hand, represent the power of knowledge that enables Christ to look upon those who believe in him with approval, as in John 10: "I know my sheep" (cf. John 10:14), which means believers. **Like fishpools,** because his eyes are filled with the waters of loving-kindness.

Your head, which is to say, the most elevated part of this Head — Christ's divinity. From it there flow the understandings and impulses of the spiritual life, into the humanity of Christ first of all, and after that to all the members of the Church. That explains why the expression **like Carmel** is added, which is a mountain rich in fruits. **The hairs** of this **head** are the apostles who first adhered to Christ the Head; and they say, **like a king's purple,** because for love of Christ their King they were made scarlet with blood by receiving the prize of martyrdom.

From all that has now been said, a conclusion is drawn:

How beautiful you are on the inside, in virtue of your faith; and how lovely on the outside, in virtue of your probity. O dearest one: which means "one redeemed at the highest price," that is, by the precious blood of Christ. For the word "dearest" means "that which is purchased at the highest price." In delights, because for his Bride the suffering of Christ opened the door of the delights of Paradise.

Your height has been likened to a palm tree, for its uprightness in justice and the height reached by its devout contemplation. And your breasts to grapes, on account of the abundance of milk they give for the nurture of the children of Christ and the Church.

I said, I will mount. Now there follows a description of the Bride's beauty as far as it concerns the special case of those who are perfected. Of these the Bridegroom says, I said, I will mount, that is, I will cause those in the Church who are perfect to mount. The palm tree, that is, to the height of contemplation. And I will grasp, that is, I will cause them to grasp, as has frequently been explained above in similar cases, its fruits, which means the sweetness that is experienced at the height of contemplation, even as the palm tree generates its fruit up at its top. And your breasts will be like grapes on the vine because they abound in the milk of sacred teaching. For in the act of contemplation, contemplatives soak up the things that they later pour out in their teaching — as is plain from the case of Paul after his rapture, and from that of many other teachers. And the scent of your mouth, that is, the renown of the teaching. Hence the apostle Paul, at 2 Corinthians 2, says, "Through us [God] spreads the fragrance of the knowledge of [Christ] everywhere, since we are the aroma of Christ to God" (2 Cor. 2:14-15), and so on. The line that follows bears on the same point:

Your throat, in which the words of the proclamation are shaped, [is] like the finest wine, intoxicating the minds of believers with the divine love. This is the wine that produces virgins: Zech. 9 (Zech. 9:17). . . .

(2) Theodoret of Cyrus

How lovely are your feet in their sandals,
 O daughter of Nadab!
The proportions of your thighs are like bracelets,
 the work of an artisan's hands. . . .
Your head sits upon you like Carmel,
 and the plaited hair of your head is like scarlet,
 a king tied up in the tresses.

[For "Nadab"] Aquila says "prince," while Symmachus has "governor." But who can this governor or this prince be if not the Holy Spirit, the Comforter? It is the Spirit, too, that says to her in the psalm, "Hear, O daughter, consider, and incline your ear; forget your people and your father's house, and the king will desire your beauty, since he is your Lord" (Ps. 44:11-12 LXX = 45:10-11). Moreover the blessed David teaches us that the title governor also belongs to the Holy Spirit when he says, "Restore to me the joy of thy salvation, and uphold me with thy governing Spirit" (Ps. 50:14 LXX = 51:12). Therefore the

Bridegroom first praises the **feet** of the Bride because they go straight and walk along the royal way, and in her sandals shine with beauty. The blessed Paul explained what the reference to **sandals** means: "and your feet shod with the preparation of the gospel of peace" (Eph. 6:15). But the prophet Isaiah also foresaw the beauty of these feet, and said, "How beautiful are the feet of those who bring the good news of peace, who bring good news of good things" (Isa. 52:7)! And in the book before us the Bridegroom uses the very same words: **How lovely are your feet, O daughter of Nadab!**

But in order that we may derive some insight not only from the translation of the name but also from the name itself, let us inquire who Nadab was. He was the son of Aaron, but his life was ended when he introduced a strange fire into the tent of God (Num. 3:2-4; cf. 1 Chron. 24:1). So too it is that we find the Lord's Bride — the Church, I mean — introducing into the divine tent a new fire, and not the fire required by the law. What is more, she took this fire from the Bridegroom himself; for "I came to cast fire upon earth, and would that it were already kindled" (Luke 12:49)! Introducing this new fire into the divine tent through the New Covenant, he cries out and says, "The old things have passed away; behold, all things have become new" (2 Cor. 5:17)! Rightly, then, does he call her "daughter of Nadab," in that she offered the sacrifice owed by human beings with the new fire. . . .

Previously the Bridegroom praised the Bride starting from her topmost part. In the present case, however, he starts from her feet and her sandals and works up to the hair of her head. And after her sandals and her feet, he marvels not at her **thighs** but at the **proportions of** her **thighs**, and says that they are like bracelets made by an artisan. For just as the latter, he says, have their stones fixed in the gold with perfect harmony, so that those who see them marvel not only at the materials of the gold and the stones but also at the skill of the goldsmith, so too each of the parts of practical virtue is adorned with harmony and proportion. For **thighs** understood figuratively signify practical virtue, because when by their means we make a journey we will what we are doing.

Thus the Bridegroom, marveling at the Bride, starts from the practical and progresses to contemplation, whereas at the beginning of the Song he took the opposite course (cf. 4:1-5). There he started with contemplation and proceeded to practice. For, he said, **Your eyes are doves**, referring in this way to the spiritual character of the soul's eye. Here, however, he marvels first at her practical virtue — and with entire justification. For when first we are enlightened [at baptism], and open the previously shut eyes of the soul, and take in the divine light, we are supported by faith. Then, in this manner, we undertake the way of practical virtue. This explains why, when he is composing his initial commendation, the Bridegroom starts from the eyes, which are the first to receive healing. Now, however, since the Bride's beauty has been perfected, he starts from the bottom with practical virtue, and progresses to contemplation while praising the loveliness of the Bride's form.

First of all he praises her **feet** and her **sandals**, and then **the proportions of** her **thighs**, that is to say, each of the things that have come to pass. But after the **thighs**, the **navel**. For **Your navel**, he says, **is like a finely wrought bowl that never lacks mixed wine.** Let us, then, set forth — if it seems appropriate — what was said about the navel of Judea by the God of the universe through the prophet Ezekiel. For divulging her licentiousness, and making display of her impiety, just as we related in the first book, God says to the prophet, "Testify to Jerusalem regarding her transgressions, and say this: 'Thus says the Lord to Jerusalem, "Your root and your birth were from the land of Canaan, your father was an Amorite, and your mother a Hittite. And as for your birth, on the day on which you were brought forth, your navel string was not cut"'" (Ezek. 16:1-4). To Jerusalem, then, what he says is "Your navel string was not cut," while to our Bride he says, **Your navel is like a finely wrought bowl that never lacks mixed wine.** For she who was brought forth out of Egypt did not cut her navel string, but drew from Egypt, as by way of a root, the iniquity of ungodliness. Our Bride, however, did not simply cut her navel string, but so deepened the cut that the entire root of idolatry was drawn out, with the result that her navel is likened to **a finely wrought bowl** and contains an unfailing supply of the **mixed wine** of joyfulness, and she never lacks the heart gladness that has been brought forth within her as the child of godliness.

Furthermore, **Your belly is a heap of grain fenced in by lilies.** That is, "The storehouses of your soul are full of hidden mysteries, whose sweet smell is as yet known only to the immature and to babes." For, he says, it is **fenced in by lilies,** in order that by means of the fence we may apprehend that something is hidden there and, by means of the lilies, perceive the sweet smell that is spread abroad from it.

Then: **Your two breasts are like two fawns, twins of a gazelle,** for the founts of your teaching, which pour forth new streams, teach sharp-sightedness and spiritual insight. For the gazelle takes its name from its sharp-sightedness, and the word "fawn" signifies something new.

Your neck is like an ivory tower. For by taking my yoke upon it, it is set free of its pitch-dark color and made white. It is also, like a tower, fearsome to enemies and, for its shining, much desired by friends.

And next: **Your eyes are like pools in Heshbon, in the gates of the daughter of a multitude.** In translating this, Aquila writes "thought" instead of "Heshbon." It follows that the Bridegroom is teaching that the vision of godly souls is **pools** that are fed by divine streams and are ceaselessly overflowing, in that through many **gates,** that is to say, mouths (for in figurative language he calls mouths **gates**), they take in the rivers: from the great Moses, and from Joshua the son of Nun and Samuel the prophet, and from David, the prophet and king, and from Isaiah and Jeremiah and Daniel and Ezekiel, and from the Twelve Prophets, and from the divine Gospels, and from the holy apostles, and from the teachers that came after them, they take in the streams of edification. That is why the Bridegroom says, **Your eyes are like pools in Heshbon, in the gates of the daughter of a multitude.** "For the insights of your soul, and the abundance of godly thoughts, are like pools that take in water from many sources, since you welcome the streams of the teaching from many mouths."

There follows: **Your nose is like a tower of Lebanon, looking upon the face of Damascus.** For Judea's **nose,** on account of its disobedient and headstrong behavior, received the threat of the law as a ring to be, so to speak, its bit and bridle, just like a butting bull, since "like a frenzied heifer, Israel is frantic" (Hos. 4:16 LXX). On the other hand, the Bride's **nose,** he says, **is like a tower of Lebanon looking upon the face of Damascus.** For it is elevated and lofty, and it takes in the sweet smell of the realm on high. Attached to the Bridegroom's perfume, she cries out, **We will run after you, toward the fragrance of your perfumes** (1:3-4). That is why she is likened to a tower set atop Mount Lebanon, **looking upon** Damascus's **face**. For seeing that, according to the blessed Paul, the Devil disguises himself as an angel of light (cf. 2 Cor. 11:14) and takes the shape of a spiritual perfume, the Bride's **nose** must of necessity "keep awake and be sober" (1 Thess. 5:6) and look upon **the face of Damascus**, lest she be deceived and abandon the true perfume and follow after that which is counterfeit and illusory. And the Holy Scripture frequently says "Damascus" when it means Gentiles and the ungodliness that then prevailed. Thus the blessed Isaiah prophesied about the birth of the Lord and spoke in the person of the Holy Spirit: "I went in to the prophetess, that is, the Virgin, and she conceived in her womb and bore a son." Then he adds: "And the Lord said to me, "Call his name 'Swiftly strip the prey, plunder speedily'; for before the child knows how to call 'Mother' or 'Father,' he will carry off the power of Damascus and the spoils of Samaria in the face of the king of the Assyrians" (Isa. 8:3-4). This means that when he is a child he will destroy the one who is figuratively called "king of the Assyrians," that is, the Devil. He will carry off "the power of Damascus," that is, he will break up the power of idolatry and will himself become ruler of those who are in captivity to the Devil. For it says, "He will carry off the power of Damascus and the spoils of Samaria." When he has liberated both those who are Jews and those who are Gentiles, and delivered them from error, and destroyed the tyrant, he will make them his own subjects. Rightly, then, does he say to the Bride, **Your nose is like a tower of Lebanon, looking upon the face of Damascus.** So take care that the Devil with his imitation of things divine does not deceive you, and resist his lie with the truth.

Then he says, **Your head is like Carmel**, which means "Filled up with all good things." For the God of the universe too says this when through the prophet he rebukes the folly of the Jews: "And I brought you into Carmel to eat of its fruit and of its good things" (Jer. 2:7 LXX). Therefore he says, "**Your head** is similar to **Carmel**, which gives birth to every kind of good thing and bears every fruit for me, its cultivator."

Then there is added: **And the plaited hair of your head is like scarlet, a king tied up in its runnings.** "For earlier on your hair was loosed and for that reason compared to **flocks of goats that have been revealed in Gilead** (4:1); now, however, it is plaited, and not only has it been plaited, but it has been treated with a wondrous dye, and your locks are likened to a king that has put on scarlet and is running back and forth in all directions." When he speaks of a plaiting together of hair that is likened to imperial scarlet he means teaching that is put together and set out coherently and harmoniously, and adorned with the blood of Christ. For no king attired in a robe of imperial scarlet shines in the same way as a teacher of godliness who weaves together the proclamation of the knowledge of God and sets it out for those who are nurtured by the truth.

(3) Apponius

How lovely are your steps in sandals,
    O daughter of the prince!

As I see it, **daughter of the prince** means the people that was set far from knowledge of the divine law and from the places where human redemption was celebrated, and so was summoned in the farthest North by teachers who came from that people which is called **sister** and **close one**, and, coming by faith in God the Almighty, "has been brought near in the blood of Christ" (Eph. 2:13). She has laid hold on this by running with the **steps** of faith and by crying out from the ends of the earth, in the voice of one who makes confession of faith, that she too is one who has rejoiced in the bodily presence of Christ. She lived for endless years without the law and had drawn far away from her true Father, her Creator. Furthermore, by sacrificing to demons and not to God, she had lost God as her Father and had been made a **daughter of the prince** of this world. Now, by taking to herself the Word made flesh through the teaching of the apostles or of teachers like them, she has become **dearest among the delights** of that people which gave birth to the apostles.

    Therefore, before all the other parts of her body, praise is first given to the loveliness **of her steps.** The reason is that it was not her "heads," the leaders and kings, who were first converted to the teaching of the apostles, but those who, being subject to kings and deprived of all power, are compared to feet. These are praised as **lovely** in that they run in the way of the divine precepts (cf. Ps. 118:32 LXX = 119:32) by furnishing leadership to the other parts of the body; yet they are praised not on the ground of the mere naked power of choice, but as sheltered and protected by the assistance of God's power: **How lovely are your steps in sandals, O daughter of the prince.** Regarding this the prophet has said, "Our help is in the name of the Lord" (Ps. 123:9 LXX = 124:8).

    Through all this we learn that, once they have turned from error to the truth, those who seem lowly in the presence of human persons of high repute are, in the presence of God, picked out as stronger persons who bear up the whole body in its weakness and, further, are revealed to be people that by their example in good works provide leadership even to kings. These folk seem to me to attain, among that people, the first fruits of the praises in virtue of the loveliness of their feet: they are imitators of those feet that, in the person of the prince of the apostles, follow Christ to heaven by their death.

(4) The *Glossa ordinaria*

How lovely are your steps in sandals!

In the earlier descriptions [of the Bride and of the Bridegroom; cf. 4:1-5; 5:11-15], the movement is downward from the top, and praise is accorded only to the upper parts of the body. Here the lower parts are also praised, and the movement is from the lower parts to the higher. The purpose of this is to show that the Church that has been assembled recently from among those who have been in a state of condemnation up till now shall nevertheless possess bodily members that are not unequal to the nobler members. In this description mention is made of **feet** because it is shown that she shall find her first beauty not in the ease and repose that are to come, but in warfare as she joins battle.

(5) Honorius of Autun

Your two breasts are like two fawns,
    twins of a gazelle.

This means: "Those who suck at the two Covenants, which are your breasts, are as zealous in the honoring of God as the two former peoples, Judean and Israelite," who were twins, that is, equal in the law of God, sons of the gazelle, which means the synagogue. He uses **breasts** for those who suck the breasts, the cause for the effect. Or else the **two breasts** are the two commandments of love, while the **two fawns**, the active and the contemplative, are the twin sons of the **gazelle**, that is, the Church.

(6) Bede the Venerable

Your height has been likened to a palm tree,
    and your breasts to grapes . . .
worthy for my Beloved to drink,
    and for his lips and teeth to chew over.

For the **height** of the Church is the rectitude of her good works, by which she disdains to be bent down to earthly lust and lifts herself wholly up to the promised heavenly goods. The apostle issues an admonition on this subject when he says, "Be watchful, stand firm in your faith, be courageous" (1 Cor. 16:13); and the Lord himself says, "I am the Lord who brought you out of the slavery with which the Egyptians oppressed you . . . so that you might walk erect" (cf. Lev. 26:13). Moreover, a palm is put into the hand of a victor; but among the ancients, whoever had conquered in a contest was crowned with a golden palm. Hence the **height** of the Bride is likened to the palm tree because she stands upright in her love of things heavenly, and every effort of believers is bent to thinking on that palm with which as a victor she is to be presented when the contest is over. Likewise, since the palm tree is bitter to the taste in its lower parts but exhibits the beauty and sweetness of its fruit in its topmost parts, the **height** of the Church, or of the soul of any believer whatsoever, is deservedly likened to the palm tree; for on this earth she sustains bitter labors for the Lord's sake, but she hopes that in heaven she will receive from the Lord a most sweet reward. Likewise, since the palm tree is dressed out in long-lived branches and keeps its leaves without replacing them, who cannot see that it contains a type of the **height** of the faith that, in the fluctuating state of the present fading age, always retains the same words of the true confession like leaves that are never going to fall, [and] to the end of the age preserves in her elect the same perfection of works that she commenced at the start, not unlike an adornment of branches?

And your breasts, he says, **have been likened to grapes. Breasts,** as has often been said, means the Church's teachers when they are ministering the milk of elementary instruction to Christ's little ones. The very same breasts, however, are likened to **grapes** when these very teachers further make known, to those to whom the elementary mysteries of his incarnation had been committed, the hidden truths of the divinity by which he is equal to the Father. Previously they had said, "We have determined 'to know nothing among you save Jesus Christ, and him crucified'" (1 Cor. 2:2). Afterward they say the same thing to those capable of deeper matters: "Theirs are the fathers, from whom Christ is descended according to the flesh, who is God over all, blessed forever" (Rom. 9:5).

As to the Bridegroom's words, **I said, I will mount the palm tree, and I will grasp its fruits,** they fit the historical era in which Solomon sang these songs — the era when in the many voices of the prophets the Lord promised that he would come in flesh to redeem the human race, when he predicted that he would, dying of his own free will, mount the tree [and] return victoriously to life when the reign of death had been destroyed. The **fruits** of the palm tree, moreover, which he said he would lay hold on, mean the later glories that followed after his ascent of the cross, that is to say, the splendors of his resurrection and ascension into the heavens, the advent of the Holy Spirit, and the salvation of the believing world. And what follows fits this interpretation nicely:

And your breasts will be like grapes on the vine, because the first teachers of the Church, the apostles, once his passion and resurrection had been completed, received much greater knowledge than they had hitherto possessed, because he appeared after his resurrection and "opened their minds so that they might understand the Scriptures" (Luke 24:45), or because, with the sending of the Spirit down from on high, he imparted to them knowledge of all languages, on the occasion when mockers said falsely, "They are filled with new wine" (Acts 2:13). But they had truly been made **like grapes on the vine,** because by the grace of spiritual gifts they had been made over in virtue of the fulfillment of the truthful teaching in which he said, "New wine is to be put into fresh wineskins, and both are preserved" (Matt. 9:17). What follows, moreover, is consistent with either interpretation, namely:

And the scent of your mouth like that of apples, your throat like the finest wine. By the **scent of** the **mouth** is meant the good repute that belongs to sound speech, but by **throat,** the work of speech dedicated to God. Each of these is worthy of praise in the catholic Church, as well as in any elect soul, because both the speech itself that instructs people when they are present and the good repute of discourse that reaches the absent, whether in written form or through those who have heard it, is known to be full of power and grace. The fact that he compares **the scent of** the Bride's **mouth** and her **throat** to apples and to wine respectively can be clarified thus: apples possess all their virtue in the very fact of being fresh and new, whereas the value of wine depends on its being aged. Consequently it is right that the voice of the Church as she is speaking, and its good repute as disseminated, be compared to these two kinds of things, for it is certain that both its initial form and its matured form provide occasions for admiration. Likewise, since the virtue and glow of the **finest** wine is better than that of **apples,** it is rightly said: **And**

the scent of your mouth like that of apples, your throat like the finest wine. Wine surpasses the pleasure of apples as much as the unmediated message of the holy Church of God excels the good repute that the speech of its hearers can spread concerning it. And when the spoken praise of the Bride had come to the point where her **throat** was said to be like **the best wine**, she snatched the word from the mouth of the Bridegroom, and she was eager to be filled rather with that; for she understood that the expression **finest wine** refers to the word of the gospel, in which alone is found eternal salvation for believers. And she says:

Worthy for my Beloved to drink, and for his lips and teeth to chew over. "The **finest wine**," she says, "to which he compared my throat, is **worthy for my Beloved** himself **to drink** because the word of the gospel that he has deigned to place in my mouth is of such sublimity that it ought not be proclaimed to the world by anyone other than the beloved Bridegroom himself." It was he after all who first appeared in flesh and through the mystery of redemption opened to the human race the way that leads to heaven; he who first proclaimed the mystery of his passion, resurrection, and ascension by which the world was saved, and then left it to those who believe in him to proclaim; he, the saving one, who drank of the chalice and thus presented it to be drunk by the Church. Nor should the words **for his lips and teeth to chew over** seem an absurd expression because they are spoken with regard to wine. To be sure, cud-chewing is more suited to solid food than to drink. In the Bride's figurative speech, however, the **lips** of the Beloved and his **teeth** are used, as shown above, to refer to holy teachers who "chew over" the **finest wine** that he himself drank in the sense that they delight to explore, through plentiful meditation, the word of grace that he taught. . . .

(7) John of Ford

I said, I will mount the palm tree,
   and I will grasp its fruits.

If, alternatively, you should understand the palm tree to be the cross of Christ, on the ground that on the cross he gloriously and powerfully triumphed over our sins and over the author of death; or if you should understand it to represent patience, which is the crown, but the concealed crown, of those engaged in the struggle; or should you take it to represent love, as I did in the previous sermon — I would be sure that you were not making a mistake. Each of these identifications has good grounds to support it, and in the end they all come to the same point. But let us for the time being understand "palm tree" to mean the cross, an interpretation that both makes plain sense to the unprejudiced mind and points to a hidden profundity of unfathomable Wisdom.

The words are: **I said, I will mount the palm tree, and I will grasp its fruits.** This is the word of the all-powerful Word, a word of great counsel (cf. Isa. 11:2), a word that reflects an eternal purpose, a word concerning the redemption of his Bride that — like the most loyal of physicians, or, better still, the sweetest of Bridegrooms — he shared with his Father from before the ages, treating of the remedy before his patient succumbed to illness.

I said, I will mount the palm tree, and I will grasp its fruits: that is his word. And what a good word it is, what a sweet word, surpassing any speech or thought whatever — inconceivable save as erupting from the depths of the Father's being into the depths of the Son's, and uttered in the same way by the Son to the Father! So great is it that it is a matter of immense merit simply to believe it, a source of great blessedness not to be offended by it, and a matter of supreme wisdom not to be blinded to it. Hear the apostle: "We preach Christ crucified, to Jews an offense, and to Gentiles, foolishness" (1 Cor. 1:23). **I will mount the palm tree**, he says: "He who descended is the same one who also ascended" (Eph. 4:10) — and it is my view that this descent of his occurred when he ascended the palm tree.

At any rate, it was from the time when "The Word became flesh" (John 1:14) that the Lord Jesus took up his cross, being from that point on, surely, "a man of sorrows and acquainted with grief" (Isa. 53:3). In my view, the Evangelist conveyed precisely this by saying, "The Word became flesh," for by the word "flesh" was meant his ability to suffer and to share with others in suffering. For what in the whole creation is more fragile than flesh, or more tender in its susceptibilities than flesh? Thus fragility bespeaks suffering, while tenderness reflects sharing with others in suffering; and the cross of Christ is put together out of these two as if they were two lengths of wood. For the true cross of Christ, as Gregory [the Great] tells us, is suffering and sharing the suffering of others — that is to say, in the body's affliction and in the mind's sharing of others' suffering — as long as this sort of cross is borne for the sake of Christ and in accordance with Christ's manner of bearing it. . . .

Further, it may be that he chose to be arrested and crucified in a garden (cf. John 18:1; 19:41) in order to point to the grace that was flowering in his joyous soul — and also so that he might, after that, be able to exhort the Bride to do the same sort of thing when she was in need or trouble, and so say to her, **I have come into my garden, my sister, my Bride; I have mixed my myrrh with my spices** (5:1). Jesus was arrested, then, not because Judas and the Jews had mutually agreed upon this, but because he himself had said, **I will mount the palm tree, and I will grasp its fruits**. That is why he was betrayed and arrested, held and tied up, taken away and put on exhibit, mocked and whipped, tried and condemned, crucified, killed, and buried.

This means that the Wisdom of God was betrayed, the Power of God was arrested; the One who contains all things (cf. Wisdom 1:7) was constrained; the One who holds the heavens in his hand (cf. Isa. 40:12) was tied up; the One who is never absent anywhere was taken away; the One who is present everywhere was put on exhibit; holiness was mocked; innocence was whipped; the One to whom justice belongs was put on trial; the sole righteous One was condemned; the One who is the God of glory was crucified; the One who is the life of those who live was killed; the One who is the salvation of the dead was buried. Behold, such are the ascents of this palm tree; and the One who said, **I will mount the palm tree**, had planned them in his heart from the beginning. Now he mounts the palm tree openly, in the sight of all, having been "lifted up" (cf. John 12:32) upon the cross that he had borne from his very conception, as has been said.

When he had been "lifted up," then, and elevated to its highest peak, he took possession of the fruit he had previously desired. Blessed is the fruit of this tree; anyone who tastes of it shall be given life's own life and shall not die. The fruit of Adam's transgression was death, for flesh and for troubled soul alike, and in the end descent to the underworld. Our first parents had more than enough of this twofold fruit of their own making, and — alas! — "they have had more than enough children and have left the remains of this fruit for their little ones" (Ps. 16:14 Vg = 17:14).

On the other hand, the One who mounted the palm tree took from it fruit of a very different sort — the fruit of joy and of immortality. To be sure, the afflictions of the world below laid siege to the soul of Jesus as he went down to its depths; but it was not possible for them to confine him and keep him in custody, nor was it possible for the flesh conceived of the Virgin and united to the Word of God to be long held captive by death. This is why he said to his Father, "For you will not leave my soul in the underworld, nor will you give your holy one to see corruption" (Ps. 15:10 Vg = 16:10). . . .

But this twofold death has already been partially "swallowed up" in the "victory" (1 Cor. 15:54) of Christ's resurrection, and on the Last Day it will be fully swallowed up; and . . . the apostle . . . scoffs at it when he says, "O death, where is your victory? O death, where is your sting" (1 Cor. 15:55)? . . . Furthermore, the Lord refers to this twofold death when he promises the righteous person that he "shall not be hurt by the second death" (Rev. 2:11). He who is the life of the living and the resurrection of the dead tasted both of these deaths — by his dying and by his descent to the underworld; by tasting it he chews it up, by chewing it he swallows it up, and in this way both deaths are "swallowed up in victory." Therefore, there is, after the twofold death, a twofold fruit of the resurrection: an endless joy that fills the soul to its brim, and a perfect incorruption that restores the body. . . .

Song 7:11-14

SEPTUAGINT	VULGATE

7:11 I belong to my Kinsman,
    and his turning is toward me.
	7:10 I belong to my Kinsman,
	    and his turning is toward me.

12 Come, my Kinsman,
    let us go out into the field,
    let us dwell among the villages.
	11 Come, my Beloved,
	    let us go out into the field,
	    let us stay among the villages.

13 Let us go early into the vineyards,
 	
    let us see if the vine has budded,
  if the bud has blossomed,
    if the pomegranate has flowered.
  There I shall give you my breasts.
	12 Let us rise in the morning early
	        [and go] to the vineyards,
	      let us see if the vine has flowered,
	    if the flowers are bringing forth fruit,
	      if the pomegranates have flowered.
	    There I shall give you my breasts.

14 The mandrakes give off their
        fragrance,
    and over our doors all fruits.
  New things in addition to old
    have I kept for you, my Kinsman.
	13 Mandrakes have given off their
	        fragrance
	      in our gates;
	    I have saved for you, my Beloved,
	      all apples, new and old.

In these four verses, the Bride is speaking, and the key question posed for interpreters was what is meant by the Bride's leading her Beloved into the "field" and "villages" and "vineyards" — terms that suggest a rural setting and a humble, not to say unsophisticated and deprived, population. Not surprisingly, then, the various exegeses stress how the perfected soul encourages the coming of the Word of God to the "weak" (Ambrose) or to deprived outsiders living in "the life-world of the nations" (Apponius), or to "poor and insignificant" souls (Theodoret).

In examining these materials, the reader should note that the "palm" was, in the ancient Mediterranean world, a symbol of victory — especially of victory in athletic contests and chariot races; and it is interesting to see how for Ambrose the image of a palm evokes the idea of a chariot, which in turn leads him to recollect a well-known image of Plato (Phaedrus 246Aff.) as portraying "chariot races of souls."

266

It is also worth noting that the mandrake plant — often associated in the ancient world with (sleep-inducing) belladonna — has a root that characteristically took the shape of a headless stick-man: a circumstance that Honorius exploits in his account of the meaning of 7:14.

(1) Ambrose of Milan

I belong to my Kinsman,
   and his turning is toward me.

Christ . . . brings the Bride to the place where the palm of victory is found when he says to her, **How fair and pleasing you have become, O love, in your delights! Your stature is like that of a palm tree.** And she for her part says, **I said, I will mount the palm tree.** But further: love itself is the palm tree, for it is in its own right the fullness of victory. Let us run, then, that we may grasp it (cf. 1 Cor. 9:24); let us run that we may attain victory. The person who attains victory climbs up the palm tree and eats of its fruit. The person who attains victory no longer runs in the race but is seated, as it is written: "He who conquers, I will grant him to sit with me on my throne, as I myself conquered and am seated with my Father on his throne" (Rev. 3:21). This explains why philosophers have given those accounts of chariot races of souls, but they could not for all that win the palm because their souls did not know the loftiness and height of the Word.

This soul, though, in whom the Word lived and dwelt, knew it, for she says, **I belong to my Kinsman, and his turning is toward me.** She has repeated this idea three times, though in different ways, in the Song of Songs. At the beginning she says, **My Kinsman belongs to me, and I belong to him; he shepherds his flock among the lilies, until the day dawns and the shadows depart** (2:16). Then she says, **I belong to my Kinsman, and my Kinsman belongs to me; he grazes his flock among the lilies** (6:3). Then at the end she says, **I belong to my Kinsman, and his turning is toward me.** In the first case, the reference is to the soul's initial schooling — that is why the words **My Kinsman belongs to me** are put first; for when he is manifesting himself, the soul too has taken on a desire to cling to God in love. In the next case, the reference is to the soul's progress; and in the third, to its perfection. In the first case, as it were in her initial schooling, the soul still sees **shadows** that have not been driven away by the revelation of the Word as he draws near, and therefore up to this point the light of the gospel has not shone forth. In the second case, without the confusion occasioned by **shadows**, she enjoys godly scents. In the third case, already perfected, she supplies to the Word a place of rest within herself, so that he may be turned to her and lean his head upon her and take his rest. Now she enjoys the recompense that earlier she had sought without being able to find it, and she invites him into her **field**, saying, **Come, my Kinsman, let us go out into the field, let us rest in the villages.**

Previously she invited him into her garden. Here she invites him into a **field** that contains not only the beauty of flowers but also wheat and barley — that is, the underpinnings of the more substantive virtues — so that he may look upon his fruits. **Let us**

rest, she says, **in the villages** to which Adam, when he had been put out of Paradise, was banished. In them he took rest, but he worked the land. It is plain, moreover, why she wanted him to go out into the field, namely, that as the Good Shepherd he might tend his sheep — lift up the weary, summon the wanderers back. For although that soul kept both new and ripened fruits for him, nevertheless there are some that are still like lambs, who have to be fed with a drink of milk. Therefore, as a perfected soul, she intervenes not for her own sake but for that of others, so that he may go forth from the bosom of the Father, so that he may come forth like a bridegroom emerging from his chamber and run his course (cf. Ps. 18:6 LXX = 19:5); so that he may not linger upon the mystic throne of the Father and in that brightness where the weak are unable to follow, but that he may be received and led into the Bride's house and her private place, that, being outside himself, he may be within us, may be our Mediator even though he be not seen by us. . . .

(2) Apponius

I [give] to my Beloved,
   and his turning [is] toward me.
Come, my Kinsman,
   let us go out into the field,
let us dwell among the villages.
Let us go early into the vineyards.

This statement is understood to come from that soul whom, by their admiration, the daughters, queens, and concubines joined in praising. To her **Beloved** she has offered the entire depth of her love and her entire will, to the point that she would make room in her thoughts for love of nothing else whatever, but would cling wholly to him. In return for this gift, **his turning toward** her, which came about through the fellowship of the incarnation, is so truly realized that "the Word became flesh" (John 1:14); and this is what she refers to now when she says, **his turning is toward me**, and in her the one Son of God is made known. In this mystery, the prophecy contained in the verse before us is seen to be fulfilled. **I [give] to my Beloved** — what do I give, if not a sanctified will? **And his turning is toward me** — and what **turning** is this unless, in accordance with his infinite goodness and his redemption of the created order, God deigned to become a human being, so that the conquered flesh, holding to the way of righteousness, might at some point overcome the Enemy, and a human being might redeem humanity — regarding which the prophet said, "A brother does not redeem, a human being redeems" (Ps. 48:8 LXX = 49:7)?

Therefore this unspotted soul, united to God, urges him that he would deign to **go out**, by way of the word of his disciples, from the dwelling place of the synagogue and the city of the Hebrew nation, in which he dwelt by his self-manifestation and by their knowledge of him, **into the field** of the great multitude of the peoples for the sake of redeeming the other nations — the nations that did not see him in the flesh; just as he declares in the Gospel when he says to the Father, "I do not pray for these only, but also for those who shall believe in me through their word" (John 17:20). By these words she urges him in particular to **go out into the** uncultivated **field**, the thorn-ridden world of the nations, to **dwell among the** ruined **villages**, the assemblies of the peoples in which they worshiped creatures instead of the Creator (Rom. 1:25), but which now, with Christ the Son of God living among them and dwelling with them, have become villages that are built up by the teaching of the apostles, that is to say, assemblies of the truth, homes for Churches, where now God the Father dwells in Christ through the Holy Spirit.

And when the Word goes out into the night of ignorance, the morning light dawns through the aforesaid teaching, pointing to the light's entrance. By this light, or in it, a salvific care and cultivation is brought to bear, whether upon the ruined **villages** mentioned above or upon the **field** that is full of brambles — just as she now says, **Come, my Beloved, let us go out into the field, let us dwell among the villages.**

When therefore the Most High was about to construct the fabric of the world, which he purposed, for his praise, to fill with human beings made after his image, he ordained in his providence — already at that point — chieftains of the angels by whom the nations, entrusted to the precise number of them, would be governed. When, plainly, to these chieftains the peoples of the nations had been distributed, out of their number, as the lot fell, Jacob became his portion and Israel "his allotted heritage" (cf. Deut. 32:8-9). Propelled by their own will, these chieftains turned to tyranny and drew a great part of his portion away into their own through the worship of idols. This lost portion of his heritage he sought out, coming as it were after many ages to the city of his portion, Jerusalem, by being born of the Virgin. He found it by dying, the spotless one for those who had been defiled; by rising from the dead, ascending the heavens, and sending the Paraclete he restored the multitude of believers, now found and released from the hands of the chieftains, to his own rule, even as he says: "The Son of Man came to seek what had been lost" (Luke 19:10), and "I was not sent save to the lost sheep of the house of Israel" (Matt. 15:24).

For he went out **into the** aforesaid **field** of the nations through the coming of the Holy Spirit, who by the fire of his own power and the luster of the apostles at once changed the night of ignorance into the light of morning by knowledge of the truth, and banished the thorns of unseemly thoughts and revelries from the aforesaid **field**. In these ways he did indeed **go out into the field**, that is, the life-world of the nations, from a people that was arrogant and took for its own the wisdom of the law of Moses, from the city where "he came to his own, and his own received him not" (John 1:11).

And when his own city had refused to receive him — which he reproached in a lament: "Jerusalem, Jerusalem, that kills the prophets and stones those who are sent to you" (Matt. 23:37) — he went out **into the field**, he dwells **among the villages**, which means among the simplest of human minds, minds that lack any eloquence of speech, in which, once the darkness of ignorance had withdrawn, the morning light, knowledge of the truth, soon began to rise because of the presence of the Holy Spirit — that is, the voice of the teachers; as she says, **Let us go early into the vineyards.**

(3) Theodoret of Cyrus

Come, my Kinsman [or Beloved],
   let us go out into the field,
   let us dwell among the villages.
Let us go early into the vineyards,
   let us see if the vine has budded,
if the bud has blossomed,
   if the pomegranate has flowered.
There I shall give you my breasts.
The mandrakes give off their fragrance,
   and over our doors all fruits.
New things in addition to old,
   my Kinsman, have I kept for you.

The Bride urges the Bridegroom to exercise care for souls that do not count for much and are also lowly, souls that he calls **field** and **villages** because they are poor and insignificant. For she does not say, "Let us go into the city," but **let us go out into the field, let us dwell among the villages. Let us go early into the vineyards, let us see if the vine has budded.** "Let us," she says, "watch over those that have only just now received the message of the gospel, to see **if the vine has budded.**"

Let us also examine those that are at a more advanced stage, "those that have not only budded but bloomed," whom in this verse she calls **blossomed.**

If the pomegranate has flowered: "whether in some souls there has appeared the beginning of love. For we have an obligation to look into things, and to provide all appropriate care. For in doing this, I shall be of service to you." **There**, she says, **I shall give you my breasts.** For you make your own whatever is meant for them, and say, "Inasmuch as you have done it for one of the least of these, you have done it for me" (Matt. 25:40).

The mandrakes give off their fragrance. The mandrake has the power to bring on sleep, as the physicians say. Since, then, we are commanded to "put to death" our "earthly members" (Col. 3:5), not in order to hand over the members themselves to death, but in order to reveal them as dead to wicked doings, it is right for her to make mention of the **mandrake** here and say, **The mandrakes give off their fragrance**, which means: "The human race has begun to fall asleep to sins." And just as those who have drunk the mandrake do not feel the motions of their bodies, so too those who drink of the cup of godly teaching are eager to put the passions to sleep.

But it is not **the mandrakes** alone that **give off their fragrance**, but also **all fruit trees over our doors**; for those who receive our teaching bear all kinds of fruit. **New things in addition to old, my Kinsman**, all that my mother has given me, **have I kept for you.** For both the commandments of the Old Covenant and the counsels of the New Covenant, which I have received from my mother, the grace of the Holy Spirit — these have I kept for you, and I have kept the deposit inviolate. What the blessed Paul writes to Timothy fits in with what is said here: "I have fought the good fight, I have finished the race, I have kept the faith. Henceforth there is laid up for me the crown of righteousness, which the Lord, the righteous judge, will award to me on that day" (2 Tim. 4:7-8). And again, there is that which the Lord says in the Gospel: "Every scribe who has been trained for the kingdom of heaven is like a householder who brings out of his treasure what is new and what is old" (Matt. 13:52).

(4) The *Glossa ordinaria*

**Let us see if the vine has flowered
[and] whether the flowers give birth to fruit.**

So that I, who am a guide of beginners, may be able to discern how those who belong to me are developing, to what extent they have made progress, so that I may understand in what way they need to be nourished.

The point is not just to see whether the vines are in bloom, but whether the flowers are becoming strong enough to bring forth fruit; for there is nothing wonderful about people's getting a start on good things, but it is wonderful indeed if, with a right intention, they persevere in doing good.

(5) Honorius of Autun

There I shall give you my breasts.

That is, in that field I shall bring forth, to honor you, all the teaching of both Covenants — which are my breasts — in order that beginners in the faith may suck from them the milk of the teaching. And after I pressed out what is in them, **the mandrakes gave off their fragrance in our gates.** Now the mandrake, as has been said, is a plant that has the form of a human body, though lacking a head, and it has many medical uses. What it stands for is the Gentile constitution, which is endowed with human reason, and also has many useful ideas to convey, but does not possess Christ, who is the "head" of believers. Upon this nature the Bridegroom sets a golden head, inasmuch as he publishes to it his Deity, which transcends all things just as gold does all the other metals, crowns it with glory and honor, and joins it to himself by the splendor of the vision of himself. Thus the **mandrakes** without heads represent the pagans apart from Christ their head, but after their own head, the Antichrist, has been displaced. These **gave off their fragrance in our gates,** that is, they provided an example of good works in the virtues by which one enters heaven for the sake of the reward of beatitude. Or else the Church's **gates** are the prophets and apostles, and in these gates **the mandrakes gave off their fragrance,** in that the pagans, once converted to Christ, spread abroad, in the teachings of the apostles and in place of heretical teachings, the renown of good belief.

"Not only **shall I give you my breasts,** but also **all fruits, new as well as old, my Kinsman, have I kept for you.**" That is to say, "Not only have I set forth the teaching of both laws to those who were then being converted, but I have also preserved for you all the works of the apostles of the new law, and all the works of the prophets of the old law," which is to say that I have done so by explaining them on your behalf to these folk — and not only the works of the aforementioned, but I have also narrated your own deeds in order; and how I wish that I had seen them with my eyes in the way that they did!

Song 8:1-4

SEPTUAGINT

8:1 Who will give you, my Kinsman,
     as a suckling at the breast
     of my mother?
Finding you outside, I will kiss you,

     and they will not look down on
     me.
2 I will take you up and bring you
     into the house of my mother,
     and into the chamber of her
     that conceived me.
I will give you to drink of spiced
     wine,
     of the juice of pomegranates.

3 His left hand is under my head,
     and his right hand will embrace
     me.
4 I adjure you, daughters of Jerusalem,
     by the powers and strengths of
     the field,
     that you stir not up nor awaken
     love until it please.

VULGATE

8:1 Who will give you to me, my Brother,
     sucking the breasts of my mother,

     so that I may find you outside and
     kiss you,
     and let no one despise me.

2 I will seize you and bring you
     into the house of my mother,
     and into the bedroom of her
     that bore me.
There you will teach me, and I will
     give you a drink of spiced wine,
     and the new wine of my
     pomegranates.

3 His left hand is under my head,
     and his right hand will embrace
     me.
4 I adjure you, daughters of Jerusalem,

     not to rouse up my beloved,
     nor make her wake up,
     until she herself wills it.

*These first four verses of chap. 8 include two that repeat the wording of an earlier
set of lines in the Song: 8:3-4 repeats 2:6-7, with its description of the Bridegroom's embrace and its prohibition addressed to "the daughters of Jerusalem."
The opening verses (8:1-2), on the other hand, introduce material that is quite
new: the picture of the Bridegroom as the Bride's suckling brother, and the pic-*

ture of the Bride as bringing her brother into her mother's dwelling to drink "spiced wine." Of these two images, the first seems to require the greatest exegetical ingenuity. For Bede, it points to the way in which the Word of God shares the nature — and is therefore the sibling — of Old Testament believers; while the "mother" who suckles him is not Mary (as one might expect) but simply humanity or human nature. Theodoret's exegesis too is governed by the idea that brother and sister share something in common; but in his case, what is shared is the Holy Spirit, the gift received at baptism both by Jesus and by believers; and the "mother," it seems, is the heavenly Jerusalem, the archetype of the Church. Honorius in his anagogical treatment of the passage sees this whole scene as a portrayal of the joys of the age to come.

(1) Theodoret of Cyrus

Who will give you, my Kinsman,
  as a suckling at the breast of my mother?
Finding you outside, I will kiss you,
  and they will not look down on me.
I will take you up and bring you
    into the house of my mother,
    and into the chamber of her that conceived me.
I will give you to drink of spiced wine,
  of the juice of pomegranates.

For he too, in his human reality, received the entire grace of the Holy Spirit. For it says, "The child Jesus grew and was strengthened by the Spirit, and the grace of God was upon him" (Luke 1:80 and 2:40). Therefore the Bride, astonished in the face of this inexpressible love for humankind, says, "You too have suckled at the breasts of my mother."

But in order that we may preserve the sequence and arrangement of what has been said, let us begin from a little before this and summarize the sense of the passage. "I received," says she, "not only **the new things** but also **the old things** of my mother, and I will keep them for you" (7:14). But you, in your great love of humanity, and taking on my nature, purposed to suckle at the same breasts as I, in order to demonstrate, in this respect too, that we are brother and sister. You suckled, however, not out of need, but to teach me how to suckle to my benefit, and through what sort of nipple to draw in grace. The reason why you came forward to be baptized was not to wipe off the dirt of your sins (for you "did no sin, nor was guile found in" your "mouth" [1 Pet. 2:22; Isa. 53:9]), nor was it to receive the grace of the all-holy Spirit (for of that you were full); but you show me what the gifts of baptism are and in what manner to suck the grace of the Spirit. The reason why the Spirit came down in the form of a dove was not to furnish you with what you did not possess (for you were full of his gifts), but so that you might show me what the gift of baptism is.

Hence I say in a mood of amazement, **Who will give you, my Kinsman, as a suck-**

ling at the breast of my mother? Drawn by this love of yours for the human race, **finding you outside, I will kiss you, and they will not look down on me. I will take you up and bring you into the house of my mother, and into the chamber of her that conceived me. I will give you to drink of spiced wine, of the juice of pomegranates.** For drunken with your love, when I find you, I will embrace you and kiss you, not only in the chamber and in the hall but also in the marketplace and in public. And those who see me behaving in this way will find no fault with me, acquainted as they are with the fire of love.

Thence, having taken you up, **I will bring you into the house of my mother, and into the chamber of her that conceived me.** But what is the **house** of the all-holy Spirit (for it is he that brought the Bride to birth) if it is not the divine temple that images the "Jerusalem that is above" (Gal. 4:26)? Those who enter it engage in free and frank converse with the Bridegroom because they have assumed the status of the Bride. And there, she says, **I will give you to drink of spiced wine, of the juice of** my **pomegranates.** By **spiced wine** is meant teaching that has been prepared with divine grace; and to the extent that it is **spiced,** it is fragrant. **The juice of pomegranates** means the benefit that is born of the fruits of love.

When the Bride has said these things to the Bridegroom, she speaks to the young maidens, saying, **His left hand is under my head, and his right hand will embrace me.** "I am above threats of punishment, and I pluck the blessings of his right hand; for this reason he places his left hand at my head and embraces me with his right hand."

(2) Bede the Venerable

Who will give you to me, my Kinsman,
    as a suckling at the breast of my mother?
And I will find you outside and kiss you,
    and now let no one despise me.
I will seize you and bring you
    into the house of my mother.

This Song testifies — in many of, indeed all, its verses, and in this place above all — that it intends nothing fleshly or literal when it speaks, but wants to be understood spiritually and typically in its entirety. For what woman can there be who would suddenly wish that her lover and beloved should not be the youth he had been but should be born all over again as her baby brother, and that he whom she had been accustomed to love as an adult might be nourished as an infant at the breasts of her mother?

The voice that speaks here, accordingly, is that of the righteous of olden times. They desired to see the Lord and Savior — whom they believed to be consubstantial with the Father and the Holy Spirit in his divinity, and whom they worshiped with the service due him — in the dress of a human being as one who is consubstantial with other human beings, so that they might see the things they had learned of through prophecy come true in the very person they had foretold. They desired to hear that most fitting utterance of their Creator, which he spoke when, with hands extended toward his disciples, he said:

"Behold my mother and my brethren" (Mark 3:34). They wanted to receive the wonderful announcement that those same disciples received after the triumph of the resurrection: "Go and tell my brethren to go to Galilee, and there they will see me" (Matt. 28:10) — a witness borne by the Beloved himself, who elsewhere says to his disciples, "Many prophets and righteous men longed to see what you see, and did not see it, and to hear what you hear, and did not hear it" (Matt. 13:17).

As to the words **a suckling at the breast of my mother**, they are not to be understood to refer to the glorious God-bearer herself. She is the one of whom it was truly said, "Blessed is the womb that bore you, and the breasts that you sucked" (Luke 11:27); and regarding her he himself says in a psalm, "From the womb of my mother you are my God" (Ps. 21:11 LXX = 22:10) — which is to say openly, "You who were my Father before the ages are also my God from the moment I began to be a human being." After all, neither Solomon nor any other righteous person of his era could call the blessed Mary his mother, when she was to be born in the world after so long a time. On the contrary, when the synagogue speaks of her mother she means the stuff of human nature — the human nature from which she herself had been born and from which she desired the Redeemer of all to be born and to be fed.

Finding you outside, I will kiss you, and now let no one despise me. The Beloved was truly within because "In the beginning was the Word, and the Word was with God, and the Word was God" (John 1:1); but in order that he might also be found outside, "The Word was made flesh and dwelt among us" (John 1:14). For the patriarchs and prophets alike saw God, but within, which is to say, in the mind's spiritual contemplation and not in the vision of the fleshly eye. They saw him, though, in an image, in the form of an angelic substance, but they were in no wise able to see his very nature, which he manifested through angels in whatever manner he chose. Accordingly, the Lawgiver himself, who merited to hear the words "I will make all my goodness pass before you" (Exod. 33:19), heard, on the other hand, "You will not be able to see my face, for no human being shall see my face and live" (Exod. 33:20). Happy indeed, then, were those who merited to repeat among themselves the words "We have seen the Messiah, which means Christ" (John 1:41); and again, "We have found him of whom Moses in the law and also the prophets wrote, Jesus of Nazareth, the son of Joseph" (John 1:45); for the words of our text — **finding you outside, I will kiss you** — fit such persons perfectly. For the synagogue has kissed the Beloved, once found, in the persons of those who have merited to see him face to face in the truth of the flesh he assumed, those who have merited to speak with him mouth to mouth. For this is the kiss — that is, that most loving gift of his mouth, and the communion of mutual comfort — that the synagogue was seeking above all in this Song when it began with the words, **Let him kiss me with the kiss of his mouth.** Properly, then, does she add in the form of a wish:

And now let no one despise me. For the Church had been despised by outsiders as an insignificant and worthless affair that had been enclosed for a long time within the narrow confines of Judea; but when with the Lord's coming in the flesh it began to spread out through all the nations, it became a source of awe to the world, threatening to fill the entire globe and to drive out the worship of all the gods. . . . The Church had also been despised by the unclean spirits; for they boasted that they had deceived the human race and dragged it down from its celestial homeland into this place of exile and into manifold calamity, and that there had not been a single human being that could exist apart from their universal dominion. But after "the mediator between God and humanity, the man Christ Jesus" (1 Tim. 2:5), came into the world and, when he had been tempted, overcame the very enemy by whose temptation the first-formed human had been defeated, he also went about doing good and curing all who had been oppressed by the Devil, and in the end by dying he destroyed "him who had the power of death" (Heb. 2:14), and bringing with him from the lower world the whole multitude of the righteous who had gone before, he led them with joy to that kingdom which the first-formed human had lost, and on the foreheads of believers he placed the sign of his victory. No longer is it for the unclean spirits to despise the life of good people; for they see themselves vanquished by a human being, and they lament the transfer of the human race to the kingdom that they had lost because of their pride. . . . Hence that ancient multitude of the elect, rightly longing for the advent of the same Lord Jesus, said: **Who will give you to me, my Brother, as a suckling at the breast of my mother? Finding you outside, I will kiss you, and now let no one despise me.**

Here there is appropriately added, **I will take you up and bring you into the house of my mother.** The synagogue speaks these words in the same way as Paul says, "We who are alive, who are left until the coming of the Lord, shall not precede those who have fallen asleep" (1 Thess. 4:15) — Paul who, though he was sure that he could not last in the flesh until the day of judgment, nevertheless, on account of his fellowship with the same body of brethren, joins himself to the number of those who will be found alive in the flesh at the advent of the Judge. And in this text, therefore, the ancient people of God speaks in the person of that portion of it that was going to see him as he appeared in the flesh: **I will take you up and bring you into the house of my mother.** "With open and faithful devotion I shall receive you as you come, and with eager desires I shall embrace your admonitions, await your promises, and, as you are returning to the heavens once the dispensation of the flesh as been completed, I shall precede you with happy torches and proclaim you to all with a joyous voice." For **the house of my mother** means the happiness of the heavenly homeland that human nature was created to inhabit, and into whose perpetual possession, if no one had sinned, the whole human race, without the intervention of death, would have passed from the delights of the Paradise in which the first human was lodged. Therefore the Church promises that she will bring the Lord into this house, not because she is able of her own strength to do this, but because in her prayers she longs that it may come to pass and in her proclamation announces that it is to be accomplished or that it has been accomplished — just as the psalmist could not exalt him to the heavens, but nevertheless said, "I will exalt you, O Lord, because you have made me your own" (Ps. 29:2 LXX = 30:1) — which amounts to saying openly, "Because you have deigned to make my frail nature your own, I publicly make proclamation of your power; for you have glorified this nature by unfaltering delight of the mind."

(3) Honorius of Autun

Who will give you, my Beloved,
   as a suckling at the breast of my mother. . . .

There [in the life of the coming age], she will see Christ in God as her brother, that is, as a human being born of the human race, who has made her his sister, that is, the co-heir of the kingdom. This brother of hers sucks at the breasts of the Church, because the Lord's humanity possesses the joy of the heavenly Jerusalem, that is, of the plenitude of the angels, and communicates it to his own. This brother, whom here she sees **outside** in the flesh, the Church finds within, in the glory of the Father. She kisses him whom she has so long desired, while she is joined to his sweetness in eternal peace. Let none **look down** upon her any longer, for she who here was a reproach for her fellow human beings and an object of contempt for the proud shall be equal to the angels (cf. Luke 20:36 and Matt. 22:30). There the Beloved, whom she long sought but scarcely ever found, she grasps with an everlasting love; and she leads him, as together with him she will enter upon the everlasting marriage, into the **house of her mother** — that is, the heavenly Jerusalem, which is the house of the angelic mother Church — and into **the chamber of her that conceived me,** that is, into the hidden place of the glory of Christ's humanity, which she will see in the glory of the Father. The Christ will teach her that which "no eye has seen, nor ear heard, nor the human heart conceived, which God has prepared for those that love him" (1 Cor. 2:9). There he will give her **a drink of spiced wine and the juice of pomegranates,** which means the full joy of angels and human beings alike. It will be like **wine** and **juice,** which provide the good cheer of the banqueters. . . . There the **left hand** of the Bridegroom will be under her head, since she will see all the world's glory under the power of Christ, who is her head; and his **right hand will embrace** her, since the company of the angels and the concord of the saints, which will be at Christ's right hand at the Judgment, will join her to themselves. In this right hand she rests from all turmoil, and none will waken her from this repose, for none can deprive her of her joy.

Song 8:5-10

SEPTUAGINT

8:5 Who is this woman that is coming
      up, all whitened,
    leaning upon her Kinsman?

  Under the apple tree I awakened you.
  There your mother was in travail
      with you,
    there she who bore you was in
      travail.
6 Set me as a seal upon your heart,
    as a seal upon your arm;
  for love is as strong as death,
    jealousy is as bitter as the grave.

  Its sparks are sparks of fire,
    its flames.
7 Much water cannot quench love,

    and rivers do not wash over it.
  If a man should give the whole of
    his livelihood for love,
    it would be utterly despised.

8 Our sister is little
    and does not have breasts.
  What shall we do for our sister
   on the day on which she is spoken to?
9 If she is a wall,
    let us build silver battlements
      upon it;

VULGATE

8:5 Who is this woman that is coming up
      from the wilderness,
    abounding in delights,
    leaning upon her Beloved?
  I raised you up under an evil tree.
  There your mother was corrupted,

    there she who bore you was
      violated.
6 Set me as a seal upon your heart,
    as a seal upon your arm;
  for love is as strong as death,
    jealousy is as unyielding as
      the grave.
  Its lamps are lamps of fire
    and of flames.
7 Many waters have not been able
    to extinguish love,
    nor shall rivers cover it over.
  If a man were to give all his house-
    hold property for love,
    people would despise him as
      nothing.
8 Our sister is little
    and does not have breasts.
  What shall we do for our sister
    on the day when she is spoken to?
9 If she is a wall,
    let us build silver battlements
      upon it;

and if she is a door,	if she is a door,		

and if she is a door,
    let us fix tablets of cedar upon it.

10 I am a wall,
    and my breasts are like towers,
  I was like one
    who finds peace in his presence.

if she is a door,
    let us strengthen it with cedar
    planks.

10 I am a wall,
    and my breasts are like a tower,
  whence I have become like one
    who seeks peace in his presence.

This is a puzzling passage for several reasons. For one thing, it is difficult to discern in it any line of thought that lends it unity: it can easily strike the reader as a collection of fragments. Moreover, it is never easy to identify the speaker. Thus in the first verse (8:5) there seem to be two speakers — some observer or body of observers, and then, in the second half of the verse, at least possibly, the Bridegroom. But then who is speaking in 8:6? Neither version makes it necessary for a reader to suppose that it is the Bride. And who are the "we" who want to do something for "our sister" (8:8)?

Other difficulties stem from problems of translation. The phrase "all whitened" in the Septuagint version of 8:5 is an error (though an error rooted in a traditional reading of the Hebrew), and the Vulgate is more correct with its "from the wilderness" (though "abounding in delights" is a gratuitous addition). In fact, the first line of 8:5 reproduces exactly the wording of 3:6 above. Again, the Vulgate version of the second half of this verse (8:5), with its talk of an "evil tree," corruption, and violation, derives from a particular way of fixing the Hebrew up to make sense; but the Septuagint version is closer in its effect to the original. It is interesting that John of Ford, even though he employs the Vulgate text, takes the Latin "sub arbore malo" ("under an evil tree") to mean "under the apple tree," and takes "apple tree" to contain an allusion back to 2:3.

Finally, the last sentence of 8:7 is ambiguous: it is not clear whether what is "despised" is the man himself or the property he gives up for love, and this circumstance gives rise to differing interpretations (as Bede carefully notes in the excerpt below).

No doubt the most complicated solution to the problems of the passage comes from Apponius below, who seems to identify the "woman that is coming up" with the lost tribes of Israel, and the observer of her arrival with the human soul of Jesus, which welcomes this arrival as the age to come dawns. Perhaps a more commonsense reading is, not surprisingly, that of Theodoret.

23. Song 8:5-10

(1) Theodoret of Cyrus

Who is this woman that is coming up, all whitened,
    leaning upon her Kinsman?
Under the apple tree I awakened you.
There your mother was in travail with you,
    there she who bore you was in travail!

They do not say "white" but "whitened," for she is black. In the case of the Bridegroom, the Bride says, **My Kinsman is shining white** (cf. 5:10), but not "whitened"; for he is white by nature. She, however, after she had been **made dark (for the sun has looked askance at me** [cf. 1:6]), was whitened, and took on the whiteness of the Bridegroom. Just as, being Light himself, he also fashioned her to be light and called her so; and, being holy himself, made her holy too; and, being resurrection, made her worthy of resurrection — so also he shares with her his native whiteness. That is why the young maidens who see her ask, **Who is this woman that is coming up, all whitened, leaning upon her Kinsman?** For guided by him and led, as it were, by his hand, she makes her ascent into the heavens and her journey toward her Beloved, assisted by her firm faith in him.

    After that the Bridegroom speaks to her and says, **Under the apple tree I awakened you. There your mother was in travail with you, there she who bore you was in travail.** We will grasp the sense of these statements if we recollect what was said by the Bride at the start of the book; for there she said to the Bridegroom, **As an apple tree among the trees of the wood, so is my Kinsman among the sons. In his shadow I rejoiced and sat down, and his fruit was sweet in my throat** (2:3). Now the shadow of the good things to come is the things that have been conferred on us in the present time — for, says the blessed Paul, "now we see as in a mirror, as in an enigma, but then face to face" (1 Cor. 13:12). The Bride therefore wanted to sit in the **shadow** of the Bridegroom, that is to say, in the **shadow** that is the "guarantee" (cf. Eph. 1:14) now given us. Necessarily, then, the Bridegroom says, **Under the apple tree I awakened you . . . , there she who bore you was in travail.** For once we believed the proclamation regarding our Savior, we came forward to God's baptism; and once we had come forward, we attained rebirth. For the grace of the Holy Spirit gave us birth, as the story in Acts attests. For when, says the author, the divine Peter addressed the people and proclaimed the message of the Savior to those who had come, those who heard the word were stunned and said to Peter, "What shall we do to be saved?" And his reply was, "Let each of you believe and be baptized in the name of our Lord Jesus Christ, and you will receive the promise of the Holy Spirit" (Acts 2:37-38). Rightly then does the Bridegroom say to the Bride: **Under the apple tree I awakened you. There your mother was in travail with you, there she who bore you was in travail.** . . .

(2) Apponius

**Who is this coming up from the desert full of delights,
leaning upon my Beloved?**

It is written concerning the Son of God in Isaiah the prophet: "He shall see the fruit of the travail of his soul and be satisfied" (Isa. 53:11). Therefore in the mystery of her suffering — in that most bitter death which is shown, by the utter cruelty of its torments, to have been brought upon her by the godless — this oft-named soul was in travail for the salvation of mortals. And it is plain that the burden of all these labors was borne not by the impassible Deity but by the soul that suffered along with the flesh. Of her it is said at the time of the passion, "My soul is very sorrowful even to death" (Matt. 26:38); and of her the prophet says, "Save my soul from the sword, my darling from the hand of the dog" (Ps. 21:21 LXX = 22:20).

This soul, after the many labors mentioned above — labors that she is shown to have undergone for the benefit of all the nations, at once by her own agency as well as through the apostles and whatever saints one might name, in whose travail hers is carried out — is lodged in secure sleep by her beloved Word of God up until the time of which the apostle spoke when he said, "Let him who restrains do so until it is removed from the midst" (2 Thess. 2:7), the time that we have previously named the unmistakable times of the Antichrist. . . .

And while for a short time that soul finds refreshment in the conversion of the folk that now is the Church throughout the world, I mean the Israel that now dwells within the Christian people, the Beloved leads the folk that under Hoshea the son of Elah, king of Ephraim, was led captive in its ten tribes into Assyria by Shalmaneser king of the Assyrians (cf. 2 Kings 17:1-6), or dispersed among various nations — leads it, as it puts its weight upon him, along the way of ascent **from the desert** (where by its sinning it got itself banished by the Devil) to the place of the kingdom of the knowledge of himself. This folk, set free from the mouth of the demons, and, now that it has come to knowledge of the glory of life everlasting, **abounding in delights**, is **leaning upon** the **Beloved** of the previously mentioned folk, whose person that matchless soul takes to her own mother in this passage.

This soul, while she rests in the deep sleep of safety, wakes from her sleep. She sees this folk putting its weight on him — that is to say, trusting and believing and putting all its hope in the one Redeemer of the world, her **Beloved** — and ascending, by making its way **from the desert** of unbelief. She shows her wonder at its swift conversion from idols to the true God by saying, **Who is this coming up from the desert full of delights, leaning upon my Beloved?** Before its conversion she did not yet know it, but now that it has been converted from the worship of idols and is coming to faith in Christ, she recognizes it by saying, **I raised you up under an evil tree. There your mother was corrupted, there she who bore you was violated.**

We plainly learn in these lines that the folk that **is coming up from the desert** signifies the ten tribes, the kingdom of Ephraim, that were brought by King Shalmaneser into captivity among the Assyrians. The prophet Jeremiah prophesied about them when he said, "A voice is heard on high, lamentation and bitter weeping, the voice of Rachel weeping for her children. She refuses to be comforted for them, because they are not" (Jer. 31:15). The word of God consoles her; it promises that there will be hope as the end approaches: "Thus says the Lord, Let your voice cease from weeping, and your eyes from tears; for your children shall return to their own borders and shall return from the land of the enemy, and there will be hope in your last days, says the Lord." For "hearing, he has heard the migration of Ephraim" (Jer. 31:16-18) — who was the son of Joseph, the son of Rachel, from whose seed came King Hoshea. The prophet then introduces the penitent cry of this folk and says in what follows, "Turn me, and I shall return, since you are the Lord my God. After you turned me, I repented" (Jer. 31:18-19). Then he answers the people in the voice of the Lord, "Set up a mirror for yourself, get hardships ready for yourself, guide your heart in the straight path in which you walk, and return, O virgin Israel" (Jer. 31:21).

The rest of the body of believers is not jealous of her as she returns in the world's end time, leaning upon the Son of God, but wonders at her and says, **Who is this coming up from the desert full of delights, leaning upon my Beloved?** She marvels at her in her ascent as though she were unknown; but now, in the verse that follows, because her faith has been ascertained, she recognizes her. She also recalls that she was once known to her among the fathers; and with her own voice she admonishes her, now that she has been awakened from the deadly sleep of unbelief, to be mindful of the holy faith and its mode of life, and to avoid the wiles of him who, among his evil deeds, **corrupted** her **mother** and **violated her who bore** her by shedding the blood of innocents. Thus she says, **I raised you up under an evil tree.** That is, by her teaching she called her, and by her example wakened her as she was sleeping under the the power of the Devil, who is the tree of death, and given to the works of death, which is the deadly sleep.

For Christ is the tree of eternal life — "to whom," says Jeremiah, "we have said, 'We shall live in your shadow among the nations'" (Lam. 4:20); and the Church says in response, **I sat under his shadow, which I had desired, and his fruit was sweet in my throat** (2:3). By the same token, the Devil, as we have said, is known to be the tree of death, and the teaching is that he is genuinely evil both in fact and in name. Should any come under the shadow of enslavement to him, there is no doubt that they will be handed over, shut up as it were within a pile of logs, to the fire of Gehenna for food. Seduced at one time by the death-dealing delight of this shadow, the Hittite nation was deprived by its own choice of its rational faculty. It nourished this people of which we are speaking on its abominations with the milk of poisoned teaching and dissolute example, even as we hear in the reproach of the prophet Ezekiel: "Son of man, make known to Jerusalem her abominations and say to her, '. . . Your Father was an Amorite, and your mother a Hittite'" (Ezek. 16:2-3). Beyond doubt the Amorite nation begat her by commending its own barbarity, the sacrifice of children to demons; and the Hittite nation nourished her on its crimes by teaching her effeminate superstitions.

For the word "mother" is not a proper but a common noun, and it is applied rather by reason of the offering of breasts than by reason of procreation. Therefore the Hittite nation, upon which Joshua the son of Nun led the people of Israel in order to destroy it from the face of the earth for its heinous crimes, but which was preserved in violation of

God's command, is called Israel's **mother** because she gave Israel to suck upon her deeds, in that by imitating all her villainies, Israel became like her. Distancing herself from the tree of life, that is, from knowledge of her Creator, she was brought **under the tree** of death by the power of the prince of the world. The latter, having once taken up with tyrannical rule, presumed in his pride to make himself the equal of Christ, and it is he whom the Church compares to the Phoenician apple — that is, the pomegranate — **tree**. Drunk upon the wine of his suasions and sunk in the sleep of death, she, like someone who is insensible, was deprived in her mind of rational understanding and simplicity — which the Hittite nation had received from her Maker so that she might not fall away from knowledge of him or turn away and retreat from him but consider that the one best and greatest God does not dwell in mines but in heaven, as has been said.

On the other hand, **she who bore** this people and **was violated** by the Devil means she in whose belly the Jewish people was led captive to Assyria with its King Hoshea the son of Elah. This **bearer**, already in a foreign land, was, not unlike the Hittite nation, overcome as if by force by two wicked enemies, to wit, by the poisoned suasions of that most destructive nation, the Assyrians, as well as those of the Devil.

(3) Honorius of Autun

I raised you up under an evil tree.
>   There your mother was corrupted,
>   there she who bore you was violated.
Set me as a seal upon your heart,
>   as a seal upon your arm;
for love is as strong as death,
>   jealousy is as unyielding as the grave.
Its lamps are lamps of fire
>   and of flames.
Many waters have not been able to extinguish love,
>   nor shall rivers cover it over.
If a man were to give all his property in exchange for love,
>   he would despise it as nothing.

This is the same as to say, "You have done well to come to me, for I raised you up when you were dead, and I set myself upon you as your Head." Moreover, the words **I raised you up under an evil tree** apply to the whole human race, which, though it lay dead beneath the tree of its transgression, has been raised up through Christ beneath the tree of the cross. **There**, to be sure, under the curse tree, **your mother was corrupted, there the one who bore you was violated.**

The **mother** of the human race is human nature, which before the sin was incorruptible, impassible, and immortal, but, once **corrupted** by the craft of the Devil, became passible and mortal. Further, **the one who bore** the human race was Eve the mother of all, who before the sin was inviolate, being stained neither by wrong desire nor by uncleanness. But she was **violated** by the serpent's suasions, and was quickly subjected to wrong desire and uncleanness and sorrow. Christ, though, restored incorruption to his mother in that, rising from the dead, he rendered human nature incorruptible. He restored **the one who bore** us in that he preserved the Virgin, **the one who bore** him, inviolate. That explains why he says, **I raised you up under an evil tree.** It is as though he were saying to the entire human race, "I have raised you up under the tree of the cross by my death, you who lay dead beneath the curse tree where your **mother**, human nature, was corrupted by the Devil when she threw away her adornment, to wit, her obedience, by eating of the forbidden apple[1] — and was for that reason condemned, because she quickly lost the privilege of incorruption and immortality. And there **the one who bore you**, Eve, was violated by the serpent when, expelled from Paradise, she lost integrity in conceiving and discovered sorrow in giving birth.

"And because I have raised you from death to life, **set me as a seal upon your heart.**" That is, "Stamp the image of me, your friend, upon your memory, just as a seal is impressed upon wax, so that you may love me even as I, who laid down my life for you, have loved you. And **set me . . . as a seal upon your arm**," that is, "stamp the example I provide upon your activities, so that you may act as I do, who have loved my enemies and have died for the ungodly."

For in fact by **seal** is meant image; by **heart**, memory; by **arm**, action. The ancients wore carved stones upon finger rings or bracelets, with which they sealed the letters they had sent to their friends, and that is the source of this analogy. Upon the seal an image is inscribed, which confers the image upon the wax that has been imprinted.

The seal is the humanity of Christ, upon which the image of Christ's divinity has been inscribed, while the wax is the human soul, shaped to the image of God. For we know that Christ, as it is written, is "the image of the invisible God" (Col. 1:15), being equal to the Father. God imprinted this image upon the human being when he created the interior human person (cf. 2 Cor. 4:16) "after the image and likeness" (Gen. 1:26-27) of God. By the image the Trinity is denoted; by the likeness, the equality; the person who forms the image of Christ in his heart is one who believes Christ to be equal to the Father. He imprints his image upon the person who believes that human nature has been united to God. That person sets the seal of Christ upon his arm who takes the example of Christ's action as something to be imitated, and who by holy and righteous living is conformed to the likeness of God. Moreover, the works of Christ that the Bride is to imitate are these: that he loved his enemies to the point of dying for the ungodly (Rom. 5:7-10).

Hence the words, **for love is as strong as death, jealousy is as bitter as the grave.** This means: "Just as death overpowers all the mighty, and therefore is mightier than all, so too love is mightier than all, which has overpowered me who am the mightiest, and brought me to death for your sake. And just as hell is stronger than all bitter things, and therefore not to be broken down, so jealousy is unconquerable — I mean my own envy, by which I envy the Devil because he possesses you, my Bride, and has inflicted cruel death upon you; for I have so loved you as to have redeemed you with my blood. There-

---

1. Only a northern European like Honorius would call the forbidden fruit (which the book of Genesis does not identify) an apple; earlier Mediterranean exegetes often speculated that it was a fig.

fore, it is fair that you should love me to the point of imitating me and undergoing death for my sake.

"And if you have love, you will be able to undergo death for my sake, because **its lamps, love's lamps, are lamps of fire and of flames.** Lamps are light bearers, and spiritual persons are love bearers — who inwardly burn with love and outwardly shine with good actions. Lamps are **of fire** when they blaze for themselves, and they flame when they give light to one's neighbors. Such persons despise pains and bodily death because they love eternal life. **Much water cannot quench love, and rivers do not wash over it.** That is, neither flattery, nor threats, nor persecutions, nor terrors overcome the lover so as to keep him from fulfilling my will. He indeed loves me, and that is why he will keep my word: "This is my commandment, that you love one another as I have loved you" (John 15:12). The analogy is taken from a great fire that neither rains nor floods can put out. By waters we understand flattery; by floods, temptations, which cannot turn spiritual persons from good to evil.

Love is more precious than anything; for **If a man should give all the property of his household in exchange for love, he would despise it as if it were nothing.** That is, if someone in full possession of reason should give everything he owns to feed the poor, and, while lacking love, should hand himself over to martyrdom in order to merit possession of God, who is love, it is as if he had given up nothing; for he will despise everything that he gave unless he himself possesses love. All this is said because it is assumed that the Bride wants to be joined to the Bridegroom and in love imitates him to the greatest possible extent; for "anyone who loves abides in God" (1 John 3:14), and "anyone who does not love abides in death" (1 John 3:14).

(4) Augustine of Hippo

Love is as strong as death.

"Go around Zion and embrace her" (Ps. 47:13 LXX = 48:12). To those who live wickedly, and in whose midst there dwells the people to whom God has been merciful, let this be said: "In your midst there is a people that lives in the right way: 'Go around Zion.'" But "go around" *how?* "Embrace her!" Do not surround her with offenses, but surround her with love — so that you may imitate those who live in the right way in your midst, and by imitating them be incorporated into Christ, whose members they are. . . .

"Place your hearts in her virtue" (Ps. 47:14 LXX = 48:13). Do not refuse her virtue in order to have "the form of religion" (cf. 2 Tim. 3:5). What is the virtue of this city? Anyone who wants to understand the virtue of this city must grasp the force of love. Love is the virtue that none can overcome. No deluge of this age, no torrents of temptation extinguish the fire of love. Concerning it Scripture says, **Love is as strong as death.** For just as, when it comes, death cannot be resisted — with whatever arts, whatever medications you may greet it — and those who are born as mortals cannot evade the fury of death; so too the world can do nothing against the fury of love. On the contrary, death is set before us as a likeness of love. For just as death achieves heights of fury in the work of destruction, so love achieves heights of fury in the work of salvation. Through love many have died to this age in order to live to God. The martyrs were on fire with this love — not in pretense, not puffed up with empty pride, not in the manner of those of whom it was said, "If I give my body to be burned, but have not love, it profits me nothing" (1 Cor. 13:3), but in the manner of those whom love of Christ and of truth brought to true suffering. What did the trials brought upon them by their raging enemies accomplish in their case? The eyes of those who wept for them did them more harm than the persecutions of their enemies. For how many parents did their children restrain so that they might not suffer! How many wives fell down on their knees to avoid becoming widows! How many children did their parents forbid to die, even as we know and read in the passion of St. Perpetua! All of these things happened. But when did tears — however abundant and with however much force they poured out — put out the fire of love? This is the "virtue" of Zion, who is elsewhere addressed in these words: "May peace be in your virtue, and abundance in your towers" (Ps. 121:7 LXX = 122:7).

(5) John of Ford

Her lamps are lamps of fire
    and of flames.

The Bridegroom is quite right when he says, **Her lamps are lamps of fire and of flames.** He wants to make it clear that they are made of a stuff very different from that of the lamps of the foolish virgins (cf. Matt. 25:2ff.); for the lamps of the latter are made of glass, and any little fall will break them. The lamps of the former, however, since they are a fiery substance, are not liable to this kind of accident. Moreover, they possess within themselves by God's grace the means of giving heat and light.

Just as charcoal once lit is customarily called fire to the extent that it takes on a fiery heat and color, so any kind of virtue, once enkindled by the fire of love, is deservedly adjudged to deserve the title of love. Patience, for example, or kindness, for example, enkindled by love, are nothing more than patient love and kindly love. So temperance and chastity, meekness, humility, and modesty, once they have caught the flame of divine love, are nothing but **lamps of fire and of flames.** If there was anything in them that was glassy and fragile, it is not consumed by the hungry flame of love, which transforms it into its own substance and gives it a firm solidity.

So they become afire, and not only afire but aflame. Yet there is something more striking in that the Bridegroom does not say, "Lamps of fire and flame," but **lamps of fire and of flames.** I think that by "fire," which is used in the singular, there is shown the single strength of the love with which God is loved. But by "flames," there is manifested the twofold power of the love with which friends are sweetly relished in God, and enemies bravely delighted in for God. Since, then, the love of God has precedence, not only because of its origin but also because of its dignity, over the former love, the Bridegroom first says **of fire,** and then **of flames.** In fact, to the degree that tinder is applied to nourish and feed it, fire creates flames, and the more strongly the love of God sets the heart on fire, love for our neighbor bursts more and more into flames. God's love is mother to love of man, and father too, and nurse.

(6) Bede the Venerable

If a man should give all the property of his household in exchange for love,
    he would despise it as if it were nothing.
Our sister is little
    and does not have breasts.
What shall we do for our sister
    on the day when she is spoken to?
If she is a wall,
    let us build silver battlements upon it;
if she is a door,
    let us strengthen it with cedar planks.
I am a wall,
    and my breasts are like a tower,
whence I have become as one
    that seeks peace in his presence.

This thought does not need to be explained in words. He himself established its truth for the apostles, and likewise, afterward, an unnumbered multitude of believers did the same by their examples — when, that is, for love of the truth, they seemed to give up everything that they properly possessed in this world and to themselves seemed to lack nothing so long as they held on to the true goods in the heavens. In the Gospel the Lord openly indicates this in two continuous parables. "The kingdom of heaven is like a treasure hidden in a field, which a man found and covered up; then in his joy he goes and sells all that he has and buys that field. Again, the kingdom of heaven is like a merchant in search of fine pearls, who, on finding one pearl of great value, went and sold all that he had and bought it" (Matt. 13:44-46). Hence that most excellent of preachers said most excellently: "Because of the surpassing worth of knowing Christ Jesus my Lord, for whose sake I have suffered loss of all things and count them as refuse in order that I may gain Christ and be found in him" (Phil. 3:8-9).

But if the text be taken to say, as certain codices have it, **will despise him**, a considerably different sense is produced: to wit, that which the apostle commends when he says, "If I give away all that I have to feed the poor, and if I deliver my body to be burned, but have not love, I gain nothing" (1 Cor. 13:3). If, then, someone gives **all the property of his household** to the poor to gain love, that is, so that he may love as if he had given nothing away, that very judge who has seen that his heart is empty of love will despise him. And although this seems the contrary of the meaning stated above, it nonetheless asserts that the virtue of love is as noble as it is necessary, and each version of the text comes to this point, that in our doings and works, their identifying mark may be that they disseminate sincere love.

Our sister is little and has no breasts. The Lord speaks these words to the synagogue as she wonders at the faith or acceptance of the Church of the Gentiles. By a great dispensation of love, he is naming her their sister, that is to say, his own sister and that of the synagogue, so that the synagogue herself may recall that she too has been made the sister of her Creator by grace, and may rejoice more and more at what has been added to her in the gift of a sister's society. Indeed, every Church of Christ gathered from either people, as well as any holy soul, is a **sister** of the Lord and Savior, not only on account of the assumption of the very same nature by which he himself became a human being, but also on account of the free gift of grace by which he gave those who believe in him the power to become children of God, so that he who was the only Son of God by nature might become "the firstborn among many brothers and sisters" (Rom. 8:29) by grace. Hence the sweetness of that word of his spoken to Mary: "Go to my brethren and say to them, I am ascending to my Father and your Father, to my God and your God" (John 20:17).

So when he says, **Our sister is little and has no breasts,** he is referring to the early years of the birth of the Gentile Church, when it was not only small from the point of view of the number of believers but also lagged behind in its readiness for the proclamation of God's word. Read the Acts of the Apostles, which covers the period from the nineteenth year of Tiberius Caesar to the fourth year of Nero, and you will find that many large groups had come to faith in response to the apostles' preaching, yet you will never find — in that whole time of about twenty-eight years — that they had preached. For the Gentile Church was small and was not up to the task of begetting or nursing children by the teaching of Christ. For this reason, the Lord admonishes the synagogue that, with sisterly love, given the health and promise of the one she delights in and her immaturity, she should provide the help and support requisite for growth.

To this he also adds the following, as if consulting in brotherly fashion about what is fitting: **What shall we do for our sister on the day that she is addressed?** The Lord addresses the Church or each elect soul when he admonishes her with regard to eternal salvation, whether by means of a private manifestation of his Spirit or by means of the public word of preachers. In such an address, supreme justice observes the extent of our strength and confers its gifts on each in proportion to the measure of human capacity. Hence he says, **What shall we do for our sister on the day that she is addressed?** — as if openly to say: "The Gentile Church is indeed small in number and is not yet strong enough to support the ministry of the word. What, then, O synagogue, does it seem to you should be done with regard to the care of that sister — to wit, our sister — at the time when I begin to address her through my apostles and the successors of the apostles? Should we entrust to her, as to one who is yet a little one, the little mysteries among the heavenly secrets? Or should we render her more mature by increments, to the extent that, as she makes progress, she can be capable of the more perfect virtues?"

When she is silent and prefers to hear what he wishes, he explains straightway what it is appropriate to do in the following manner by adding: **If she is a wall, let us build silver battlements upon it; if she is a door, let us fix planks of cedar upon it.**

In Holy Scripture it is customary for the Lord himself to be designated quite frequently by the term "wall" or "gate." He is rightly called a wall because he fortifies his

Church on every side lest it be ravaged by enemies; and he is rightly called a door because it is only through him that we enter either this society that is the Church or the bulwarks of the everlasting kingdom. For he says of himself, "I am the door of the sheep; if anyone enters by me, he will be saved" (John 10:9); and again, "No one comes to the Father save through me" (John 14:6). Concerning him, the prophet, predicting the future gifts of the Church, says, "He set in her wall and breastwork" (cf. Isa. 26:2) — "wall" meaning the Lord himself as he appears in flesh, and "breastwork" meaning, on the other hand, the prophetic revelation that by predicting his incarnation from the beginning of the world greatly assisted the building of the Church. Truly he who by becoming manifest in flesh deigned to make the Church his **sister**, also himself conferred upon her participation in his name, with the result that she was called both "wall" and "gate" — "wall" in those who, supplied with greater learning and with the power of the Spirit, were able to fortify the minds of believers against the attacks of those in error and defend them boldly with arms by resisting wickedness; but "gate" in those who, though less instructed for the purposes of repelling the sophistries of heretics or pagans, nevertheless, being wholesomely imbued with the plain catholic faith, opened wide by their preaching the entrance to the kingdom for those who were willing, and introduced them, by the mystery of the second birth, into the halls of eternal life. In the same way, he does not shrink from assigning other designations that refer to virtues to the same more perfect members of his Bride, designations that are certainly characteristic of himself, as, for example, "You are the light of the world" (Matt. 5:14), and again, "Behold, I send you out as sheep in the midst of wolves" (Matt. 10:16), seeing that he himself is "the true light that enlightens everyone who comes into the world" (John 1:9), and that he is the spotless and unsullied Lamb who has taken away the sins of the world.

If then, he says, our sister **is a wall, let us build silver battlements upon it** — as if he said openly, "If the Gentile Church is in certain of its members capable of opposing the teachings of wrong-headed individuals because it has men that are intelligent speakers, whether they are skilled in virtue of a natural talent or a philosophical education, I would in no wise desire to deprive them of the teaching office save that we would prefer to assist them by providing them with the books of the Holy Scriptures, with whose help they can the more easily and powerfully guard any weak or uninstructed persons against the snares of erroneous teaching or corrupt example"; for the **silver battlements** are the high points of the divine words, of which it says above, **Your neck is like a tower of David that was built with battlements** (4:4), and again in the psalm, "The words of the Lord are pure words, silver tried with fire on the ground" (Ps. 11:7 Vg = 12:6).

If she is a door let us fix tablets of cedar upon it. "If there are in her people who understand how to imbue little ones with the word of plain teaching, and how to bring them into the hidden places of a holy way of life, let us set before them the unfading examples of the righteous who preceded them, with the help of which they can fulfill the above-mentioned office in a better and more effective manner." Now since it is often said that cedars denote the virtues of the elect, the figure of the **tablets** expresses their breadth of heart, in which they hold the memory of the heavenly words, of which the prophet says, "I have run in the way of your commandments when you broadened my heart" (Ps. 118:32 Vg = 119:32). He was teaching that he had been adorned with these **tablets**, and the apostle wanted his hearers to be adorned with them, for he said, "Our mouth is open to you, Corinthians; our heart is broadened. You are not made narrow by us, but you are made narrow by your own inward feelings, having the same reward. As to children I say, broaden your hearts also" (2 Cor. 6:11-13). Hence the Word also admonishes the lover of wisdom, saying, "Write her upon the tablet of your heart" (Prov. 7:3).

And the Church, hearing these counsels or promises addressed to her by her Redeemer, no longer awaits the approval or response of the synagogue to whom she was speaking, and answers him devoutly, **I am a wall, and my breasts are like a tower, whence I have become like one who seeks peace in his presence.** "Rightly am I named a wall: I have been put together out of 'living stones' (1 Pet. 2:5); I have been unified by the bond of love; I have been set upon an immovable foundation; I cannot be cast down by any blow of a heretical battering ram. For God's foundation stands firm, having this as its seal: 'The Lord knows those who are his.' But within me there are those who, endowed with a greater grace, transcend, as a tower does a wall, the common life of the faithful by the distinctive loftiness of their virtues; and these like breasts nurse the little ones and the weak in faith with the milk of a plainer exhortation, and, by their uncommon speaking ability, like a steady tower repel all the missiles of the wrongheaded.

"All of these things I was able to possess by the choice of my free will; but it is of his own gift that I have received that by which I have become in his presence like one who finds peace — which is to say, that by which he has deigned to bestow on me the gift of his peace by the word of reconciliation. For by my diligence I was not able either to come into the presence of him from whom I had departed very far or to recover the peace that I had lost; but with great gratitude I have accepted it when it was offered by him. . . ."

(7) The *Glossa ordinaria*

I have become like one
  who seeks peace in his presence.

"I do well to say **one who seeks peace**, for in that peace of which I spoke a vineyard was established by the peacemaking Christ, a vineyard that was foretold of old by the Law and the Prophets." This peace did not embrace solely the single people of the Jews. On the contrary, it contains many peoples brought together out of the whole world, not in virtue of any human merits, but in virtue of that peace between God and humanity which Christ came to create.

Song 8:11-14

8:11 A vineyard belonged to Solomon
     in Beelamon.
     He put it into the hands of
     keepers.
     A man brings a thousand pieces of
     silver for its fruit.

12 My vineyard, mine, is before my eyes.
     The thousand is yours, Solomon,

     and two hundred for those that
     keep your fruit.

13 You that are seated in the gardens,
     your companions are attentive to
     what you say;
     make me hear.

14 Flee, my Kinsman,
     and be made like the gazelle,
     or the young stag
     upon the mountains of spices.

8:11 The peaceful one had a vineyard in
     that which contains people.
     He put it into the hands of
     keepers.
     A man will bring a thousand
     pieces of silver for its fruit.

12 My vineyard is in my presence.
     The thousand belongs to your
     peaceful one,
     and two hundred to those who
     guard its fruits.

13 You who live in the gardens,
     friends are listening;

     make me hear your voice.

14 Flee, my Beloved,
     and be like the gazelle,
     or the young of stags
     upon the mountains of spices.

The first two verses of this difficult and apparently disjointed section relate that Solomon (whose name the Vulgate translates as if it were an ordinary word and not a name: "the peaceful one") had a vineyard in a place called Baal-hamon — a place no one seems able to locate. (Perhaps for this reason, the Vulgate also translates "Baal-hamon" for what its two words mean as common nouns: "Lord of a multitude." Thus "in Baal-hamon" comes out in the Latin version as "in that which contains people.") We then learn that he farmed it out to tenants, who received "a thousand pieces of silver" for its produce, of which they kept twenty percent for themselves.

*   Given the customary interpretation of the symbol of the vineyard in the*

Song, it is natural that it should be taken to refer to Israel (as in the Jewish Targum) or to the Church (as in most Christian interpretations; see the passage from Bede below). The "thousand pieces of silver" are then the price of the eternal goods that the garden's "plants" produce, which, as Bede understands it, is the salvation of the souls who are "planted" in the garden.

It is not clear whether Ambrose, in his comment on the following two verses (8:13-14), would connect them with the account of Solomon's vineyard or treat them as independent of it. The use of the word "garden" seems, however, to mark the beginning of a new scene, and Ambrose takes it as a reference to the original Paradise, from which the human race has been exiled, but where Christ sits and converses with the heavenly host of angelic creatures.

(1) Bede the Venerable

The peaceful one had a vineyard in that which contains people.
    He put it in the hands of keepers.
    A man brings a thousand pieces of silver for its fruit.
My vineyard is in my presence.
    The thousand belongs to your peaceful one,
    And two hundred to those who guard its fruit.

The peaceful one whom she names is, moreover, her very own Bridegroom and Beloved, the "Everlasting Father, Prince of Peace" (Isa. 9:6), whose role and character Solomon imaged, in respect both of his name and of the peaceful condition of his kingdom. In this peace of his, this same One **had a vineyard**, in that through his very own grace the catholic Church throughout the world was built up for him, the Church of which mention is made in a great many scriptural passages, but most obviously in the Gospel parable in which it is said: "The kingdom of heaven is like a householder who went out early in the morning to hire laborers for his vineyard," etc. (Matt. 20:1). There, by the persons of the laborers that came at the third, sixth, ninth, and eleventh hours, it is palpably shown that the same Church of Christ is cultivated by the unwearied work of spiritual teachers throughout the span of the present age (which is what the space of one day represents).

Further still, **the peaceful one had a vineyard in that**, that is, **in that** *peace* about which he had predicted that in his presence the vineyard would come to be as it were a creator of peace, since whoever cares nothing for peace does not belong to the Church of Christ even though he appear to confess Christ and to obey his commands. For "his place has been established in peace" (Ps. 75:3 Vg = 76:2); and the apostle says, "Strive for peace with all men, and the holiness without which no one will see the Lord" (Heb. 12:14). . . .

He put it into the hands of keepers. A man brings a thousand pieces of silver for its fruit. For the keepers of the Church are the prophets; the keepers are the apostles; the keepers are the successors of the prophets and apostles who by divine command have been provided at different times in the world's history for the Church's governance; the keepers are the armies of the heavenly host, which exercise care for the condition of the

Church at every point in the age that is passing, to make sure that she is not disturbed by the incursion of malicious agents, whether human beings or spirits. And **a man brings a thousand pieces of silver for the fruit** of this vineyard in that every individual that has been perfected gives up everything proper to this world for the sake of possessing the kingdom of heaven; for the fruit of labors undertaken in the temporal order for the Lord's sake is reception with the Lord of the eternal rest and eternal kingdom of which he himself says, "I . . . appointed you that you should go and bear fruit and that your fruit should abide" (John 15:16) — that is, that you should work and receive your reward, and that the reward itself may never come to an end.

Further: Scripture is accustomed to call a person of perfected virtue **man**; for a **man** [*vir* in Latin] is so called by derivation from the word "virtue" [*vir-tus*]; and this true **man**, that is, a mind that is lofty on account of virtue, brings a thousand pieces of silver for the fruit of this vineyard in that he gives up all his temporal possessions in order to acquire eternal goods. For by the reference to silver coins he denotes every kind of property that must be given up, while by the number "one thousand" — which is perfect and complete — the whole world is denoted. Thus the thousand pieces of silver that a man is said to bring to pay for the fruit of this vineyard point to the whole world of things that the perfected give up for the sake of the Lord; and while at times this does not amount to much in the way of riches, it is great and plentiful in the estimation of the One who weighs not the quantity of the goods surrendered but the intent of the giver. Moreover, this is the same teaching that is asserted above in other words: **If a man were to give all his household property for love, he would despise it as if it were nothing** (Song 8:7). If, then, in this passage, the thousand pieces of silver stand for all the household property that is given up, the love that in our heavenly homeland is honored forever, even when other charisms have ceased (cf. 1 Cor. 13:8), is itself the fruit of the vineyard by which the blessed ones, who now "hunger and thirst for righteousness" (Matt. 5:6) while working in that same vineyard, will then abundantly be fed.

There then follows a word of the peaceful One himself, in which he indicates how great a care he has for his holy vineyard, the Church, what it is that he is storing up for those who give up their possessions, and what in the way of special recompense he is arranging to award to the **keepers** of the vineyard, that is, the teachers.

My vineyard is in my presence, he says; **the thousand belongs to your peaceful one, and two hundred to those who guard its fruits.** You have truly shown, he says, that I handed my vineyard over to keepers who would cultivate it with their words and their examples alike; you surely know that I have thus committed the care of it to keepers so that I myself may unceasingly attend to what goes on in it, note with what mind and what diligence each individual labors in it, and discern, finally, how many of the adversaries' hidden snares and open attacks he suffers. And what more? "Behold, I am" with it "always, to the close of the age" (Matt. 28:20). But when that time comes, I shall appropriately recompense all who worked in my vineyard, or on behalf of my vineyard, or against my vineyard.

Those who, to gain its fruit, that is, to gain the hope of a supernal inheritance, have administered all the goods they could possess or acquire in the world and given them to the poor shall gain the secure reality of their hope, and indeed in the heavens they shall receive much greater things than they had known how to hope for — namely, "What no eye hath seen, nor ear heard, nor the heart of man conceived, what God has prepared for those who love him" (1 Cor. 2:9). Those, however, who acted as keepers of the vineyard by their preaching or by glowing with exalted deeds will be accorded double the reward of the rest of the righteous. That is why the angel says to Daniel, "And those who are wise shall shine like the brightness of the firmament; and those who turn many to righteousness, like the stars for ever and ever" (Dan. 12:3).

(2) Ambrose of Milan

You who live in the gardens,
  friends are listening;
  make me hear your voice.
Flee, my Kinsman,
  and be made like the gazelle,
or the young of stags
  upon the mountains of spices.

For she was delighted that Christ was sitting **in the gardens**, and that friends there **in the gardens** were intent upon his words. Those friends, however, were from heavenly places — Archangels, or Dominations and Thrones; for the human beings had been expelled from Paradise on account of their disobedience to heavenly commands, and so hitherto the Church had not been able to hear his voice, which she desired to hear. That is why she said, **let your voice make its way to me.** Hence if we want him to sit within us, let us too be locked and fortified, let us bring forth the flowers of the virtues, the sweetness of grace, so that we may be able to hear the Lord Jesus as he converses with the angels.

But it would turn out to be the case that when the Church had come to its fullness, it would be tested by various persecutions; and for this reason, when she was being delighted by the grace of the Word, she at once discerned the snares of the persecutors; and because she feared them more for her Bridegroom than for herself, or else because the persecutors preferred to seek Christ out within us, she says:

Flee, my Kinsman, and be made like the gazelle, or the young of stags upon the mountains of spices. He flees on account of the weak, who are not able to bear the heavier trials. That is why it is written that we flee from city to city, and if they persecute us in this city, we flee to another (cf. Matt. 10:23). It is, then, as we have said, on account of those who are weak that he flees the persecutors; or else he flees from the lowest depths and passes over to **the mountains of spices** — he who, because of the witness he bore in his martyrdom, can carry with him the perfume of resurrection.

The **mountains of spices** are the saints. Christ takes refuge with them; for "His foundation is upon the holy mountains" (Ps. 86:1 LXX = 87:1). He takes refuge with those who are his steadfast foundations. In us he flees; in them, he dwells in a place that is safe. Therefore Paul is a mountain of spices, for he can say, "We are the fragrance of Christ to God" (2 Cor. 2:15). David is a mountain of spices, the fragrance of whose prayer ascended to the Lord, and so he says, "Let my prayer be set forth in your sight as incense" (Ps. 140:2 LXX = 141:2).

(3) The *Glossa ordinaria*

You who live in the gardens,
  friends are listening;
  make me hear your voice.

The Church — or some faithful soul or other — dwells **in the gardens**; and she is already filled with the greenness of hope and good works. Yet the hope that this world breeds is dry and parched, for all the things that people love here wither away swiftly. Hence she who dwells **in the gardens** must make the Bridegroom hear her voice; that is, the more she speaks what is good in her preaching, the more delighted is the One she desires, because **friends are listening,** which is to say: all the elect desire to hear the words of life so that they may be restored to the life of their celestial homeland.

(4) John of Ford

Flee, my Beloved,
  and be like the gazelle
or the young stag
  upon the mountains of spices.

There is no doubt at all that these are words spoken by the Bride. She is saying good-bye to the Bridegroom and following after him as he leaves for some mysterious locale. And if the words make reference to her at the time when she was the Lamb's new Bride, a bride that married him in the early days when he was still with us, then the meaning of the words is easy to grasp. For the spouse says, "Because I have spoken these things to you, sorrow has filled your hearts" (John 16:6) — pointing to the swift realization of his words. And he added, "But I tell you the truth, it is in your interest that I go. If I do not go, the Advocate will not come to you; but if I go, I will send him to you" (John 16:7).

What do you make of this? Surely that his Beloved was doing everything possible to hold Jesus back even though he wanted to go away and return to his Father; for she could not hear so much as a word about his departure without sorrow's filling her heart. He, on the other hand, was desirous of leaving, though she held him back with such determination. Consequently, since he was going where he had to go, he wanted to go with her permission and her blessing. So he employed those persuasive words, which embodied not a human but a heavenly wisdom, and did it with such great effect that in the end he obtained her thankful agreement to the very thing he had so greatly desired a little earlier. . . . So, in the face of Jesus' grand promises, she gave up the sorrow that had filled her heart and made space for joy. To Jesus as he was getting ready to depart she gave her hand, and to the Holy Spirit, who had been promised her, she entrusted the fullness of her hope.

Surely these words — **Flee, my Beloved** — can now be assigned a straightforward sense. If, she says, this represents your will, and this is what my welfare requires, what reason, my Beloved, do you have for remaining with me? You have persuaded me not only to put up with your flight but to covet it, and so you must not stay with me for a minute more. If your remaining means that the Holy Spirit is delayed, why prolong your stay? **Flee, my Beloved!** You have promised that you will send your Holy Spirit, and I shall be clothed with him from on high (cf. Luke 24:49), and I am hopeful that in him you will be closer to me than in this bodily presence of yours. . . . Remove your body of flesh and in that way make a place for the Holy Spirit, and I shall be able to say: "the Spirit before our face is Christ our God; because even if we knew Christ according to the flesh, now we know him so no longer" (2 Cor. 5:16). . . .

There follows: **and be like the gazelle or the young stag.** The gazelle and the young stag are by nature quick, but it is no problem to capture them, the former being guileless, and the latter weak because of its age; and they are lovable because of their gentleness.

Now it is plain that the Bride wants to compare her beloved to these animals, but only **upon the mountain of spices**, that is, upon and above the angelic spirits. She seems to be telling him (though in other words): Hurry, my beloved, and with all the speed you can muster exalt the lowly nature of our human condition up above the great height of the heavenly spirits. Hasten to set our poor nature at the right hand of Majesty. Not only am I moved by the principle that governs my own progress — in that the Spirit cannot be given to me until you are glorified — but the very hope of your glorification drives me strongly to desire it. . . .

Flee, therefore, make a dash for the things of heaven. Return again to your own place, which is the bosom of your omnipotent Father. Deliver to your eternal Father the product of your obedience, show him the victorious banners of your passion, bring the glory of your cross to heaven itself. Let your life-giving blood, as it cries out for your Church, strike the heart of your Father. Let those **mountains of spices** wonder at you when you are lifted high above the top of the mountains.

Authors of Works Excerpted

Ambrose of Milan (339-97). Ambrose was elected bishop of Milan, the imperial capital of the West, during his tenure as governor of the Roman province of Aemilia-Liguria in northern Italy. At the time he was still a catechumen. Baptized and ordained in 374, he was a strong defender of Nicene orthodoxy. He was also — a rare distinction among western bishops — fluent in Greek; and alongside his many other achievements, he made his knowledge of Greek biblical commentators, and especially of Origen, available to his Latin-speaking contemporaries. He wrote no formal commentary on the Song of Songs, but referred to it regularly in his exegetical and catechetical writings, and in one treatise, *On Isaac*, treated much of the text in order.

Apponius. This writer is known only by his name (sometimes spelled "Aponius," but not in the earliest manuscripts of his work) and by his commentary on the Song of Songs, with which both Gregory the Great (d. 604) and Bede the Venerable (d. 735) were acquainted. There seems no doubt that the commentary, which is complete, was originally written in the West, probably in Italy, in the early 5th century; and the author was in all likelihood a monk.

Augustine of Hippo (354-430), a student and teacher of rhetoric who stemmed from North Africa, was converted in 386 and baptized by Ambrose of Milan in 387. He sought a retired life of reading, contemplation, and prayer, but was quickly seized and ordained a presbyter at Hippo Regius, a port city of Numidia. Not much later, after the death of the bishop there, Augustine succeeded him. Through his active episcopate, his many writings in many genres, and his participation in the Donatist and Pelagian controversies, Augustine became a — perhaps *the* — principal teacher of the medieval Latin church and indeed of both Protestants and Catholics during and after the Reformation. He had clearly given much thought to the Song of Songs, but comments on it only in passing in works that treat of other subjects.

Bede the Venerable (673-735) was a Benedictine monk of the Abbey at Jarrow, on the River Tyne in Northumbria. A learned scholar, he wrote not only commentaries on books of the Bible but also the famous *Ecclesiastical History of the English Nation* — and also a history of his own monastery. His commentaries drew on earlier Latin authors, for example, Gregory I, Augustine, Jerome, and Ambrose; but he did not lack independence of mind.

Bernard of Clairvaux (1090-1153), was the founder of the famous Cistercian abbey at Clairvaux. In the course of his career he became, through his connections with the papacy, a leader of the wider church. A combative aspect of Bernard's character emerged at once in his stern orthodoxy, which led to the notorious condemnation of Abelard in 1140, and in his preaching of the second crusade. Quite another emerged in his famous treatise *De diligendo Deo*, which reveals the mystical side of Bernard — as do his eighty-six deservedly beloved *Sermons on the Song of Songs* (which cover no more than the first two chapters of the Song and the first verse of the third).

Cyprian of Carthage (d. 258). Thascius Caecilianus Cyprianus, like Tertullian, whom he called "the teacher," was a rhetorician by profession. Converted to Christianity, he was chosen bishop of Carthage in 249, just months before the beginning of the Decian persecution, during which he governed the Carthaginian church from exile, and after which he showed himself a decisive leader of all the African churches in a period when disagreements and schisms were occasioned by differences over the treatment of the many Christians who had fallen away during the persecution. When persecution was renewed under Emperor Valerian, Cyprian himself was martyred.

Cyril of Alexandria (d. 444) was the nephew of Theophilus, patriarch of Alexandria 385-412, and inherited from him not merely the episcopal throne of Alexandria, but also something of an addiction to controversy. He exhibited this by his dedicated opposition to Judaism and Neoplatonism, but above all by his hostility to the see of Constantinople — and in particular to Nestorius, the Antiochene monk who, like John Chrysostom in the days of Theophilus, had moved from Antioch to head the church there. Nestorius questioned the correctness of the title *theotokos* ("God-bearer," "mother of God") as it had been applied to the Virgin Mary. This outraged Cyril and opened a christological debate that was concluded (if not settled) only by four ecumenical councils. Cyril in his notable commentary on the Gospel of John and other writings offers interpretations of isolated verses of the Song of Songs.

Gregory the Great (ca. 540-604; bishop of Rome, 590-604). Gregory was the offspring of a Roman Christian family of senatorial rank. After a brief public career and the death of his father, he disposed of his inheritance by founding and endowing six monasteries in Sicily and one in Rome, the latter on the site of his family home, where he himself became a monk. Popes Benedict I and Pelagius II employed him, now a deacon, as their representative to the imperial court in Constantinople. He succeeded Pelagius II as Pope in 590, to become an energetic, practical, and thoughtful administrator of his see and a principal guide of his posterity — medieval Latin Christianity. His *Commentary on the Song of Songs*, which is incomplete, can count only as one of his minor works; but its preface, largely translated here, was influential long after his death.

Gregory of Elvira. The dates of Gregory's birth and death are uncertain, but he was a Spanish contemporary of the Cappadocian fathers, and he died sometime after 392. Bishop of Elvira (near Granada), he was a radical defender of the Nicene cause in the last stages of the Arian controversy.

Gregory of Nyssa (ca. 330-95) was a younger brother of Basil the Great and a principal contributor to the settlement of the Arian controversy at the Council of Constantinople in 381. His best-known work was a series of treatises collectively titled *Against Eunomius,* which were written in response to the arguments of a neo-Arian bishop; but his *Great Catechism* and his dialogue *On the Soul and the Resurrection* are equally well known. The *Homilies on the Song of Songs,* which of course never made it to the end of the Song (he got as far as 6:9), were delivered toward the end of his life.

"Honorius of Autun" (Honorius Augustodunensis). At the end of his work *On the Luminaries of the Church,* an otherwise nameless monk of the Benedictine order who flourished in the first half of the 12th century identified himself as "Honorius," located himself in Autun (in Burgundy), and described himself as a priest and a scholar. There is little doubt that this account of himself, for whatever reason, deliberately falsified both his name and his place of residence. The likelihood is that the greater part of his writing career was spent at the abbey of St. James at Ratisbon in Germany, a Benedictine house of British foundation where the monks were permitted to be solitaries in the Celtic manner. He may well have been of British origin, and he may have begun his monastic life at Canterbury under the tutelage of Anselm. His — complete and systematic — commentary on The Song of Songs was only one of a large number of works in which, without seeking originality, he sought to summarize and synthesize the theological learning of his day.

Hugh of St.-Victor (ca. 1096-1141) became a monk of the distinguished house of St.-Victor in Paris in 1115, shortly after its foundation by William of Champeaux. Later its prior, he was a theological thinker in the Augustinian and Neoplatonist tradition, best known for his work *On the Sacraments* — or better perhaps *Mysteries* — of the Christian Faith.

John of Ford (ca. 1145–ca. 1214) was born near Axminster in the south of Devonshire and at an early age joined the (Cistercian) monastic community at Ford, in the same vicinity. He was Prior of Ford Abbey, then Abbot of a daughter community of Ford at Bindon, and finally, until his death, Abbot of the community at Ford itself. His *120 Sermons on the Last Part of the Song of Songs,* written during the final ten years of his life, was intended to complete the work of Bernard of Clairvaux — and of course that of Gilbert of Hoyland, who had himself taken up the task Bernard's death had left unfinished. John's sermons begin with Song 5:1.

Nicholas of Lyra (d. 1340) was a member of the Franciscan order who taught at the University of Paris. Unlike anyone else in this list, he read Hebrew and was directly acquainted with the work of many Jewish exegetes, especially that of "Rashi" (Rabbi Solomon Isaacson). He took a stand against the allegorism fashionable in the biblical exegesis of his day, and his *Postillae* — notes on the whole of the Bible — sought the precise literal sense of the Scriptures, though what he meant by "literal sense" in the case of the Song of Songs was not what a modern commentator would take that phrase to signify.

Nilus of Ancyra (d. ca. 430) was the abbot or archimandrite of a monastery near Ancyra, the modern Ankara in Turkey. His letters indicate that he was a disciple of John Chrysostom. He wrote works on the monastic life, and much of his correspondence has been preserved, though a great deal of what has been ascribed to him over the centuries was spurious. His commentary on the Song of Songs is in process of being edited, and the excerpts in this collection are taken from the first volume of this still incomplete edition.

Origen, called Adamantius (ca. 185-253). One of the most learned and original thinkers ever to grace the Christian movement, Origen was born in Alexandria of Christian parents; and after the martyrdom of his father in 202, he undertook to support his family by teaching. With the approval of Bishop Demetrius, he headed a catechetical school, eventually handing over the elementary work to an assistant while he busied himself with advanced subjects — especially biblical exegesis — and advanced pupils. When he and Demetrius fell out, he settled at Caesarea Maritima, having earlier been ordained a presbyter by Palestinian bishops who admired his expositions of the Scriptures. Among his many careful and formal commentaries on books of the Old and New Testaments was one on the Song of Songs, written at Athens and Caesarea, of which we now possess, besides Origen's lengthy preface, only the first three books (they cover Song 1:1–2:15) in a Latin translation by Rufinus of Aquileia (410). During the persecutions under Emperor Decius (251ff.) Origen was imprisoned and tortured for his faith, and died in Tyre shortly after his release.

Philo of Carpasius (fl. ca. 400) is another case of an author of whom little or nothing is known. In the course of the last quarter of the 4th century, he was made bishop of Carpasius, in Cyprus, probably at the instance of Epiphanius of Salamis. His *Commentary on the Song of Songs* is the only work ascribed to him that is certainly authentic.

Richard of St.-Victor (d. 1173) was a Briton who belonged to the house of St.-Victor in Paris, where he was a disciple of Hugh of St.-Victor. A theologian of contemplative disposition, his major work was his treatise *On the Trinity*, but he also wrote a number of exegetical works.

Rupert of Deutz (ca. 1070-1129) was a Benedictine monk and scholar who became Abbot of the monastery at Deutz (in the vicinity of Cologne) around 1120. He opposed the "new" theology of the schools and defended the traditional Benedictine style with its interest in the spiritual life. Apart from his commentary on the Song of Songs, notable for its identification of the Bride with the Virgin Mary, his writings included treatises on the Eucharist and on the Christian year *(De officiis)* as well as other scriptural commentaries.

Theodoret of Cyrus (ca. 393–ca. 458) was born in Syrian Antioch of wealthy Christian parents. Educated in monastic schools, he joined a monastic community but shortly thereafter was made — against his will — bishop of Cyrus, a city north and east of Antioch on the River Orontes (423). He was an active defender of Nestorius and a prominent participant in the Nestorian controversy. Deposed himself at the "Robber Synod" of Ephesus in 449, he was restored at the Council of Chalcedon in 451 after grudgingly accepting Nestorius's condemnation. In addition to his writings on apologetics and christology, he wrote commentaries on an extensive range of Old Testament books — commentaries that admirably illustrate the Antiochene style of exegesis, though his commentary on the Song of Songs — one of the few early commentaries that we have in complete form — follows in the footsteps of Origen.

William of St. Thierry (ca. 1085–ca. 1148) was a lifelong Benedictine who became Abbot of St. Thierry (in the vicinity of Rheims) in 1119. After sixteen years he renounced this office and became a simple monk in the new Cistercian monastery at Signy in the Ardennes forest. A friend of Bernard of Clairvaux, he was also a lifelong student and wrote extensively on subjects having to do with theology and the spiritual life.

Sources of Texts Translated

1. Abbreviations of Source Titles

CCCM	*Corpus Christianorum. Continuatio Mediaevalis.* Turnhout (Belgium): Brepols, 1971ff.
CCSL	*Corpus Christianorum. Series Latina.* Turnhout (Belgium): Brepols, 1953ff.
CIJE	P. E. Pusey, ed., *S.P.N. Cyrilli Archiepiscopi Alexandrini in Joannis Evangelium.* 2 vols. Oxford: Clarendon, 1872 (repr. Brussels, 1965).
CIP	P. E. Pusey, ed., *S.P.N. Cyrilli Archiepiscopi Alexandrini in XII Prophetas.* 2 vols. Oxford: Clarendon, 1868 (repr. Brussels, 1965).
CSEL	*Corpus scriptorum ecclesiasticorum latinorum.* Vienna, 1866ff.
Fontes 3	J. Schmitz, ed. and trans., *Ambrosius: De sacramentis, De mysteriis.* Fontes Christiani 3. Freiburg and New York: Herder, 1990.
GCS	*Die griechischen christlichen Schriftsteller der ersten drei Jahrhunderte* 33 (Origenes 8). Berlin, 1925.
GNO	Werner Jaeger, ed., *Gregorii Nysseni opera.* Leiden: E. J. Brill, 1960.
Green	R. P. H. Green, ed., *Augustine: De doctrina christiana.* Oxford: Clarendon, 1995.
Kiecker	J. G. Kiecker, ed. and trans., *The Postilla of Nicholas of Lyra on the Song of Songs.* Milwaukee: Marquette University, 1998.
PG	J.-P. Migne, ed., *Patrologiae cursus completus . . . series graeca.* 161 vols. Paris, 1857-66.
PL	J.-P. Migne, ed., *Patrologiae cursus completus . . . series latina.* 221 vols. Paris, 1844-64.
SBO	J. Leclerq, et al., ed., *Sancti Bernardi Opera.* Romae: Editiones Cistercienses, 1957ff.
SC	*Sources chrétiennes.* Paris: Éditions du Cerf, 1948ff.

2. Sources of Individual Excerpts

1. Prefaces and Title (Song 1:1)

(1) Origen, *Commentarium in Canticum Canticorum*, Preface, in *GCS* 33:61-71.
(2) Gregory the Great, *Expositio in Canticis Canticorum* 1-5, 9, in *CCSL* 144:3-8, 12-13.
(3) William of St. Thierry, *Expositio in Cantica Canticorum*, in *CCCM* 87:21-30.
(4) Honorius of Autun, *Expositio in Cantica Canticorum* 1, in *PL* 172:359B-D.
(5) Origen, *Commentarium*, Preface, in *GCS* 33:79-80.
(6) Gregory of Nyssa, *Homiliae XV in Canticum Canticorum* 1, in *GNO* 6:26-27.

2. Song 1:2-4

(1) Origen, *Commentarium* 1, in *GCS* 33:89-91.
(2) Gregory of Nyssa, *Homiliae* 1, in *GNO* 6:32-33.
(3) Bernard of Clairvaux, *Sermones in Cantica Canticorum* 2.3, in *SBO* 1:9-10.
(4) Bernard of Clairvaux, *Sermones* 9.2, in *SBO* 1:43.
(5) Honorius of Autun, *Expositio* 1, in *PL* 172:359D-361B.
(6) Rupert of Deutz, *In Cantica Canticorum Commentariorum Libri* 1, in *CCCM* 26:10-11.
(7) Nicholas of Lyra, *Postilla on the Song of Songs*, in Kiecker: 34, 36.
(8) Origen, *Commentarium* 1, in *GCS* 33:93.
(9) Gregory the Great, *Expositio* 13, in *CCSL* 144:15.
(10) Nilus of Ancyra, *Commentarium in Canticum Canticorum* 4-5, in *SC* 403:133-35.
(11) William of St. Thierry, *Expositio* 5.36-37, in *CCCM* 87:37-38.
(12) *Glossa ordinaria*, in *CCCM* 170.22:85.
(13) Gregory of Nyssa, *Homiliae* 1, in *GNO* 6:35-36.
(14) Gregory the Great, *Expositio* 14, in *CCSL* 144:16.
(15) Origen, *Commentarium* 1, in *GCS* 33:101-2.
(16) Gregory of Nyssa, *Homiliae* 1, in *GNO* 6:36-38.
(17) Gregory the Great, *Expositio* 21, in *CCSL* 144:23.
(18) Ambrose of Milan, *De mysteriis* 5.28–6.29, in *Fontes* 3:226.
(19) Apollinarius of Laodicea, in Procopius, *Epitome* (*PG* 87:1552A).
(20) Theodoret of Cyrus, *Interpretatio in Canticum Canticorum*, in *PG* 81:65B-68B.
(21) Origen, *Commentarium* 1, in *GCS* 33:108-9.
(22) Gregory the Great, *Expositio* 26, in *CCSL* 144:27-28.
(23) Gregory of Nyssa, *Homiliae* 1, in *GNO* 6:41-42.

3. Song 1:5-8

(1) Origen, *Commentarium* 2, in *GCS* 33:113-14.
(2) Gregory of Nyssa, *Homiliae* 2, in *GNO* 6:48-49.
(3) Bernard of Clairvaux, *Sermones* 27.2-4, in *SBO* 1:183-84.
(4) William of St. Thierry, *Expositio* 8.44-45, in *CCCM* 87:41-42.
(5) Bede the Venerable, *Expositio in Cantica Canticorum*, in *CCSL* 119b:195-96.

(6) Gregory of Nyssa, *Homiliae* 2, in *GNO* 6:50-51.

(7) Gregory the Great, *Expositio* 33, in *CCSL* 144:34.

(8) Gregory of Nyssa, *Homiliae* 2, in *GNO* 6:54-57.

(9) Apponius, *In Canticum Canticorum Expositio* 1.47-49, in *CCSL* 19:33-34.

(10) Origen, *Commentarium* 2, in *GCS* 33:134.

(11) Augustine of Hippo, *Sermones* 46.33-37, in *PL* 38:289-92.

(12) Apponius, *Expositio* 2.1-2, 5, in *SC* 420:226-30, 235.

(13) Nilus of Ancyra, *Commentarium* 18, in *SC* 403:170-72.

(14) Origen, *Commentarium* 2, in *GCS* 33:136-37.

(15) Cyril of Alexandria, *In Johannis Evangelium*, in *CIJE* 1:236-37.

4. Song 1:8-12a

(1) Origen, *Commentarium* 2, in *GCS* 33:141-42, 143, 145-46.

(2) Augustine of Hippo, *Enarrationes in Psalmos* 66:4, in *CCSL* 39:861.

(3) Nilus of Ancyra, *Commentarium* 1.21, in *SC* 403:178-80.

(4) Bernard of Clairvaux, *Sermones* 36.5-7, in *SBO* 2:7-8.

(5) Origen, *Commentarium* 2, in *GCS* 33:151-53.

(6) Gregory of Nyssa, *Homiliae* 3, in *GNO* 6:73-75.

(7) Apponius, *Expositio* 3.1-3, in *CCSL* 19:60-61.

(8) Theodoret of Cyrus, *Interpretatio*, in *PG* 81:77A-D.

(9) Nilus of Ancyra, *Commentarium* 26, in *SC* 403:191-95.

(10) William of St. Thierry, *Expositio* 14.67-68, in *CCCM* 87:56.

(11) Origen, *Commentarium* 2, in *GCS* 33:156-62.

(12) Gregory of Nyssa, *Homiliae* 3, in *GNO* 6:83-87.

(13) Gregory of Elvira, *In Canticum Canticorum* 2.38-43, in *CCSL* 69:190-92.

(14) Philo of Carpasius, *Expositio in Canticum Canticorum* 23-24, in *PG* 40:54AB.

5. Song 1:12b-14

(1) Origen, *Commentarium* 2, in *GCS* 33:168-69.

(2) Gregory of Nyssa, *Homiliae* 3, in *GNO* 6:88-90.

(3) Nilus of Ancyra, *Commentarium* 1.29, in *SC* 403:202-6.

(4) Philo of Carpasius, *Expositio*, in *PG* 40:54CD.

(5) Origen, *Commentarium* 2, in *GCS* 33:170.

(6) Nilus of Ancyra, *Commentarium* 1.30-31, in *SC* 403:208-18.

(7) Ambrose of Milan, *In Psalmum CXVIII* 3.8, in *CSEL* 62:44-45.

(8) Theodoret of Cyrus, *Interpretatio*, in *PG* 71:81C-84B.

(9) Apponius, *Expositio* 3.16-18, in *CCSL* 19:69-70.

(10) The *Glossa ordinaria*, in *CCCM* 170.22:129.

6. Song 1:15-17

(1) Origen, *Commentarium* 3, in *GCS* 33:172-74.

(2) Bernard of Clairvaux, *Sermones* 45.7-8, in *SBO* 2:54-55.

(3) William of St. Thierry, *Expositio* 18.84-88, in *CCCM* 87:65-67.

(4) Apponius, *Expositio* 3.19, in *CCSL* 19:70-71.

(5) Gregory of Elvira, *In Canticum* 3.10-11, in *CCSL* 69:194-95.

(6) Apponius, *Interpretatio* 3.20-22, in *CCSL* 19:71-73.

(7) Gregory of Elvira, *In Canticum* 3.12-16, in *CCSL* 19:195-96.

(8) Gregory of Nyssa, *Homiliae* 4, in *GNO* 6:107-9.

(9) *Glossa ordinaria*, in *CCCM* 170.22:137.

7. *Song 2:1-2*

(1) Origen, *Commentarium* 3, in *GCS* 33:177-79.

(2) Philo of Carpasius, *Enarratio*, in *PG* 40:60BC.

(3) Theodoret of Cyrus, *Interpretatio*, in *PG* 81:85BD.

(4) Nilus of Ancyra, *Commentarium* 1.39-41, in *SC* 403:234-44.

(5) Rupert of Deutz, *PG* 168:858D-859A

(6) *Glossa ordinaria*, in *CCCM* 170.22:141.

(7) Augustine of Hippo, *Enarrationes in Psalmos* 47, in *CCSL* 38:545.

8. *Song 2:3-7*

(1) Gregory of Nyssa, *Homiliae* 4, in *GNO* 6:116-18.

(2) Origen, *Commentarium* 3, in *GCS* 33:181-84.

(3) Apponius, *Expositio* 3.36-41, in *CCSL* 19:82-85.

(4) Theodoret of Cyrus, *Interpretatio*, in *PG* 81:90AD.

(5) William of St. Thierry, *Expositio* 24.110-113, in *CCCM* 87:80-82.

(6) Nilus of Ancyra, *Commentarium* 45, in *SC* 403:254-56.

(7) Augustine of Hippo, *Sermones* 21.3, in *PL* 38:143-44.

(8) Origen, *Commentary* 3, in *GCS* 33:193-97.

(9) Bede the Venerable, *Expositio*, in *CCSL* 119b:215.

(10) Nilus of Ancyra, *Commentarium* 49-52, in *SC* 403:264-74.

9. *Song 2:8-15*

(1) Origen, *Commentarium* 3, in *GCS* 33:201, 202-3.

(2) Theodoret of Cyrus, *Interpretatio* in *PG* 81:96C-100A.

(3) Gregory of Nyssa, *Homiliae* 5, in *GNO* 6:144-45.

(4) Apponius, *Expositio* 4.16-17, in *CCSL* 19:96-97.

(5) Ambrose of Milan, *De Isaac* 4.32-37, in *CSEL* 32.1.2:661-64.

(6) Gregory of Nyssa, *Homiliae* 5, in *GNO* 6:151-54, 155-56.

(7) William of St. Thierry, *Expositio* 35.160-62, in *CCCM* 87:160-62.

(8) Origen, *Commentarium* 3, in *GCS* 33:235-39.

(9) Gregory of Nyssa, *Homiliae* 5, in *GNO* 6:164-68.

(10) Augustine of Hippo, *Sermones* 164.3, in *PL* 38:1640-642.

(11) Nilus of Ancyra, *Commentarium* 63-67, in *SC* 403:312-24.

(12) Bernard of Clairvaux, *Sermones* 67.8-10, in *SBO* 2:193-94.

10. Song 3:1-5

(1) Gregory of Nyssa, *Homiliae* 6, in *GNO* 6:180-84.

(2) Gregory of Elvira, *In Canticum* 5.5-14, in *CCSL* 69:208-10.

(3) Rupert of Deutz, *Commentariorum Libri* 3, in *CCCM* 26:57-59.

(4) Richard of St.-Victor, *In Cantica Canticorum Explicatio* 5, in *PL* 196:419-20.

(5) Gregory of Nyssa, *Homiliae* 4, in *GNO* 6:129-35.

11. Song 3:6-11

(1) Theodoret of Cyrus, *Interpretatio,* in *PG* 81:118C-119C

(2) Ambrose of Milan, *De Isaac* 5.44-46, in *CCSL* 32.1.2:668-71.

(3) Apponius, *Expositio* 5.25-26, in *CCSL* 19:126-27.

(4) Rupert of Deutz, *Commentariorum Libri* 2, in *CCCM* 26:61-62.

(5) Gregory of Nyssa, *Homiliae* 7, in *GNO* 6:211-14.

(6) Rupert of Deutz, *Commentariorum Libri* 3, in *CCCM* 26:68.

12. Song 4:1-8

(1) Ambrose of Milan, *De mysteriis* 34-35, 37-40, in *Fontes* 3:230, 232-34.

(2) Augustine of Hippo, *De doctrina christiana* 2.11-13 and *Enarrationes in Psalmos* 3 in *CCSL* 38:10-11.

(2) Apponius, *Interpretatio* 7.1-34, in *CCSL* 19:139.

(4) Bede the Venerable, *Expositio* 2, in *CCSL* 119b:244-45.

(5) Rupert of Deutz, *Libri Commentariorum* 3, in *CCCM* 26:71.

(6 Gregory of Nyssa, *Homiliae* 7, in *GNO* 6:224-28.

(7 Apponius, *Expositio* 6.9-12, in *CCSL* 19:142-43.

(8 Honorius of Autun, *Expositio* 2, in *PL* 172:413A-414A.

(9 Apponius, *Expositio* 6.26-34, in *CCSL* 19:148-51.

(10 Gregory of Nyssa, *Homiliae* 7, in *GNO* 6:242-44.

(11) Hugo of St. Victor, *De amore sponsi ad sponsam,* in *PL* 176:987B-992B.

(12) Augustine of Hippo, *Enarrationes in Psalmos* 67, in *CCSL* 39:898-99.

(13) Richard of St.-Victor, *Explicatio,* in *PL* 196:478D-482C.

13. Song 4:9-15

(1) Gregory of Nyssa, *Homiliae* 8, in *GNO* 6:253-60.

(2) Theodoret of Cyrus, *Interpretatio,* in *PG* 81:137D-140A.

(3) *Glossa ordinaria,* in *CCCM* 170.22:249, 251.

(4) Richard of St.-Victor, *Explicatio,* in *PL* 196:485C-487C.

(5) Rupert of Deutz, *Libri Commentariorum* 3, in *CCCM* 26:82-83.

(6) Honorius of Autun, *Expositio* 2, in *PL* 172:423C-426D.

(7) *Glossa ordinaria*, in *CCCM* 170.22:265.

14. Song 4:16–5:1

(1) Theodoret of Cyrus, *Interpretatio*, in *PG* 81:148A-149A.

(2) Gregory of Nyssa, *Homiliae* 10, in *GNO* 6:298-302.

(3) Bede the Venerable, *Expositio*, in *CCSL* 119b:270-71.

(4) Rupert of Deutz, *Commentariorum Libri* 4, in *CCCM* 26:92-93.

(5) Cyril of Alexandria, *In Joelem*, in *CIP* 1:298-99.

15. Song 5:2-8

(1) Theodoret of Cyrus, *Interpretatio*, in *PG* 81:149B-152B.

(2) Apponius, *Expositio* 8.1-7, in *CCSL* 19:181-84.

(3) Richard of St.-Victor, *Explicatio*, in *PL* 196:503C-504C, 505B-507A.

(4) Gregory of Nyssa, *Homiliae* 11, in *GNO* 6:327-32.

(5) Gregory of Nyssa, *Homiliae* 12, in *GNO* 6:353-56.

(6) Ambrose of Milan, *De Isaac* 6.55-56, in *CSEL* 32.1.2:679-80.

(7) Honorius of Autun, *Expositio*, in *PL* 172:437C-439B.

16. Song 5:9-16

(1) Richard of St.-Victor, *Explicatio*, in *PL* 196:508B-509B.

(2) Theodoret of Cyrus, *Interpretatio*, in *PG* 81:156C-160A.

(3) John of Ford, *CXX Sermones in ultimam partem Cantici Canticorum* 7.3-5, in *CCCM* 17: 75-77.

(4) John of Ford, *Sermones* 14.4-6, in *CCCM* 17:127-30.

(5) *Glossa ordinaria*, in *CCCM* 170.22:301.

(6) Apponius, *Expositio* 8.37-39, in *CCSL* 19:196-97.

(7) Gregory of Nyssa, *Homiliae* 13, in *GNO* 6:393-98.

(8) Theodoret of Cyrus, *Interpretatio*, in *PG* 81:160D-161B.

(9) Ambrose of Milan, *In Psalmum CXVIII* 10.17, in *CSEL* 62:213

(10) Honorius of Autun, *Expositio*, in *PL* 172:441B-444C.

(11) Richard of St.-Victor, *Explicatio*, in *PL* 196:518B-519C.

17. Song 6:1-3

(1) Gregory of Nyssa, *Homiliae* 15, in *GNO* 6:434-41.

(2) Honorius of Autun, *Expositio*, in *PL* 172:445A-446A.

18. Song 6:4-9

(1) Theodoret of Cyrus, *Interpretatio*, in *PG* 81:165D-168D.

(2) Ambrose of Milan, *De Isaac* 7.57, in *CSEL* 32.1.2:681-82.

(3) Theodoret of Cyrus, *Interpretatio*, in *PG* 81:168D-169A.

(4) Augustine of Hippo, in *CCSL* 38:10-11.

(5) Cyprian of Carthage, *De unitate ecclesiae catholicae* 4.

(6) Apponius, *Expositio* 9.22-27, in *CCSL* 19:223-25.

(7) Bede the Venerable, *Expositio* 4, in *CCSL* 119b:309-10.

19. Song 6:10–7:1

(1) Theodoret of Cyrus, *Interpretatio*, in *PG* 81:176B-177C.

(2) Apponius, *Interpretatio* 9.33-35, in *CCSL* 19:227-28.

(3) *Glossa ordinaria*, in *CCCM* 170.22:336.

(4) Ambrose of Milan, *De Isaac* 8.64-66, in *CSEL* 32.1.2:687-89.

(5) Honorius of Autun, *Expositio*, in *PL* 172:453B-455D.

(6) Nicholas of Lyra, *Postilla*, in Kiecker: 98.

(7) Theodoret of Cyrus, *Interpretatio*, in *PG* 81:184C-185C.

20. Song 7:2-12

(1) Nicholas of Lyra, *Postilla*, in Kiecker: 100, 102-6.

(2) Theodoret of Cyrus, *Interpretatio*, in *PG* 81:185C-193C.

(3) Apponius, *Expositio* 10.2-4, in *CCSL* 19:238-39.

(4) *Glossa ordinaria*, in *CCCM* 170.22:349.

(5) Honorius of Autun, *Expositio*, in *PL* 172:458AB.

(6) Bede the Venerable, *Expositio*, in *CCSL* 119b:329-31.

(7) John of Ford, *Sermones* 83.1-2, 8-9, in *CCCM* 18:569-70, 573-74.

21. Song 7:11-14

(1) Ambrose of Milan, *De Isaac* 8.66-69, in *CSEL* 32.1.2:689-91.

(2) Apponius, *Expositio* 11.1-4, in *CCSL* 19:256-58.

(3) Theodoret of Cyrus, *Interpretatio*, in *PG* 81:197B-200B.

(4) *Glossa ordinaria*, in *CCCM* 170.22:376.

(5) Honorius of Autun, *Expositio in Cantica Cantorum*, in *PL* 172:472C-473A.

22. Song 8:1-4

(1) Theodoret of Cyrus, *Interpretatio*, in *PG* 81:200B-201C.

(2) Bede the Venerable, *Expositio*, in *CCSL* 119b:337-40.

(3) Honorius of Autun, *Expositio*, in *PL* 172:477C-478A.

23. Song 8:5-10

(1) Theodoret of Cyrus, *Interpretatio*, in *PG* 81:202C.

Index of Subjects

Africa, 48-50, 185

Age, present, 12, 61, 120, 150, 156, 158, 166, 226, 281, 293; to come, 82, 94, 111, 139; consummation of the age, 123, 245, 277

Allegory, xii-xiii, xviii, 8, 9, 23, 65-67, 124, 135-36, 157, 161, 185, 205, 275. *See also* Enigma, Numerology, Type

Anagogy, 6, 24, 27-28, 119

Angelic, describing ascetic way of life, 234

Angels, 21, 24, 52, 61, 65, 72, 124, 132, 136, 139, 141-42, 177, 183, 278, 295; ministers of God, 199, 217; of the nations, 52, 269; as Powers, 93, 112, 128, 144, 156, 297

Antichrist, 271, 282

Apostles, assignment of, 94, 128, 138; authors of Church's books, 222; defenders and guardians of the Church, 164, 293; martyrs, 77, 255; recipients of knowledge, 262; teachers, 34-35, 258; teaching and practice of, 41, 52, 79, 88, 118, 260; unity of, represented by Peter, 238; witnesses, 148-49

Apparent Good, 45

Aquila, 147, 258

Ascent, from unbelief to faith, 282; of soul to God, 150, 281

Ascetics, 50, 51, 61, 185, 186, 249

Askesis, 162, 223-24, 234, 249. *See also* Philosophy

Baptism, 77, 139, 158, 198; baptismal interrogation, 33; Christ's, 96, 140, 245, 274; and circumcision, 249; creates intimacy with Christ, 53; enlightenment, 257; gift of the Spirit in, 34, 74, 79; identification with Christ, 138, 171, 189; rebirth, 40, 200, 281, 290; sanctification and purification, 59, 201; seal, 121; washing and forgiveness of sins, 52, 74, 157, 184

Bible. *See* Scriptures

Bishop, 85, 162, 293, 294; prelates, 186, 224

Blindness, spiritual, 8. *See also* Ignorance

Blood, of Christ, 94, 138, 150, 211, 250, 256, 259, 285, 297

Body, 162; bodily desire, 8, 206; concerns of, 130; constraints of, 150; holiness of, 132; resurrection of, 150

Bridegroom, identified with the Word of God, 2

Carnal, 202, 226, 230; vice, 51

Charity, 36. *See also* Love

Chastity, 51, 61, 69, 121, 163, 166, 183, 185, 186, 223, 225, 255, 256

Choice. *See* Freedom

Christ, 121, 185; divinity of, 22, 76, 141, 182, 211, 212, 250, 255, 262; freedom from sin, 211; light, 211-12, 213; mediator, 22, 215, 268; offices of priest, king, and prophet, 163-64; person of, 22, 59, 86, 141; titles of, 7, 29, 108; union of divinity and humanity, 147, 151, 182, 212; work of, 110, 119-20, 151, 167, 239, 263, 277, 281. *See also* Incarnation, Son of God, Truth, Word

Church, 138; assembly of all the saints, 21, 191; Christ's body, 178-79; composition of, 230, 240; existing from the beginning, 65; of the Gentiles, 39, 151, 158, 289; oppressed and despised, 43, 116; of the patriarchs and prophets, 153; sanctified by baptism, 59; unity of, 50, 238, 241

Commandments, 10, 23, 31, 180

Compassion, 181, 264

Confessors, 69, 162, 183, 248

Index of Names

Index of Names

Theodoret of Cyrus, xx, 34-35, 62-63, 78, 93, 104-5, 115, 117-18, 146-49, 177, 180, 189-90, 196-97, 210, 280, 281, 212-13, 221, 233-34, 235-38, 243, 244-45, 251-52, 254, 256-59, 266, 270-71, 274-75, 280, 281

Theodotion, xv

William of St. Thierry, 1, 10-17, 29-30, 42-43, 64-65, 83-85, 105-6, 123-24

Index of Scripture